CONTENTS

ACKNOWLEDGEMENTS

The sources for this work were primarily interviews, along with surviving documentation, newspaper reports and suchlike. Much of this source material proved to be problematic. The Rás has generated many myths, some of which have become established in people's consciousness as reality. Printed sources, particularly from the earlier period, were strongly influenced by promotional material issued by the Rás organisers. Newspaper reports tended to deal solely with the happenings of stages, not always accurately and in a sanitised manner that did little to reveal the more extensive dramas being played out. Given these considerations, every effort has been made to corroborate the detail in this work from a number of sources.

The cycling community in Ireland is relatively small and intimate, and it is understandable that, in many cases, interviewees requested that opinions expressed about their contemporaries should be dealt with confidentially. Many quotations are therefore not ascribed to their source.

The work was buoyed up by the goodwill, support and practical assistance of a great many people, and by the consensus that the story of the Rás deserved and needed to be recorded. It was a great pleasure and honour to meet so many people associated with the event, but it is a regret that, due to the necessary limits of a book such as this, much remains untold.

I am very grateful for the generous assistance of the following: Steve Abbott, Dan Ahern, Jack Barrett, Dick Barry, Tim Barry, Gerry Beggs, John Blackwell, Liam Brick, Ann Brolly, Mary Cahill, Richie Cahill, Gerry Campbell, Tim Carey, Con Carr, Patrick Casey, Philip Cassidy, John Caulfield, Ian Chivers, Colm Christle, Mick Christle, Larry Clarke, Noel Clarke, Celine Collins, Eoin Concannon, Michael Concannon, Brian Connaughton, Gearóid Costello, Michael Costello, Joan Curtin, Dan Curtin, Cormac Daly, Eoin Daly, Hannah Daly, Ursula

Daly, Edward Dawson, Dermot Dignam, Séamus Donnegan, Séamus Downey, Peter Doyle, Eamon Duffy, Michael Duggan, Cara Finnegan, Paudi Fitzgerald, Alice Flanagan, Batty Flynn, Ian Gallagher, John Galvin, Frank Gibson, Geno (John) Goddard, Giuseppe Guerini, Timmy Griffin, Clare Hackett, Pat Healy, Eddie Hoolihan, Gabriel Howard, Steve Howells, John Ibbotson, Simon Jones, Brian Kenneally, Pádraig Kenneally (*Kerry's Eye*), Billy Kennedy, Séamus Kennedy, Ray Kennedy, Billy Kerr, Mick Kilcourse, Christy Kimmage, Kevin Kimmage, Gerry Kinsella, Eddie Lacey, Seán Lally, Tim Lane, 'Tosh' (Thomas) Lavery, Steve Lawless, Keith Lawton, Ronnie Long, Declan Lonergan, Joe Lonergan, May Lonergan, Denis Lynch, Tom Lynch, Micheál Mac Aonghusa, Alasdair MacLennan, Gene Mangan, John Mangan, Padraig Marrey, Joe McAloon, Jim McArdle, Cormac McCann, Norman McClusky, Rita McCormack, John McCormack, Paul McCormack, Brian McCormack, Tommy McGowan, Grace McKenna, Oliver McKenna, Mickey McKenna, Jim McQuaid, Kieron McQuaid, Pat McQuaid, Brian Monaghan, Paddy Moriarty, Shay Murphy, Lorcan Murphy, Mick Murphy, Eugene Murtagh, Colm Nulty, Mick Nulty, Con O'Brien, Phil O'Brien, Paddy O'Callaghan, Brendan Doherty, Denis O'Connell, Phil O'Connor, Mike O'Donaghue, Patrick O'Donaghue, Micheál Ó Dubhfláine, Jimmy O'Flynn, Richard O'Gormon, Shay O'Hanlon, Noreen O'Mahoney, John O'Mahoney, Tony O'Neill, John O'Reilly, Donie O'Shea, Tom O'Shea, Finn O'Sullivan, Lorraine O'Sullivan, Stephen O'Sullivan, Séamus Ó Tuathaile, David Peelo, Bobby Power, Pat Power, Gerry Rea, Christy Riordan, Andrew Roche, Bunny Roche, Larry Roche, Stephen Roche, Frédéric Rostaing, Sally Ryan, Ann Sheehan, Harry Shine, Kevin Simms, Kerry Sloane, Stephen Spratt, Ian Steel, John 'Súli' Sullivan, Damien Switzer, Neil Taggart, Emanuel Thackaberry, Bob Thom, Jack Watson, Louis White, Ronnie Williams, Peter Wedge, Anthony Wood.

PHOTOGRAPHIC ACKNOWLEDGEMENTS

There is a great shortage of photographs from the early years of the Rás and 'action' shots are especially rare. This can be seen as a reflection of the poor economic circumstances prevailing at the time, along with the lack of commercial sponsorship and associated photographers. Apart from this lack of general pictures, images of some of the event's greatest riders are even rare – for example, it proved impossible to find an image of Shay O'Hanlon and Paddy Flanagan in action together, or of members of the great ICF team of 1974.

The Rás organisers did commission the Dublin photographic agency, Lensman, to cover the first decade of the Rás but its images are confined to start and finish scenes in Dublin. Interestingly, Lensman did not cover the 1956 Rás – the year of the 'Cookstown Incident'. Curiously, however, it is evident from newspapers of the day that a photographer was on hand to record some of the 'Cookstown' scenes. Even though these images were widely distributed to newspapers at the time by the Irish News Agency (a state-established body now defunct), it is equally curious that it has not been possible to find out who the photographer was and that no original print has materialised. Hence, the images from that stage reproduced here are of poor quality from surviving newspaper cuttings.

Some individual photographers did produce significant early pictures. For example, McMonagle's of Killarney made a striking series of images of the Rás in the Kerry mountains in the late 1950s and some of these were reproduced in later NCA publications. However, this collection was not available for this publication. Similarly, Pádraig Kenneally took an impressive range of early Rás images in Tralee and the Kenneally (*Kerry's Eye*) collection was generously made available to this book.

In the 1960s, an amateur Dublin photographer, Bill Mooney, began working on the Rás as a favour to Joe Christle and he was the main source of Rás photographs for many years, producing a very large collection of images. Unfortunately, the entire Mooney collection of negatives was later destroyed. It is likely that many of the photographs made available for this book by individuals originated from the Mooney collection.

Because of these circumstances, some of the important images available from the early years of the Rás are from 'snapshots' taken by followers and spectators, such as those of Donie O'Shea and John O'Reilly, some of which are reproduced here.

With the influence of more organised commercial sponsorship, the Inpho Photography agency was commissioned to cover the Rás in 1984 and has continued to do so since then. The Inpho collection has generously been made available to this book, with most of the images being the work of Lorraine O'Sullivan.

Hopefully, the release of this book will unearth other pictures that will help fill the visual record of Irish cycling.

Many people went to a great deal of effort to provide images for this book and I am very grateful to the following for providing the following pictures:

(note: where there are multiple images on a page, they are indicated clockwise, from left to right); page 6, 7, 9, 10, 11, 12, 19, 25, 26, 32, 46 (bottom right), 59, 122 (bottom), 141, 153, 298 (bottom), Colm Christle; p. 17, from the *Irish History Quarterly Review*; p. 21, John Goddard; p. 33, 41, 85, 92, 111 (top right), 119 (bottom), 121, 133, 157, p. 147 (newspaper cutting – original source unknown) Gene Mangan; p. 35, Paddy O'Callaghan; p. 37, 39, 42, 43, 54, 57, 83, 84, 289, 291 Pádraig Kennelly (*Kerry's Eye*); p. 45, 47, from newspapers cuttings – source unknown; p. 48, Kerry Sloane; p. 50, 51, Donie O'Shea; p. 50 (bottom left) from newspaper cuttings – source unknown; p. 52, 60, Ronnie Williams; p. 55, 208, Paddy O'Callaghan; p. 63, 65, 309 (right), Phil O'Connor; p. 67, 298 (top), John O'Reilly; p. 73, 81, Christy Riordan; p. 78, Jimmy O'Flynn; p. 81, *Kerryman/Corkman*; p. 89, 167, Shay O'Hanlon; p. 91, from an NCA publication; p. 92, 175, Larry Clarke; p. 93, Gabriel Howard; p. 96, 177, 185, 186, 192, 195, Alice Flanagan; p. 98, Kerry Sloane; p.100, Ray Kennedy; p.102, 103, 106, 108,

109, 110, 113, 143, Shay O'Hanlon; p. 117, 302, John O'Reilly/John Goddard; p. 120, *Corkman/Kerryman*; p.122, *Corkman/Kerryman* (left), from an NCA publication – original source unknown (right); p. 123, 124, 186 (bottom), Jack Barrett; p. 136, Brian Connaughton; p. 146, 150, 213, Colm Nulty; p. 169, 319, Gabriel Howard; p. 170, 171, 178, 180, Mike O'Donaghue; p. 182, 197, 203, 211, 214, 223, 227, 229, Sally Ryan; p. 198, Séamus Kennedy; p. 230, www.fbdmilkras.com; p. 231–253 (top), 254–281 (top), 300, 284, 304, 305 (bottom), 307, 311–318, 321–327, Inpho; p. 253 (bottom) John Blackwell; p. 247 (bottom), Frank Gibson; p. 292, Gerry Rea; p. 305 (top), Phil Leigh.

INTRODUCTION

The Rás bunch in triumphant mood with the tricolour they 'recaptured' from the RUC during a fracas near Lurgan.

As a typical Irish child of the 1950s, 1960s and 1970s, I found the Rás to be something powerful that wove its way through my youthful consciousness and left a distinct imprint. It had a special aura, a flavour of something grand and epic.

The arrival of the Rás Tailteann every few years was a significant local event, to be discussed and anticipated with enthusiasm. Waiting at the roadside for the Rás to arrive from far-flung places, we would stare in awe as the fleeting bunch skimmed past on its marathon journey. We would try, usually unsuccessfully, to catch a glimpse of the local man, an individual who, in parochial communities, would always carry the distinction of having ridden the Rás. And at a time when many sporting heroes were local heroes, the national figures of the Rás – cyclists such as Mangan, O'Hanlon and Flanagan – were superstars of their day, men of great stature within Irish sport.

The magical grip of the Rás stretched far beyond my impressionable young mind. Probably the most physically demanding sporting event in the country, it touched the psyche of the sporting nation from its inception and became the subject of the dreams and aspirations of Irish cyclists. For the leading riders, success in the Rás was the ultimate prize. For the ordinary rider, the race itself was the prize. The event endured, in spite of much turbulence and unfavourable circumstances, and had increased greatly in scale and sophistication by the time it entered the élite UCI (Union Cycliste Internationale) calendar of international races in 2001.

Though the public profile of the Rás has declined in an era of saturation media coverage of sporting events, the race retains its essential qualities and remains unique as a stage race. Nevertheless, there was no significant written source of information about the Rás and, while it developed a rich oral tradition, much of this folklore had more than a hint of myth and fable. Still, it gave a tantalising hint of a fascinating true story that might lie beneath. With the fiftieth anniversary of the first Rás in 2002, it seemed fitting that the story of this national sporting treasure, and of the people who created it, should be chronicled.

This resultant work was not intended, nor does it claim, to be the definitive history of the event. Rather, while giving an overview of fifty editions, it endeavours to convey the essence of the Rás through an examination of particular individuals and incidents, and its significance not only within Irish sporting history but also its part in the wider history of Ireland and its parallels with the evolution of the nation. Therefore, the degree to which certain individuals or events are, or are not, examined in this work is not a reflection on their relative significance in the overall history of the Rás. Because of its nature, the story of the Rás will have an appeal beyond followers of competitive cycling. Therefore, as the text inevitably includes cycling terminology which may not be familiar to some readers, a 'Cycling Glossary' of these terms is provided. Similarly, for the non-Irish reader, a 'Non-cycling Glossary' provides explanations for words and expressions of a strictly Irish context. The acronyms of various organisations also crop up regularly and the origin of these is explained in the text as they arise. The section entitled 'Rás Timeline and Related Events' will also assist in understanding these.

The task of researching and writing this book proved much more challenging than anticipated. Given the complex origin of the event within the fractious political divisions of the country and the strong ideological overtones in the early decades of the Rás, it quickly became evident it was much more than a bike race. It also became clear that it would be difficult to produce an in-depth, chronological history of the Rás. A total of 486 stages were fought out between the first event in 1953 and the fiftieth Rás in 2002. Each one of those produced its own stories and drama, each was significant to the riders involved and each has its own unique place in the history of the Rás. Every one of the thousands of participating riders has his own individual story and saw events through a unique personal perspective. It's clear that a full account of the Rás would fill many volumes.

There was always a certain risk to the project – the possibility that once one began to scratch beneath the veneer of anecdotal tales one might discover a myth based on fallacy and delusion. In fact, the opposite was the case and the investigation of the Rás – its time, its people and the wider political, social and sporting issues that surrounded it – quickly began to reveal a rich, previously unrecorded story with powerful characters whose feet were certainly not made of clay. Therefore, I hope this book will succeed, to some degree, in adequately documenting what must be one of the great untold stories of Irish sport and of the world of cycling.

RÁS TIMELINE AND RELATED EVENTS

1947 The world governing body of cycling, the UCI (Union Cycliste Internationale), decrees that the NCA (National Cycling Association) must confine its area of jurisdiction to the 26 counties of 'Éire'. The NCA, a 32-county body, refuses and is expelled from the UCI.

1949 A minority of Irish clubs break away from the NCA and form a new association that confines itself to the 26 counties. It is called the CRE (Cumann Rothaíochta na hÉireann) and obtains international recognition from the UCI.

1953 The first Rás Tailteann is run by the NCA as a two-day event.

1954 The first eight-day Rás.

1958 Gene Mangan achieves four consecutive stage wins.

1963 The first foreign national team participates, from Poland.

1966 The Rás becomes a ten-day event.

1967 Shay O'Hanlon gets his third consecutive Rás win.

The CRE changes its name to ICF (Irish Cycling Federation).

1972 The last Rás to be organised by Joe Christle, the event's original prime mover.

1973 Discussions begin between the CRE and ICF on possible unification.

The Rás is organised by a committee, and Jim Kelly is the first of a succession of Race Directors.

1974 An ICF team participates in the Rás for the first time.

The Rás becomes a nine-day event.

There is more active commercial sponsorship and becomes the 'Discover Ireland – Be Active Be Alive Rás Tailteann'.

1978 The Irish Cycling Tripartite Committee (ICTC) is formed from the different cycling organisations to jointly administer cycling in Ireland.

1979 Riders from the three cycling bodies in Ireland compete in the Rás for the first time.

The Rás is called 'The Health Race'. It is won by Stephen Roche.

1981 Rás entitled the 'Tirolia Rás Tailteann'.

1983 Dermot Dignam takes overall charge of the event, and it become the 'Dairy Rás Tailteann'.

1984 It becomes the 'FBD Milk Rás'.

1987 As a result of the work of the ICTC, the Irish cycling bodies formally unify and become the Federation of Irish Cyclists (FIC).

1990 The Rás enters the UCI calendar and is moved back to May.

1993 The Rás is no longer in the UCI calendar.

2001 The Rás again enters the UCI calendar at a 2.5 ranking, and becomes an eight-day event.

2002 The event's golden jubilee.

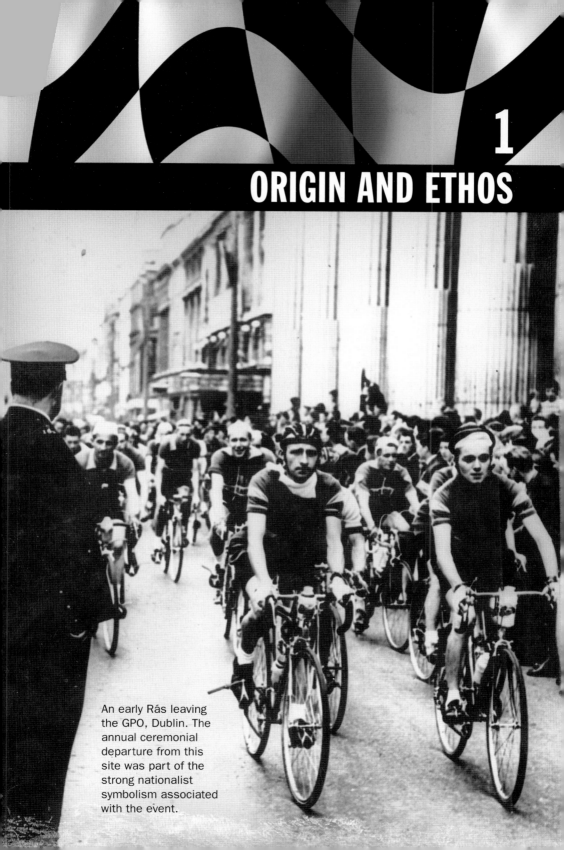

1
ORIGIN AND ETHOS

An early Rás leaving the GPO, Dublin. The annual ceremonial departure from this site was part of the strong nationalist symbolism associated with the event.

The Rás had a modest beginning. On 19 September 1953, 52 riders assembled in O'Connell Street in Dublin on a wet Saturday afternoon. It was a two-day affair, from Dublin to Wexford and back, totalling 200 miles (320km). The riders had feelings of both anticipation and trepidation, as there was little tradition of 'mass-start' road racing in Ireland and few, if any, of them had previously ridden a stage race.

To the casual observer, there was an unusual element of showmanship at the start, with a strong cultural dimension. The two days were to be a strong blend of athleticism, nationalist symbolism, and razzmatazz, reflecting a strategy that was to eventually establish the Rás as a powerful Irish sporting institution.

By choosing to call it the Rás Tailteann, its founders associated the event, and those involved, with the characteristics of the ancient Tailteann Games. This Celtic sporting and cultural festival was held on the Plain of Tailte in County Meath in prehistoric times, a form of Celtic Olympics that pre-dated the ancient Greek Games by centuries. In the late nineteenth and early twentieth centuries, when emerging Irish nationalism was forming its identity, the period of the Tailteann Games represented a golden era of Irish nationhood. The name chosen for this new event – Rás Tailteann – clearly had sporting, cultural and nationalistic connotations.

The start was in front of the GPO (General Post Office), again symbolically significant as it had been the headquarters of the Irish Volunteers during the 1916 Rising. A group from the race entered the building and laid a wreath at the statue of Cúchulainn, the legendary hero of the ancient Irish sagas who had died heroically in defence of his homeland. The nobility, integrity and generosity of spirit of the Fianna were being associated with the event. When the group emerged from the building, a dedication was read out to the 'Youth of Ireland honouring nationhood'. This referred to the cyclists, all members of the NCA (National Cycling Association) and banned from international competition because their association refused to recognise the partition of Ireland. Hence, they were presented as upholders of core republican principles.

The Rás was started by the Lord Mayor of Dublin and set out on the 90-mile (144 km) first stage, to Wexford, in strong wind and heavy rain. Much of the route was littered with leaves and branches, and the riders had to negotiate a fallen tree in Wicklow. Colm Christle, from the Gate Cycling Club in Dublin, did much chasing to bring back an early break, but Mick Carr, from Carrigtohill in Cork, broke away at Enniscorthy and won the first Rás stage by 34 seconds.

Colm Christle and his friend Phil Clarke were well-known riders from the Gate Club and roomed together in a boarding house in Wexford that night. They were

'To the youth of Ireland honouring nationhood.' Start of the first Rás, O'Connell Street, Dublin, 1953: (left–right) Lord Mayor of Dublin, Alderman Timmins, John O'Reilly, Pat Murphy; standing behind Pat Murphy is Bart Bastable, a Radio Éireann commentator.

in good condition and had ambitions of winning the event. Christle was the reigning NCA 100-mile road champion and, earlier that year, he and Clarke had cycled to Italy to watch Fausto Coppi's attempt to add the World Championship to his three Giro d'Italia and one Tour de France wins. They treated it as a training exercise and rode hard, doing 'bit 'n' bit' from Calais across northern France, into Switzerland, over the Gothard Pass and south to Lugano in Italy. 500,000 Italians lined the circuit and Christle and Clarke saw Coppi make a famous break to win the historic race.

During the Rás, many of the boarding houses lacked drying facilities and Colm Christle was pulling on his wet cycling jersey the following morning when his brother and race organiser, Joe, came to their room. In simple terms, he told them he had little money for prizes and that one of them must win the race so as to extricate him from his difficulty. Joe Christle was usually listened to without argument and it was understood as an instruction.

The Christles were key figures in the event. The sons of a small farmer from County Offaly who came to Dublin to work in the Guinness brewery, they inherited a strong sporting and nationalist tradition and five of them became absorbed in cycling. The Christian Brothers, who were unashamedly nationalist,

Pat Murphy (Gate Club) and the Lord Mayor of Wexford at a ceremony at the Pikeman statue, Wexford, 1953. The rider to the right of the cameraman is Mick Carr of Cork and the rider to the left, with cap, is Christy (Kitt) Dunne from the Harp Club in Dublin.

influenced them in primary school. One teacher in particular, Br O'Shea from Dingle, was an admirer of the Cúchulainn legend and the Pearse vision portraying the Irish nation as free and Gaelic, independent and strong. At secondary school in St James' Street CBS, a further influence was Jack Sweeney, a noted athletics coach of his time who dreamt of reviving the Tailteann Games. The Cúchulainn and Tailteann ideals took root in Joe Christle's mind.

The second stage was again preceded by ceremony and a wreath was laid at the monument in Wexford commemorating the pikemen of the 1798 Rebellion. It was a 110-mile (176km) return route to Dublin. Colm Christle was reluctant to make an early move as he had a slight cold from the previous day, but by New Ross, a group of three had built up a lead of two minutes. Christle caught them and went into the lead for the KOH (King of the Hills) at his mother's native Leighlin Bridge in County Carlow. A group of nine eventually developed at the front, including Kerry Sloane, who was later to be instrumental in developing the Rás. Christle began to cramp in both legs and measured his effort, but was driven by determination. Naturally competitive as an athlete, his brother's instructions to win the non-existent prize provided additional motivation. And as a member of the Christle family, he was ideologically motivated and keenly aware that the Rás Tailteann was a visionary concept, crucial to the survival of his cycling organisation and the political, cultural and sporting aspirations that it represented.

'Who wears the wreath that shall forever be green.' NCA president, Jim Killean, presenting the prize of a wreath of laurels to the winner of the first Rás, Colm Christle. The laurels were picked at Aonach Tailte, the site of the ancient Tailteann Games. To the left is Pat Kenna, from Carlow, who was second. The rider between Christle and Killean is Pat Murphy, who performed the wreath-laying ceremonies during the race. On the far right is Andy 'Ando' Christle, brother of Joe and Colm; he was killed in the Rás the following year.

Christle punctured near Carlow, but a rider from Navan, Frank Reilly, gave him his front wheel. A Kerry rider, who had been the main driving force in the bunch, 'sat up' and delayed the group until Christle regained contact. Christle later learned the rider's name – Paudi Fitzgerald – and was to repay this act of generosity three years later when Fitzgerald was attempting to win the 1956 Rás. Some early attempts were made to get away from the lead bunch, but Christle, conscious of the danger of cramp in his legs, bided his time until the finish on the Crumlin Road. Leo Collins led out the sprint, but Christle was first over the line to win the inaugural Rás.[1]

The 'prize-giving' took place in the Iveagh Grounds pavilion where Jim Killean, president of the NCA, presented Colm with his trophy – a wreath of laurels picked at Aonach Tailte, the site of the original Tailteann Games. Quoting James Fintan Lalor, Killean said it represented 'the wreath that shall forever be green' – a reference to the endurance of republican values.[2] That evening, there was a Rás céilí in the Mansion House, the venue for the first Dáil in 1919. At the next NCA Congress, the first three riders were presented with miniature flag-poles carrying the tricolour. Colm Christle had to wait twenty-five years for his 'prize', when he was presented with a substitute winner's trophy during the Rás of 1978.

Following the precedent set in the first Rás of 1953, the GPO on O'Connell Street in Dublin became the traditional starting place of the Rás.

While most of the riders considered the first Rás Tailteann as no more than a good and novel two-day bike race, it was, in fact, an interim step towards the development of a major Irish stage race by individuals within the NCA. The concept was conceived within a complex political and sporting context, and it received impetus from three principal, coinciding and interrelated forces.

Firstly, cycling administration in Ireland had become embroiled in wider political issues in which the Rás concept was to become a weapon. This situation had evolved from the historical developments following the War of Independence of 1919–22. The country was then partitioned into Northern Ireland – the 'Six Counties' – and the Irish Free State – the 'twenty-six Counties', later to become the Republic of Ireland, or Éire. A tragic and bitter Civil War was fought in 1923, with Partition a central issue, an emotive and acrimonious subject which was to give rise to violence at various times until the end of the century.

Cycling administration became entangled in the Partition issue and, by the 1950s, a fractious situation had developed. This evolution was convoluted and complex, but an overview of its unfolding is central to an understanding of the origin of the Rás and its development over the following thirty years.

The early administration of athletics and cycling in Ireland was under the auspices of the GAA (Gaelic Athletic Association). Following the establishment of the Irish Free State in 1922, power was divested to the NACA (National Athletics and Cycling Association). The NACA, a 32-county organisation, retained strong links with the GAA and shared its republican ethos. Later, in 1938, responsibility for the administration of cycling was divested to the NCA (National Cycling Association), also a 32-county organisation. There was little distinction between the three associations in many parts of the country – the same individuals were involved in administration, most of them nationalist and republican in outlook.

The issue was further complicated by the existence of the Northern Ireland Cycling Federation (NICF), under the administration of the British National Cyclists' Union (BNCU). A more serious division developed in Irish cycling in 1947 when the BNCU proposed a motion to the world governing body of cycling – the UCI – that the NCA confine its area of jurisdiction to the twenty-six counties. The motion recognised official state boundaries and was strongly resisted by the NCA as its acceptance would have amounted to an endorsement of Partition. The British vigorously pursued the motion and, with the support of the block of Commonwealth votes, it was passed by the UCI.

This scenario, in fact, was being repeated across the international scene and more than twenty country associations were to be expelled from the UCI. Examined in a broader context, it might be seen as part of the new order being imposed in post-war Europe, with an insistence that political borders be recognised in all aspects. In Ireland, however, Partition was still a contentious issue. The Constitution of the Irish Republic claimed jurisdiction over the entire island of Ireland and the British presence was widely viewed as an 'occupation' of Ireland – a final barrier to full Irish nationhood and a united Ireland. The IRA (Irish Republican Army) continued to pursue its military campaign, with a degree of support from some sections of the population.

The UCI ruling was seen by the NCA as a product of British 'guile' and yet another British-promoted conspiracy against the interests of Irish nationalism. It was a setback for the republican cause and the NCA refused to comply with it. The association was expelled from the UCI and its members banned from international competitions, including the Olympics and World Championships. This situation had its precedent in athletics, with Pat O'Callaghan and Bob Tisdall being unable to defend their Olympic titles in Berlin in 1936.

The situation further escalated in 1949 when most of the Dublin-based clubs broke away from the NCA to form an association that would confine its jurisdiction to the Republic of Ireland. Calling itself the CRE (Cumann Rothaíochta na hÉireann), it sought international recognition from the UCI. This was granted, with the support of Britain, and precipitated a bitter split within Irish cycling that was not formally resolved until 1978. A residual antagonism continued long after and the scars only began to disappear as a new generation emerged, unencumbered by the historical burdens of previous eras.

The new CRE posed a considerable threat to the NCA. The major Dublin clubs joined it, taking with them whatever sponsorship money was available. Individual leading riders, anxious for international competition, were also lost to the CRE, including John Lackey and Karl McCarthy. With more international exposure, the CRE was forward-looking and primarily interested in top-quality road racing. The NCA remained strong outside of Dublin and robustly resisted attempts by the CRE to expand into the provinces. Many NCA administrators were experienced in political struggle and had the support of a powerful nationalist network. While the NCA prevailed as the much stronger organisation, it remained relatively insular and conservative, and concentrated on grass-track-racing, then the most popular form of competitive cycling in Ireland.

There were other, more subtle differences. Speaking about the NCA members in general, one former CRE member observed: 'They had a rooted Irishness in them – they were born into it.' Furthermore, the NCA had a rural and working-class base, while the CRE was city-based and its members somewhat urbane. As one individual put it: 'The NCA riders wore dark socks.' In other words, they were outside the Pale and thought of as 'culchies' by the CRE.

In a move that further vexed the NCA, the CRE entered into negotiations with the British Cycling Federation (BCF), resulting in the establishment of the NICF, an adjunct to the BCF for the purpose of administering cycling in Northern Ireland.

Considerable rancour and hostility developed between the NCA and CRE, driven mainly by the NCA hierarchy's view that the CRE had compromised republican principles and was undermining the honourable stand being made by NCA members. This position was summarised by Joe Christle in his speech at the 1798 monument in Wexford during the first Rás:

> In the field of sport, we could never be denied complete independence. No doubt, we could lose certain privileges by maintaining that independence, but we prefer national honour to international dishonour.

NCA publicity depicted the CRE as pro-British and the level of spite that was to develop is illustrated by the adjectives scattered throughout an article in the 1961 Rás programme; CRE members were described as 'reprobates', 'traitors', 'scabs', 'deserters', 'brood of vipers' and 'shoneens'. NCA riders frequently shouted such insults at CRE members on the roads of Dublin. The CRE, on the other hand, saw itself as conforming to the constitutional situation in Ireland and to international conventions in sports administration. Its members were chiefly interested in road racing at the highest level and its sporting motivation transcended politics. While the CRE resented the NCA's efforts to stifle its work, it was reasonably satisfied with the high level of competition available to its members.

On the road during the first two-day Rás of 1953: (left–right) Barney O'Brien, Kevin Simms, Willie Cooper, Philip Clarke (white cap), Colm Christle.

This split, and the resultant battle between the two organisations, was one of the primary motivations for the development of the Rás concept. Such an event would create a high-profile, national race to match the prestige and challenge of international competition available to CRE members. This strategy, however, was not formally developed within the NCA and might not have come to fruition without a second, crucial element – the personality factor.

There emerged within the NCA at that time a number of young, forceful and idealistic figures with the imagination, resolve and tenacity to force the concept through the conservative and obstinate NCA bureaucracy. Two individuals – Joe Christle and Kerry Sloane, both in their early twenties – were to emerge as prime movers. Joe Christle was a charismatic visionary, a superb organiser and publicist, and the driving force behind the Rás. Like a benevolent dictator, he was to forge the Rás' character and dominate it for twenty years. Though not especially motivated as a competitive cyclist, he loved cycling and was happy touring on his own. Even when financially comfortable in later years, he could leave for Europe on the spur of the moment with just his bike and the contents of his saddlebag.

Joe Christle's commitment to cycling was just one facet of a remarkable life. After leaving school, he worked for Bord na Móna, studied at night and qualified as a certified and cost accountant. Later, he earned a degree in law, was called to the Bar and subsequently acquired a degree in philosophy. He lectured in Law and Accounting at the College of Commerce, Dublin, where his development of courses was regarded as 'mould-breaking'. He was very active in Sinn Féin and the IRA, and was editor of the *United Irishman* (later to become *An Phoblacht*). He was also a member of the Gaelic League executive and organised a National Students' Council in UCD (University College Dublin) in 1954. Trade unionism was another of his interests and he was, on several occasions, elected by ESB (Electricity Supply Board) workers as their representative on the company's statutory tribunal.

Christle was an independent thinker whose political philosophy was greatly influenced by his reading of revolutionary writers such as Voltaire, Rousseau, James Fintan Lalor, John Mitchell and Thomas Davis. He believed the whole island of Ireland was one nation and his life was guided by the pursuit of the ideal of 'nationhood'. Sinn Féin objectives and Fenian beliefs were his guiding principles. He advocated republicanism, not merely as a set of laws and rules, but as a way of life. His vision of Ireland was

... a Nation where we desire to substitute morality for egotism, principles for usages, merit for intrigue, genius for cleverness, truth for splendour. A Nation wherein the welfare of every individual shall be assured and wherein the resources shall be the source of public welfare and not the monstrous opulence of the privileged few.[3]

The sporting aspect of his life was embedded in this wider philosophy. His bitter resentment towards the CRE was fuelled by his belief that they had betrayed these principles for material gain, such as better prizes and international competition: 'Hence the defection of so many ambitious men, who abandoned the Republic because they did not commence the journey to arrive at the same object as the Founders.'[4]

Christle had a forceful, dominating personality and, as an activist, had little patience with the constraints of organisational bureaucracy. In his book, *The IRA*, Tim Pat Coogan described him as follows:

Joe Christle has a quality that I can only describe as 'whoosh' – energy, anarchy, male supremacy and learning all canalised into a brand of patriotism that finds its outlet in everything from fomenting strikes and laying up explosives to bicycle racing. Apart from organising the marathon round-Ireland Rás Tailteann he cycles twenty miles before work every day himself. His home is

Joe Christle was an excellent publicist and orator. This picture of him addressing a student rally, taken shortly before the raid on Gough Barracks, County Armagh, in 1954, illustrates one of his many interests. The placards are written in three languages, with one quoting the opening line of Virgil's *Aeneid*, so appropriate to Christle – *Arma virumque cano*, which translates as 'This is a tale of arms and men'.

continually in turmoil. Phones ring. People rush in and out. Beethoven booms from the record player. Large men in track-suits carry bicycles through the hall. (Like most things surrounding Christle, there is more purpose to the activity than meets the eye) ...[5]

Coogan is probably referring here to Christle's involvement with the St James' Gate Cycling Club, which he founded in 1949 at a time when the NCA was on its knees in Dublin. Commonly referred to as the 'Gate', it produced some of the outstanding contributors to the Rás, including Philip Clarke, Colm and Mick Christle, and Dermot Dignam. Some of its members were republican activists and there was an understanding within cycling circles that a core of Gate individuals were active in the IRA at that time.

Following the formation of the CRE, Christle used the Gate club to seed the revival of the NCA in the Dublin region. As it gained in strength, he spawned similar clubs by instructing some of his more able lieutenants to leave the Gate and organise elsewhere. For example, when the Tailteann Club defected *en masse* to the CRE, Christle sent John O'Reilly to organise a new NCA Tailteann Club in the same region. The Clann Brugha[6] and Setanta[7] clubs had similar origins and produced great Rás riders such as Shay O'Hanlon, Seán Dillon and Sonny Cullen. In addition, Christle was promoting high-profile events to bolster the NCA.

Kerry Sloane brought a different perspective to the Rás ideal. From a middle-class background, he attended UCC (University College Cork), where he was introduced to cycling by Karl McCarthy – a noted Cork cyclist of that era. Sloane took part in the extensive programme of track events around County Cork before emigrating to Britain upon graduation in 1951. There, he joined the NCU (National Cycling Union), but having little enthusiasm for the time-trialling focus of English cycling, transferred to the BLRC (British League of Racing Cyclists). Like the NCA at home, with which he maintained ties, the BLRC was also a disaffected organisation: its innovative development of road racing had brought it into conflict with the British cycling establishment. When Sloane returned to Ireland in 1953, he took a commission in the Irish army. That autumn, he was elected road racing secretary of the NCA. He had been significantly influenced by the BLRC's involvement in good-quality road racing and his administrative post within the NCA placed him in a good position to promote the Rás idea.

The development of a large stage race might have been inevitable anyway, given the third factor – the emerging interest in 'mass-start' road racing. Prior to the 1950s, this had enjoyed little popularity in Ireland and time trialling was never to have the broad appeal that it had in Britain. Grass-track-racing was the main

1955: The Gate Cycling Club was one of the main driving forces behind the early Rás: (back row, left–right) Joe Christle, Jim Ennis, Mick Christle, Brendan Christle, Pat O'Brien; (front row, left–right) Colm Christle, Jacky Cullen, Davie O'Brien, Des Kavanagh, Harry O'Toole King.

The bike, a Jack Taylor, was the machine used by Colm Christle in the first Rás of 1953. Note the upturned saddle, the elongated frame because of shallow frame angles, the long wheel-base and the relatively low saddle height. This was a typical set-up of its day. Note also the lamp-holder on the front fork. The bike had gears, described then by Christle as 'an unreliable novelty'.

competitive activity and it thrived in much of the country. The post-war revival of racing in Europe, however, led to cyclists taking a growing interest in events such as the Tour de France. The increasing penetration of the 'wireless' and newspapers contributed to this and many of those who were being drawn to road racing at the time refer to the influence of magazines and their stories of great continental road heroes, such as Fausto Coppi.

The gradual development of road racing in Ireland centred on Dublin. The CRE initiated the 'Coast to Coast' race in 1950, from Dublin to Galway and back, with top English riders competing. Interest in stage racing in Ireland was further stimulated when the Tour of Britain began in 1951. A twelve-day event sponsored by the *Daily Express*, it was run by the BLRC and, given the BLRC's estrangement from the UCI, a five-man NCA team was permitted to compete in the race. Karl McCarthy's ninth place created considerable interest and, in 1952, Joe Christle came up with the 'International Tour Revenge' – a 100-mile race around the Phoenix Park. Many of the top English trade teams competed, including Viking, BSA and Pennine. The presence of such professional riders provoked a lively debate – a controversy that would later resurface in the Rás.

The CRE ran a successful Dublin–Belfast–Dublin two-day event in 1952 and there was a further significant development in 1953 when a government-sponsored cultural festival, 'An Tóstal', included sports. The CRE took the opportunity to run a high-profile four-day race. The event was a success and led to the Tour of Ireland in 1954. The Tour was equally successful, despite attempts by NCA members to sabotage it in Kerry by spreading tacks on the road near Farranfore.

Sloane and Christle, separately, saw the writing on the wall – there was a steady movement toward road racing and the CRE was considerably more advanced in this regard. While they were interested in such racing because of its challenge and attractiveness in pure cycling terms, Sloane and Christle identified the need for a popular stage race as being central to the long-term survival of the NCA.

Collaboration between Sloane and Christle did not begin until after the first two-day Rás of 1953. In later years, a story in *Gaelic Weekly* gave a colourful account of how they originally met and developed the Rás plan, but this was typical of much of the later NCA promotion – fanciful and romantic, and only loosely based on facts. Both had actually been working on the idea independently. Christle had been trying to promote the idea prior to 1953 and there were reports that the *Daily Express*, stimulated by the success of the Tour of Britain, was interested in sponsoring an Irish stage race. The proposal was debated at a stormy meeting of the NCA's congress in 1952, but the idea of an English paper sponsoring an NCA event never had a chance of success. Discussions with the *Irish Press* also fell through.

Kerry Sloane was also trying to develop a stage race, which he intended to call Rás na nGael, and he called a meeting to discuss it in autumn 1953. Though he received little support, he continued planning. Meanwhile, Christle and his followers decided to develop the 1953 Rás idea; they envisaged a larger event that would still emphasise the Gaelic and 32-county theme. Later that year, Christle and Sloane discussed the matter for the first time and agreed to develop the project jointly, even without a sponsor. In general terms, the concept was relatively simple. They planned a high-profile stage race, modelled on the Tour de France but adapted to the Irish context and the aims of the NCA. Without a sponsor, they would depend on the support of the people, mainly through a reliance on committees in the towns the race would visit.

Given the flux of sporting and political developments within Irish cycling, the Rás Tailteann concept was timely and its ethos blended well with national sentiment at that time. Nevertheless, there were considerable barriers to overcome before the concept could be brought to fruition. Parochialism, conservatism and economic deprivation prevailed throughout the country, and the NCA hierarchy considered it an extravagant dream. Many clubs were sceptical and cautious. To many, it was an unrealistic abstraction beyond their grasp, and an enormous challenge lay ahead for its instigators.

2

THE FIRST EIGHT-DAY RÁS

The stages finished in the evenings in the early Rásanna[8], bringing large crowds to the stage-ends after the day's work was over. Here, Geno (John) Goddard of the Exiles team arrives in Tralee, 1962.

The first 'real' Rás, as a multi-stage event, dates from 1954, but the objectives, ethos and name had been clearly established by Joe Christle in 1953, when the organisers of the event, and most of those competing, had been conscious of a new beginning. The planning and development of the 1954 race was based on the previously established ideals and objectives, and their projection onto the eight-day event distinguished the Rás as more than just another multi-stage bike race in the European tradition.

Equally, the way in which Christle and Sloane developed the Rás to meet the particular strategic needs of the NCA helped to give the event a unique character. They displayed considerable acumen in the way they recognised and interpreted the subtleties of the sporting, social and political landscape of Ireland at that time, and their consummate adaptation of a bike race to that context accounted greatly for the enormous success of the Rás within a three-year period.

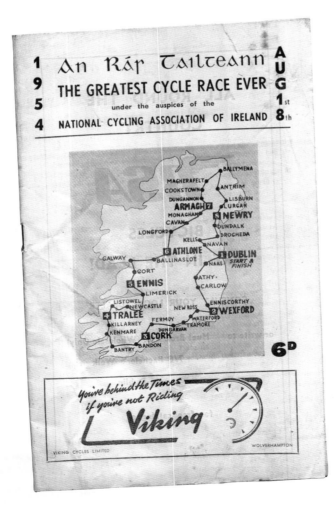

First Rás programme, 1954.

Christle brilliantly displayed one aspect of this strategy in his foreword, in Irish, in the Rás programme of 1954. Here, as in the first Rás, he associated the NCA riders and their cause with the warrior-like qualities and integrity of the Fianna in the ancient Irish sagas, and portrayed the race as part of the process of achieving national destiny. Christle began with a classic quote from the ancient sagas which described the three qualities that were the source of the Fianna victories:

Glaine ár gcroi,
Neart ár ngéag,
Agus beart de réir ár mbriathar.

(The purity of our heart,
The strength of our limbs,
And our actions according to our word.)

He then expanded these three themes to present his message:

Each cyclist in this race is certainly a true example of cleanliness of heart as he has trained strenuously to attain mental and physical perfection for this enormous venture. It is known to all that a young man cannot train athletically and carouse at the same time, therefore the lives of these youths are as committed as those of monks.

Regarding 'strength of limb', there isn't a sport in the world more difficult than a long race such as this. More energy is required for the Rás Tailteann than for the marathon itself. The cyclists will be approximately 40 or 50 hours in the saddle. Each one of them will need bravery and spirit, agility and style. On observing these young men racing, one would think that winning was uppermost in their minds, but this is not the case. Like the ancient heroes, victory is not their main aim but to participate in the competition. These cyclists are members of the Irish National Cycling Association and therefore put the honour of Ireland before prizes and international competition. Because they were not prepared to yield to England or to renounce their people in the six counties, they were expelled from the International Association through British treachery. These youths must stay at home from international competition because they were unwilling to go abroad and represent the Irish nation as 26 counties. Yet, we are proud that they did not yield to the threats and guile of England. They are suffering for their nationhood, but they are loyal to the cause of Ireland, acting according to their word.[9]

The organisers gradually developed other key strategies during this period which laid solid foundations for the ongoing success of the event. To bring the race to the people, it was routed through the rural heartlands; the stages would end in the evenings when the people were free to watch; the distances would be at the outer limits of the riders' capabilities; they formed close alliances with key individuals and groupings in the provincial towns; it would be an event for the Irish Diaspora and it was initially hoped to bring exiles' teams from as far as Australia and the US; and the Rás would be an independent entity, not subject to the bureaucratic vagaries of the NCA governing body. Some of the teams in 1954 were club-based, but the following year, they adopted the GAA inter-county model, leading to passionate rivalry.

The originality, creativity and vision of the organisers was matched by much hard work and close attention to detail. Sloane and Christle formed a good working relationship, with Sloane recognising Christle's single-mindedness and prepared to operate within his *modus operandi* – things would have to be done Christle's way, or not at all. Sloane accepted this because he recognised that anything Christle committed himself to doing would be done thoroughly.

The fact that Sloane, an army officer, and Christle, a suspected IRA activist, were working closely together aroused curiosity. Christle made no attempt to exploit the connection and Sloan's army superiors never raised the subject with him. Sloane swore allegiance to the Irish Constitution and did not share Christle's more extreme political outlook. However, like the vast majority of people in the twenty-six counties at the time, he aspired towards a 32-county republic and was therefore strongly supportive of the NCA position.

Supported by key workers, such as John O'Reilly and Jack Barrett, the immediate organisational tasks facing Christle and Sloane were the route and stage ends, and to persuade clubs and County Boards to enter teams. Stage-end committees were relied upon to look after much of the local detail, such as accommodation and promotion. This strategy, developed through a combination of idealism and pragmatism, created a vital, long-term bond between the Rás and its followers. Many of the riders, for example, stayed in private houses as guests of cycling enthusiasts, and the cultural events run in association with stage finishes, such as Irish dancing displays and hurling competitions, involved local organisations and added to the atmosphere. The Rás quickly became a significant community event.

The organisers chose provincial towns that had reliable and sympathetic organisers with a strong support network available to them. This was usually a coalition of GAA, NCA, NACA and local republicans. A network of good, local

Irish culture was constantly emphasised in the early Rásanna as part of the event's wider role of promoting the concept of 'nationhood'. Hurling competitions were organised by stage-end committees to coincide with the Rás, and Irish-dancing exhibitions were frequently held. Here, in 1963, the rather coy dancers meet a French team.

organisers developed and was to last for decades. Key organisers included Tadhg Crowley in Killarney, Bill Hyland in Clonmel, the Monaghan brothers in Newry and Leo Collins in Meath. Christle generally made initial contact with the local organisations by letter or telephone and others made follow-up visits. Sloane combined his organisational work with training for the event; for example, he cycled from Dublin to Athlone and from Cork to Tralee to meet stage-end organisers. Both Christle and Sloane had a flair for promotion and information was regularly drip-fed to the local and national press. Sloane asked clubs to request their local corporations or county councils to lobby for the Rás to be brought to their regions; this created a local news item and an awareness of the event.

A main sponsor could not be found but this did not deter them. Christle wrote that it would be the 'people's race' and that, in some vague and unspecified way, the support of the people would carry it through. However, the enthusiasm and energy of the organisers was matched by scepticism and some cynicism. Doubt existed at all levels in the NCA, from the grassroots to the Executive Council, and the event might never have received NCA approval without the persuasion of its president, Jim Killean, who was to be a vital ally of Christle's.

Killean, a man of strong personality and greatly respected, dominated the NCA. He had fought in Seán McKeown's Flying Column in the War of Independence and took the anti-Treaty side in the Civil War. He was a central figure in the reorganisation of the IRA after the Civil War, reached a very high rank and was imprisoned on both sides of the border. In spite of this level of activity, he became a prominent cyclist in the 1930s. He was elected president of the NCA in 1947 and his first major challenge was to rally the association following the split in cycling. His empathy with Christle's wider agenda is illustrated by his uncompromising view of the role of cycling within the national question:

> Nationality must always come before cycling and if compromises are to be made they may be made on cycling issues, but never on the broader National Issues at stake.[10]

Killean's stature and personality were vital in coaxing approval for the Rás Tailteann from the staid NCA Executive Council. Then in his fifties, Killean showed remarkable foresight in supporting Sloane and Christle, and he also had an important role in moderating their youthful exuberance. In Sloane's words, 'Killean was the bridge between the impetuous young fellows and the sleepy ould fellows. They were obsessed with the idea that we would bankrupt the NCA, and the Rás would never have happened without Killean.' Even then, the Rás Tailteann only received a grudging consent, conditional on the absence of any financial dependence on the NCA. In addition, the completed arrangements would be subject to final approval by the Executive Council a week before the start. Only then could the race proceed. The Executive Council's attitude may have been coloured by the fact that the Rás structure was autonomous and was apparently not accountable to the NCA.

There were widespread misgivings about the ability of NCA riders to race 1,000 miles in eight days. In the entire NCA at the time, there were, perhaps, no more than half a dozen riders who had raced for more than three days. The idea was ridiculed by some CRE elements and this became a powerfully persuasive tool for Christle and Sloane. They argued that the NCA needed to hold its own against the CRE, that the national identity needed the Rás and that it was going to be the best race in the country. By and large, the riders eventually, but cautiously, bought into the event. The lure of being selected on a county team was effective, as the honour of wearing the county jersey was highly regarded. Comparisons were being made with the Tour de France and it was seen as an opportunity for riders to emulate their continental heroes. Some counties even began to run longer road races to prepare riders for the event.

The tactical cat-and-mouse game with the CRE continued. The battle between the NCA's Rás Tailteann and the CRE's Tour of Ireland seemed unevenly matched. The Tour of Ireland had the top road men in Ireland, supplemented by top English riders and officials. It also had adequate sponsorship. None of this could be said of the Rás. Nevertheless, the first tactical round went to the Rás. Christle and Sloane kept details vague until the CRE unveiled its plans for the Tour of Ireland. It was to be a seven-day event, including one rest day, covering 600 miles (960km). Only then were details of the Rás announced. It would be a continuous eight-day race of 1,000 miles (1,600km). The CRE was panicked into making a tactical blunder. In an attempt to match the Rás, the Tour of Ireland was changed to seven full days, covering 800 miles (1,280km) and would be held in April. There were two major flaws with the new plan – it was too early in the year for amateur riders to attain adequate fitness and it did not allow for the uncertainties of the weather. The event was a shambles for precisely these reasons – there was an initial high attrition rate and then, on a day that entered Irish cycling folklore, the race was struck by a snowstorm. The remainder of the field was decimated, with riders climbing off their bikes and seeking shelter in roadside houses. Only six eventually finished.

Preparations for the Rás continued. Without a major sponsor, various fund-raising activities were organised, including raffles and dances. Sloane sent press releases to the newspapers with ongoing updates, for which he sought a donation 'equivalent to the cost of a free-lance report'. Notwithstanding the huge voluntary effort being made, it nevertheless remained a mystery as to how the race was financed without significant sponsorship, even considering the shoestring nature of the event. Christle, however, had another important ally in Pádraig O'Keeffe, Secretary General of the GAA.

O'Keeffe, a veteran of the War of Independence, was a strong supporter of the Irish language, culture and nationalist movement. In the early years of the Rás, he and Christle forged strong formal links between the Rás and the GAA. Given the NCA Executive Council's hesitancy about the Rás in 1954, however, it could hardly have been expected that the GAA would provide strong financial support and its records for that year detail a donation to the Rás of just £50. Christle, in later years, told a confidant that O'Keeffe had surreptitiously made additional and significant GAA funds available, enabling the race to succeed. Sloane, however, provided an alternative insight on the subject:

> That was a bluff – while we got good moral support from the GAA and plenty of practical help around the country, we were disappointed with the funds. But we could not say that. You see, we were fighting a battle on two fronts – with the CRE on one side and the conservative elements in the NCA on the other. In trying to bring along our own people it was important to give the impression that we were getting strong support, and we deliberately put out the word that the GAA was backing us financially.

Christle's vision, hard work, organisational abilities and craftiness are evident throughout this period, and it's difficult to envisage where time and energy were found for developing the Rás, given the commitments in his wider life. He was working full-time whilst studying for his law degree. He was also deeply involved in other organisations, including the IRA. For example, on the morning of 12

The first 'real' Rás, as a multi-stage event, dates from 1954, but the objectives and ethos had been clearly established in 1953. Widespread misgivings prevailed about the ability of NCA riders to complete the race. The field was composed of provincial, county and club teams, along with individuals. Ulster was the only provincial team: (left–right) Séamus Devlin, Séamus McGreevy, Pat Lavery, Pat Rodgers, Brian Monaghan.

June 1954, during the frenzied run up to the Rás, he sat an exam in Dublin. Later that day, he took part in a spectacular IRA raid on Gough Barracks, County Armagh, in which a large quantity of munitions was captured. He was back in Dublin that night, commanding the lorry that brought the weapons across the border.[11]

Three weeks before the race, only thirteen cyclists had entered. Kerry Sloane later admitted that there were serious misgivings about it going ahead. Nevertheless, sixty riders lined up for the start. There were six county teams, four club teams, two provincial teams and a number of individual entries. In recognition of the important role of the GAA, Pádraig O'Keeffe was given the honour of starting the race in front of the GPO. He dropped the flag and the great adventure began.

For many, it was to be a baptism of fire. Besides the fitness element, many of the teams were tactically naïve and lacked experience of the organisation or strategies of teamwork and stage racing. While the Dublin-based riders and certain individuals had some experience, most were thrown in at the deep end. Those counties that had run some longer races in preparation lacked long-established road riders to whom other riders would have served an apprenticeship in the normal course of events. Little attention was paid to food and diet, and the team support varied greatly. For some of the teams, it was even an effort to scrounge a support vehicle for the race.

Nevertheless, it was new and exciting, the organisers were youthful, energetic and inspiring, and a great sense of anticipation and vitality surrounded the event. The race set out on the 103 miles (165km) to Wexford, with Mick and Colm Christle from the Gate club as favourites, along with Terry Carmody from Kerry and Con Carr from Kildare. However, a nineteen-year-old mechanic from the National Cycling Club in Dublin, Joe O'Brien, stole a march and won the stage into Wexford.

O'Brien had the advantage of being in the best-managed team of the race. Jack Sweeney, the National Cycling Club boss, ran an efficient outfit that concentrated on road racing and he had the remarkable foresight of bringing Percy Stallard from England as an advisor for the event. Stallard was the founder of the BLRC and is now considered to be the father of mass-start racing in England. He represented England in the World Championships three times in the 1930s, with a best position of seventh. With Stallard and Sweeney, O'Brien's team had the best management available at the time.

On the second stage to Cork, 'Big' Willie O'Brien, the Cork team leader, was denied a home win when Mick Christle beat him in a sprint on the Grand Parade after spending more than six hours on the road. Cecil O'Reilly from Antrim took the Yellow Jersey[12] from O'Brien. Following the race, the riders changed at the city's public swimming baths where they were visited by George Harding, who offered any necessary assistance. Harding, a mild-mannered man, owned a well-known bike shop in the city and had been instrumental in some Cork riders joining the CRE. Unsurprisingly, some of the riders were hostile to him and he ended up in the pool.

The third stage, to Tralee, was to be another rain-soaked, six-hour race. The Jersey changed hands again when Terry Carmody got a home win from Philip Clarke in front of an enormous crowd, estimated by various newspapers at between 10,000 and 20,000 people. But as the throng savoured the atmosphere and celebrated Carmody's win, a tragedy was unfolding back along the road. Andy 'Ando' Christle, Joe's brother, had returned from England to help with the race and was driving a motorbike. His brother, Colm, who was competing in the race, had suffered a number of punctures and was late arriving. Andy left the finish in Tralee to go and meet him, but collided with a car a few miles outside the town and was killed. Colm saw the accident but at the time did not realise it was his brother. Andy Christle[13] was the first of three men to die during the first fifty years of the Rás.

Andy's death was a terrible tragedy for the Christles and a bitter blow to the Gate club and the Rás. All the Christles and Gate members retired. Kerry Sloane, who was competing, pulled out and took over from Joe Christle as Race Director.

The race left for Ennis the next day. Carmody's spell as race leader came to an ignominious end at the bridge in Listowel. Seeing some of his family and supporters on the bridge, he raised both hands in a sign of triumph and to display the Yellow Jersey. He wobbled, hit the parapet hard and crashed heavily. A youthful team-mate from Kerry, Gene Mangan, waited for him and they chased in vain for the rest of the day but never regained contact. This was a second hugely frustrating stage for Mangan – another team-mate, Paudi Fitzgerald, had fallen on tram tracks as the race was leaving Dublin and since Fitzgerald was considered to be a prospective race winner in Kerry, Mangan had also waited for him. They had spent over 100 miles (160km) chasing in vain.

The Rás had its first and longest ever time trial on the following day – 40 miles (64km) from Ennis to Galway – and it produced the overall winner, along with the first Rás controversy. The timekeeper's car punctured between the start and finishing points, and a dispute arose from a claim that he was not at the finish when some of the riders crossed the line. The timekeeper insisted he saw the last riders crossing the line as he arrived and that he had timed them from the moving car. Joe O'Brien was credited as the winner and he regained the Yellow Jersey. This incident illustrates the apparent sophistication of the organisation masked its fragile and shoestring nature. Jim Killean, for example, the timekeeper, drove his own car and at his own expense; the jeep carrying a cameraman had been cadged from the competing army team; and a céilí band toured with the race, partly to provide much-needed income from stage-end dances each evening.

The strain was now telling on some of the riders. Long, rain-soaked stages of over six hours, distorted leather saddles from constant wettings, poor food and unreliable support, indifferent digs with the sharing of beds and lack of drying facilities, the physical attrition and lack of mental preparation all combined to result in abandonments. It proved too much for the precocious, seventeen-year-old Gene Mangan. Having spent two of the first four days chasing on his own with team-mates and affected by the shock death in the race, he led a mutiny in the Kerry camp over poor conditions, and three of his team decamped in Galway. The number of riders to give up was never officially announced, but up to nineteen eventually abandoned, including the Gate riders.

With a strong and well-managed team, O'Brien – who took two stages in succession – and the National club gained a stranglehold on the event and went on to win the individual and team prizes. The race made the symbolically important journey across the border for stage ends at Armagh and Newry, and the all-important 32-county dimension was bolstered when Joe McIvor, the sole rider representing Tyrone, won the final stage into the Phoenix Park in Dublin.

Even though the 1,000-mile (1,600km) figure was regularly cited, the first eight-day Rás recorded 906.25 miles (1,450km). The average speed was 23.2 mph (37.1 km/h), and the slowest stage, 128 miles (205km) from Cork to Wexford in wet weather, averaged 20.8 mph (33.2 km/h). Sixteen-year-old Willie Kennedy from the Tailteann Club finished the event. The winner, nineteen-year-old Joe O'Brien from Dublin, had been suffering from pain in his back during the race. It continued to bother him and he did not ride another Rás. It transpired he had cancer in his spine and he died at a young age.

The Rás organisers cultivated athlete-warrior symbolism – this Cúchulainn image was used in early Rás promotional material.

The first multi-stage Rás was an overwhelming success. As a novelty and spectacle, it had attracted some large crowds. There had been nothing like it before and it caught the imagination of the public who were astonished and enthralled at the idea that local men could race 1,000 miles in eight days. At a time when most heroes were local heroes, the attraction of seeing local men in action was very strong. As Rás finishers, the riders became men of esteem in their communities.

The event presented a colossal athletic challenge to the riders and many found the racing exceptionally hard. There were large time-gaps – 25 minutes separated first and tenth rider on GC (General Classification) – and to finish the Rás was considered a badge of distinction. For the NCA, it was a triumph and an all-Ireland triumph at that. The Rás had achieved its objective of creating an event with the status and attraction necessary to keep riders in the association. Christle, Sloane and the NCA – experts at promotion – exploited the success of the Rás to the full. They cultivated the warrior-athlete figure and created the iconic 'Men of the Rás' image which took hold in the riders' and public's imaginations.

The Rás also proved to be a highly successful social event and – at a time when most people seldom left their native parish – was an entirely new experience for many of the riders. An *esprit de corps* was felt by the participants in the race, and bonhomie and camaraderie developed amongst the entire entourage over the eight days. The race dances and close intermingling with the local communities at stage ends generated an atmosphere of fun which was to become a hallmark of the Rás.

Most of the riders and officials involved in 1954 were won over by the event and determined to do it again. They left for home with a new appreciation of the demands of stage racing and a determination to be better prepared the following year. A transformation of competitive cycling in many regions got under way and a series of classic races developed from around this time – Rás Luimní, Rás Uladh, Rás Laighean and Rás Glanmire.

Road racing might have become the dominant form of competitive cycling in Ireland even without the Rás, but the 1954 race was undoubtedly a watershed in Irish cycling and stimulated an explosion in road racing. Within a couple of years, the cycling landscape was irreversibly changing. An article in a 1960 issue of *Bikes and Bikemen* bemoaned the decline in track racing:

A strange disease is sweeping the country, it is long distance-itis. Those suffering from it have the hallucination that anything less than one hundred miles is not bicycle racing and that track-racing is only for scrubbers.[14]

But there was to be no turning back of the clock. From 1954 on, the Rás became the primary motivating force for competitive Irish cyclists and the pivotal event around which the entire racing year revolved.

3

CONSOLIDATION

Gene Mangan
with supporters
following his 1955 Rás
win, three days before his
nineteenth birthday. The
rider standing to his right
is his team-mate
John Switzer.

With the practical feasibility of the Rás well established in 1954 and the various bureaucratic hurdles overcome, the organisers were able to focus on improving the event. In 1955, support became more readily available. The GAA connection was formalised and an NCA press release happily announced that the GAA Central Council, as 'fellow Gaels', had given the race its official blessing and sent 'a substantial cheque'. The GAA records show this to be £100, but it's possible that Pádraig O'Keeffe, president of the GAA, made more available unofficially. The GAA also presented a new Rás trophy, Corn Cathal Brugha, modelled on the McCarthy Cup presented to the winners of the All-Ireland hurling final. Highly-prized All-Ireland GAA medals were also provided as prizes. Individual GAA County Boards supported some county teams while Bord Fáilte donated £250.

Throughout the country, riders and County Boards were making their own preparations. Fund-raising was under way and long-distance races began to spring up in many places. The craft of road racing was being quickly learned in the school of practical experience and the intense rivalry amongst those hoping to be selected for county teams spiced up the racing scene.

Sixty riders started the 1955 Rás and the entire procession had more of the trappings of a large stage race than it had the previous year. Loudspeakers, a broom-wagon, press reporters and team motorbikes added to the spectacle and the race attracted a huge following from the beginning. Inter-county competition was tremendous and a mammoth battle unfolded between Kerry and Dublin to further excite interest – many of the newspaper reports of the day gave team results priority over individual placings. On completion of the 1955 event eight days later, the Rás had consolidated its position and was firmly established as a major national sporting event. The race also produced Ireland's first road racing superstar, in the form of the eighteen-year-old Gene Mangan from Kerry.

Mangan and bikes were synonymous from a young age. Apart from the mechanical fascination, cycling became a vent for his individuality and single-mindedness, and satisfied his competitive streak. It also became an instrument in the process of carving out an identity separate from his father, whose notable record in rugby and golf created expectations. In his native Killorglin, Mangan's reputation on a bike developed when he was young. Speeding down the hill in the town, with his feet on the saddle, drew some attention. A high-speed collision with a horse left the youngster unscathed, but the horse had to be put down. One of his more notable escapades was to ride across the lumpy, rough-hewn parapet of the eight-arch bridge that dominates the town. He ensured a good audience by timing his performance for after Mass, when the townspeople would be passing,

Ronnie Long from the Limerick team heads the leading break crossing the Shannon at Sarsfield's Bridge, Limerick, 1955. He is followed by Séamus Healy (Tipperary), Tom Gerrard (Meath), Paddy O'Callaghan (Kerry).Ollie Brawn (Limerick-team manager) is on the first motorbike.

and coinciding it with low tide, thereby leaving the spectators in little doubt that a fall would almost certainly result in his death.

Biking was becoming inexorably linked with his persona but, in spite of his antics, the need to find expression through the bike remained stifled. Circumstances changed dramatically for him, at the age of fourteen, over a school disciplinary matter. Constantly flouting a school rule that all pupils had to be indoors at 7 pm during term, one night he was involved in a near-collision with the principal's wife. He was paraded before the entire school assembly the next morning and asked to undertake that he would stay off his bike until the summer holidays. For Mangan, this was too much. To the consternation of all, he refused and fled into the Kerry mountains, on his bike, in the depths of winter.

When he was brought back, three days later, his father had come to a better realisation of the significance of the bike for his son and offered a compromise that would also resolve the school-disciplinary problem – if Gene wanted to cycle, he could do so by riding to a school in Tralee each day – a return journey of 34 miles (54km) with 1,600 feet (488m) of climbing. Gene demanded a new racing bike as part of the bargain and specified a Hobbs of Barbican from the Rutland bike shop in Dublin. He was dispatched by train to the care of an aunt and made his purchase. Instead of returning by train as expected, he headed for Kerry on his new bike, departing on a Saturday evening. He rode 60 miles (96km) to Mountrath before nightfall and cycled the remaining 140 miles (224km) to Killorglin on Sunday. The following day, Gene made his first journey to school in Tralee. Thus began his journey, with a bike, into the wider world.

Mangan began competing immediately on road and track, and won the first Kerry road championship[15] in 1952 at the age of fifteen, and won again in 1953. He emigrated to England after the Rás in 1954. While he continued to compete and train there, he was not considered a rider in good form when he returned for the 1955 Rás. That year, Denis O'Connor, of the confident and experienced Dublin team, won the first stage, to Newry. Mick Palmer, from Mayo, broke a chain when he was away in a crucial break and his eventual third place might otherwise have been different.

The second, mammoth 140-mile (224km) stage, from Newry to Sligo, was significant for Mangan in that he avoided losing the race. Every stage race has a defining moment from which the eventual victory can be traced, something usually highlighted in subsequent analysis. Yet many of the Rás victories, such as Mangan's in 1955, can be traced to equally significant, but more low-key moments, in an earlier part of the race when defeat was avoided. These incidents often require more mental ruggedness than the winning moves or the defence of a lead. They often occur early in a race, when the only pressure on a rider is the weight of his own ambition or the fear of failure. In such cases, the seemingly inexorable unfolding of events is defied, the 'inevitable' not conceded. Such moments require a mix of courage and talent, or the need for individual character to overcome the collective will of a bunch.

These critical moments in Rásanna were usually tied up with 'Rás breaks'. Decisive breaks, with large time-gaps, were to be a feature of the event. Such a break developed during this second stage and Mangan was not in it. When the gap reached five minutes, he made one of those crucial moves that overcomes defeat – he broke free from the bunch, alone, and time trialled for 75 miles (120km) to cut the deficit to the lead group to two minutes. The main bunch came in another three minutes behind – his chances of eventual victory would almost certainly have been over had he still been in it.

On the third stage, from Sligo to Westport, Mangan and the Dublin rider, Steve Abbott, were to have the first of their head-to-head sprints that were to be a feature of the race. These were a sub-plot in the greater Dublin-versus-Kerry drama and aroused great public interest – like two full-forwards going for goal, their arrival was eagerly anticipated at stage ends. Mangan defeated Abbott in the first duel, at Westport, but Abbott had the satisfaction of winning in Mangan's home territory in Tralee and in front of an enormous crowd.

The head-to-head sprints between Steve Abbott of Dublin and Gene Mangan of Kerry were a feature of the 1955 Rás and a sub-plot in the greater Dublin-versus-Kerry rivalry. Here, Abbott beats Mangan into Tralee on stage 5.

The next stage marked the first visit of the Rás to the Kerry mountains, a battlefield that was to feature in most subsequent events. The cohesive Kerry team had decided to move against O'Connor, who had held the Jersey from the beginning, and Mangan attacked from the line in Tralee. He broke an axle on Moll's Gap, but his team-mate, Paddy O'Callaghan, was on hand to give Mangan his bike. Then he punctured on the 'Tunnel Road', heading for the prime at the summit – he won on a flat front tyre. Switching to the spare bike of a team-mate – Paudi Fitzgerald – Mangan gave chase to the leading group. The ferocity of his descent into Glengarriff, where he caught them, became part of Kerry's cycling folklore, with one newspaper describing him as having descended 'on wings'. By the end of the stage, O'Connor had lost the Jersey to fellow Dubliner, Steve Abbott, and Mangan had gone into second place at just 11 seconds.

Mangan took the Jersey with typical aplomb on the second-last day, to Wexford. At Carrick-on-Suir, he jumped from a chasing group containing Abbott, got across to the lead bunch on his own in 30 miles (48km), and won the sprint to the finish. Now in yellow, Mangan put the yellow tape on his handlebars that he had brought from England in anticipation of victory.

Given that he was now the likely race winner, as well as the leader of the probable winning team, he decided that the normal accommodation arranged by the Kerry manger, Liam Brick, was not appropriate for their status in the Rás. He led the team to the best hotel that he could find in Wexford, leaving the unfortunate Brick to worry about finding the funds necessary for such unknown extravagance.

The Kerry team carefully marked every Dublin rider on the road to Dublin the following day and successfully defended the team-prize and Mangan's lead. At eighteen years of age, he was to be the youngest rider ever to win the Rás.

It was the first, high-profile exposure of Mangan's tactical brilliance, supreme style and devastating speed. One contemporary, who had been challenging him for the Jersey, described him as a greyhound, bounding from bunch to bunch; another, who was later to become a Rás winner himself, but of the more rugged style, said that comparing Mangan and himself was like comparing a racehorse to a donkey.

The response to the 1955 Rás was unprecedented in Irish cycling and the reaction in Kerry illustrated how deeply it had entered the public consciousness in so short a time. The drama and scale of the event was hugely impressive and the courage and endurance of the riders was widely written about in epic and heroic terms.

The Rás was firmly established and hugely popular by the end of the second, eight-day event in 1955. The victorious Kerry team was brought into Tralee on a truck and given a huge reception. The group on the truck: (left–right) Jimmy Leahy (Kerry support), Liam Brick (Kerry manager), Gene Mangan (Rás winner), Jack Lacey (president of Tralee Cycling Club), Jackie Connor, Paddy O'Callaghan, Paudi Fitzgerald, unknown.

The Kerry team toured the county and its reception was matched only by those of All-Ireland-winning football teams. There were processions, civic receptions and massive crowds wherever it went. Even the third-place rider, Mick Palmer, was greeted by bonfires in his native Westport. The extent of its impact can be illustrated by one example. In 1955, a young Kerry football team beat a fancied Dublin side in the All-Ireland final, a game that is considered to be one of Kerry's greatest footballing victories. Yet, that year's recipient of the Bishop Moynihan Trophy – essentially 'Kerry sportsperson of the year' – was an eighteen-year-old cyclist, Gene Mangan.

For the NCA, the 1955 Rás was another wonderful sporting and strategic success, and Gene Mangan, as a young cycling star, was a valuable asset. Mangan, however, also became an important test of the Rás. Given his track, time trial and road victories, he was an obvious candidate for international competition and it was inevitable that joining the CRE would be suggested to him. Not being from a strong republican family, he had no ideological ties to the NCA. Would the Rás' stature and aura counter the attraction of international representation? Could the Rás realise one of its intended objectives of retaining top road men in the NCA?

Mangan remained in the NCA fold. He was intimidated by the prospect of being branded a 'traitor', and the healthy domestic racing scene satisfied his competitive needs. The NCA's promotional acumen also ensured that his public profile remained high and that he received the acclamation which his undoubted talent deserved.

Mangan soon learned that being a leading NCA figure brought expectations and obligations other than sporting. Within a few weeks of his Rás win, he found himself in an Italian jail. The background to this extraordinary development was the increasing frustration felt by the NCA at its inability to represent Ireland and a resultant degree of entrenchment and belligerence towards the CRE. An illustration of this was when English riders preparing to compete in the CRE's 1955 Tour of Ireland received telegrams on the eve of their departure announcing that the event had been cancelled – part of the NCA's uncompromising campaign to sabotage the event. At the same time, other tensions arose from increased IRA activity in Northern Ireland, which was to culminate in the 'Border Campaign' of 1956–62. Given the NCA leadership at the time, it was inevitable that the distinction between cycling and politics would be blurred even more. The case of the Gate rider, Philip Clarke, illustrates this.

A prominent Gate rider who had ridden with the club in the first two Rásanna, Clarke was also in the IRA and close to Joe Christle. In an attempt to replicate the spectacular raid on Gough Barracks, the IRA launched an elaborate attack on

Go dtugaidh Dia neart is bua dhuit,
Fuinneamh tréan, ceacht is clú dhuit,
Rath is séan i gcleasa lúith dhuit,
Is ceart i gcúis na h-Éireann.

(May God give strength and victory to you,
Great energy and fame to you,
Success and satisfaction in athleticism to you,
And justice in the cause of Ireland.)

Seán Ó Néill, May 1958 –
from *The Gene Mangan Story*

The NCA's promotional acumen, combined with the aura that surrounded the Rás Tailteann, ensured great acclaim for the stars of the day.

Omagh army barracks, County Tyrone, in October 1954. Joe Christle, Philip Clarke, Pat Murphy[16] and other Gate members were involved, but the foray went wrong. Christle was wounded in an exchange of fire with British troops and Clarke was captured and sentenced to ten years in jail. Given the republican tradition of cherishing prisoners and exploiting their captivity, Sinn Féin decided to enter prisoners as candidates in the Westminster elections. Christle's reputation had been much enhanced in republican circles by the courage and leadership he had displayed in the Omagh fight and this helped him secure a nomination for Philip Clarke for the Fermanagh–South Tyrone constituency. Clarke was subsequently elected as an MP but was disqualified because of his conviction. He was also elected vice-president of the NCA and the number one jersey was reserved for him in the Rás until the end of the decade. He became an NCA *cause célèbre*, and a surrogate voice of the NCA republican element within Irish cycling.

Within this atmosphere of increasing agitation, the NCA decided to use the World Cycling Championships in Frascati, near Rome, as an international stage to air its grievances. It selected and sent an 'Irish' team, even though the CRE was the UCI-recognised team for the race.[17] Mangan's Rás win ensured he was picked for the NCA team and, because of his naïvety about political matters, he assumed that he would actually be racing for Ireland. The other members of the team – Séamus McGreevy from County Down, Bernie O'Brien from Kildare and Mick

Some county teams quickly became quite sophisticated for their day. The Kerry contingent, for example, had a van (above), car (facing page, top) and motorbike (below) to support the riders in 1956. Such arrangements were often fickle, however, depending on the circumstances involved. Kerry was out of the Rás the following year due to internal wrangling. Above left (left–right): Donie O'Shea and Mossie Cantillon. Below: Mossie Cantillon, Tom Fitzgerald (Paudi's father), Johnny Switzer, Donie O'Shea.

A Rás group in the 1950s.

Christle from Dublin – were committed and experienced supporters of the cause, and probably a lot wiser about the true nature of the mission. The team did infiltrate to the start but were spotted. When attempts were made to eject them, observed by the Pope, Mick Christle traded blows with CRE riders and then with the Italian police. The team members were all arrested, put into jail and made the desired international headlines, thus promoting the NCA and republican cause.

While it was a coup for the NCA, it had unwelcome repercussions for Mangan. His family was deeply unhappy about his role in the event and he was not able to return to his job in England because of the publicity and his 'association' with republicanism. He eventually settled in Dublin where he was offered a job on condition that he join the National Cycling Club, under the control of a noted NCA figure, Jack Sweeney. The National suited Mangan – it concentrated on road racing and was well organised. Its patron and president was the Taoiseach, Seán Lemass.

Apart from a spell racing in France, Mangan was an integral part of the Rás for the next twenty years. He wove a particular style through the fabric of the race and won a total of twelve stages. He was one of a group of riders – including Ben McKenna, Paddy Flanagan and Shay O'Hanlon – emerging onto the road racing scene around this time and who contributed immeasurably to the Rás. They were all rounded cyclists, in track, road and time trial, and each had particular qualities of style and character that were admired and valued, and which made them distinctive beyond the reputations gained solely from winning. Those particular qualities found their best expression in the Rás and their greatest link with the public was through the Rás. The Rás, therefore, was the medium through which they were to become legends and where their endeavour and mode of accomplishment was so valued in the sporting public's consciousness that the word 'great' became attached to their names. In this way, the 'Great' Gene Mangan, the 'Great' Ben McKenna, the 'Great' Paddy Flanagan and the 'Great' Shay O'Hanlon emerged from the Rás, beginning with Mangan's performance in 1955.

CONFLICT

Jackie Connor of Kerry in defiant pose after the 'recapture' of the tricolour from the RUC near Lurgan, County Armagh. Note his bike set-up, with long frame and very low saddle.

The quasi-political element of the Rás was to impact on the 1956 event, as it had in the previous years, and embroil the race in one of the more memorable episodes in its fifty-year history.

By 1956, Joe Christle was becoming an irritant to the IRA leadership on a number of counts. He was something of a loose cannon, pulling off various stunts without authorisation and, more significantly, becoming the focus for a group of younger, more militant Dublin IRA men who were impatient with the leadership's lack of action on the North. The IRA GHQ (General Headquarters) felt Christle was somewhat beyond its control and therefore dangerous, and he was expelled on a technicality. Christle held a meeting in Dalkey and founded a new organisation, Óglaigh na hÉireann. Up to half of the IRA activists in Dublin were said to have joined him and it became a serious issue for the IRA in the run-up to its planned Border Campaign later in the year. Various mediation efforts were made but the Christle group later joined up with Saor Uladh, another splinter group which operated along the border under Liam Kelly. Jim Killean and Pat Murphy were also active with this grouping.

In the midst of these developments, Christle was organising the 1956 Rás. The jailed Philip Clarke became a voice for Christle's ideology in cycling circles and the first page of the 1956 Rás programme had a photograph of Clarke being taken from Belfast High Court, along with the following message:

> From his cell in Belfast Jail, he says to Rás Tailteann competitors: 'As sportsmen I congratulate you for upholding National Unity: as soldiers I trust you will strive to attain National Sovereignty.' (Philip Clarke, TD)[18]

The average Rás rider did not consider himself to be a 'soldier', and definitely not in the literal sense. While there was a core of republican activists in the NCA, most were just competitive cyclists without political ideology beyond the general republican aspiration of the population at large. The 'message', however, was clear and, perhaps, portentous. During the second stage in 1956, from Newry to Armagh, the riders found themselves behind a lead car, occupied by Joe Christle and John O'Reilly, that was defiantly flying a large Irish tricolour. Under the Flags and Emblems Act (Northern Ireland) of 1954, the tricolour was suppressed in Northern Ireland. Where any police officer considered a flag or emblem likely to lead to a breach of the peace, the Act empowered the officer to 'require the person displaying the flag or emblem to remove it', or for the officer himself to 'remove and detain' it. Trouble had previously broken out at a number of NCA races where the flag had been flown. In Newry, in 1954, for example, fighting broke out

A scene near Lurgan, County Armagh, following the fracas over the flying of the tricolour. The known individuals are (from the left) Paddy O'Callaghan, Donie O'Shea (Kerry-support team, in white overalls), Colm Christle (foreground), Brian Monaghan (behind Christle to left), Bernie O'Brien (no. 24), John O'Reilly (in black with cap).

between NCA riders and the RUC (Royal Ulster Constabulary), during which the police had used batons.

Shortly into the stage from Newry to Armagh – an anti-clockwise loop around Lough Neagh – the first of a series of incidents occurred that became known collectively as the 'Cookstown incident'. A policeman stopped the lead car near Banbridge and ordered the tricolour flag to be removed. Christle and O'Reilly refused and drove away before any of the riders came up to them. Further along, outside Lurgan, the police blocked the road and again ordered the removal of the flag. Tension rose on this occasion, as riders and officials came up to the lead car and milled around. As one newspaper tactfully reported, there were 'vocal recriminations of a political nature'. John O'Reilly was then struck in the mouth with a stick wielded by a police inspector. The police tried to seize the flag and a fracas ensued during which the flag pole was broken. Christle regained the flag and held onto it, surrounded by cyclists. Jim Killean began negotiations with the RUC, arguing that the flag was not likely to lead to a breach of the peace and was therefore legal. The arrival of a tender-load of police added to the tension. The police were adamant that the race would not proceed while the flag was flown,

The Rás bunch in triumphant mood with the tricolour they 'recaptured' from the RUC during a fracas near Lurgan in 1956. The flag pole had been broken in the mêlée. The stage was cancelled in protest at the RUC not allowing the flag to be flown and the riders were cycling the route in protest. Retribution was pending, however, and they were riding into an RUC and unionist ambush at Cookstown. (Left–right) Frank Ward, Dublin (with glasses), Natty Fahy (note hand in plaster-cast), Paddy Moriarty (Kerry), Peter Sweeney (Dublin, no. 22), Ben McKenna (Meath, no. 25), Johnny Switzer (Kerry), Paddy O'Callaghan (Kerry), Cecil Donoghue (Dublin, in Yellow Jersey), Denis O'Connor (with dark glasses) and John Landers (from Kerry, riding with Cork team). The man in the dark top, at Paddy Moriarty's right shoulder, is Tommy Flanagan (Navan).

prompting Christle to announce the abandonment of the stage in protest – the only Rás stage ever to have been abandoned. The riders, he declared, would ride the rest of the route, but only as a protest demonstration.

The cavalcade moved out, with the cyclists riding tempo, and police tenders gathered both in front and behind. Paddy O'Callaghan, a republican activist from Kerry, is especially remembered for leading the bunch in the singing of republican songs, including 'A Nation Once Again'. They continued around Lough Neagh, through Randlestown and Magherafelt. Before Cookstown, O'Callaghan provoked matters further when he led an attempt to remove a Union Jack from a telegraph pole, in retaliation for the police attempting to seize the tricolour. The police foiled their efforts and one of the riders was struck with a baton. The incident heightened tension considerably and was frightening for some of the riders.

When they reached the outskirts of Cookstown, they found the road blocked by police. A large group of hostile unionist residents was also waiting. The police ordered the removal of various placards and emblems from the vehicles, and tension rose on all sides. Political slogans were shouted, a bottle was thrown at the race, the hostile crowd, joined by police with swinging batons, rushed the cyclists and serious fighting broke out. The mêlée ebbed and flowed for approximately twenty minutes, with the Kerry team coming in for particular attention as their colours closely resembled those of the tricolour. One of their number, Jimmy Leahy, was badly beaten.

The memories of some of those who were at Cookstown present three overriding impressions from the episode – firstly, and predominantly, there were feelings of real fear and vulnerability; secondly, the screaming of the unionist women, some of whom threw hot water at the riders as they tried to exit the scene; and thirdly, intense annoyance at the race having been interrupted.

A number of riders were reported to have been injured and put into vehicles, and the remainder eventually moved to the safety of the nationalist end of the town, either individually or in small groups, through a narrow gauntlet of locals who continued to make random attacks. There, the race regrouped and rode the rest of the stage heavily escorted by police. There was a certain elation, common to groups in the aftermath of having conducted themselves well in action. They reached Armagh towards nightfall and received a warm reception from its predominantly nationalist population.

The NCA leadership immediately set about maximising the publicity value of the event and it made front-page headlines throughout the country the following day. Jim Killean prepared a formal protest to the Stormont government and Paddy O'Callaghan contacted Kerry colleagues with instructions to have a Union Jack on hand for the homecoming of the team to Tralee.

The following day, the race was neutralised leaving Armagh and had a heavy police escort to the border. Tension remained high and there were a number of isolated incidents – the flag was again flown for a time and individual cars were stopped and forced to remove emblems. The Rás regrouped in Monaghan, where the race proper got under way to Ballina in the west, 136 miles (218km) away. The total distance for the day was 153 miles (254km), including the neutralised section. The stage to Ballina is remembered by many participants as one of the most gruelling Rás stages they ever experienced. Some riders were on their bikes for over eight hours, due to a combination of the neutralised section from Armagh to Monaghan, the delays in beginning the race and the demands of the stage itself, which went through five counties. The weather was bad, too, with wind and rain.

Newry, the morning after the 'Cookstown Incident' and prior to the start of the stage to Ballina. Mossie Cantillon (centre) and Donie O'Shea (right), with the tricolour that had become a trophy. Posing for the photograph with them is the guest-house owner.

The Middletown border crossing, County Armagh, the day after the 'Cookstown incident' – the Ulster team is forced to remove a tricolour pennant before leaving Northern Ireland.

Paudi Fitzgerald and Con Carr (right) at the start of stage 3 in Ballina, 1956. Carr, the oldest man in the race at thirty-eight, was the race leader having won the confused stage the previous day when they rode an estimated 153 miles (254km) from Armagh, the day after 'Cookstown'. Fitzgerald almost abandoned that day but went on to win two stages and the Rás. The car was owned by Fitzgerald's father, who was a carpenter – hence the wooden bike rack. Con Carr had to be taken to hospital after the first stage in 1960 when he struck a cow during the sprint.

Added to this, some groups of riders went astray because of confusion over the route – the stage was re-routed in order to avoid entering Northern Ireland again at Enniskillen. One of those to lose time over this was John Keane of the Exiles team.

News of Cookstown had reached Ballina and a large crowd was waiting. Con Carr from Kildare, the oldest man in the field at thirty-eight, won the stage late in the evening. Groups straggled to the finish well after dark and burning tar-barrels were put out on the approaches to guide the riders in. Carr had gone into yellow in Ballina but, without strong support, could not contain a series of Kerry attacks launched from the start of the following stage, to Nenagh. Paudi Fitzgerald, who

Ronnie Williams of the Dublin team receives the Yellow Jersey from the Kerry Manager, Liam Brick, in Tralee, 1956. Many notable characters of the rival Dublin and Kerry teams of the period are present: (left–right) Denis O'Connor (Dublin, Yellow Jersey holder for five stages in 1955), Paudi Fitzgerald (Kerry, two stage wins and outright winner in 1956), Liam Brick (Kerry manager), Cecil Donoghue (Dublin, one stage win and Yellow Jersey holder for two stages in 1956), Ronnie Williams (Dublin, Yellow Jersey holder for one stage in 1956) and Matt Sands (Dublin manager).

went on to win the race, was in the midst of the action but was, in fact, very lucky to have been still in the race at that point. Like Mangan the previous year, Fitzgerald just avoided defeat in the early stages of the Rás. He had been in the break with Carr the previous day from Monaghan, but the group eventually disintegrated from exhaustion until just three riders were left. Then, in an advanced stage of fatigue and with only 10 miles to go, Fitzgerald climbed off the bike and tried to abandon.

Fitzgerald, who came from Lispole in the middle of the Dingle Peninsula, had come to road racing through the usual route of local track-racing and progressed to the Kerry team through a combination of talent and huge training miles. Fortified with porridge and a raw egg in sherry at dawn – prepared by his mother – he would train over the Conor Pass or around Slea Head on his way to work, followed by longer evening routes. Weekends might include a trip to an aunt in

Macroom, via Kenmare, Glengarriff and the Pass of Kemaneagh. He was a well-established rider in 1956, but came to the Rás with a residual frustration from the previous three years. He felt that he might have won in 1953 had he attacked the punctured Colm Christle instead of waiting. In 1954, he was left unsupported at a crucial stage after half of his team had absconded and he had crashed and hurt himself in 1955.

Team support was crucial to Fitzgerald when he tried to abandon and, as in many Rásanna to follow, was vital in saving the eventual win. Supporters put him back on the bike, and he struggled to the finish at the back of a following group. When he was bathed, fed and massaged, they forced him to ride a few miles in low gears. They got him up early the following morning, again riding in low gears for half an hour. By the time the fourth stage started for Nenagh, Fitzgerald was fully recovered and finished second behind Gene Mangan. At the next stage end, in Tralee, an oil tanker was left onto the finishing straight, causing confusion and danger, but Fitzgerald was most successful in negotiating the obstacle and won. Ronnie Williams from Dublin went into yellow in Tralee, but Fitzgerald attacked him on the following stage to Kenmare, dropped him in the Kerry mountains and won his second consecutive stage.

Though Fitzgerald had dropped Williams, John Keane, from the Exiles team, stuck with him. At this point, Keane was the only survivor of the Exiles, who were without a car or support, and had been trying to get around as best they could. Keane, originally from County Roscommon, was then labouring in England. He won the KOH in bad fog at Coomakista and went into yellow by just twenty seconds in Kenmare. He was the first man from Connacht to wear the Yellow Jersey in the Rás.

Fitzgerald's instructions, on the second-last stage to Nenagh, were simple. He was to attack Keane in the mountains and be more than twenty seconds ahead of him into Clonmel, 133 miles (213km) away. Fitzgerald went clear on his own over the 'county bounds', and was over four minutes up at Mallow. He took a wrong turn shortly outside the town, heading for Mitchelstown rather than Fermoy, and took another wrong turn before Fermoy. A group of eight, including Keane and Mangan, came up to him at Glanworth. He had lost the time advantage gained on his sole effort from Kenmare. The leading bunch disintegrated as various riders tried to jump clear and Mangan went away to eventually win the stage. Fitzgerald and Keane were left behind with a smaller group. There was a stalemate, as Fitzgerald could not break clear of Keane. Keane started to tease him and they began to argue and then tussled with each other. Their managers and the other riders eventually got the group on the move again but Fitzgerald still failed to break

Emotions were running very high in Tralee when the Kerry Rás team returned after the 1956 'Cookstown incident'. Here, Donie O'Shea (left) and Paddy O'Callaghan – standing on the roof of a bus – are burning a Union Jack said to have been captured by the riders. The flag, in fact, was procured from a local travel agent for the occasion. O'Callaghan, a republican activist, had been prominent in the 'Cookstown incident'. O'Shea, who was driving a Kerry support car, quietly slipped away from the mêlée near Lurgan to smash the headlights of police tenders.

free. When the bunch came across a funeral in a village outside Mitchelstown, Fitzgerald took his chance, attacking up the left side of the cortège. Keane responded by chasing on the other side but got held up amongst the mourners. Fitzgerald was free. He got out of sight around bends and was over six minutes ahead of Keane into Clonmel. He was now race leader, with a comfortable margin for the final stage to Dublin.

While this winning move was unfolding, another row had developed further back, at Mallow, where Ronnie Williams had got into a fight with his Dublin manager, Matt Sands. Williams was tired from the efforts of defending his Jersey the previous day and felt that his team might have done more to help. He was frustrated with the Dublin tactics that saw them losing a commanding team lead to Kerry and was further frustrated with tactics during his chase of Fitzgerald. He

The tricolour that had been re-captured from the Northern Ireland police toured the county as a trophy with the winning Kerry team.

got off his bike near the railway bridge at Mallow and demanded his gear from the manager. Sands was not pleased that one of his best riders was abandoning and a wrestling match ensued at the side of the road. Williams eventually got his gear, walked up to the railway station and took the next train home. The battle between Kerry and Dublin was over.

Fitzgerald held his lead to Dublin and Kerry's dominance was sealed when Paddy Moriarty won the last stage. Kerry had won the team and individual prize, and all but two stages. The celebrations in Kerry equalled those of the previous year and again demonstrated the enormous popularity that the Rás had achieved. The reception in the strongly republican town of Tralee was highly emotive, focusing strongly on the 'victory' at Cookstown. Fiery speeches were made – one speaker assured the crowd that each member of the Kerry team was prepared to defend the tricolour with his life if necessary and that, hopefully, it would be flying for good over Cookstown some day. The tricolour recaptured from the RUC was displayed and a Union Jack, which was claimed to have been captured by the cyclists, was burned on top of a bus.

The tone of some of the reporting on the Cookstown incident by the regional newspapers had fuelled this atmosphere – much of it referred to the presence and defeat of 'B-men', or 'B-Specials' – members of the Ulster Special Constabulary, a heavily armed and notoriously sectarian reserve police force, feared and loathed in equal measure by the nationalist population. One report read like a Hollywood script, with the outnumbered 'cowboys' riding through hostile territory, being attacked, their wagons encircled, beating off the attackers in a 'fierce fight' and riding away victorious.

The wider implications of Cookstown cannot, however, be trivialised. It occurred at a time when elements in the IRA, led by Christle, were seeking more militant action and Cookstown may have been a motivating factor in that process. The IRA Border Campaign formally began a few months later, in December 1956, and lasted until 1962. Christle's military adventures were confined to the 'Kelly/ Christle group', and mainly involved the blowing up of police and customs buildings across the border.

Although there is no direct evidence that Christle deliberately engineered the Cookstown incident, the flying of the tricolour at the head of a high-profile race, in probable contravention of the Flags and Emblems Act and at a time of heightened border security was highly provocative. He must have expected at least some level of trouble in the circumstances. Cookstown was the type of stunt and defiant statement at which he excelled, and the belligerent NCA tone, exemplified by Philip Clarke's 'message' prior to the Rás, adds weight to the suggestion that the incident was a welcome expression of the NCA leadership's position. To argue, however, that NCA riders were mere pawns, manipulated for the wider political interests of the NCA's hierarchy, would be an over-simplification given the intricate socio-political complexities of Ireland at the time. A number of cyclists and NCA officials were certainly involved in the IRA, but the vast majority of the riders were more interested in how Cookstown affected their performance in the race. But like most of the Irish population at the time, the riders supported, in principle, the political thrust of the NCA. One rider expressed in simple, unsophisticated terms, how that general sentiment fitted with Cookstown: 'It was our flag, the flag of our federation and our country – we had the right to carry it in our own country and they could all f—k off.'

Paudi
Fitzgerald:
'A jewel that
was left in
the ground.'

Like Gene Mangan's Rás win the previous year, the 1956 Rás had an epilogue
for the winner. Paudi Fitzgerald's victory resulted in his selection on an NCA Irish
cycling team, this time bound for the Olympic Games in Melbourne and again
with the intention of highlighting the NCA grievance of being excluded from the
competition. Tommy Flanagan, the National League Champion, was also chosen,
along with Tom Gerrard from Meath, who was in Australia at the time.

As in Rome, the riders infiltrated the start of the race, were identified and
ejected with great publicity. They had the assistance of a well-organised expatriate
group that distributed thousands of leaflets arguing the case in Christle's
unmistakable style: 'Must we, as Irishmen, beg crumbs from England's table, so

that we may eat on Mount Olympus?' Their mission, however, had additional objectives. They were instructed to remove every Union Jack they could find, which they duly did, and – in keeping with the hard-line approach – were instructed to extinguish the Olympic flame in protest at their exclusion. However, on discovering that the flame was an engineering structure too large and sophisticated for the mission, that part of the plan was abandoned. To Fitzgerald's relief, what would have been an historical moment in Olympic history was avoided.

While the Melbourne mission was relatively successful from the NCA point of view, it was overshadowed by Ronnie Delany's win in the mile and especially by the fact that his gold medal was won for 'Éire', a 26-county entity.

The three-month round trip to Melbourne, via the US, was a wonderful experience for the young man from west Kerry and Fitzgerald was fêted on three continents. In contrast to Mangan, victory in the Rás and his heightened profile were not enough to satisfy Fitzgerald's competitive will. Having won the Rás, it no longer offered motivation. His horizons were broader and he wanted to test the limits of his ability on the world stage. But his family were staunch republicans – both parents had been active in the War of Independence – and joining the CRE was not an option for Fitzgerald.

It was also a time when Fitzgerald was trying to decide the direction of his life. With his cycling aspirations frustrated, he became disillusioned, though not resentful, and cycling became less influential in his decision making. He competed half-heartedly for a while in 1957, before emigrating to the building sites of London. Commenting on Fitzgerald, one of his racing contemporaries said: 'Fitzgerald was a jewel that was left in the ground.' From an athletic point of view, he was shackled by the circumstances of his time. The Rás, equally moulded by circumstance, could not provide an adequate release.

5

A UNIQUE RACE

A young Rás hopeful in 1964.

The Rás faced a number of predicaments in 1957 and was weak in organisational terms. Nevertheless, according to Kerry Sloane, it was the year that marked the coming of age of the event.

A sequence of factors led to the problems, beginning with the imprisonment of Joe Christle for republican activities. This prevented him from any involvement in the detailed planning or running of the event and the NCA congress appointed Jimmy Leahy of Kerry as Race Director. He had been involved in three previous Rásanna but then unexpectedly resigned and left the Rás in limbo with just a few weeks to go. This was a crisis, but Steve Abbott from Dublin launched into the enormous organisational job with a seemingly impossible time scale. To compound his difficulties, Abbott was then faced with a major decision when the Northern Ireland Minister for Home Affairs banned the race from entering the North. Armagh was the planned destination for the first stage.

From jail, Joe Christle sent instructions to Abbott to take the race across the border in defiance of the official ban. This placed Abbott in a dilemma. The situation in the North had deteriorated significantly since the 'Cookstown Incident' of the previous year – for example, 12,000 'B-Specials' had been mobilised on account of the Border Campaign and a military curfew was placed on Newry the week after the Rás was to have passed through. Abbott travelled to Belfast to appeal the decision and made a public issue of it, but the ban was not reversed. He then decided not to bring the Rás into confrontation with the Northern authorities and re-routed the first stage.

The organisation of the 1957 event inevitably suffered with this confused background, but Abbott had played an important role in ensuring the continuity of the Rás at a vulnerable time. He was to continue as Race Director again in 1958, and also rode in the event both years.

Frank Ward of Dublin was a favourite coming into the event, having won a stage the previous year and coming second overall. Also, the Kerry team was not competing due to internal wrangling. Ward did win the first stage and went into yellow. Instead of going into the North, this stage was re-routed and went over the Wicklow Mountains and back to Dublin. A small breakaway developed early and remained clear all day. Along with Ward, it included a seventeen-year-old Ben McKenna who was competing in the second of his twenty-one Rásanna. The break also contained an even more novice Gerry Rea from Cork who, at the age of nineteen, had changed from grass track to road racing to ride the event. Rea was to have one of the best rides of any Cork rider in the Rás – he would have worn the Yellow Jersey but for the minute's bonus per stage for the Yellow Jersey holder

Crashes were just one of the difficulties to be coped with during Rásanna.

and was lying second when he hit a spectator in the sprint into Clonakilty. He was injured in the subsequent crash but managed to finish fifth overall.

McKenna won the second stage and took the lead from Ward, but Ward took the third and fifth stages, and his eventual win was decisive. McKenna finished third, the first step in a sequence that was to see him coming second the following year and first in 1959.

The nature of the racing in 1957 was significant in terms of the development of the Rás. Writing two years later, in a special NCA publication to celebrate the organisation's twenty-first birthday, Sloane said that Ward was a worthy winner as the 1957 Rás had been the best to date from a tactical point of view. Any residual hesitation and tentativeness in the riders' minds about their ability to compete over the eight days had now vanished, leading to a more fully committed and aggressive approach:

> There was now a large group of cyclists completely confident in their own ability to ride the eight days all out. The timid riding of previous races was out and it was a go-all-the-way race from start to finish … every man in the race seemed prepared to have a go.

The character of the racing, as described by Sloane, was subsequently regarded as being somewhat peculiar to the Rás. It came to be characterised by a lack of conventional tactics and a flamboyance, spontaneity, sense of bravado and fierceness of competition that often left foreign riders baffled and sometimes floundering. An attempt to explain and understand this uniqueness may help to set the scene for the following years of the Rás.

Typically, a Rás stage – leaving any small town in Ireland for over 100 miles of racing on rough, country roads, in rain, hail, wind or heat – would begin with somebody going for glory the moment the stage began. Perhaps it would be an explosion of years of pent-up Rás ambition, or an attempt to get to the bottom of the next mountain early so as to cut the inevitable losses on the climb. It could be for many different reasons but it inevitably set the pattern for the day: 'volleys of attacks' constantly launching from the front, break-aways developing, followed by desperate chases with many riders just hanging on in sheer desperation. Others would be left scattered back along the road, eventually collecting in groups and trying to limit their losses.

Sometimes the race would settle, but usually not for long. The contenders might make what they hoped would be the vital move. It might be a group of local riders trying to be first to go through their native parish or village. And there were always the opportunists, hoping that, if they got up the road, a group of strong riders would eventually come up to them and provide an easier ride to the finish in their slip-stream. For the lucky county rider, such a move might put him onto the coveted first sheet of the GC or place him first in his team. And always, there was the outside chance that he could be in that decisive 'Rás break' that might come in ten or fifteen minutes ahead of the bunch. Being in such a break might ensure a top-ten finish for a county rider – a distinction that he would always carry with pride.

In recent years, an insight into the characteristics of the Rás and its impact on riders has been provided by Web-based diaries of participants. These can be particularly descriptive and intuitive because, in the new era of laptop computers and Internet cafés, they are sometimes written within hours of stages when the emotion and tension of competition is still strong and the writing less reticent. Sometimes, they are composed by foreign riders with a broad experience of stage racing. These modern-day commentaries closely mirror the oral views of riders from previous eras and demonstrate how remarkably resilient and unique the Rás has been. Equally significant is the fact that these commentaries are by 'ordinary' competitors, as it's these 'foot soldiers' who gave the Rás much of its unique flavour.

Paul Pickup from England, after his participation in 2000, described the Rás as 'a truly great race'. Like many riders attempting to portray the Rás experience, he referred to it as 'a real love-hate affair', accompanied by a great sense of achievement just to have survived it:

Antony Wood, a Canadian with Irish roots, first came to Ireland to ride the Rás in 1992. His failure to finish 'haunted' him and he returned four years later, but the Gap of Mamore almost broke him again – 'By the time I arrived at the finish in Buncrana, six minutes behind the winning group, I was utterly in ruins. I crossed the finish line and just collapsed against the kerb-side, making no effort to conceal my tears of frustration and exhaustion.' However, the will to become one of the 'Men of the Rás' prevailed and Wood survived to Dublin.

> You can be really suffering, hanging on in there, knowing, at the back of your mind what is still to come, but the whole thing just rolls along and you can't help but be engulfed by it.

Antony Wood, a Canadian with Irish roots, first came to Ireland to ride the Rás in 1992. His introspective account of the experience gives a valuable 'outsider's' perspective. One of his first observations was on the weather:

> … for the better part of each day, we rode through driving wind and rain, with the temperature hovering around twelve Celsius. And just when things appeared to be improving, the skies unleashed the hail. My hands became so numb towards the finish of the second stage that shifting gears was very near impossible and some unlucky riders, dropping back to their team cars in the cavalcade to find warmer clothing, never made it back to the peloton. Some were to struggle in an hour or more off the pace.

The aggression of the racing came as a shock to him – the 'all-out' approach noted by Sloane in 1957 was still embedded in the Rás. On the third day, an Irish rider dumped Wood in the ditch while both were fighting for refuge behind the same wheel on one of the desperate chases. The 'broken roads', the narrowness of the descents and the unending attacks began to take their toll. By the fifth stage

> … the culmination of 'chewing the bars' for over 800km in five days had finally begun to take its toll. I was sure the stage would never end, which made the

endless volleys of attacks and chases seem all the more painful. More than anything, the misery was psychological. It was clear my legs were lacking, but I simply could not fathom how these riders found the strength to attack repeatedly mile after mile, day after day.

Wood's account does not do justice to his true condition. The dirt and grit thrown onto his shorts by his back wheel during the constant days of riding in rain had caused horrible chafing and bleeding, and he endured a lot of pain to try and finish. His manager had unsuccessfully tried to persuade him to abandon. However, his race finished on the second-last day on Mt Leinster when he injured his Achilles tendon. He observed the finish from the side of the street:

To the rest of the survivors of this epic race, there must have been no greater relief than crossing that final finish line. For nine days, they had braved the rugged terrain of Ireland, persevering in the most appalling conditions imaginable. They had raced over 1,300km, ascended seventeen major climbs and visited nearly every county of the nation, often traversing bone-jarring roads more suited to livestock. Now it was over and the relief on the ebullient faces of the survivors almost obscured the fatigue in their bloodshot eyes. Somehow, despite knowing full well the indescribable pain and suffering endured by all those brave lads, I couldn't help but envy them. Standing in the sunshine beside the finish line in Dún Laoghaire, I resolved, then and there, to one day join the immortal ranks of the 'Men of the Rás'.[19]

Wood's failure to finish the Rás 'haunted' him and he made a personal vow to return. Four years later, in 1996, he came back 'to lay the ghost to rest'. That was an Olympic year and he discovered that the good riders intended to impress their national selection committees, resulting in 'one brutally competitive race'. His relative lack of Rás experience showed up early on when he assumed that the race would follow the more usual course of a stage race:

I had opted to ride conservatively, naïvely thinking those with ambitions of riding well during the last few days would do the same. It was already too late when I realised the endless series of attacks and chases had taken a large group of riders some ten minutes up the road. It was only the second day and already I could see my chances of doing well quickly slipping away.

The Donegal mountains nearly broke him, particularly the Gap of Mamore:

Gap of Mamore, County Donegal – one of the more notorious climbs that frequently appears on the Rás route.

For the first time in ten years of racing, I was confronted with a grade so steep that I was forced to dismount and walk my bike. By the time I arrived at the finish in Buncrana, six minutes behind the winning group, I was utterly in ruins. I crossed the finish line and just collapsed against the kerb-side, making no effort to conceal my tears of frustration and exhaustion.

The following day, another stage through the Donegal mountains began as normal: 'The stage began at a blistering pace, as had become the custom, with seemingly endless volleys of attacks launched into the wind and rain.' Going over the Glengesh Pass, he developed the impression that he was 'in the company of truly special men'. The Donegal mountains sorted out the race: 'At this point, it no longer mattered. This was a death march and there were two more days to survive.' He began to struggle on the second-last stage, into Newry:

The slightest of grades become mountains, the gentlest breeze became a gale. Never before have I experienced such overwhelming fatigue. I have no recollection of the final dozen kilometres into Newry.

However, he survived for the final stage:

No longer able to sleep, barely able to force food down my throat and coughing sickly yellow fluid from my lungs, I mounted my bicycle for the final chapter of this epic … when at last I crossed the finish line for the final time, the relief was indescribable. I couldn't care less that I had finished 42nd overall … all that mattered was that I had survived. I had at last become one of the 'Men of the Rás'.

Wood had been a victim of an obsessive quality that the Rás had for Irish riders from its beginning, and this has endured during its first fifty years. J. P. Partland, a US rider, also described how this need to finish had overcome him by the third-last day of his first Rás in 2000:

I didn't think it would be so hard. Not thinking was the only way to survive. My goal was to finish the stage on time, to start tomorrow and to finish tomorrow, so that I can start the ceremonial *criterium* on Sunday. A few days ago, I could have been cut [outside the time limit] and I would have been only mildly disappointed. Now, I'll slay so I can make it to Sunday.

Nobody climbed off the bike in the Rás unless they really had to – a bad day at the back of the bunch. Date and location unknown.

Riders have always had this 'love-hate relationship' with the Rás. They loved to ride and finish it, and their season was incomplete without it. Yet, when participating, many hated the event for the suffering it imposed. They felt inadequate as riders unless competing in it and kept coming back without fully understanding why they wilfully endured such suffering. From its beginning, the Rás drew Irish riders under its spell and, like some migratory instinct, there was an urge to not only ride the Rás, but also to 'do something' in the Rás. This extraordinary grip on the psyche of the Irish riders was partly responsible for the tactical uniqueness and peculiarities of the event.

Nobody climbed off the bike in the Rás unless they really had to and this led to sights of the most amazing hardship, primarily amongst ordinary riders just trying to complete the event. Myles McCorry, from the 2001 County Armagh team, described his need to fully finish the final *criterium* even though he would technically have finished the Rás had he pulled out when lapped:

> If you get dropped and lapped you get a time and a finish, but if I was pulled out I wouldn't feel like I finished. So followed the hardest 60 minutes of bike riding of my life. After 20 minutes I was dead, nothing left, nothing could help me. It was like holding on to a cliff edge for my life. Passing riders who lost

contact, cutting corners to gain places. Wrenching on the bars and hitting the pedals off the ground to keep in. Fighting for survival. Never again. When I saw two laps to go I knew they wouldn't lap me and the last lap was glorious. I stopped hearing my heart rate in my ear and heard the people cheering. I clicked it up to the fifteen [changed down gear] and felt the sun on the polished spokes. I saw the line and rolled in. Finished, delighted and fecked.

Those that abandoned the Rás often saw themselves as incomplete riders and their failure, often through injury, became a self-imposed cloud over their heads for the rest of the season. The Rás developed an influence that shaped the pattern of the racing season and, for some, became a dominating influence in their lives and defined them as individuals. In any given year, there may have been no more than ten riders with the speed and power to win the Rás, and perhaps no more than twenty who had a realistic chance of winning a stage. This did not matter to the bulk of riders, who spent most of their spare, precious, daylight hours of winter hammering out 2–3,000 miles in bleak weather. To survive the circuit, you had to 'get the miles into your legs'.

While many knew that they would suffer every day of the Rás – perhaps struggling in between 10 and 30 minutes behind the stage-winner – they entered the Rás with their own goal or aspiration and with that need to 'do something' – to contribute to the event; to be part-author of the story; to make an impression, however small. The reminiscences of ordinary Rás riders reveal this powerfully: the memory and satisfaction of the day one contributed in the Rás; the day he helped a team-mate or friend to bring back that dangerous break; when he was in the vital, decisive break; the day he went over a mountain with O'Hanlon; the time he gave his wheel to a stranded contender.

Much of the Rás' character was moulded by the mass of Irish county riders, who made the Rás what it is. Perhaps, over the course of the race, there would be one day when the county rider was feeling good and he would make his move. This was not normally planned or articulated and when the attempt came, was usually spontaneous, unpredictable and opportunistic. With perhaps a hundred riders in this frame of mind, a fierceness and unpredictability of racing, quite uncommon elsewhere, was typical of the Rás. It is these Irish riders who give the Rás its character – always watching, waiting, analysing and trying to get into the right moves. They would not look impressive, they would not have reputations and might not get a good result from one end of the year to the next, but they held a belief that their day would eventually come in the Rás.

There was a certain category of opportunist whom the better riders found intensely irritating – the 'bleeders', 'leeches' and 'scrubbers'; in more recent times, they have been christened the 'cling-ons' (as in Klingons from *Star Trek*). These 'cling-on' to the better riders – those that generate breaks – and 'bleed' them. They might occasionally go to the front of a bunch, but always with reservation of energy. Then, when the workers in the group are exhausted and the break loses its momentum, they hop on to the next group and 'bleed' them, too. They might never get a top-ten stage finish, but could sneak into the top thirty in the Rás without ever having ridden strongly at the front of a bunch – without having truly sacrificed or having taken a real risk.

Then, of course, there was always the dream of a 'no-hoper' winning a stage of the Rás. Such dreams were sustained by stories of exceptional and legendary finishes which became part of Rás folklore – Gabriel Howard's win into Birr in 1965, the fruit of twenty-one completed Rásanna; Mick Grimes, supposedly nearing fifty years of age, being the only non-Russian to win a stage in 1970; Joe Cashin's solo win into Limerick in 1975 when he earned the title of 'Dashing Joe Cashin'; and Seán Lally, at fifty years of age, almost sneaking a stage win into Letterkenny in 1991.

Yet another category of rider added to the diversity of the race: very good riders who would know that they were not in their best form in a given year, but would make that one supreme effort to 'do something' significant. Given the demanding nature of top-level competitive cycling, the truly amateur rider can realistically expect to be in top competitive condition for only a small number of years – perhaps five at the most. The normal demands of work and daily life severely limit the amateur's ability to remain in the condition that allows him to perform to the limits of his ability. That period in which most cyclists fully mature physically – from their mid- to late-twenties – can coincide with the most demanding period of his life in terms of career and family. This group of riders was always a significant element in the Rás – knowing that they were not fit enough to win or even to get a high placing in a particular year, but always willing to make that one do-or-die effort to snatch a stage win – and perhaps blow the race apart in the process.

With the contribution of these various groups, the pattern of the racing is unrelenting – day after day, for the duration of the race, an all-out, frantic effort from start to finish is made; the hundreds of miles are tackled with courage and aggression, for up to ten days. It's an exhausting type of racing – jumping and chasing and stalling – and much more draining and sapping, both in energy and morale, than those stage races with a constant higher average speed.

This style contrasts sharply with the controlled stage racing on the continent. Many seasoned foreign riders found that they could dismiss the average Irish county rider in the Rás, but only for four or five days. Bad roads and bad weather often helped to wear them down, but more often, it was the unrelenting nature of the racing – the defiance of racing logic with repeated and relentless attacks, mile after mile, day after day, with no respite and with every gap in the race being filled or bridged by the Irish county riders. As Antony Wood described, this would eventually lead to a kind of 'psychological misery', bewilderment and frustration for many of the foreign riders.

While some of these tactical features of the Rás are relatively easy to describe, it's more difficult to provide analyses of why the Rás became such a powerful and distinctive force, and how it developed such a unique flavour. It is inadequate to say, as some do, that it is simply a magical phenomenon that makes unremarkable riders do extraordinary things. It has also been ascribed to the Irish temperament, with an irreverence for discipline, order and convention. The early years of its development, in relative isolation and uncorrupted by outside influence, might also be considered.

While each of these explanations may be relevant to some limited degree, other contributory factors should be taken into account. It's been characteristic of the Rás that the riders are not of a common standard. Stage races are often categorised by standard – recently with the help of a UCI points system – and teams more usually enter races suitable for their level of ability. Consequently, the riders fall into a narrow category. This was never so in the Rás. The average club man would be racing against seasoned internationals, while county teams ride against foreign teams. This structure affected the normal tactical approach.

Unwritten rules developed to accommodate this range of abilities. There was an understanding, for example, that racing rules strictly applied to everyone on the first sheet of GC, but leniency and the officials' judgement came into play thereafter. The rule on time limit, for instance, would normally apply, whereby riders are eliminated if they finish outside of a time calculated as a percentage of the stage-winner's time. However, riders would commonly be reinstated on appeal.

The nature of most of the Irish county teams was another significant factor in shaping the Rás character. Apart from exceptional cases, such as Dublin in the early 1960s and Tipperary in the 1980s, county teams encompass a broad range of talent. Most may have just one or two very good riders, the remainder being of very mixed abilities, including those who are content to do no more than ride and finish the Rás. In many cases, the teams were not cohesive and sometimes suffered from indifferent management and organisation. Therefore, without six good riders, teams were not strong enough to control or dominate races, or even to provide significant support to well-placed team members.

In addition to this, the rivalries that build up over years of local competition cannot easily be put aside for the duration of the Rás and riders may be reluctant to sacrifice their Rás for a team-mate who, for the rest of the year, is a keen rival. The loyalty of the team-mate could not always be relied upon, even in the national team, as will be seen. Riders in the Rás, therefore, have to be self-reliant, go beyond their teams to develop alliances and be opportunistic in exploiting any chances that emerge during the race. This, in turn, adds a very significant human dimension to the Rás and much of its story is shaped by the personal interaction of the riders and by the tensions that arise and are exacerbated by the stresses and strains of days of demanding competition and enormous personal stakes. Important, too, are the complex interplay of loyalties, constantly ebbing and flowing; the suspicions and jealousies; the fluid nature of allegiances and cliques; the 'pay-backs', both negative and positive – all are central to the Rás and added significantly to the richness of its history. These factors were also the source for many of the 'Rás breaks' – decisive breaks, with big time gaps that determined the final outcome of many Rásanna.

While most approached the Rás with a deadly earnestness, there was always a 'Laughing Group' whose mission was simply to get around the course and often with as much fun as possible. In the first few decades, for example, a group of riders would always enjoy the Rás dances at stage ends. A number of teams would be somewhat ramshackle in preparation and organisation, prompting the rival CRE to caricature the entire Rás as 'a bunch of farmers riding bikes'. But this element contributed greatly to the ambience of the Rás and their escapades became part its folklore. In 1975, for example, Patsy Crowley from Cork fell while he was wearing the KOH Jersey. His team-mate, Denis O'Connell, came back to help him and they were working all out to get back to the lead bunch when their manager came up in his car to encourage them. Crowley's frustration exploded and, in rather impolite terms, he told the manager where to go – and O'Connell concurred. The manager drove away and both riders pushed on, but coming round the next bend in the road, they passed their suitcases in the ditch – they had been jettisoned from the team car by a manager with wounded pride. Every stage generated such folklore – much of it satirical – but humbled or lowly-placed riders never felt undervalued or excluded in the Rás. The renowned camaraderie and bonhomie of the Rás was exemplified, perhaps, by the famous 'night-stages'.[20]

In addition to each of these tangible factors, the Rás had indefinable, 'magical' qualities, most powerfully evidenced by the hold it had on the riders and the enormous public popularity it achieved in certain parts of the country. It can also be identified through the statements of riders. Following his participation in the 2001 Rás, the US rider, Peter Wedge, wrote that 'this race is like no other Euro stage race that I have done', and the English rider, John Ibbotson, concluded after the same Rás that 'everyone who enjoys racing should try and move heaven and earth to do this race'.[21]

The sum of many subtle and intangible factors – the urge to perform, its strong political ethos, its aura, its connection with the people – has undoubtedly made the Rás the special event it is. There is little doubt also that the vision for the Rás Tailteann – as articulated by its founders – was central to its development. Those who took up the torch following the Christle era were faithful to that vision.

Joe Christle's publicity efforts in the early years were enormously important – his attention to detail in this regard was meticulous, at both national and local levels. He wrote much of the copy himself for national newspapers, in a format and style that was usable to journalists, and had it delivered to their desks. Equally, the volume and standard of material circulated within the NCA is very impressive, even by today's standards. This publicity effort helped to make heroes out of every Rás man and not just the stars – to simply finish the race admitted a competitor into the ranks of the 'Men of the Rás'.

Equally important was the social and economic context of Ireland in the 1950s and 1960s from which the Rás emerged. The Rás brought colour and light to this setting, and created the potential for ordinary men to become national heroes. The story of the legendary 'Iron Man' best exemplifies this.

6

THE 'IRON MAN'

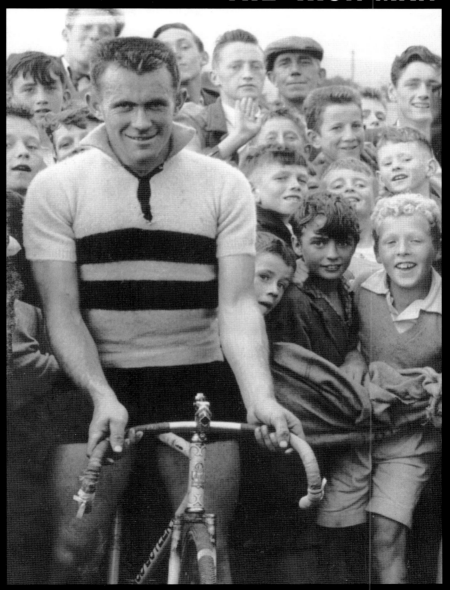

Mick Murphy as a celebrity at a track meeting in Castleisland after his 1958 Rás win.

Banteer is a small village west of Mallow in County Cork, where the rich farmland of the Blackwater Valley meets the Boggeragh Mountains. Two miles from the village, where the road to Cork city begins to rise for Nadd mountain, lies the crumbling and ivy-covered remains of a ball alley. Here, in the rural and parochial Ireland of the 1950s, the local men gathered in the summer evenings when the day's farm-work was done. Life did not change much in rural Ireland in those times and anything out of the ordinary was a source of local interest and speculation. In spring 1958, the curiosity of this gathering was aroused by the regular appearance of an unknown cyclist, head down and going south towards Nadd mountain. While his unfamiliarity was of interest in itself, the fact that he did not return intensified curiosity. Some, it is said, stayed on later and later – well into the dark of the night – but still, the cyclist was not seen returning.

The mystery rider was Mick Murphy, a 24-year-old migrant farm labourer from an impoverished farming community near Caherciveen in south Kerry. He was unknown to the locals as he had come to Banteer to prepare for the 1958 Rás Tailteann and his regular evening spin past the ball alley took him over the mountain and back to Banteer, via Mallow, on a 50-mile (80km) circular route. However, within a few weeks, local curiosity was to be satisfied when Murphy became a national sporting sensation by emerging from nowhere to win the Rás in such spectacular fashion that it made him one of the most enigmatic legends in Irish sporting history.

Legends abound about Murphy – of his feats on the bike and of his eccentricities – and his path to the 1958 Rás is as extraordinary as his winning of the event itself. Some of the contemporary newspaper accounts of the race raise niggling doubts about their accuracy and brings to mind the saying that 'the truth should never spoil a good story'. The superlative headlines of the *Kerryman* described Murphy as a 'sensation', 'mile-a-minute Murphy' and 'fabulous'. Its stories depicted a hitherto unknown cyclist romping away from the bunch, seemingly at will. They outlined how, punctured and unsupported at the side of the road, he grabbed a common bicycle from a spectator, chased and caught the bunch. They described almost daily crashes that left Murphy bruised and bloodied, needing hospital treatment at the end of a stage and being strapped to his bike the following morning. They tell of the 'Great' Gene Mangan giving his bike to Murphy after a crash and thus forfeiting his own Rás chances. And, after all this, Murphy was still able to ride away from the bunch on the very last day, stay in front for over 100 miles (160km), and eventually win the Rás by almost five minutes! Even if the *Kerryman* reports might be excused for being slightly partisan, the extraordinary nature of Murphy's win is verified elsewhere – the *Cork Examiner* referred to 'a truly magnificent performance', the *Irish Independent* described Murphy as 'incredibly durable', and the usually constrained and measured language of *The Irish Times* gave way to such adjectives as 'remarkable' and 'fantastic'.

Mick Murphy was born near Caherciveen in 1934 into a small hill farm that supported seven cows, an acre of potatoes and an acre of oats. His mentality was to be greatly shaped by the austerity and frugality of the physical, economic and social environment of his youth. On what he described as the 'mean and bad' land of the region, it was common for young children to contribute to the labour-intensive farm work, and he got little schooling. At the age of twelve, he was adding £3 per week to the farm income by drawing turf from the bogs with a donkey and creel during the 'Emergency' of the Second World War. He was taught to read and write by his mother, and through reading he developed an interest in the world beyond – a trait that was to be central to his eventual athletic success.

Murphy's introduction to athletics came through a neighbouring farmer, Joe Burke, who was interested in circus acting and who performed in the various touring circuses that regularly visited the locality. Murphy became Burke's assistant and apprentice, and one of Murphy's earliest memories, on the day before his First Holy Communion, is of a row that developed when his mother stumbled across Burke practising one of his tricks – walking around his farmyard with a ladder balanced on his chin and the young Murphy tied to the top of it.

Newspaper headlines of the day hinted at something extraordinary about the 1958 Rás.

At twelve, Murphy was initiated by Burke into the circus world – a realm of professional performers who were part of a network that stretched across Europe. They introduced Murphy to sophisticated training techniques, weight training and an awareness of diet. The circus people also let him have access to books on training, which he studied intently. He built up a gym and training circuit at home, and developed a life-long interest in weight training.

One of Murphy's early competitive successes was in running. There was an abundance of sports and 'flapper' meetings in Kerry and Cork at the time – it was at the beginning of the parish-carnival era. The flapper meetings were organised locally, outside the jurisdiction of any athletics governing body, and offered good cash prizes – at a time when a farm labourer might earn around £4 per week, he could win up to £2 at a big event. Prizes were given at sports meetings and Murphy sold these for cash. He also competed in football and boxing, suffering permanent damage to his hearing in a fight with a heavyweight opponent.

Between 1954 and 1956, Murphy travelled on a common bike for weeks on end, competing at sports and flapper meetings, sleeping in hay barns and supplementing his winnings by performing his circus acts on the streets of towns and villages. He liked performing as a form of expression – walking up a ladder on his hands and fire eating were his specialities.

His training techniques continued to develop and he enrolled in a number of correspondence courses on training methods. He continued to receive training information from abroad through his circus contacts – mostly from Russia – and he developed a strong interest in diet. He became an advocate of raw food and ate uncooked cereals, eggs, vegetables, cows' blood and meat – there are tales of him in Caherciveen, cycling away from the butcher's shop, eating the steak as he went. He bought mail-order herbal remedies for ailments and injuries.

Murphy was given a 100-yard handicap in a mile running race in Sneem in 1956 and failed to win a prize. Seeing an end to his income from running, he turned to cycling. He was very successful at common-bike grass-track racing throughout Kerry in 1956 and was becoming renowned for the huge distances he was cycling to events. It was quite common for him to ride 60 miles (96km) to a meeting, compete, then ride home again on the same day. Inspired by the sight of the exotic 'Tralee boys' riding to track meetings in Caherciveen, carrying their lightweight track bikes across their shoulders, as well as the relatively new Rás which he saw going thorough south Kerry, he made the decision to become a 'proper cyclist' at the end of the 1956 season. He believed he had the right recipe – the most advanced international training methods and dietary information available, as well as complete confidence in his own ability. The only missing ingredient was a proper road racing bike, but he began a winter training regime on his common bike – 50 miles (80km) on week nights, usually to Milltown and back, with up to 100 miles (160km) on Sundays, over circuits that included most of the big climbs in the Kerry mountains. He trained a lot at night, partly because he had a peculiarity of being very secretive, but also because daylight was largely reserved for working. He continued to work wherever he could, mainly labouring in the bogs, quarries, roads and farms of the region, and he developed a reputation for stooking enormous amounts of turf.

His 1957 season went well. Murphy's first proper road race was the 25-mile Time Trial Championship of Kerry in 1957. Competing on a borrowed racing bike, he took a wrong turn and came last. He bought his first road bike at a track meeting in Currow for £10 – a 'Viking' in poor condition which Johnny Switzer from Tralee had used in the 1955 Rás. His first road win was the 50-mile championship of Kerry, a victory he attributed to having spent 16 shillings – the equivalent of a day's wage for a labourer – on a hotel room rather than riding to the race that morning.

The winter of 1957–58 was a difficult and decisive time for Murphy. Intending to concentrate on cycling and to win the 1958 Rás Tailteann, he maintained his gruelling training schedule – he ate his Christmas dinner out of his pocket at the top of the Healy Pass, 60 miles (96km) from home. But the conflict between his cycling ambitions and the drudgery and toil of his work made him unsettled. This, combined with his unorthodox lifestyle and single-minded attitudes, led to increasing tension at home to the point where he eventually had to leave.

In the tradition of the *spailpíns* – landless peasants from the southwestern seaboard who had attended the hiring fares of Castleisland and Newcastle West and gone into 'service' in the rich farmlands of east Limerick and north Cork – Murphy looked towards Cork for work and shelter. Banteer was his preferred destination, even though it was in the neighbouring county and a world away from the south Kerry of the 1950s. He had encountered Banteer in sporting folklore and in his reading, and he thought that it must have been the centre of the sporting world – a place where his aspirations would be respected and supported. It had the best cinder cycling track in Ireland and was associated with sporting heroes such as Olympic gold-medal winners, Dr Pat O'Callaghan and Denis Horgan. It was also the home of the mock-heroic athletic champion, satirised in the ballad, 'The Bould Thady Quill'.

On Easter Saturday 1958, Murphy packed his only belongings into an old grain sack, mounted his bike, traversed the Iveragh Peninsula via the passes of Ballaghisheen and Beallaghbeama, and rode into Kenmare. He carried on through

Kilgarvan and Barradubh, and eventually arrived in Banteer. Somewhat disappointed, he found a small, typical Irish village. Undeterred, he walked into the local shop and announced his arrival and intention – 'I'm a cyclist, where's the track?'

The Blackwater valley was indeed a new world to him – here he found lush landscape, modern farming methods, unionised farm labour with work ending at 6 pm, and farmers who treated workers well. Most of all, he found the place peaceful. He quickly secured farm work and based his training on Nadd Mountain, thus giving rise to the curiosity of the locals. Much of his riding was again done at night. He was desperate for the use of a gym, the cornerstone of his training, and set about preparing one. He selected a secluded spot in a wooded area near Mallow Racecourse. From a neighbouring farm, he took two half-hundredweights – 56-pound (25 kilos) iron weights commonly used on weighing scales at the time – and he took two similar 28-pound (12.6 kilos) weights from a shop in the village. He used socks filled with sand for the smaller weights. Believing in the qualities of goats' milk because of the variety of herbs they ate, he took a goat from near Kilgarvan and brought it to his lair in a sling made of sacks. He also installed some hay as temporary bedding. From this base, he launched his assault on the 1958 Rás.

Early in the summer of 1958, Murphy suffered a serious loss of form that shattered his self-confidence and deeply upset him. He had left home and structured his life around his preparations, and had publicised himself to a certain extent. He now had poor form at track meetings and felt that he was being ridiculed. Racked with self-doubt, he decided he could not combine adequate training and rest with the regime of a farm labourer. He gave up his job, retreated to his woodland lair to rest and concentrated on his training on Nadd mountain.

Murphy performed his circus tricks in Cork city to pay for the enormous quantities of food that he was eating; he was also consuming huge amounts of milk mixed at various times with raw eggs, honey, glucose, cows' blood and a juice that he extracted from the stems of nettles. He bought pasteurised milk in shops as he was cautious about a tuberculosis scare at the time.

One of the typical legends about Murphy – recounting how he cycled the Rás route before the event, in the opposite direction – probably comes from an episode of this time. Rumour reached him that he was not going to be chosen for the Kerry team because of his loss of form. He became desperate for money to enable him to enter the Rás, perhaps individually or by buying into another team. He also needed funds to sustain himself while he trained, so he turned to his circus contacts to borrow money that he might later work off. He cycled as far as Galway, looking for the circus, but when he learned that it was probably in Donegal, he decided to return home. He made the return journey via Kildare, a jaunt that took him four or five days in all. Cyclists, with their usual network of contacts and their suspicions about rivals' training, received reports of various sightings and the story grew that he was going around the Rás route in reverse direction.

From his woodland lair, Murphy trained, performed his acts and worked part time with various farmers around the Banteer region in the run up to the Rás. His form returned and

1953: the banked, cinder track at Banteer, north Cork. It was one of Ireland's most advanced tracks at a time when track racing was the main form of cycling competition. A 5-mile race is in progress. Mick Murphy came to Banteer to prepare for the 1958 Rás.

his win in the longest stage of Rás Mumhan ensured his place in the Kerry Rás team. His final two-week preparation took place while in an FCA (Fórsa Cosainte Áitiuil – army reserve) training camp at Kilworth, near Mitchelstown. He would finish at 4 pm, train for three to four hours, sleep for a few hours in his den, train again during the night, rest again, then ride back to camp to report for 9 am. On the Friday morning before the Rás, he left his lair in the Blackwater valley for the last time and rode to Harding's bike shop in Cork to get a few bits and pieces for his machine. He then undertook the 70-mile (112km) ride to Castleisland where he was to be picked up on Saturday, the day before the race. As he expressed it himself, 'All the years of hardship and training had created an animal that the Rás wouldn't be able to tame'.

A detailed investigation of the 1958 Rás confirms that much of what was written in the newspapers of the time – and the folklore that subsequently developed – was indeed exaggerated. Nevertheless, it all originated in actual fact and the scale of the embellishment is an indication of the remarkable nature of the real events. Gene Mangan was one of the favourites but was heavily marked on the first 100-mile (160km) stage, from Dublin to Wexford, especially by the Dublin team. It was Kerry's eighteen-year-old Dan Ahern and the unknown Murphy that got away, both in their first Rás, with Ahern taking the stage. Murphy is reported to have had his first crash on this stage, about two miles outside Wexford – he clipped a bridge and his shorts were torn, but he came in second.

Monday's second stage – 120 miles (192km), from Wexford to Kilkenny – allowed Murphy's riding prowess to be seen nationally for the first time. He was reported to have simply ridden away from the bunch and 'strolled' into Kilkenny on his own. Murphy's performance demonstrated not only his strength, but also his single-mindedness and disregard for established etiquette and team strategy. Murphy powered away from the bunch after Carrick-on-Suir, leaving behind his team-mate in the Yellow Jersey. Ben McKenna of Meath went with him, followed by Gene Mangan, another Kerryman. Two strong Kerry riders had now abandoned the Yellow Jersey to his fate in the bunch. Murphy simply rode McKenna off and had a 3-minute lead at the Glenbower KOH. He arrived at the finish on his own, followed by McKenna at 58 seconds, with Mangan third. The unknown rider was now in yellow, after a performance that left the Rás astonished.

Murphy rode away from the stage finish at Kilkenny and disappeared for a while. This occurred a number of times during the Rás and led to another part of the Murphy legend – that he did 30-mile (48km) training spins after the stages. Murphy had, in fact, become dependent on his weight-training and diet, and he rode out into the countryside, wearing his newly-won Yellow Jersey, until he found a stone wall. He did his weight-training with suitably sized stones in a field for an hour. Then, using a small penknife he carried in his sock, Murphy found a docile cow, bled a vein in its neck into his water-bottle and drank the blood. Having read that African warriors had drank cows' blood for a thousand years, he did it regularly. Also, there was a tradition in parts of Kerry of bleeding cows in times of want, especially on Sundays, leading to the expression that 'Kerry cows know Sunday'. Murphy performed his 'transfusion' three times during the Rás.

The third stage – 120 miles (192km) from Kilkenny to Clonakilty – gave rise to one of the more remarkable events in the history of the Rás, from which the Murphy legend really dates. He had wanted to lead the race going through Cork city and had the field strung out behind him on the climb at Watergrasshill. His free-wheel mechanism failed on the run down into Glanmire, however, and he rolled to a stop. The bunch passed and he saw the 'Dublin boys massing to the front' as they assessed the situation. With no sign of his team car, Murphy watched the race disappear up the road and with it his Rás hopes.

The race gone, he stood in despair. Then, from a gap up the road, two cows emerged, followed by a farmer casually rolling a bike with his left hand on the handlebar. In the words of one report at the time, 'instincts dictated reaction'.

Mick Murphy in the Yellow Jersey at the finish of stage 3 in Clonakilty, County Cork, 1958. He has the team's spare bike which replaced the common bike he hijacked near Watergrasshill. It's a Mercian bike, which Gene Mangan borrowed for the event as a spare for the team. The Cyclo Benelux front gear changer can be seen on the seat tube, underneath the saddle. It was operated by leaning down and twisting it. The standard gearing was 46–48 front rings with a 14–16–18–20–23 rear block. It weighed 25 pounds (11.25 kilos) and had Michelin 25 high-pressure clincher tyres.

Without thinking, he sprinted, jumped, landed cleanly on the bike and was gone even before the farmer realised what was happening. The bike was too big for him and under-geared, but he happily set out on the chase.

Murphy did not catch the bunch on the common bike as was reported and the length of the chase was relatively short – probably between five and ten miles, but enough time was saved to keep him in contention. It is not clear as to why he received no assistance from his team, but the team car had been at the rear of the race attending to Gene Mangan, who was having one of the most torrid days of his career – he was in danger of dropping out of the race as a result of a crash, two punctures and illness. He finished second-last on the stage, half an hour down, and fell from third to thirtieth place. Such was Mangan's condition, the NCA chairman, Jim Killean, came to him that night and requested him to abandon the following day if he was not going well – he did not want Mangan to cross into his native Kerry in the state he had been in that day.

When the team car had dealt with Mangan, it eventually met with a bewildered farmer holding Murphy's bike. They retrieved it, caught up with Murphy and gave him the spare bike. He went through Cork city – again on his own and fearing that he would get lost – and rode into west Cork. After 40 miles (64km) of chasing, he caught sight of the car cavalcade on the outskirts of Clonakilty and closed with the bunch at the finish. He lost no time on the stage.

The fourth stage, from Clonakilty to Tralee – 115 miles (184km) – was to be even more dramatic. Murphy had been anticipating the Kerry mountains with relish – he admired the great Charly Gaul of Luxembourg who won the Tour de France the same year and he desired the King of the Hills prize as much as the Yellow Jersey. He was away with a group of about ten, including Mangan, and was in his element in his familiar mountains. In wet, squally weather, he struck a bridge on a downhill bend near Glengarriff, crashing heavily on his left shoulder and hip, and damaging his bike. Mangan gave him his bike without hesitation, a situation reminiscent of Paddy O'Callaghan giving his bike to Mangan on Moll's Gap in 1955, helping Mangan to his eventual victory.

Murphy lost little time and caught the bunch on the climb to Turner's Rock on the 'Tunnel Road'. It took some time before the effects of the adrenalin from the crash wore off and pain took over – he first realised that he was in serious trouble crossing the bridge into Kenmare. Séamus Devlin of Tyrone tried to get away on Moll's Gap, but Murphy contained the attack. The Dublin team launched further attacks before Killarney. Devlin eventually escaped. Meanwhile, Gene Mangan, who had lost five minutes waiting for the car to come up with the spare bike, was having one of his great rides. He left the bunch on the climb out of

Glengarriff and got across to the leaders outside Killarney, making up the five minutes he had lost at the side of the road. Devlin went on to win, but Mangan's presence steadied the situation in the leading bunch.

Large crowds had come from all over Kerry to see the stage-end, as Murphy's ride had now become national news. They saw Mangan narrowly beaten into third place – an indication that his form was returning and of what was to come – but Murphy's arrival, in eighth place, resulted in high drama – he was torn and bleeding, cycling with one hand and in obvious pain. He had a suspected broken collar-bone, and the town was rife with excitement and speculation as to whether he could continue and if he could last the 111 miles (178km) to Nenagh the following day. Mangan's generosity was given lavish praise and he, in turn, described Murphy as 'an iron man' – a name that was to stick. Murphy was taken to hospital and reports of his injury varied from a dislocated shoulder, to a broken shoulder, to a bruised shoulder with torn ligaments. A reticent Murphy did not encourage inquiry, making a judgement of his true condition difficult. He was in obvious distress at the start of the fourth stage, however, and had difficulty putting on the Yellow Jersey. When pressed on the detail of Murphy's condition at the start of that stage, one team member – Eddie Lacey – over forty years later, depicted Murphy's condition simply and descriptively: 'They helped him onto his bike,

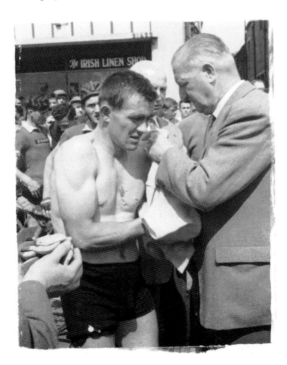

Mick Murphy having difficulty in putting on the Yellow Jersey in Tralee at the beginning of stage four. His upper-body strength, somewhat unusual for a cyclist, is clearly evident. His legs were comparatively small. His holy medal is temporarily pinned to his torn shorts. The Jersey is being presented by Dr Eamon O'Sullivan who came from an old republican and sporting family – he was trainer of the Kerry Gaelic football team and was head of the NACA in Kerry. As such, he typified the nationalist-based sporting and political network that sustained the Rás in its early years.

There is obvious anxiety as Mick Murphy is supported at the start of stage in Tralee by the Kerry manager, Liam Brick (right) and Micheál Ó Loinsigh, chairman of the Tralee stage-end committee. Murphy had fallen heavily the previous day. 'They helped him onto his bike, they put his hands on the bars, they strapped in his feet, they held him up until the start and then they pushed him off.'

they put his hands on the bars, they strapped in his feet, they held him up until the start and then they pushed him off.'

The fourth stage was a bad day for Murphy. He floated at the back of the bunch and dropped off occasionally. Gene Mangan and Dan Ahern helped him as much as they could. They got brandy for him from the car, which he mixed with tea. He felt better after this. Ben McKenna attacked between Limerick and Nenagh and gained over a minute. Mangan went with him to mark him and won the sprint so easily from McKenna and Paddy Flanagan that the judges gave him five seconds. It was the first of his four consecutive stage wins. The main bunch came in a little over a minute afterwards, with Murphy seventh from the front. He vomited at the finish but he had again saved the Yellow Jersey. In the early years of the Rás, the race leader was given a minute bonus for each day he held the Yellow Jersey and this helped to increase his margin daily.

Murphy was recovering. On Friday's sixth stage – 120 miles (192km) from Nenagh to Castlebar – he left the main bunch shortly before the finish to gain ten seconds. Mangan again won, with 45 yards to spare over Eamon Ryan of Kildare. The pattern of the race was again evident on the second-last, 100-mile (160km) stage, from Castlebar to Sligo. Murphy rode away from the bunch and had a minute advantage when he crashed near Castlerea. Again, he was without support. He stood up but fell forward onto his bike. This worried him as he had been told in his boxing days never to get up if he fell forward as it was considered a sign of concussion. He probably was concussed, because when he remounted, having

At the end of the sixth stage into Castlebar, 1958. Eamon Ryan of Kildare (left) was second. Cathal O'Reilly (centre) of Dublin was third on the stage and finished third overall, behind Murphy and Ben McKenna. He was also leader of the victorious Dublin team. It was the second of Gene Mangan's (right) four consecutive stage wins – a feat that was never to be repeated in the Rás and was even more remarkable considering that stage wins were a secondary consideration to protecting Mick Murphy's lead. In a performance that *The Irish Times* called 'remarkable', Murphy left the main bunch towards the end of this stage and finished fifth.

straightened his handlebars, he rode the wrong way. The chasing riders were startled when they met the Yellow Jersey coming towards them and they shouted at Murphy and pointed in the opposite direction. Still confused, and suspecting some kind of trick, he rode on, but the next group of riders persuaded him to turn around. He got the hunger knock later for want of food and felt that his lead was seriously under threat. Eventually, he got food, survived and arrived with the main bunch into Sligo.

Though he was reported to have numbness in his hands and difficulty controlling his bike at times, Murphy took the final, 140-mile (224km) stage, from Sligo to Dublin, by the scruff of the neck, despite his lead of three minutes, 54 seconds. Shortly after Sligo, he again rode away from the bunch, followed by two Meathmen – Ben McKenna and Willie Heasley. Mangan came up to them after another epic chase – he had left the chasing group when it was five minutes down in Mullingar, 50 miles (80km) from the finish, and he caught the leading group over 35 miles (56km). It was two Kerrymen verses two Meathmen, heading for the finish in Dublin, and both Kerrymen were convinced they could win the stage. They exchanged words on the matter on the road. Mangan took his fourth consecutive stage and Murphy won the Rás by four minutes, 44 seconds.

The 1958 Rás was yet another triumph for Kerry, following the successes of 1955 and 1956, and the team was greeted with the usual civic reception in Tralee, followed by bonfire-lit tours to the home towns of the team members. Disappointment at losing the team prize to arch rivals, Dublin, was tempered by the compensation of new Rás records – Kerry held the Jersey from start to finish, they had won six stages and Gene Mangan won four stages in a row – a feat that was never to be repeated in the Rás and was even more remarkable considering that stage wins were a secondary consideration to protecting Murphy's lead. But most of all, Kerry had produced the indestructible 'Iron Man', whose appearances now drew crowds all over the county.

Mick Murphy went back home to Caherciveen after the Rás and again survived on whatever labouring work he could find in the region. Contrary to myth, he was not a 'one-Rás wonder' – he won two stages in the 1959 Rás and came third overall in 1960 as well as winning the KOH category. Economic circumstances ended his cycling career. There were financial difficulties at home and he failed to get work on the drainage of the river Maine – one of a number of large schemes in the 1950s and 1960s intended to provide employment as well as improve drainage.

He found farm work in Kildare but then decided to emigrate. Before doing so, he rode down to Banteer to collect the medals and newspaper cuttings that he

Mick Murphy (left) as a celebrity at a track meeting in Castleisland after his 1958 Rás win. He's on a Claud Butler Olympic Sprint – Gene Mangan sold it to Dan Ahern when he went to France in 1958. It has a Major Taylor adjustable handlebar stem. Jerome Dorgan of Blarney Cycling Club is on Murphy's right – his bike is being supported by Dan Ahern, who was on Murphy's Rás team.

had stashed away. Short of money, he collected his weights from their hiding place and performed outside Banteer church after mass. Wearing a mask, he walked around the road, balancing a bystander's bike on his chin, and challenged his audience to follow him in lifting the 'half-hundredweights' with their *luidíns* (small fingers).

Murphy then rode back to Kildare, sold his gear, emigrated to the building sites in London in November 1960, and never raced on a bike again. In all, he had competed on the road for just four years.

Mick Murphy was stoical, intelligent and creative – an individualist and singular in every respect. He was also unique in physique for an élite cyclist – he was small in stature with massive upper-body strength, but with seemingly small and underdeveloped legs. He was described as 'barrel-chested', and had laughing, mischievous eyes. Liam Brick, the Kerry manager, in his descriptive and colloquial Kerry style, summarised Murphy thus: 'He was small, sturdy, desperate strong and he could pedal from morning 'til night.' He had great recuperative powers and the long stages of the era suited his style. Murphy fancied himself as a climber and loved the mountains, but 'strength' is the most common description of him. His strength was indeed truly immense – his simple strategy was to jump to the front, turn on the power and wear off his opponents with grinding attrition. There are numerous examples of Murphy riding away from groups of the very best riders. Shay O'Hanlon, the most successful Rás rider ever, encountered Murphy as their careers briefly overlapped and he related one encounter with Murphy that left him 'rattled'. This arose from a stage into Clonmel in the 1960 Rás Mumhan, where O'Hanlon, in yellow and with the help of two other very good riders, including Ronnie Williams from Dublin, tried to contain an attack from Murphy. Despite being at his very best and having good help, he could not bring Murphy back an inch. His enormous effort left O'Hanlon stretched out on the street in Clonmel, totally exhausted and seriously questioning why he should submit his body to such punishing extremes.

Yet, in spite of his accomplishment, Murphy had limitations as a racer. His tactical repertoire was limited and he was not generally admired as a stylish rider. He rode with a unique style – a fast cadence, interspersed with pauses, that was likened in appearance to that of a trotting pony. Dick Barry, who rode against him, observed:

> He had a way of pedalling the bike – he'd do ten strokes and then free wheel. He cracked up a lot of fellows the way he went – he wasn't smooth at all – a very erratic rider and you couldn't have a rhythm in a break with him.

Neither could he ride close to a wheel and when he came back into a line, he would leave a gap from the rider in front. This was both irritating and disconcerting for riders behind him, as they were always expecting a break to go from beyond the gap. It also meant that he seldom got shelter.

There were contrasts between Murphy and some of his team-mates, originating in background and outlook. He viewed himself as a total athlete in all respects, with the best professional preparation available, and he had little tolerance or patience for the shortcomings of others. He would not conform to the discipline or etiquette of team racing and contributed little to team strategy or the needs of his team-mates. He would not ride to instructions with which he disagreed and was described colloquially as 'headstrong' or 'impossible to manage'. He was reticent, shrewd and had a suspicious nature, born out of his background – he could not accept that advice was for his benefit rather than for the selfish advantage of the giver. He kept to himself and nobody knew what he was planning or thinking. He considered that his team should have given him more support in 1958, with the exception of Mangan whom, he said, had 'backed me to the hilt'. On the other hand, his team considered that he could not have won without its support and that Dan Ahern, in particular, had been invaluable to him. Certainly, Murphy was left unsupported at least three times as race leader in difficulty. But the absence of support illustrates the entirely different conditions that prevailed in the Rás in the 1950s. Kerry had one car to cover nine widely spaced-out riders. With a strong emphasis on the county-team placings, all the highly placed team members had to be supported. There was no radio or telephone communication and no neutral-service vehicles.

The Rás values 'characters' as much as gifted cyclists and Murphy combined both in great measure. Cycling is a sport in which individualism thrives and Murphy's idiosyncrasies complemented his athletic ability to produce one of the great Rás men. Equally, the disparities between Murphy and his team-mates were not an issue in the Kerry Rás team of 1958. Still in its early years, there was euphoria surrounding the event, with an associated spirit of generosity and co-operation.

When the members of the great Kerry teams of the 1950s meet at the ceremonies held in their honour from time to time, discussion quickly and inevitably turns to Mick Murphy, the 'Iron Man', a shooting star that briefly but brilliantly flashed across the Irish sporting scene, illuminated the Rás and faded just as quickly to leave one of the most enduring and enigmatic legends of the Rás.

Everything considered, Mick Murphy's 1958 Rás win must rank as one of the truly epic feats of Irish sporting history.

7

SAVAGE ROAD MEN

Shay O'Hanlon, the most successful rider in the history of the Rás.

Ben McKenna finally won the Rás in 1959. A native of Julianstown in County Meath, McKenna had a typical rural background of the time and did various labouring jobs around his locality. Picking potatoes was one of his main occupations before he won the Rás.

The first stage of the 1959 race, to Dundalk, was won by Cecil Donoghue of Dublin and he became race leader. This led to a difference of views in the Dublin team. The conventional wisdom of the time was that the Jersey could not be defended for the duration of the Rás, even with the one-minute bonus per stage for the holder. The Dublin team, therefore, wanted Donoghue to concede the Jersey. This tactic had worked for Frank Ward in 1957 – he lost it after the first stage but won it back on stage five and retained it until the end. Donoghue disagreed strongly with this strategy – he was a good and experienced rider and Dublin had a strong team. Nevertheless, custom prevailed and the Jersey was conceded the following day. It was never regained.

The early threat to McKenna came from Mick Palmer, from Westport in County Mayo. Palmer had ridden the first Rás in 1953 though he initially resisted road racing in favour of the more familiar grass-track competition. Like many of his time, he succumbed to the road-racing 'bug', and was to become one of Connacht's greatest road men in spite of much difficulty in getting to events during the 1950s. He attributed his success to twice-daily training sessions during the season – he normally rode 30 miles (48km) each morning before work.

Palmer crashed on the first stage while trying to avoid a child running across the road and Dermot Dignam, a nineteen-year-old from Dublin, in his first Rás, went down with him. Palmer, however, won the second stage, to Longford, and took over the lead. He then had the prospect of a dream finish, wearing the Yellow Jersey into his native Westport at the end of the following stage. Dublin team strategy and his own lack of concentration were to conspire against him. Denis McGrath, a sixteen-year-old Dublin rider in his first Rás and with a reputation for being 'a bit contrary', was given the job of 'sitting' on Palmer's wheel for the day. He performed his mission with such dedication that Palmer transferred his focus from retaining the Jersey to getting rid of McGrath. It degenerated into a feud and, at one point, Palmer stopped and cycled in a circle around the road – even then, McGrath stayed on his wheel. What could have been a glorious home-coming turned into a somewhat ignominious stage end, with Palmer arriving well behind the bunch and losing his Yellow Jersey. He did, however, have some consolation in winning the next stage to Ennis. Shay O'Hanlon from Dublin, just a month short of his eighteenth birthday and in his first Rás, was third on that stage.

Ben McKenna finally won the Rás in 1959. He first rode it in 1956 at the age of sixteen, came third in 1957 at the age of seventeen, second at the age of eighteen in 1958 and finally, in 1959 – at the age of nineteen – he won the Rás. He rode twenty-one Rásanna in all and came second three times. Note his bandaged hand from a fall that threatened his lead.

McKenna's winning move came on the fifth stage, from Ennis to Tralee. Along with Ronnie Williams and Shay Murphy, from Dublin, and Johnny Guerin, from Tipperary, he broke away in the climb before Castleisland. Williams and Murphy tried to set up the sprint between them but muddled it, allowing McKenna take the win and the Yellow Jersey. He defended the lead well on the next stage to Fermoy, with good assistance from Gerry Keogh, but fell about nine miles (14.5km) from the finish. Williams and the other Dublin riders attacked and took some time off him.

The second-last stage, to Waterford, precipitated an important change in the Rás. Ronnie Williams made his bid for yellow and, when the general classification was calculated, was just one second behind McKenna on time difference. However, because of the race leader's bonus of a minute per stage, he was 61 seconds behind on the official GC. McKenna held the Jersey on the final stage and afterwards acknowledged the assistance of Mick Palmer on the Wicklow Gap. His eventual margin of victory remained 61 seconds over Williams. This result highlighted the potential inequity of the bonus system, as there was a good possibility that Williams might have won in its absence. Though the established practice in stage races of the time, it was eliminated the following year in the Rás.

McKenna's win was the pinnacle of one of the most distinguished of Rás careers. He rode twenty-one Rásanna between 1956 and 1977 – he missed one year when he rode to France to see the Tour. He was sixteen years old in his first Rás, seventeen when he came third, eighteen when he came second and nineteen when he won. During his Rás career, he won nine Yellow Jerseys and four stages. In all, he came second three times and was third once. He also achieved many top-ten finishes in spite of the fact that he was not regarded as a great climber or sprinter. Like many of the very good early Rás men, he possessed the excellent recuperative powers that were especially necessary during that era of long stages.[22]

In addition to these achievements, McKenna's approach to racing won him esteem in the eyes of his contemporaries. He had a style and character that was especially admired in the Rás – a rider with great strength and the courage to use it to its limit, along with a willingness to drive from the front without expectation or obligation from those behind. His *modus operandi* was to do his own work and to keep going and going, riding hard, all day long. He was the type of rider who would string the field out in a long line behind him and maintain it like that for

Frank Reilly was one of numerous strong Meath riders from the 1960s and 1970s. Here he wins a 129-mile (206 km) stage into his home town of Navan in 1964. Reilly was a member of the Navan Road Club that claims association with four Rás winners – Brian Connaughton, Séamus Kennedy, Philip Cassidy and Kevin Kimmage. Reilly's support motorcycle was driven by Larry Dunne with passenger Jimmy Gough.

as long as necessary, until it would eventually snap. If he missed the break, McKenna might chase for 50 miles (80km) with the bunch on his wheel, so as not to concede a second more than was necessary. He had a 'never-say-die' attitude and rode with an integrity that earned great respect.

McKenna epitomised the type of rider who has a special appeal, not only to Rás riders, but to followers of road racing universally. This is not simply the admiration of finesse or style. It is, rather, an emotional response to a type of character who expresses himself, or makes a statement of what he is, through a particular type of strategy and style – a rider who simply puts his head down, makes everyone suffer as much as he is prepared to suffer himself and leaves the final outcome between those who are willing and able to endure the most. These are the hard men of the hard road, the 'animals' or, as expressed by John Lackey,[23] 'the savage road men'.

McKenna was this type of racer and the first such rider from Meath to come to prominence in the Rás. Thus, he began a great Meath tradition of gritty, gutsy and determined road racing – a tradition upheld by other Meath riders in the Rás, such as Brian Connaughton, Séamus Kennedy, Mick and Colm Nulty, and Philip Cassidy. McKenna rode his last Rás in 1977 as a member of the only veteran team

'Always at the head of whatever group he was in, be it bunch or break. Never stinting, never a wheel-sucker, never unsporting, always willing.' Ben McKenna (left), with fellow Meathman, Gabriel Howard, in the 1964 Rás.

to have ridden in the event. He also became president of the NCA. Following his death in 1992, Gene Mangan, one of his great rivals, wrote a brief obituary that summarised McKenna's qualities:

> I first saw Ben in the 1956 Rás, tall and lean with what I always considered an 'ungainly' position on the bike. Sitting low, big gears, saddle cocked upwards, riding his favourite bike – an all-chrome 'Hill Special'. This is how I remember him through twenty-one Rásanna. Always at the head of whatever group he was in, be it bunch or break. Never stinting, never a wheel-sucker, never unsporting, always willing. He remained that way in the bunch and in the National Cycling Association, in the Gardaí and in the family, until his untimely death. We are all sorry that we were not more like you Ben.

The Ben McKenna Award is now presented to the best young rider in the Rás in honour of McKenna's memory.

The 1950s gave way to the 1960s and, with the CRE relentless in its efforts to keep the NCA internationally isolated, Joe Christle considered a possible international dimension to the Rás. He recognised the need for international connections and competition – there had been strong demand for this within the NCA. Without it, the standard of riding had a false ceiling and there was a natural need for the athletes to extend themselves. The attraction of foreign competition was also needed to counter the CRE's advantages in this regard.

Christle was well fitted for this challenge. He was broad minded and well travelled – his wife was French and his children were bi-national. He had kept contact with other disaffected associations, as far back as the Tour of Britain in 1951, and when, in 1952, he had invited BLRC teams to the International Tour Revenge in Dublin, he held at least one meeting in his home with very influential English officials, including Percy Stallard, Bob Thom and Ian Steele.[24]

Like the NCA, many of these associations had political overtones and were non-conformist *vis-à-vis* the new world political order following the Second World War. Many had left-wing or communist sympathies and support, something that could have been damaging to the NCA in Ireland if its association with these overseas organisations became too overt. It fell to Kerry Sloane to find this international outlet and he was given the grandiose title of 'International Secretary' – a largely redundant job, as no such competition existed. He looked to the alternative, well-organised associations in Europe, one of the most powerful of which was the FSGT (Féderation Sportive et Gymnique du Travail), a left-wing, workers' organisation closely associated with the trade union and communist movement. It ran a high-profile international event, the Grand Prix de l'Humanité, sponsored by the *Humanité* newspaper, an organ of the French Communist Party which enjoyed a very large circulation.

Following their performance in the 1959 Rás, a team of four riders was sent to the Humanité, with Sloane as manager. They were Ben McKenna, Ronnie Williams, Gerry Meehan and Cecil Donoghue. This initial link was to be very productive for the Rás, beginning with the visit of a Polish team in 1963. The exchange was to develop and increase in importance as the Eastern Bloc became more powerful within the UCI towards the 1970s. These international alliances were to prove significant in the eventual unification of Irish cycling.

A further, though less successful international dimension was added in 1959 when Gene Mangan went to France with aspirations to ride professionally. He was the first NCA road man to do so and was encouraged by Joe Christle and Jack Sweeney, the influential boss of Mangan's club. Getting a legitimate UCI race licence was, however, a problem, as Mangan was not a member of an association affiliated to the UCI. The Taoiseach, Seán Lemass, patron and president of the National Club, made a written representation for Mangan through the Irish embassy in Paris. This was unsuccessful.

Mangan eventually made his way to northern Spain and then to the south of France. Using his middle name of Laurence and a local address, and with the help of local connections, 'Laurence Mangan' obtained an 'independent-licence'[25] in a regional French cycling federation office in the south of France. Cycling success raised his profile and when news of his progress reached Ireland, the secretary of the CRE was sent to northern Spain to seek him out and investigate. This was an important issue for the CRE as a successful career for Mangan would have damaged the CRE's version of the propaganda battle between the two organisations – that the NCA was composed of second-rate riders. It would also have undermined their position as the legitimate UCI-recognised body in Ireland.

Following representation from the CRE, the UCI in Paris queried Mangan's licence and he found it increasingly difficult to enter races. He realised he would eventually be snuffed out unless he joined the CRE and become fully legitimate under UCI rules. But he had 'come too far down the road with the NCA' to leave the association. He returned home, demoralised and unfulfilled, and abandoned his hope of a continental career. For such riders, the Rás was an important outlet and this brought an added significance and competitiveness to the event.

The 1960s began for the Rás as it was to continue – dominated by the battle between the two Herculean figures of the Rás, Paddy Flanagan and Shay O'Hanlon. Between them, they were to win six Rásanna during that decade.

Paddy Flanagan is congratulated by Tom Barry – the famous IRA guerrilla leader during the War of Independence. Christle always tried to have local dignitaries at stage-ends.

O'Hanlon was a young sensation in 1960 and a favourite for the event of that year. Dan Ahern of Kerry beat him into second place on the first stage. Another contender, Con Carr of Kildare, struck a cow in the sprint and was taken to hospital.

Flanagan won the next, 109-mile (175km) stage to Castlebar and took the Yellow Jersey. O'Hanlon made an all-out bid to take over the lead from him on the third day, over 110 miles (176km) of rough roads between Castlebar and Tuam. In the process, they produced a classic Rás stage. From the initial attacks, a leading group of four developed and stayed in front for almost 100 miles (160km). A group of twenty were chasing, including Paddy Flanagan and his brother, Ned. Further back, O'Hanlon's plans were unravelling, primarily due to three punctures.

O'Hanlon nevertheless continued the chase and caught the main chasing group which included the Flanagan brothers. He immediately attacked and jumped away from them on his own. A huge chase ensued in defence of the Jersey, led by the Flanagans and their team-mates, Murt Logan and Eamon Ryan. Only ten riders from the group survived and the leading break was swallowed up in the process. The chase got to within 500 metres of O'Hanlon, but the gap was not closing. Ned Flanagan went to the front and closed it on his own, producing one of the finest of his many rides in defence of Paddy. O'Hanlon attacked yet again and got away once more, with Ned on his wheel. O'Hanlon eventually won from Ned – the first of his twenty-four stage wins in the Rás – and Paddy came in 40 seconds later to retain the race lead.

Dan Ahern took the fourth stage – his second – and went into second place, but the Kildare team took firm control for the rest of the race.

The young O'Hanlon became very frustrated at what he perceived as an anti-Dublin bias in the bunch. From his perspective, riders unconnected to Kildare were going forward, at random, to close gaps for Flanagan, while he had to do his own work. Two factors, at least, may help to explain this. The first is contained in the following observation, made by a Meath rider, on the prevailing attitude towards the Dublin team in his first Rás in 1962:

> Dublin were the common enemy then. They were smart and quick-witted and street-wise. We were country lads. There was that divide – you would like anyone to win but Dublin.

As well as this, the less experienced O'Hanlon lacked some of Flanagan's great ability to mobilise other riders to his advantage. There are numerous stories illustrating this, one of which originated from this race, though in Rás legend it has many variations. It is said that Flanagan, fearing an attack on Moll's Gap, casually asked Seán Dillon of Dublin if he was going for the big KOH prize on the climb. Dillon did not know about a prize and Flanagan told him there was a big barometer for the first rider over the top. Dillon duly obliged by pursuing the non-existent prize and kept the speed of the ascent high enough to deter attackers.

For O'Hanlon, frustration ruled over reason on the descent of Moll's Gap and he went down recklessly fast in anticipation of a Meath rider, who had been sitting on his wheel all day, going off the road if he tried to stay with him. They both successfully negotiated the descent, but Ned Flanagan was not as lucky and flew over the edge at the 'Round-of-Beef', a notorious bend on the fastest part of the descent. Some of the Kerry riders, familiar with this feature of the road, took some satisfaction in luring unpopular rivals into it at speed. Ned had to be taken to hospital and did not finish.

Kerry Sloane, a key figure in the origination and early development of the Rás. He was third in the first two-day Rás in 1953. This picture is from 1955 when he rode with Kildare.

The last stage, from Kilkenny to Dublin, went through Flanagan's home county of Kildare and was long remembered by many who rode in it. It was a triumphant procession for Flanagan, surrounded by his team in lily-white jerseys. As they rode through Athy, Monasterevin, Kildare, Newbridge and Naas, huge crowds acclaimed the new Rás hero.

Kerry Sloane went to the Congo in 1960 as part of Ireland's first United Nations peace-keeping force and had no further involvement in the Rás. O'Hanlon and Flanagan were again favourites in 1961 and their battle was keenly anticipated. Nevertheless, a complete outsider was to take the honours in a race that was to clearly illustrate the intricate and fickle nature of team dynamics in the Rás. It also saw the most dominating performance ever produced by a county team in the event.

On the first stage to Cavan, a group of four escaped from the bunch – O'Hanlon, Flanagan, Dermot Dignam from Dublin and Murt Logan from Kildare. Dignam challenged Flanagan in the final metres of the sprint, with O'Hanlon shouting from behind, urging him on to beat Flanagan, who won. It was Dignam's day in the Rás – one of those precious moments cherished by Rás veterans – in this case, getting to the line with two giants of the road, contesting the win with Flanagan, with O'Hanlon yelling encouragement.

Flanagan and O'Hanlon were obvious favourites now, but matters took a peculiar twist the next day, and Mick Christle was to have the lead role in the drama. Mick Christle was Joe's brother and one of his right-hand men. A stalwart of the Gate cycling club and of the Rás organisation, he was fiercely loyal to Joe, the NCA and the republican cause. He began competitive cycling in his twenties, having previously played hurling for Dublin. Physical training and exercise were a daily ritual – he was interested in physical fitness for its own sake. He organised winter training sessions, including a specialised cycling training camp in Carlow. He was always very fit and well prepared. Equally important was his approach to racing – he was mentally strong and focused. Dermot Dignam much regretted that he had not come under Mick's influence sooner in his racing career, and John 'Jacko' Mangan, who won the Rás in 1972 and raced for a decade in France, attributed much of his success to the mental strength he absorbed from the Christle

Mick Christle was the right-hand man of his brother, Joe. A very strong and mentally focused rider, with a wily cycling brain, he is credited with orchestrating the legendary break in 1961 that arrived into Castlebar 22 minutes ahead of the main bunch. This led to Tom Finn's eventual win.

circle, especially Mick. O'Hanlon also acknowledged Mick's contribution to the crucial development of his mentality. Séamus Kennedy, who won the Rás in 1978, said of him:

> Mick Christle, in my opinion, was twenty years ahead of his time as a coach. He started a training camp outside Carlow and I went there. I did a whole winter's weight training under him and it definitely brought me on tremendously. I think that was what made me – as a coach he had a tremendous effect on my career … he was from the hard school – he taught me about how to take hardship and to survive. He was definitely twenty years ahead of his time.

Mick Christle was a congenial and popular character, but his convivial nature masked a shrewd and wily cycling brain. He disliked ostentatious riders and delighted in outwitting them. He was one of the great 'fixers' of the Rás, always planning and plotting, and excelled at organising strong riders not thought to be in contention to slip away in seemingly harmless breaks. They often turned out to be otherwise.

Dermot Dignam and Christle trained together for the 1961 Rás – they took every Tuesday and Thursday off work and rode up to 170 miles (272km) in training sessions. On one occasion, they did two separate 100-mile (160km) trips in the same day. On the eve of the second stage in the 1961 Rás, Christle knew he had 'the legs' and the stamina for the long road into Connacht.

As in most county teams, there were some tensions in the Dublin camp. There was great rivalry between the Gate and the Clann Brugha clubs – the Gate members resented what they perceived as an air of superiority on the part of Clann Brugha – and no love was lost between the rival riders. Mick Christle, a member of the Gate club, was captain of the Dublin team, while O'Hanlon, from Clann Brugha, was arguably the best rider in the team. There was an expectation among some of the Clann Brugha riders that O'Hanlon would be the number one in the team and would be supported as such. Christle, though team captain, was not consulted on this.

The second stage was 132 miles (210km), from Navan to Castlebar, and almost immediately, riders launched the usual attacks. Christle was one of the first to go and various riders slipped away up the road. It has always been speculated that this was a classic Mick Christle plan and that he had choreographed the break. O'Hanlon and Flanagan, and most of their team-mates, were preoccupied with marking each other and did not see the danger, even when Ben McKenna and Eamon Ryan of Tipperary went away. It did not seem as though it was a dangerous break and they did not react.

Christle had other ideas. He organised a group of eighteen into a cohesive team and urged them on. The time gap gradually opened and was five minutes at

The legendary Rás break of 1961 going through Longford. Ray Kennedy is leading and Mick Christle, who is credited with masterminding the break because of tensions in the Dublin team, is second (wearing white cap and dark glasses). John Caulfield is the rider on the right. The main contenders, including Paddy Flanagan and Shay O'Hanlon, were stranded in the main bunch and the break arrived at the stage end in Castlebar eighteen minutes ahead. It was the foundation for Tom Finn's eventual win. There was a cattle fair in Longford and the riders became liberally spattered with cow dung.

Longford where a cattle fair ensured a bigger crowd than normal, along with a liberal spattering of cow dung for the riders from the manure-littered streets. Though the gap was rising, the bunch did not react. They crossed the Shannon and Christle drove the break relentlessly into Connacht, steadily losing weaker men. The gap eventually grew to an astonishing 22 minutes before the main bunch realised the break was 'gone for the day'. Too late, the contenders saw the danger and the Dublin and Kildare teams even joined forces to try and reduce the damage. They had little success and seven survivors of one of the most legendary breaks in the Rás arrived into Castlebar 18 minutes ahead. Alan Dillon won the sprint and put himself into yellow; McKenna was second, Tom Finn of Dublin third and Mick Christle fourth.

Tom Finn took over the race lead the following day by dint of his time cushion on that break. He was a good county rider, but was not considered a Rás contender. The Dublin manager, Archie Williams, held a team meeting and demanded that the team rally behind him. They agreed, but O'Hanlon insisted that, while he would ride for Finn, he would retain the right to challenge for the Yellow Jersey as long as it did not provide an advantage to any rider outside the Dublin team. This was accepted etiquette – you could compete against a team-mate for the Jersey or a stage as long as outside rivals did not benefit in the process.

Finn's greatest threat was from Ben McKenna, especially on the time trial between Killarney and Kenmare, but Finn held on well, albeit with a reduced margin. McKenna was not the only threat and O'Hanlon kept whittling away at his lead. A break by himself and Seán Dillon for almost the entire stage from Kenmare to Clonakilty gained five minutes. O'Hanlon won what was to be the first of three consecutive stages and his win on the next stage came at the end of the longest ever in the Rás – 154 wet miles (246km), from Clonakilty to Wexford.

By then, the Dublin team had taken a complete and unprecedented stranglehold on the race. They contained every move and the last two days became a procession, to such an extent that the Dublin manager bought ice cream for the team which they ate on the road. O'Hanlon, however, made his move on the Wicklow Gap during the final stage. With almost four minutes to gain, he jumped away with Seán Dillon, opened a sizeable gap and went all out to take the race lead. Then, the manager came up and told them that Finn was being pressed hard by Ben McKenna in the bunch and that they should stop riding and help him. O'Hanlon was now in a dilemma and, in a way, was 'snookered'. McKenna was only 27 seconds behind Finn, and if he could get away from Finn in the mountains and if O'Hanlon, in turn, did not get far enough away from McKenna, then McKenna might win. He was also conscious of the fact the team manager was in

Dublin had very strong Rás teams in the early 1960s. This photograph, taken in the Eamon Ceannt Stadium in 1964, includes five of the six Dublin riders who filled the top eight places in the 1961 Rás (Ben McKenna and Paddy Flanagan were the other two): (left–right) Shay O'Hanlon, Bob Naylor, Jim Ludden, Denis Magrath, Brendan Magennis, Jimmy Kennedy, Sonny Cullen, Tom Finn, Mick Christle, Dermot Dignam.

the same club as Finn and the question arose as to whether his instruction might be favouring Finn. Having considered the situation, O'Hanlon concluded that the manager's instruction was the logical course of action and he and Dillon stopped riding to await Finn. Contrary to Rás legend, they did not go back down the mountain for him. O'Hanlon later won the stage, his third in a row, and Tom Finn won the Rás Tailteann.

An anonymous writer in *Bikes and Bikemen* later bemoaned the lack of courage in the bunch on the final two days: 'It is a pity that Con Carr, Mick Murphy or Paddy O'Callaghan were not there, for they would not have sat quietly under the Dublin whip for two days.' While this commentary may have indicated a typical regard for individual, attacking riding in preference to strong team performances in the Rás, it could not take away from what was an exceptional and record-making team achievement. Indeed, it was an era of dominance by the Dublin team and, as well as being the fifth in a series of six successive team wins in the Rás, 1961 was the most emphatic team performance in the history of the event. All six Dublin riders were in the top eight places.[26]

While it was a triumph for Dublin and for Tom Finn, 1961 was another frustration for O'Hanlon, heaped upon the frustration of the previous year. Deeply analytical, and deeply competitive, O'Hanlon reconsidered his approach to the Rás and, in the process, crossed an important threshold in the development of his racing mentality. He vowed to himself that he would attack the 1962 Rás with a renewed determination and strategy. Not only would he win the event, he would also make a solo entrance to the Phoenix Park on the final day and cross the finishing line on his own.

Three key figures in the early history of the Rás at the prize-giving in 1962: (left–right). Jim Killean, Shay O'Hanlon and Joe Christle.

'O'Hanlon rode alone' is one of the more perceptive observations of Shay O'Hanlon, as offered by one of his contemporaries. Rás veterans generally like to reminisce about the great Rás riders of their era and, like any sport, the exploits of past masters and the revisiting in the mind's eye of epic sporting scenes leads to a flow of descriptive and colourful discussion. Enquiry about Shay O'Hanlon, however, provokes a perceptible difference in reaction – a response that hints at an elusive dimension difficult to articulate. His peers, in attempting to describe his qualities as a rider, sometimes struggle to find superlatives; emotion is visibly stirred, while the body language suggests a slight discomfort at an inability to adequately express their sense of him – 'What can you say about O'Hanlon?' Personal reminiscences are quickly reverted to – scenes that are burned in the memories of those who rode with him and which might illustrate those subtle qualities: 'I'll never forget the day …'

Four outright wins, twenty-four stage wins and thirty-seven Yellow Jerseys powerfully demonstrate his stature as the most successful Rás rider ever. Such bare statistics, however, merely provide evidence of a phenomenal physical capacity and do little to reveal an equally remarkable intellect. Like the efforts of his peers to signify the essence of O'Hanlon through examples of his feats, the revisiting of a few of the seminal scenes from his Rás career may provide some fleeting illustrations of his combination of acumen and athletic ability which, arguably, produced the most dominant rider ever in Irish domestic cycling.

The Phoenix Park, 1962, is one such scene. It is the end of the final stage of the Rás and O'Hanlon rides into the park, on his own, wearing the Yellow Jersey. He is well ahead of the field and almost twenty minutes clear of the next-placed rider on GC. The usual enormous crowd is there to witness the finish and he is on his own to fully savour it – there is no distraction of a contested sprint as he crosses the line. This exhibition is telling enough in itself, but its real significance lies in the fact that it is the clinical, calculated execution of a Rás-win scenario which O'Hanlon conceived twelve months previously when, frustrated at being denied a win by an unlucky roll of the tactical dice, he resolved to cap his first Rás victory in precisely this way.

The first stage of the 1965 Rás, from Dublin to Monaghan, is the arena for another such illustrative scene. O'Hanlon is riding comfortably in a lead bunch. One of the Dublin support team, Mick Glancy, comes up to the group on a motorcycle and makes eye contact with O'Hanlon. With a gesture of his head, he urges him to attack. It is not considered wise to assume the burden of the Yellow Jersey on the first stage and O'Hanlon shakes his head at Glancy, who then retreats. But Glancy returns and the scene is repeated, except that at the second urging,

O'Hanlon accepts the advice. He wins the first stage and takes the Yellow Jersey. Then he retains it, for a full three years. From the first stage in 1965, to the final stage in 1967, the combined efforts of all of his rivals are unable to wrest the Jersey from his back and no other man wears it in the Rás for these three years.

The 1961 Rás provides what is, perhaps, the most telling image of all. Mick Christle has orchestrated the break into Castlebar that has left most of the field, including O'Hanlon, 18 minutes down. To all observers, the race is effectively over for anybody who has missed the decisive move. It is evening, the fluster of the day has died down and O'Hanlon is resting in his room.[27] He takes a copy of the GC sheet and studies it. There are eighteen men ahead of him on the list, some with an 18-minute advantage. The nineteen-year-old then ticks off names, one by one, as he resolves to overtake each of the eighteen over the next seven stages. An average gain of approximately 2.5 minutes per stage, sustained for seven days, should be beyond the expectation of any rider. But this he effectively achieves and gets to within 1 minute 40 seconds of the leader, Tom Finn, at the Wicklow Gap on the final day. Team loyalty forces him to forego further gain when he is instructed by his manager to assist Finn, his team-mate. This GC sheet, still in existence and with O'Hanlon's notes and marks on it, is possibly the most striking, almost chilling, metaphor for the phenomenon that was 'O'Hanlon'.

Shay O'Hanlon was Dublin-born and christened Séamus – the derivative Sé was also used. To cyclists, he was always known as O'Hanlon and, in some Dublin cycling circles, simply 'O'H'. To the media and the public, he was Shay. As a schoolboy, he joined his local Clann Brugha Club. His family had little inkling of his enormous potential and, at one point, his father forbade him completely from cycling when he arrived home from a day-long trip well after dark – O'Hanlon had taken a school friend on one of his excursions into the Wicklow Mountains but did not fully understand the limits of a normal youngster. His companion became exhausted and had to be pushed much of the way home. Jim Killean intervened on his behalf – O'Hanlon's father and Killean had been comrades in the War of Independence and this connection saved O'Hanlon's fledgling cycling career.

By the time he was sixteen, O'Hanlon was going to the Phoenix Park and challenging some of the top Dublin riders in training sessions – he was intensely competitive from the beginning. He began racing in 1958 and travelled with the Rás that year, selling programmes and doing other such jobs. The event then had enormous prestige in the Irish sporting calendar, but O'Hanlon had no sense of its short history – to him, it might have been there forever.

Shay O'Hanlon (left) and Mick Murphy at the end of the 1959 Rás. They fought out the final stage in the Dublin mountains and Murphy, winner of the previous Rás, prevailed. The seventeen-year-old O'Hanlon, in his first Rás, was second on the stage. Dr Eamon O'Sullivan, chairman of the Kerry NCA County Board, is in the background.

He entered his first Rás in 1959, a month short of his eighteenth birthday. He intended to win, but youthful exuberance and the excitement of the first stage overcame him. He rode aggressively, as if on a single-stage race, 'blew up', lost twenty minutes and finished in eighty-fourth position. Undeterred, he began clawing back time during the week and challenged for the last stage in the familiar Wicklow Mountains. He was denied a stage win by the 'Iron Man', Mick Murphy, who had won the Rás the previous year, but O'Hanlon nevertheless finished second on the stage and thirteenth overall.

Cyclists noted O'Hanlon's extensive training during the winter of 1959–60, leading to much speculation about his potential for the coming season. This was answered with a stunning early-season display – he won seven races in a row, including road races, time trials and three-day events. He also won the prestigious Caltex Award for best cyclist of the year. Nevertheless, he was thwarted by Paddy Flanagan, who gained the first of his three Rás wins. It was the beginning of one of the great rivalries of the Rás and a long-term battle that lasted around twenty-five years.

In 1961 there were more brilliant performances from O'Hanlon and he was to win the Caltex Award again. Early in the season, he created a sensation by breaking the 2-hour barrier in the 50-mile time trial. This had never been achieved in Ireland and was only achieved in Britain in 1947. The NCA record had stood at 2.03.47 for many years until O'Hanlon reduced it to 2.01.40 in a competition in 1960 and, in the process, knocked 1 second off Shay Elliott's 'official' CRE Irish record. In a special challenge to his own record in May 1960, O'Hanlon broke the magical 2-hour barrier at 1.59.28, in unfavourable conditions. This display of form helped make him favourite for the 1961 Rás, but defeat by Tom Finn was another blow, not softened by his three consecutive stage wins.

O'Hanlon's approach to the 1962 Rás was greatly influenced by the circumstances which had conspired to frustrate his hopes of victory in the previous three editions of the event. From these defeats, a strategy evolved that was relatively simple, with no tactical fineries or grand team strategy – if other riders were to beat him, they had to catch him first and then they had to get away from him. In that year's Rás, O'Hanlon made a solo, all-out, frontal attack on the race, charging relentlessly from the front, every day. Help was not anticipated or expected and regarded as a bonus if provided. He took the lead on the second day, but a conventional, prudent defence of the Yellow Jersey was a concept he refused to entertain – he rode each stage as if it were an individual, single-stage race that had to be won, and without any conservation of energy.

It was a tactical approach that could only have been contemplated by somebody who was either very naïve, desperate, or self-assured regarding his ability. In this case, a potent combination of desperation and self-assurance produced an explosive performance. He was 'head and shoulders' above everyone else, and vastly superior to the best efforts of any team or any combination of rivals. He held the race lead for seven days, won four stages and finished 19 minutes 4 seconds in front – the biggest winning margin ever. It was the finest individual display ever produced in the Rás.

This win was not entirely without difficulty and a team-mate, Sonny Cullen, was his main threat over the first few days. Cullen and Jimmy Kennedy had transferred from the CRE to the NCA that year following a petty argument over not being allowed to keep their Irish jerseys after competing in the World Championships. Cullen was a former CRE national champion and he and Kennedy were friends. Among the hard-core NCA riders, there was a certain resentment of former CRE riders and a feeling that their transfer of allegiance was motivated less by ideology than by the prospect of easier prizes in supposedly inferior races. Along with this, there was a concern that a Rás win by a former CRE rider might give credence to the CRE claim that the Rás standard was inferior to the CRE's Tour of Ireland. This put extra pressure on O'Hanlon. Cullen kept chipping away at his lead and got to within two minutes, but by the time they reached the mountains, the contest was over. Exactly as he had visualised a year

Sonny Cullen following Shay O'Hanlon on the third stage, into Castlebar, 1962. Cullen won this and also the fifth stage into Tralee. Though a team-mate of O'Hanlon, Cullen was his main threat in the early part of the race and the fact that he had come back from the CRE put some extra pressure on O'Hanlon. Note O'Hanlon's unorthodox position on the bike. His saddle is forward and his head is over the front fork. Even though wearing the Yellow Jersey, he is still carrying a spare tubular tyre and pump.

earlier, O'Hanlon made a defining statement to himself, and to everyone else, by arriving on his own at the Phoenix Park finish.

As with Gene Mangan, the cycling hero of his youth, the lure of French racing now had to be satisfied and, in 1963, with the assistance of Joe Christle, O'Hanlon went to the Perpignan region, where Mangan had previously been based. As with Mangan's situation, there was a difficulty with his licence, so Christle contrived to print a licence for him, using the Irish version of NCA – Gaelchumann Rothaíochta na hÉireann. This was confusingly similar to the Irish version of the CRE – Cumann Rothaíochta na hÉireann – and O'Hanlon raced successfully under this guise for a full season. But it was no more than a stop-gap measure and, like Mangan, O'Hanlon was faced with the option of either joining the CRE or abandoning any serious ambitions of a professional career on the continent. Given his family's republican background and his own loyalty to the NCA, he returned home at the end of the season.

What O'Hanlon and Mangan might have achieved in different circumstances remains one of the speculative questions from the history of Irish cycling. The denial of this potential, together with the personal cost to the individual, provides a compelling argument against a political role for sportspeople. Many feel their treatment was unjust and exploitative. An equally compelling and contrary

Above: Phoenix Park, 1962: Shay O'Hanlon comes in alone to win the Rás. O'Hanlon conceived this Rás win scenario twelve months previously when, frustrated at being denied victory by an unlucky roll of the tactical dice, he resolved to cap his first Rás victory in precisely this fashion. He launched a straightforward frontal assault on the Rás every day, won four stages, finished on his own as planned and had the biggest ever winning margin in the Rás – 19 minute 4 seconds. It was the finest individual performance in the history of the event.

Below: Shay O'Hanlon with Jim Killean following his 1962 Rás win.

argument, however, is that the considered and wilful decision of such athletes to make a sacrifice demonstrated the virtue and legitimacy of the cause.

The true personal cost of their allegiance can only be surmised as, for both men, cycling was integral to their self-identity and individuality. They had to reconcile themselves to untested and unfulfilled aspirations due to political beliefs, and to being both champions and casualties of a wider ideological struggle. Thus, they became true amateurs, without even the hope of representing Ireland at Olympic or World Championship level. They slipped back into the NCA domestic scene and became typical family men, with cycling inevitably subordinated to work and domestic demands. To be able to ride the Rás during their annual holidays offered welcome consolation. Yet, their sacrifice was not completely without recompense. Christle and the NCA were highly conscious of their role as champions of the NCA and they enjoyed an enormous public profile due to Christle's promotional ability and efforts. It was a two-way relationship. Shay O'Hanlon, in a reflection years later, turned to Gray's 'Elegy' to express his estimation of the obscurity and lost opportunity that might have been their lot without Christle's efforts and the role of the Rás:

Full many a gem of purest ray serene
The dark unfathom'd caves of ocean bear:
Full many a flower is born to blush unseen,
And waste its sweetness on the desert air.

O'Hanlon sold his bike before leaving France at the end of 1963 and arrived home to Ireland almost penniless. It was February before he was able to begin training properly and he was not fully prepared for the 1964 Rás. That was to be Paddy Flanagan's year – he got his second win and the Caltex Award for best cyclist of the year.

The 1964 Rás was also remembered for an intrepid stage win by Gene Mangan. Though not very fit that year, he studied the finish of the first stage, into Carlow, and noted that although the finish was on a new road, the old road – running alongside – was still open. Mangan perceived an opportunity. It was a bunch finish, with Mangan at the back, but coming to the line, he jumped onto the old road to pass the bunch. His line went wrong, however, and he somehow ended up on the footpath while passing the bunch. He only jumped off, in the lead, when the footpath became too crowded with spectators, but he had won the stage and the Yellow Jersey. His method was criticised by some as it was supposed to be a road race and footpaths should not be allowed. But his tactic was generally admired for

Gene Mangan, the first national cycling celebrity to emerge from the Rás, won his last stage in 1966. Though he never repeated his 1955 victory, Mangan won twelve stages in all, wove a distinctive imprint through the fabric of the race and was an integral part of the event over the 23-year period in which he competed.

Shay O'Hanlon, wearing the victor's laurel wreath, signing autographs after his 1962 win. Mick Christle is in the background.

its boldness. Nevertheless, he took a hammering the next day because of his lack of fitness and, to add to his many unique distinctions in the Rás, he became the first of only two men to abandon the event while wearing the Yellow Jersey and the only uninjured leader to do so. O'Hanlon, though not fully fit by his own standards, still managed to win two stages.

The 1965 Rás was the beginning of O'Hanlon's three-year domination of the event. Interestingly, he himself considered his best period as a rider to have been from 1960–63. Nevertheless, O'Hanlon's unbroken run of Yellow Jerseys, from 1965–67, remains his most outstanding achievement. He began the 1965 race as determined as he had been in 1962 and rode to win every stage even though he was race leader from the first day. Paddy Flanagan did not ride, as he had left to work in England, but it was still a difficult race for O'Hanlon. On several occasions, the race seemed lost due to tactical errors, yet he always managed to claw his way back into contention. He won four stages and his final winning margin from Seán Lally was almost eight minutes.

O'Hanlon had a French team to contend with in 1966, led by Jean Bellay, a former professional who had completed the Tour de France. The French riders were an exotic addition to the Rás and a product of Christle's efforts to give the event an international dimension as well as to improve the NCA standard through exposure to a high standard of racing. Joe Christle's decision to extend the race to ten days was welcomed by O'Hanlon and other strong riders, but added considerably to the challenge for the average riders. But though the duration was increased, there was a significant shift in emphasis to shorter stages. Christle explained his reasoning in a press release:

> The long mileage had often been criticised as too severe for amateurs and as making the race into an endurance test … in the early years of the Rás it was not unusual for a rider to go into a house along the road, have a meal and a rest and then set off again … now speed replaces endurance, although it will still take exceptional stamina …

As well as the French, O'Hanlon had Paddy Flanagan to grapple with again, along with Mike O'Donaghue of Carlow and Jimmy Kennedy of Dublin. Gene Mangan also caused problems. He set his own agenda, attacking early and often, forcing O'Hanlon and any other contenders to respond to his initiative. He won three stages in the process – one of these was into Killarney. He also won the next stage – a circuit-race around the streets of Killarney town that was the fastest Rás stage ever at that point. Motivated by a huge crowd, a prime on every lap and a cash prize of £20, they rode the 50km (31.25 miles) in less than an hour.

A win in the first stage – a 26-mile (41km) time trial into Navan – had given O'Hanlon the race lead and a time-cushion that provided the foundation for his ultimate win – he eventually had more than 4 minutes to spare over Bellay. From O'Hanlon's point of view, 1966 also raised an uncomfortable question. On a stage to Ballinasloe, a group of riders – including some of the French – was ahead, while O'Hanlon, in yellow, was further back. When the race went astray, it was stopped to get it back on course. Some were dubious about this as O'Hanlon may have received an advantage. Such was O'Hanlon's sportsmanship, it continued to bother him and the question was never fully resolved to his satisfaction.

He had strong opposition again in 1967. Along with another French team, the main threats came from Paddy Flanagan, Ben McKenna, Mike O'Donaghue, Jimmy Kennedy and John Dorgan from Cork. Nevertheless, it was one of those races where everything went well – he made no major tactical mistakes, there were no disastrous punctures or crashes and he won from a Frenchman, Pierre Ropert, by over 8 minutes.

Lord Moyne of Guinness congratulating Shay O'Hanlon following his win in 1966. This is a rather incongruous image, with Christle, a revolutionary socialist republican, sharing the podium with Lord Moyne, a peer of the British House of Lords and one of the Guinness family – Ireland's foremost capitalists. Lord Moyne had come to the Phoenix Park to see the end of the race and approached a Rás official, Jack Barrett, because he was employed by Guinness and was working from one of its vans. Having established that Barrett was involved with the race (he was Director of Publicity), Lord Moyne asked if he might meet O'Hanlon. Christle then invited him onto the podium. From the left: Jack Barrett (Director of Publicity), Joe Christle, Lord Moyne, Shay O'Hanlon, Séamus Ó Riain (President of the GAA), Jim Killean (President of the NCA).

O'Hanlon's four victories in the Rás were the greatest expression of an extraordinary talent in Irish sport – a blend of many qualities. Like any athlete at that level, he was extremely competitive and accepted defeat poorly. A companion remembered himself and O'Hanlon cycling home from a race, when O'Hanlon threw a trophy over a ditch in disgust at it being for third place. This natural talent and competitiveness was complemented by a high degree of ordered, methodical and analytical thinking. He attended to every detail and his methods took no account of fashion or convention. His position on the bike, for example, was very unusual – his saddle was very far forward so that he sat over the bottom bracket. In France, he was expected to ride a conventional set up, but reverted to his normal habits when he returned home because he did not see any good reason to change. But when he returned to France in 1966 to ride in the Humanité, he bought a book by Jean Bobet[28] and changed his position and diet accordingly, corresponding to Bobet's clearly outlined reasoning. His training was equally structured, rigorous and thorough. He did great distance work in the winter – something he did not look on as a chore. Rather, his approach was to enjoy it as a form of fast touring – long, pleasurable trips through the countryside in the company of friends.

Of most significance, however, was O'Hanlon's mental approach. As early as 1959, O'Hanlon was getting into decisive breaks and, though able to work in them, he was unable to achieve consistent results. Having analysed his performance, he concluded that, since his training was adequate, his mental attitude would have to change if he was to be successful. He became a firm believer in the 'mind over matter' maxim and had a policy of never thinking negatively – he did not allow himself to contemplate defeat as he believed in the 'self-fulfilling prophecy'. His mental discipline made it impossible to frustrate him, even under intense pressure – 'You could sit on him, drag him, pull him or haul him, but he'd never lose his temper.' He had a forward-looking perspective and was a keen observer, thinker and student of the mind and body. He was advanced in what later became known as the discipline of sports psychology.

The comment that 'O'Hanlon rode alone' expresses much more than his self-reliance, limited support and the fact that he had to do more riding than most to achieve his Rás wins – it also throws some subtle light on his psychological disposition vis-à-vis his interaction with other riders. While genial and cheerful in character, he kept private his thoughts about racing. He confided in no one and never revealed how easy or difficult a race was. As one peer remarked, 'His mind was a deep well.' That 'well' concealed an insecurity about racing which was disguised by his outwardly confident demeanour. While seen as dominant and assured, he felt vulnerable and hunted on the bike. His expectations of himself verged on paranoia and everybody was a perceived threat – potential predators ready to pounce if he dropped his guard or made a mistake. Such fear provokes defensive reaction, but he converted this to a positive, aggressive type of riding.

This detachment, combined with his phenomenal ability, created an enigma. One county rider, who had only known O'Hanlon by reputation, shared accommodation with him on a couple of occasions during a Rás and noticed that he brought some unfamiliar food to breakfast each morning. The rider became preoccupied with this and thought that if he could only find out what O'Hanlon was eating, he would discover the key to success. But he could not summon the courage to ask. Years later, when continental tastes became common in Ireland, he recognised muesli as the food which so perturbed him when he had thought it unique to O'Hanlon. In order to anticipate conditions on each part of a stage, O'Hanlon listened for the wind direction and speed in the weather forecast, and studied maps carefully. This led to speculation that he adjusted his breakfast

Shay O'Hanlon on his own after a crash on the final circuit in 1967, the year of his third consecutive Rás win. With two laps remaining of the final circuit in the Phoenix Park, he fell on a corner and was initially stunned. Another rider, Joe Roche, stopped, gave O'Hanlon his bike and got him going again. Roche's father was killed in a motorcycle accident in the Rás four years previously, in 1963.

accordingly, using a secret formula to balance his food intake to correspond with the anticipated energy expenditure during the stage.

Yet another belief emerged, that O'Hanlon deliberately set out to psychologically destroy his main rivals. It was vaguely postulated that he achieved this by luring them into long, gruelling trips in vile winter weather into the Wicklow Mountains. There, he would display his strength and power, and they were left in awe and forever lost any confidence in their ability to attack him. Whatever its validity, the theory gained credence, and when the young John Mangan was brought to Dublin by his mentors, they would not allow him to train with O'Hanlon – 'That fellow will destroy you.'

During the 1960s and early 1970s, when at his best, O'Hanlon had an enormous stature in the Rás. He was tremendously strong and was an excellent time trialist and sprinter. He could attack at will, jumping from the bunch with great aggression and power. There are numerous examples of him leaving the *peloton* and bridging, with apparent ease, a 5-minute gap to a leading break. Many such breaks were driven by a dread of O'Hanlon getting up to them because they knew that, if he arrived, he would 'crucify' them – 'Is he coming … any sign of him?' they would ask, without any need to elaborate on who the 'he' was.

He could lead from the front, sometimes endlessly. On leaving Ballinasloe in 1967, he made one of his usual surges at the start and a few riders went with him. An unexpected gap of almost a minute opened quickly and he was faced with the decision of conceding the advantage or keep going all the way to the end at Castleisland, 113 miles (180km) away. It was an indication of his mental courage that he chose to stay out in front and go for the stage win from that distance. Various riders made it up and did some work, before dropping away again, but his physical strength and courage, and the ability to endure what must have been considerable suffering, was exemplified by his role in holding off the whole chasing bunch, including a French team which was to win six stages, for the entire 4 hours and 42 minutes it took him to win the stage.

Such performances inspired admiration and, to his generation of riders, O'Hanlon was a Titan of the Rás. He was greatly respected and his dominance not resented. He wore the mantle of greatness with unassuming grace, was scrupulously fair and 'he spoke with his pedals'. He became a benchmark by which riders measured their performance and they could articulate, by reference to O'Hanlon, where they lay on the spectrum of development and achievement. The average Rás rider would return home a proud and fulfilled man if he could talk about the day he was in the break with O'Hanlon. More ambitious riders would try and ride with him to gauge their level of progress – how far they could work against him or could they last in the break until the finish? When a rider gained the confidence and ability to 'take on' O'Hanlon, he had crossed an important psychological threshold and knew that he had progressed into the élite ranks; one of the many compliments made about Paddy Flanagan was that he had no fear of O'Hanlon.

After his 'three-in-a-row', O'Hanlon was to remain at the forefront of the Rás until the mid-1970s – he came to depend less on his strength, became very tactically astute and won five further stages up to 1975. He wore the Yellow Jersey again in 1973. To O'Hanlon – as to most of the riders – there was more to the Rás than stage wins and Yellow Jerseys, and he continued to ride in it up to 1984, the twenty-third event he started.[29] In all, he spent about six months of his life simply riding the Rás.

FROM BEHIND THE IRON CURTAIN

Trying to escape the Poles – Sonny Cullen (leading) and Geno Goddard, 1963.

The participation of a Polish team in the 1963 Rás Tailteann was a landmark for the event. Along with other teams from behind the Iron Curtain – Czechoslovakia in 1968 and Russia in 1970 – they brought prestige and an international dimension to the Rás and the NCA, and challenged a complacency that had developed amongst the home riders and raised the Rás to a new level of competition.

The following extract from the Rás programme, written by Joe Christle, expressed the political significance of the coming of the Poles:

In 1963 the barriers erected by England and propped by Seoiníns to keep Ireland out of International racing began to collapse under the pressure of An Rás. A Polish team travelled to Ireland in defiance of 'Official' threats and competed in the Rás. In doing so, the NCA gained a powerful and valuable ally to support the reasonable claim that Ireland is bounded by God's seas and not Acts of England's Parliament.

While the Poles' apparent 'defiance' of the UCI directive did indeed appear to be a radical statement of support for the NCA, the Poles had not been made aware that they were coming to an 'unofficial' event. This, of course, did not deter Christle's exploitation of the visit in the propaganda battle and the circumstances of their coming are indicative of his vision and shrewdness.

While the event was very popular in the early 1960s, Christle was not satisfied to let it rest on its laurels and bask in its huge domestic, if isolated, success. As part of this progressive approach, he would have to break the international blockade, imposed because of the NCA's 32-county stance. Christle's strategy for dealing with this matter was never generally known within the NCA or the Rás organisation. While he directed a band of willing and able helpers, he shared his strategic thinking or planning with very few. He ran the Rás by himself and kept it independent of any NCA control. Perhaps the conspiratorial nature of his republican activities led him to operate the republican 'need-to-know' principle in relation to the Rás. Indeed, given the ongoing battle with the cycling establishment, there was a constant atmosphere of intrigue and a real need for secrecy. In the case of the Poles, for example, had the CRE been forewarned, it would undoubtedly have made strenuous efforts through the UCI to have the visit blocked.

The participation of the Poles developed from contacts maintained with the French FSGT[30] since the early 1950s, especially through the Grand Prix de l'Humanité. The link with the BLRC was also important in bringing the Polish team to Ireland. Teams from the BLRC attended the International Tour Revenge in Dublin in 1951 and 1952,[31] and Bob Thom came as manager of the professional Viking team from England. By the early 1960s, the BLRC had become reconciled with the UCI and Thom had been manager of the British national road race team on many occasions. He therefore had connections in European cycling and an empathy with those who had been alienated from the UCI in the 1950s. The Polish cycling federation was another organisation to have come back into the UCI fold and, on behalf of Christle, Thom introduced the idea of a Polish team visiting the Rás to a Mr Golebiewske, a senior figure in the Polish federation. The rest of the arrangements were made between Christle and the Poles, but both Thom and Christle neglected to mention to Golebiewske that the Rás was 'illegal' in UCI terms.

The arrival of the Poles achieved all that Christle could have hoped for and the event was a resounding success. Sadly, though, a Dublin-team helper, Donal Roche, was to die in a motorcycle accident during the race. The Polish team was a colourful, radical and exciting addition to the event, their domination of the race a jolt to the bulk of the riders. It was their first exposure to such levels of competition and to such highly refined tactical team riding. The newspaper previews did not anticipate their impact,[32] and to the Irish riders, the Poles set an unbelievable pace – 'It was like riding against five O'Hanlons' was the opinion of one participant.

The first stage was closely contested and a group of eight came to the line together. It was won by a Pole, Mikolajczyk, whilst John 'Geno' Goddard from the Exiles[33] team was second. Dan Ahern, from Kerry, was third. Another Pole, Linde, took the second stage and the Poles took the first three places on the third stage.

The lack of a strong, well-organised and tactically astute Irish team to counter experienced foreign teams was a feature of the Rás then, and would be the case for a long time to come. Ad hoc efforts were often the only response and the first of these began at the end of the third stage, in Tuam, when Gene Mangan and Mick Christle took the initiative. They held a meeting of select riders

Dan Ahern, considered to be one of the best riders to never have won the Rás. He was twice second, and also third and fifth. Ahern provided the main Irish challenge to the first foreign national team in the Rás – the Poles in 1963.

Sonny Cullen pips Jimmy Kennedy into Castleisland in 1963. This stage win was the result of the first of many plots by gangs of Irish riders against dominant foreign teams. They gave the Poles the slip for one day.

and organised a group to 'mark' the Poles on the following stage to Castleisland. It was the first of many such covert and unofficial Irish 'teams' created to counter foreign teams down through the years. In this case, the plan was crude enough – they divided the Poles between them and each agreed to 'sit on' his assigned man, while some of the Polish 'danger men' got two markers.

The strategy, albeit a negative one, succeeded in disconcerting the Poles in the short term. Two groups of about twenty-five riders got away in the early stages to Castleisland and every attempt made by the Poles to escape from the main bunch was thwarted. There was no Pole in the first six places, the race leader finished almost 9 minutes down and Sonny Cullen won the stage, narrowly beating Jimmy Kennedy. Geno Goddard from the Exiles team took the Yellow Jersey from the Pole, Mikolajczyk.

Four Poles in the lead bunch at the foot of the Coomakista climb in the Kerry mountains. Christy Kimmage is second. Zbigniew Glowaty (on the left, looking around) was the eventual winner. Dan Ahern (seventh rider, partially hidden) was the only Irish rider to stay with the Poles on the Kerry climbs.

For this stage, Dan Ahern from Kerry had been assigned to watch Zbigniew Glowaty, one of the lower-placed Poles. He noticed that Glowaty did not even change down to his lower chain ring on the Barnagh Gap before Castleisland and this hint of form led him to conclude that Glowaty was the real danger man. He decided to keep him within his sights for the rest of the race. Ahern's judgement proved correct when Glowaty made his move the next day, on the 112-mile (180km) Ring of Kerry. The tactics of the previous day could not work in the Kerry mountains and Glowaty – supported by a team-mate – went away on the climb of Coomakista. Ahern was the only Irish rider able to survive with them for the remainder of the stage. Glowaty won into Killarney, ahead of Ahern, and became race leader.

Above left: Following a duel in the Kerry mountains, Glowaty beat Ahern into Killarney. However, Ahern was to turn the tables in Clonmel the next day.

Above right: Dan Ahern beating the Pole and eventual race winner, Zbigniew Glowaty, into Clonmel in 1963. The Poles initially disputed the result until this press photograph was developed in the town that evening. Posted in the window of the local cinema, a queue formed to see it.

Ahern again tracked Glowaty on the following stage, into Clonmel and they contested the sprint. The judges awarded the win to Ahern but it was close enough for the Poles to question the verdict. A picture of the finish, taken by one of the press photographers, was processed in the town that evening and posted in the window of the local cinema. The queue that formed to see it were left in no doubt – it showed a dramatic win by Ahern, by half the width of the line.

Ahern stayed with Glowaty on the next stage, to Gorey, which was won by Christy Kimmage. Glowaty had a 1 minute 52 seconds advantage over Ahern at the beginning of the final stage, which was to take one of its typical routes through the Wicklow Mountains. Archie Williams, who had been riding very well all week, made an early attack at Avoca while the main contenders were being cautious before the big climbs. He was soon brought back. Dave Kenny from the Exiles team made another attack and got away, but he took a wrong turning at Rathdrum and lost his advantage. Meanwhile, Ahern was waiting until the very last opportunity. He launched his attack on Glowaty and made his bid for glory on

Clonmel, 1963: Five Poles, including Glowaty, lined up behind Christle's Race Director's car at the start of the second-last stage.

the steepest part of the Wicklow Gap. He broke free and began to get away. At the summit, the race lead was dramatically in the balance as they began the descent and the last 30-mile (48km) scramble for Dublin. However, the lack of team help for Ahern made the final difference – the Poles regrouped, chased Ahern and caught him just before the entrance to the Phoenix Park.

Ahern was a reserved man who did not make excuses and it was therefore little known that he had fallen on one of the two hump-back bridges on the descent of the Wicklow Gap. He damaged his gears which kept slipping on the run into Dublin. The enormous crowd lining the final stages of the route from the Islandbridge gates of the Phoenix Park witnessed Christy Kimmage win the final sprint. His second stage win in a row was a good reward for having joined the NCA from the CRE just to ride the Rás. Zbigniew Glowaty's overall victory made him the first foreign rider to win the Rás Tailteann.

The first foreign winner of the Rás, Zbigniew Glowaty from Poland, throws his bouquet into the crowd in the Phoenix Park, 1963. While there was a big risk in bringing a 'communist' team to the Rás in the Ireland of the 1960s, the participation of the Poles was very successful and a landmark in the history of the event.

Dan Ahern's challenge to Glowaty on the Wicklow Gap was one of the high points of his Rás career and he is considered by many to be one of the best Rás riders never to have won the Rás. He was second twice and also came third and fifth.[34] Commenting on Ahern's performance in the 1963 Rás, an anonymous writer in the 1970 Rás programme commented: 'Any class of team support and the Rás was his.' While the Kerry team could not have been expected to mount a challenge to the Polish national team, the remark did highlight the lack of an NCA national-team strategy to challenge foreign teams. This deficiency was to exaggerate the apparent gap between the top NCA riders and their Continental counterparts. The foreign teams consisted of top-class riders, experienced in international competition and riding as well-managed and cohesive units. They were the equivalent of professional riders, with the full support of communist regimes that sought sporting success as an endorsement of their political systems – for them, it was a matter of international prestige. In the Rás, relatively few Irish riders were good enough to pose a threat and these, for the most part, lacked international-level tactical experience and were preoccupied with more parochial rivalries. Their response to the foreigners, therefore, tended to be disjointed and fragmented.

The Poles suffered no repercussions for breaking the UCI ban by attending the Rás in 1963 – they were too powerful in world cycling terms to be censured for attending a remote race at the edge of Europe. When they met again after the Rás, Golebiewske reprimanded Bob Thom for not alerting him to the fact that it was an 'illegal' race. The reproach was, however, light-hearted – they had been treated so well and enjoyed themselves so much, Golebiewske said, that it had been well worth it.

The Exiles team did not have such immunity – they were pursued through the system by the CRE and each rider was suspended from his federation in England for varying periods. Geno Goddard, for example, who had taken the Yellow Jersey from the Poles for one stage, was banned for six months, beginning in January 1964.

Regardless of Christle's grander strategies, most Rás riders were glad to be rid of the Poles and reverted to their native rivalries, with Flanagan and O'Hanlon winning the Rás over the next four years. Christle, however, continued to develop the international challenge and brought teams from the French FSGT in 1966 and 1967. While these were very experienced and well organised, the Irish riders could compete with them and they had an important role in maintaining the standard of the Rás. They would probably have won both of these events were it not for O'Hanlon.

Other pressures were brought to bear on the NCA and the Rás during this period. In 1966, after a lapse since the late 1950s, the CRE reactivated the Tour of Ireland as a six-day event, with strong English teams competing. Then, in 1967, the CRE changed its name to the Irish Cycling Federation (ICF). The name change was largely cosmetic, but the 'new' federation was vigorously marketed as a fresh beginning in Irish cycling. The NCA lost some riders to it, leading to much acrimony and ill will. Paddy and Ned Flanagan were the most high-profile riders to defect.

Hard on the heel of these developments, Christle brought a very strong team from Czechoslovakia in 1968 and the first Irish Rás team was formed to challenge the Czechs. It consisted of Mike O'Donaghue (Carlow), Benny Donnelly (Antrim), Kevin Dolan (Louth), Séamus Kennedy (Meath), Shay O'Hanlon (Dublin) and Tony Ryan (Tipperary). From a modern perspective, this hastily arranged national team was poorly organised and hopelessly incoherent. The individual riders' results counted for placings for their respective county teams as well as for the national team. This was probably to placate County Boards over concerns that the drawing of the best riders to a national team would weaken their county teams. While Mick Christle was Irish-team manager, he had no separate team accommodation or transport and had no contact with his riders during the stages. They travelled, lodged and ate with their respective county teams, but were then expected to race against them. The Rás programme made no mention of an Irish team and it was not until the third stage that the GC sheets made reference to it. From stage 3, Benny Donnelly's results, for example, were given as 'Ireland and Antrim'. In effect, they were riding for two teams and this inevitably led to divided loyalties and lack of co-ordination.

Most of the riders were probably not ready for the idea of an Irish team in the Rás. The bulk of them were still operating within narrow and deeply embedded inter-county, inter-personal and inter-clique rivalries – those qualities that had helped make the race so successful – and this national team was one of the first, faltering steps in developing mentalities towards a broader perspective.

Those complacent attitudes were rocked on the very first day, as the difference in standard between the Irish and Czechs was even more apparent than the disparity with the Poles and the shock to the Irish correspondingly more pronounced – 'I was flabbergasted and shocked,' remembered one of the Irish team. 'The Czechs worked us over on the road to Newry and it was all over on the first day.' On that first stage, the Czechs initially sent two men up the road, followed by two others and, finally, the remaining two. They then joined forces: four of them arrived at the line together, followed by the remaining two – the nearest bunch of Irish riders arrived 3.5 minutes down.

The pattern was repeated the next day, to Ballyjamesduff, and again on the third day, to Ballinasloe. By then, three different Czechs had been race leaders – it seemed as if they were taking turns with the Yellow Jersey. According to one newspaper reporter, this eventually convinced the Irish team to discard their county affiliations and develop some kind of a unified response. As with the Poles, the Irish riders were assigned different Czechs to mark. This approach upset the Czechs the following day, on the road to Spiddal. Mike O'Donaghue's man became so frustrated with O'Donaghue sitting on his wheel all day that he stopped on the side of the road. O'Donaghue stopped with him and they stood beside each other, the Czech remonstrating with him. O'Donaghue did not understand the language but the message was clear. Eventually, feeling foolish, they moved off, with O'Donaghue resuming his place on the Czech's wheel.

While there was no concerted or organised effort to intimidate or spoil the Czechs, isolated incidents did occur. A Cork rider, for example, tried to put his pump into the back spokes of one of the Czechs' bikes, but the pump went straight through and clattered harmlessly on the road. The Czech – the much larger of the two – caught the Corkman by the back of the jersey, shook him and dismissively pushed him into the ditch.

The Irish team tactics had some measure of success and they placed three riders in a seven-man leading group into Spiddal. While Zelenka finished clear, Séamus Kennedy challenged another Czech for second place, while Benny Donnelly and Mike O'Donaghue were also placed. The Czechs' frustration with the Irish 'sitting' tactics boiled over when the main bunch came in. Hrazdira, the victim of O'Hanlon's attentions all day, became agitated when they arrived at the finish. A fracas erupted in which O'Hanlon, Hrazdira and others became involved. O'Hanlon's wife was in the crowd and she stood by her man, kicking Hrazdira in the shins.

From the start the following day, the six Czechs immediately charged to the front of the 114-mile (182km) stage from Spiddal to Abbeyfeale. They were determined to get out of the main bunch and avoid a repetition of the previous day's tactics – they probably also intended to teach the Irish a lesson. The move had been anticipated, however, and five of the Irish team got away with them. A seventeen-man group eventually arrived in Abbeyfeale and Shay O'Hanlon won the sprint – the only Irish win against the Czechs and one of the best and most memorable finishes of his Rás career.

Nevertheless, the Czech superiority was reasserted – Hrazdira got away on the next stage to Dingle and, in a virtuoso display of solo riding, finished over 8 minutes ahead. Their dominance was maintained for the rest of the race and the six Czechs took the first six places overall on GC. Séamus Kennedy was the first Irishman to finish, in seventh place.

As with the Poles, the disparity in standard was accentuated by circumstances. The Czechs were full-time, world-class riders and approached the Rás with ruthless efficiency. When Irish riders later met some of the Czechs at the Humanité, they learned that they had treated the race very seriously and came with the best team with the intention of never letting up or giving any concessions. It was not just the top Irish riders who had been taught a lesson – of the eighty-two starters, only fifty-five finished – the highest casualty rate ever in the Rás. It was a rude awakening for all concerned, especially those riders who had both aspiration and ability – 'That was our first wake-up call, ever,' remembered one of the Irish team.

Nonetheless, the lesson was not lost. While there was considerable resistance amongst many of the rank-and-file NCA cyclists to foreign teams, their presence did have the desired effect of exposing Irish riders to a standard of racing that they would otherwise not have encountered. This raised expectations accordingly. In Meath, for instance, the experience led to much thought and discussion among a large number of very good riders cycling for Meath teams around that time, among them Noel and Larry Clarke, Mick Creighton, Mick and Colm Nulty, Brian Connaughton, Christy Reynolds and Séamus Kennedy. Three of this generation of Meath riders went on to win the Rás.

In order to further improve the standard of NCA riders, Joe Christle initiated the Stephens' Project[35] in 1969 with the aim of getting more experience on the continent for promising young riders. With the assistance of Leo Collins, Christle provided an estate car and a caravan, and Christy Reynolds, Benny Donnelly, Andy Stynes and Séamus Kennedy set out for a season's racing. They began with FSGT races in the south of France, and then moved up to Paris. With the help of contacts, they managed to acquire UCI licences and spent the remainder of the season riding on the tough Belgian circuit. The experience was to be of benefit to them, and especially to Kennedy, when they returned home to face a Russian team in the 1970 Rás.

Christle's most ambitious international project was to bring a Russian team to the Rás. Russia was one of the two most powerful nations in the world, with an enormous sports programme that had a central role in maintaining its international prestige. In 1969, Christle sent Séamas Ó Tuathaile to the Grand Prix de l'Humanité in France with specific instructions to meet Russian cycling officials and to initiate negotiations. Ó Tuathaile was typical of Christle's team – able and competent, interested in cycling and committed to the NCA cause. He had begun assisting Christle in organising the Rás in the mid-1960s, and remained involved until the end of the Christle era.

Ó Tuathaile duly made contact with Russian officials and arranged a meeting. He could speak some French, and a Frenchman, who could speak some Slavonic, acted as translator. Ó Tuathaile had his strategy well prepared. The Cold War was at its height during this period, and with the USSR and the USA vying for world ideological domination, sporting success was seen as evidence of the merit of one system over another. Consequently, sport and principle were strongly connected.[36] Ó Tuathaile therefore opened on an ideological tack, giving a brief outline of Irish history and the discrimination heaped upon the NCA because of continuing British 'imperialist' involvement in Irish affairs. He reminded them of how comrade Vladimir Ilyich Lenin had praised James Connolly and his comrades in 1916, how he had defended them against allegations that they had engaged in no more than a putsch, and how he had expressed regret that socialist Europe had not risen in their support. Ó Tuathaile then declared that the 1970 Rás would be dedicated to Lenin and that it might therefore be appropriate for a Soviet team to attend.

Vodka was soon produced by the Russians (as the Soviets were commonly known in Ireland) and various toasts were drunk to Connolly, Lenin, et al. Ó Tuathaile did not drink much – he needed a clear head to articulate how Ireland was a small sporting nation and that, perhaps, a team from just one of the Soviet republics, rather than a full USSR team, might be appropriate. In the circumstances – the French had by then introduced cognac to the proceedings – it's not surprising that there was some confusion on this point.

Following further negotiations during and after the Humanité, and a visit to the Soviet embassy in London by Christle, agreement was reached – the Russians would send a team of four officials and six riders. The 'team' included an official from the Soviet embassy in London. As part of the agreement, the Rás organisation would provide food, lodgings and transport for the Russians. In addition, they demanded expenses of US \$2 per person, per day, as a condition of their participation – their need for foreign currency was indicative of the direction in which the Soviet economy was drifting.

Given the Soviets' careful preparation for the event, a political decision must have been made to defy the UCI deliberately by attending the Rás. The Soviet federation was becoming powerful within the UCI at this time and its ideological empathy with the NCA's position – and the attractive manner in which the invitation had been framed – must have outweighed UCI considerations. The decision may also have been related to the 'Troubles' in Northern Ireland which erupted in 1968. The NCA was ideologically linked through its nationalist and 32-county ethos, and the Eastern Bloc countries had hoped the Troubles would be a de-stabilising influence in capitalist Britain. Equally, negotiations on the establishment of formal diplomatic relations between the USSR and Ireland were ongoing at the time, and this might also have been a factor.

On the domestic front, the impending arrival of the Soviets raised a very serious problem for the NCA. In the conservative and Catholic Ireland of the late 1960s, there was rampant paranoia regarding communism – any allegation of association with communism, or even the espousing of vague socialist principles, could be very damaging. Christle was very well aware of this: he had been a candidate in a local election but was denounced by the priest at his local church and accused of being a communist sympathiser – a death-knell to his ambitions of public representation.

Elements hostile to the NCA raised the issue of the NCA bringing communists to Ireland, but Leo Collins, from Navan, came up with a solution. There was a large seminary near Navan run by the missionary Dalgan Fathers and the seminarians were on holidays at the time of the Rás. It was arranged to house the Russians there and this association with a Catholic religious order was an insurance against any further attack. It also solved the very practical problem of accommodating the Russians and proved an ideal base for their orientation period before the race.

The Rás programme was delicately balanced that year. By the early 1960s, it had become an important vehicle for delivering the NCA message and for expressing its nationalist ethos. A great deal of attention was paid to its content, most of it written in Christle's unmistakable style. From 1960, he would dedicate each year's race to a particular historical individual or event strongly associated with Irish nationalism and republicanism. The Rás was dedicated to such diverse figures and institutions as Roger Casement,[37] St Patrick, the Irish Christian Brothers and the Fenians. In 1966, the fiftieth anniversary of the 1916 Rising, each stage of the Rás was named after one of the revolutionary leaders. The programme also carried many articles reflecting Christle's socio-political interests, ranging from the hanging of Barnes and McCormack[38] to Apartheid in South Africa. The dedication of the 1970 Rás to Lenin was a tribute to the Russians' participation and probably influenced by Christle's own socialist leanings. It could have been very dangerous, but Christle's balancing of this with an equal association with James Connolly made it politically safe. Connolly, one of the leaders of the 1916 Rising, was executed by the British authorities. He was an influential socialist thinker, whose writings had helped inspire Christle's brand of socialist republicanism. The 1970 programme made reference for the first time to the wave of violence sweeping across Northern Ireland and compared Lenin's description of the 1913 Lockout[39] to events in the Bogside.[40]

The participation of the Russians made a big impact on the public and the media. They were a huge attraction around the country and larger crowds than usual came to see the race, many just to see the Russians. As expected, they dominated the racing and the standard of their world-class riders was exemplified by the presence of Gainan Saidchuchin. He had been one of the leading figures in the Peace Race during its 1960s heyday.[41] In addition to his overall Peace Race victory in 1962, he was a key member of four winning teams and also won the climber's jersey and four stages.

In the first stage, to Oldcastle, Alexander Gysiatnikov of Russia came first, followed by another Russian, with Séamus Kennedy third. Another Russian followed him and Christy Reynolds was fifth. This set the trend for the race – Russians dominating, with Gysiatnikov holding the Yellow Jersey until the end

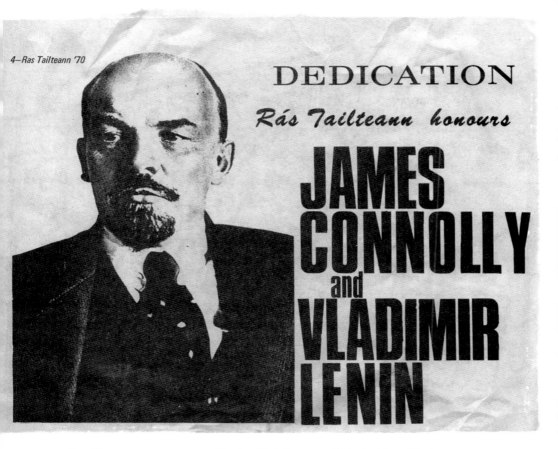

DEDICATION

Rás Tailteann honours

JAMES CONNOLLY and VLADIMIR LENIN

The Rás programme was used by Joe Christle as a vehicle for his political messages. The 1970 programme was delicately balanced – while the dedication of the 1970 Rás to Lenin was probably influenced by his socialist leanings and as a strategy to entice a 'Russian' team to the event, it was politically very risky with paranoia about communism rampant in the 1960s. However, an equal association with James Connolly – one of the leaders of the 1916 Rising whose writings had influenced Christle's thinking – made it politically safe.

and Meath, especially Kennedy, providing the main opposition. Despite the Russian dominance, some of the strong Irish riders found they could ride with them but were again tactically outclassed. In a stage across the west, for instance, with a strong cross-wind on exposed roads, the Russians and some French riders escaped in *echelons*. The Irish riders had never seen *echelons* before and could not comprehend what was happening. They lacked an understanding of finer nuances that could only come with widespread experience.

On the second stage, to Gort, the Russians took the first five places, followed again by four Meathmen, along with John Mangan from Kerry. Despite the rivalry, there was a good atmosphere and everybody got on well with the Russians. The day of the fifth stage, into Killarney, was Saidchuchin's birthday and he won the stage, though closely pressed by Kennedy. He again won an evening stage around the streets of Killarney in which Johnny Lonergan from Tipperary won six primes and came second. A birthday party was organised for Saidchuchin that night in the Russians' hotel at which one of the more memorable stage wins of the Rás was masterminded.

Gene Mangan was not riding as he was recovering from a crash but, in typical fashion, was a central actor, even off the bike. He was driving the Russian official group, which included the team manager, an official from the Russian Embassy in London who spoke English and acted as translator, and an official from the Russian cycling federation. As the race wore on and the Russian domination became more and more apparent, Mangan suggested to the Russian manager that they would never be invited back to the Rás if an Irishman failed to win a stage. When the riders had left Saidchuchin's birthday party and had gone to bed, and when the hotel bar closed to the public and the 'night stage' began in earnest, everybody became merry, except Mangan, who did not drink. He again pressed the Russian manager about a stage win for an Irishman. Eventually, in the midst of the banter and fun, the Russian threw up his hands and said that they could have a stage win if an Irishman could arm-wrestle and beat one of the Russians. He must have been confident because it was later learned that his choice for the contest was a former European boxing champion. Mangan got Gerry Keogh out of bed. Considered one of the strong men of cycling, he was driving the Russian mechanic and gear in a jeep.

The contestants faced each other across a table, locked hands and began the contest. Neither was able to shift the other and, after about 10 minutes of stalemate, both men were showing signs of distress with the Russian, especially, becoming more and more red. The Russian manager became concerned, jumped up and stopped the contest. Mangan immediately claimed victory but the Russian disagreed, saying that the contest had been stopped with no outcome. Mangan had a fundamental, almost childlike sense of right and wrong, becoming obstinate and truculent if he felt he was being cheated. Consequently, an argument ensued over the disputed outcome.

On the following stage, to Castletownbere, where Gysiatnikov won his fourth stage, Mangan continued to whinge and gripe, demanding the stage win as the agreed prize for the contest, and he repeated his demand on the eighth stage, to Dungarvan. Eventually, the Russian gave a sigh and examined the GC sheet. After a long time, he said 'OK,' pointed to a name on the list and indicated to Mangan to send that man up the road. At first, Mangan thought it was a joke because the name pointed to was that of Mick Grimes. Nobody knew what age Grimes was but he had been riding the Rás for so long that everybody affectionately referred

'Pop' (Mick) Grimes, the oldest man in the 1970 race, passing a prime on his way to the only non-Russian stage win. He is thought to be the oldest stage winner in the history of the Rás. The Honda 50 support bike was driven by Ollie Shaughnessy.

to him as 'Pop' Grimes. It was generally thought that he was close to fifty. His son had ridden in the Rás the previous year but had not come back, leading to the joke that 'Pop' Grimes was so old that even his children had given up riding the Rás. He was from County Louth but had not been able to get on the team because of his age and was riding with the Cavan team. 'That's the oldest man in the race,' Mangan protested, but the Russian was unmoved. Mangan then understood his logic and realised he had been outwitted – it was the longest stage in the race, at 132 miles (211km), with nearly 90 miles (144km) still remaining and it was unlikely that Grimes could stay out on his own for so long. Even if he did, a win by Grimes would be no loss of face for the Russians.

The Russian manager then spoke with one of his riders, Grimes was summoned back to the car and Mangan told him to go up the road. Grimes thought it was a joke or some kind of a trick, and would not take Mangan seriously at first. Mangan cursed at him and he eventually made his move.

And so, on a small hill outside Bandon, 'Pop' Grimes attacked the Russians.

Grimes, in fact, was only forty-one years old. While this was considered ancient in cycling circles at that time, he was a good, strong and very determined rider. He had been employed at a cement factory in Drogheda but the building industry throughout Ireland had been crippled by a very long cement strike and Grimes had done a huge amount of training. He powered away from the rolling bunch and was 3 minutes up at Cork. He had stretched that to 4.5 at Midleton and retained the advantage to Youghal. Then, after being over 60 miles (96km) alone, he began to tire on the last, and hardest, 19 miles (30.5km), to Dungarvan. To make matters worse, one of the Russians – Lavrushkin – broke ranks and began to chase hard. Grimes doggedly held him off, by just 37 seconds, with the bunch storming in 43 seconds later.

Though everybody realised there was something odd about the circumstances of Grimes' win, there was no resentment and it illustrated the two-faceted nature of the Rás, where deadly competition could always make room for the eccentric, the 'character' and the fun. Moreover, the solo ride of over 80 miles (128km) was an epic piece of riding for an ordinary Rás contestant, and it was not by any means slow – in that Rás, it was faster than three other stages, over shorter distances. In all probability, Grimes punished the Russians for their error of judgement in underestimating his considerable ability.

The Russians won the final two stages and Alexander Gysiatnikov, the overall winner, was the only man besides Shay O'Hanlon to wear the Yellow Jersey for the entire race. They also filled the top six places on GC. A Frenchman was seventh and Meath riders took the next three places – Reynolds, Kennedy[42] and Colm

Nulty. Unlike 1968, when the Czechs came, there was no Irish team to challenge the Russians and it is not clear why the 1968 experiment was not developed.

For most Rás riders during the 1960s, the Russians, and previously the Poles and Czechs, were temporary aberrations in the natural order of things. The Rás was firmly established and hugely popular, and there was no pressure for change. As envisaged at its inception, the Rás was thriving on inter-county and local rivalries. Joe Christle, however, had foreseen the need to progress and it was a considerable achievement to bring world-class teams to what, in the grand order of things, was a small and remote event. Furthermore, he managed to do this in defiance of the world governing body and the official federation at home.

This was a process of broadening horizons. Certainly, it had its shortcomings and Shay O'Hanlon's stance in 1970 was a manifestation of this. He heard about the expected arrival of the Russian team only a short time before the race and became very disgruntled. Stung by what he considered to have been a poorly prepared and feeble response to the Czechs, he felt that the sudden Russian presence would produce an entirely different race than the one for which he had prepared. This, he felt, was disrespectful to dedicated athletes and he could not do himself justice under these circumstances. Consequently, though conscious that he was exposing himself to accusations of cowardice in the face of the Russians, he decided not to compromise his own standards of planning and preparation for expected competition, and stayed at home.

Examined in retrospect, many of the riders who rode against those teams from behind the Iron Curtain realised that, regardless of the difference in standards, the Irish were ill-equipped, both tactically and organisationally. This was inevitable, given not only the relative isolation but also the fact that NCA road racing was still a very young sport in Ireland, lacking high-level experience, an international outlook, and the long apprenticeship necessary to develop fully what is a very complex sporting activity.

This period was an embryonic phase in the building of a national team in the Rás and the initial steps in its eventual passage to a full international event. These foreign teams had the intended impact on the better riders and the late 1960s saw the transition to what might be regarded as the second generation of great Rás riders – the emergence of a new cohort, much influenced by this top-level exposure. Kennedy, the Nultys, Connaughton, 'Jacko' Mangan and O'Donaghue were some of the names of the 1970s, a period of intense competition and personal rivalries in the Rás, and a period in which Irish cycling was to undergo fundamental change.

The coming decade would also herald a situation almost unimaginable at the end of the 1960s – the full participation in the Rás of what were then CRE/ICF riders, the beginning of the eventual reunification of Irish cycling and a gradual dissipation of acrimony and bitterness. However, matters were to become much worse before they began to improve.

These developments were to bring a whole new element to the Rás – leading Irish cycling dynasties, such as the McCormacks and McQuaids, great CRE/ICF champions like Peter Doyle, and new, developing legends, such as Stephen Roche.

'Rarely has there been such a graceful exit': Brian Connaughton, at the age of thirty-eight, getting his only stage win in the last Rás stage that he rode. It was seventeen years after his first Rás. The second rider is Mick McKenna.

For many riders, there was a freshness to the 1969 Rás. O'Hanlon had enjoyed a clear run from 1965–67 and the Czechs swept the board in 1968. In 1969, since there was no dominating foreign team and with O'Hanlon appearing beatable, there was everything to play for. This period also saw the emergence of a new wave of great Rás names – powerful personalities were to dominate for many years to come, whose keen inter-personal rivalries further magnified the racing peculiarities of the Rás. This led, in 1969, to one of the more unusual stages during which the Meath rider, Brian Connaughton, took the Yellow Jersey and went on to win the event. In the process, he was reputedly reborn as a rider.

During his first six years of competitive cycling, Connaughton never won a race. Then, in 1969, he had his first win – the Rás Tailteann. Naturally, without a previous winning record, he was not considered a contender – when he first took the Yellow Jersey in 1969, one newspaper delicately referred to him as having been 'rather unconsidered'. After his victory, he went on to have many classic successes and was to be one of the dominant forces in the Rás for another decade. The impression therefore developed that Connaughton's experience of winning a Rás, in some vague way, released a previously trapped quality and transformed him from an ordinary rider into an exceptional one. The reality, however, was more complex and his story illustrated how amateurs, having to work in ordinary jobs whilst competing in such a demanding sport, had to undergo a fundamental alteration of mind set in order to reach their optimum potential and have any hope of Rás success.

The performance of riders in the Rás was often determined not so much by their inherent cycling ability but by their attitude to themselves as athletes and the wider circumstance of their lives at any particular time. In many cases, the most significant element was mind set – whether they viewed themselves in essence as cyclists, or as individuals who cycled. Then, finding an equilibrium between the demands of cycling and the other demands of an amateur's life was crucial.

For Connaughton, as a young rider beginning his career in the early 1960s, the Rás was the pinnacle of cycling ambition, and to finish it would be comparable, in his eyes, to climbing Mount Everest. His first chance came in 1964, at the age of twenty-one, but he was not particularly well prepared. As a trainee Garda in Templemore, 'square-bashing', rather than cycling, was his main physical activity. He was elated when he survived the first stage to Carlow and finished at the back of the bunch.

He was a 'work-horse' that year, in the great battle between his team-mate, Ben McKenna, and Paddy Flanagan, and in the parallel struggle for the team prize. He found the event very tough but, in spite of a bad crash halfway through, he managed to finish. He was now smitten with the Rás. Like most young lads of the time, his first experience of the event revealed a new and wonderful world. It was also a broadening of horizons and something of a culture shock – his first time staying in a hotel, the novelty of being served food in a dining-room, visiting previously unknown parts of the country, huge crowds at stage ends to see the exotic riders who, in the spectators' reckoning, had ridden from far-flung places. Many would mingle with the riders, listening to their strange accents, inquiring about the places they had come from and engaging in inquisitive discussion. With Connaughton, because he was from County Meath, these inquiries often reverted to land, football and cattle.

Connaughton missed the 1965 Rás due to illness. The demands of moving to Dublin as a young Garda and the weeks of continuous night shifts ruled out the following year's event. He had to wait until 1967 for his next opportunity, the year of O'Hanlon's third consecutive win and his great battle with Paddy Flanagan and the French. Connaughton was a good, strong rider then, much improved from his first event, and with ambitions of 'doing something' in the Rás. He attacked towards the end of the second stage, into Monaghan, with the intention of winning, but was amazed at how quickly the leading riders brought him back and counter attacked. He was stunned at their strength and power, and realised that courage and determination alone were not enough to achieve something in the Rás. He crashed again later in the week, while in eleventh place, and was forced to abandon, with bitter disappointment.

He suffered a loss of form early in 1968 and his pride and confidence was dented when he was not selected on either of Meath's Rás teams. Nevertheless, he got his Rás chance from a local, enterprising privateer who put his own Meath team into the event. While great fun initially, the team began to disintegrate for want of funds and planning. His meal, for example, after the eighth stage at Crosshaven, was two slices of white bread and a few bits of cheese. The following evening, in Carrick-on-Suir, at the end of a bitterly cold and wet stage, there was nowhere to change clothes or even to stay. After changing on the side of the street, he went to a nearby pub with another member of the team, seeking some shelter and heat. One of the customers eventually took them home, fed them and gave them a bed for the night.

That was the year of the Czechs and another salutary lesson for Connaughton. He arrived into Dingle with a group, at the end of a hot, hard stage and, as they were rolling to the finish, he spotted the race leader, Hrazdira, already down by the seaside, relaxed, assured and enjoying the cool seawater. The contrast with his own exhausted condition brought a realisation of the great gulf between the Irish and Czech cyclists. Equally, as he observed the Czech team's sophistication, he realised how rudimentary some of the Irish riders were, with 'primitive' pumps, for example, and still turning bikes upside down on the road to change wheels. In this sense, it was an important Rás for Connaughton. Delighted to be able to race against the best amateurs in the world, he realised that he was getting stronger as the week wore on and found that he was able to ride with the Czechs towards the end. This gave him great hope and exemplified the benefits of Christle's plans in this regard – the Czechs were a barometer with which the aspiring riders could gauge their level of performance, and raise their expectations accordingly. He also came to appreciate the importance of the Rás in allowing him freedom from the restraints of normal life for one week of the year, allowing him to devote himself totally to bike racing and play the role of a professional rider.

Connaughton learned from these experiences and became determined to change his approach to cycling, but received a setback when he was knocked from his bike later in the season. Then, in January 1969, after a six-month break and overweight, he had, for the first time, both the opportunity and application to set up a meaningful training regime. Unlike his previous rather haphazard approach, he established a structured and disciplined routine of training, working, resting and eating, which he followed diligently. As with many Rás winners up to then, much of this was based on his own intuition and study of training methods, rather than any formal coaching. The crucial factor, however, was that he had altered his mind-set and found the optimum equilibrium between the day-to-day demands on an amateur rider and his ability to prepare sufficiently to reach his full potential. Finally, he came under the wing of a mentor, Frank Reilly, who gave him a belief in his ability to win the Rás in 1969.

The improvement brought by this new approach came as a surprise to Connaughton and he began the 1969 Rás in much better condition than before. His room-mate, Séamus Kennedy, won the first stage and took the race lead. In their room that night, Connaughton sat admiring the Yellow Jersey, coveting it and longing to wear it, for even one day. Kennedy fell on loose chippings on a freshly tarred road the next day, cut himself horribly and lost the Jersey to another of the new generation of riders – Mike O'Donaghue from Carlow. The pattern of the race was now taking shape and it was a confused one. Pat Healy, a Kerry rider in his first Rás, summed it up in an understated way: 'The main feature of that Rás was the tactics – they were kind of complicated.'

The strong Meath contingent had decided to 'nail down' O'Hanlon and they had plenty of able men to do it. The other top riders were also watching each other to a greater extent than usual and were reluctant to develop any initiative that might also benefit a rival. It was typical Rás fare – riders trying to jump away and being pounced on, or riders getting away, not working together and the breaks collapsing because particular individuals were, or were not, in them. The bunch was stalling and it was frustrating stuff for the determined, strong and more pro-active riders, who might attack a dozen times and still not get away.

On the third stage, into Ballina, Connaughton laid the foundation for his eventual win. What happened was typical of many Rás wins – a day, early in the race, when apparently inevitable defeat was avoided by a strain of resoluteness that cut against the collective ethos. A break quickly developed, containing an extremely good rider from Tipperary, Johnny Lonergan, and none of the contenders in the bunch would settle down and chase or allow any other group to do so either. The gap grew steadily and it appeared as if it was going to be one of those decisive Rás stages. Despairing at the 'pulling and dragging' in the bunch, and not willing to concede to the seemingly certain course of events, Connaughton launched himself from the bunch, broke free and gave chase. He gathered up some random riders on the road and organised a cohesive pursuit. They did not reach the break, but the vital minutes saved were to be critical in putting Connaughton into the Yellow Jersey on the following, somewhat infamous and rather bizarre stage, into Gort.

Along with Connaughton, the other pivotal figure in that drama was the eighteen-year-old 'Jacko' Mangan from Kerry. While officially referred to as John Mangan, he was known locally as Jack and always referred to as 'Jacko' by cyclists. He grew up on a farm at the foot of the MacGillycuddy's Reeks, near Killorglin in County Kerry and, as was natural for a Kerry youngster, began playing football at an early age. He found, however, that when he and his companions would be racing to the football field on their bikes, he could beat much older boys, even when carrying a friend on the crossbar. In spite of this, he had no interest in competitive cycling, but the formative experience of seeing Gene Mangan win two Rás stages in Killarney in 1966 inspired him to take up the sport.

John Mangan, a rider of fierce ruggedness and determination.

Gene, whom he later learned was a distant relative, saw John racing in Kerry and immediately recognised a quality in the youngster that he admired. He took him under his wing and encouraged him to move to Dublin to experience better racing. He stayed with Gene initially, who also arranged a job. Within a year of taking up cycling, aged just seventeen, John Mangan was riding in the Rás. That was 1968, the year of the Czechs and, in spite of their dominance, the young Mangan was a sensation. He finished sixth in a stage into Dingle and was the fourth-best Irish rider overall.

He continued to develop as a competitor of fierce ruggedness and determination. Even as a junior rider, it was not unusual for him to leave home for the Ring of Kerry at 5 am so that he would be back in time to help with the day's work on the family farm. He became 'a man for the hard road' – very tough and immensely strong, both physically and in character, always giving his full effort and not suffering fools gladly. Reputations meant nothing to him and any rider that beat him became a target – after the 1968 Rás, for instance, the seventeen-year-old was heard to comment on the all-conquering Czechs: 'Wait till next year and I'll sort out those fellas.'

Having won a number of prestigious races prior to the 1969 Rás, including Rás Connachta, he found himself a marked man and lost time on the Ballina stage, where Connaughton had gained vital minutes.

The day after, on the fourth, 97-mile (155km) stage to Gort – in heavy rain and gusting wind – Mangan and Connaughton were again in the main bunch, while a small group was away, gaining time. The main riders were once more focused on countering their rivals rather than taking any concerted initiatives and the bunch was stalling yet again. Both Connaughton and Mangan were determined not to be confined by these negative manoeuvrings and Mangan conspired with Kevin Dolan of Louth to break free. They attacked simultaneously, on different sides of the road. Mangan escaped and Connaughton went with him. They began chasing the leading break, in pouring rain, and gathered up Frank Dames of Dublin on the way. They caught the break beyond Castlebar and, soon after, Mangan attacked again and powered away. Only Connaughton could stay with him and they began building up a lead.

Meanwhile, the 'argy-bargy' in the bunch was degenerating into a negative cycle of sitting and blocking, mainly between Dublin and Meath riders, and no group would agree to chase or let rivals leave the bunch. Consequently, all of the big names and their respective camp followers lost out – O'Hanlon from Dublin, Benny Donnelly from Antrim, Gene Mangan from Kerry, Mike O'Donaghue from Carlow, Colm Nulty and Séamus Kennedy from Meath. It continued for

Johnny Lonergan (left) lost the Yellow Jersey to Brian Connaughton in the dramatic stage to Gort in 1969. A very good, classy rider, he came second overall in 1969 and won two Rás stages. The date and location of this stage-end picture, which includes a youthful-looking Shay O'Hanlon (centre), is unknown, but it probably dates from 1961 when Lonergan had one of his stage wins.

mile after mile until they eventually wore each other out psychologically and the bunch fell into a gloomy and lethargic truce. They completed the stage almost at touring pace.

At the head of the race, Jacko was trying to gain time and ride back into contention, but could not shake off Connaughton who had started sitting on him before Galway. Then Connaughton found himself without food – the sugar lumps that he normally carried had dissolved in the heavy rain – and Mangan eventually dropped him after Oranmore, about 10 miles (16km) from the finish. Connaughton got his sugar supply replenished and curtailed the loss to Mangan to 1 minute 56 seconds The main bunch rolled in 32 minutes 45 seconds after the winner – the biggest such gap ever in the Rás.

Mangan's stage win was one of the more brilliant rides of any young competitor in the Rás and Connaughton's determination over two days, and his tenacity in containing Mangan's eventual margin into Gort, put him in the lead with a commanding margin of 5 minutes 17 seconds over second-placed Johnny Lonergan of Tipperary. He was finally wearing the coveted Yellow Jersey.

The race was effectively in tatters now, following the débâcle in the main bunch, and all the leading men, apart from John Mangan and Lonergan, were over 40 minutes down. Reactions varied. O'Hanlon was exasperated with the conduct of the bunch, which he considered farcical, and felt there was no further point in continuing. He decided to take the train home. However, he was dissuaded by the argument that his abandonment in such circumstances would create a sensation and bring disrepute to the Rás.

Other contenders were also disillusioned and some of these like-minded riders formed a loose coalition and agreed that, for the remainder of the race, they would deny Meath any further stage wins, would not hinder each other and would be sympathetic to each getting a stage win. O'Hanlon joined in the scheme and, over the next six days, the remaining stages were won by members of this gang – Johnny Lonergan, Shay O'Hanlon, Mike O'Donaghue, Benny Donnelly and Vincent Sheridan. In all, O'Donaghue won three stages, as well as two seconds and a third.

In Gort, on the evening of the fourth stage, there was some initial doubt about Connaughton's ability to hold the Jersey and a strong attack was expected from John Mangan on the following stage to Kerry. But Connaughton had a large gap and the support of two strong Meath teams that now closed ranks and rode hard for him. Colm Nulty, especially, did a lot of work and Mangan was never again allowed to get away. Also, with the Yellow Jersey on his back, Connaughton grew in confidence and strength as the race progressed. On the penultimate day, going over Mount Leinster, Johnny Lonergan tried to break the Meath control of the race and was trying to jump away. Connaughton rode up beside him and simply said, 'Watch it Johnny, or you'll lose your second place'. Meath's dominance was the strongest team display since Dublin and Tom Finn won in 1961. As well as Connaughton's individual prize, both Meath teams took the first two placings in the team category.

Following this win, Connaughton continued to blossom as a rider. As well as being strong, determined and aggressive, and always wanting to be at the front, he had made the important mental transition necessary to have any hope of success in the Rás – the change in mentality from being amateur in all respects, to being an amateur with a fully committed approach that put cycling at the core of his life. The stature of being a Rás winner no doubt further contributed to that process.

Connaughton again wore the Yellow Jersey for two stages in 1977, against a very strong Russian team. Though well placed in stage and Rás finishes many times, he lacked sprinting speed and a stage win eluded him for a long time. Then, at the age of thirty-eight, seventeen years after his first Rás, he won the final stage in 1981 – the last Rás stage he ever rode. 'Rarely,' wrote the sports reporter, David Walsh, 'has there been such a graceful exit.'

The Russians dominated the 1970 Rás but the struggle for dominance by domestic rivals was resumed with a vengeance in 1971. A strong threat was expected from the Frenchman, Jean Louis Marionneau, who had been first man next to the Russians and well ahead of the nearest Irishman, but he was not to prove a serious challenge.

1971 is best remembered for a remarkable clash, not only between the Kerry and Meath teams, but also for internal disputes within both teams that, in turn, were to be partially responsible for further extraordinary Rás episodes. This 1971 event and the subsequent fall-out well illustrated the intricacies and subtleties of inter-personal rivalries common to the Rás. Controversy within teams was not unusual – as well as natural competitiveness and the single-minded nature of top riders, it was fuelled by the huge honour and prestige at stake in the Rás, and was most likely to occur where the team had a number of possible contenders but no clearly defined leader. In such cases, it was somewhat of a lottery as to which individual made the best, or luckiest move in the first few stages and established himself in the best position from where he could expect and demand loyalty and support from the others. The first few days were, therefore, a critical time during which the team 'sorted themselves out' and the dominant rider emerged.

Meath had all the constituents of such a powerful but inherently volatile team. Cycling was very strong in the county but divided into various factions, one centred in Stamullen, another in Navan and yet another based around the Nulty brothers. This gave rise to strong competition within the county – 'There used to be war at the Meath County Championship – it was the hardest and dirtiest race of the year.' The Meath team was therefore a potentially unstable mix. Its A-team had three individuals who saw themselves as definite contenders for the overall prize – Colm Nulty, Séamus Kennedy and Brian Connaughton. The other three – Noel and Larry Clarke, and T. P. O'Reilly – were also very good and ambitious riders, while the B-team would have been considered a strong team in itself and included the still very effective Ben McKenna. Other Meath riders, who could not get on the A or B-teams, were dispersed through other county teams.

Kerry was almost equally powerful, and had a definite favourite in John Mangan. Batty Flynn had also emerged from Killorglin as a fresh, young, rising star with devastating speed. And a third man in the Killorglin club, Pat Healy, had emerged from the Black Valley, deep in the Kerry mountains, to be a rider of great promise. Gene Mangan, the wise old head of the team, was the fourth member from Killorglin, and Batty Flynn and John Mangan were then living in his house in Dublin. He viewed them as his protégés and had directed their preparation for the Rás. Michael Moriarty, also from Killorglin, and Matt Lacey from a strong

Above: The 1971 winner, Colm Nulty (with the Rás trophy) and 'Miss Savings', Mary O'Callaghan.

Below: The Meath riders in this picture, taken after Colm Nulty's win in 1971, were outstanding Rás riders of their era. It includes three Rás winners from Meath. (left–right) T. P. O'Reilly, Séamus Kennedy, Mary O'Callaghan ('Miss Savings'), Colm Nulty, Brian Connaughton, Larry Clarke. Noel Clarke was also in the team but is not in the photograph.

Tralee cycling family made up the rest of the team. It was managed by Paddy O'Callaghan, a veteran of the 1950s.

Gene Mangan was in the autumn of his career – it was seventeen years since his first Rás – and Kerry planned a win for him on the first stage into Dunleer. Batty Flynn, the man with the greatest speed in the Kerry team, was to lead him out, but Ben McKenna, never considered a sprinter, beat Flynn – perhaps the sweetest of four stage wins of his Rás career, as well as his ninth Yellow Jersey.

John Mangan won the second stage, into Clones, and became race leader. The next stage, to Sligo, was a day of hard, tense and intricate racing with the first 40 miles (64km) over narrow, twisting roads, conducive to quickly developing breakaways. John Mangan crashed after 20 miles (32km) and had to chase hard for most of 30 miles (48km) to regain contact. Nulty punctured at the halfway stage but lost little time.

The decisive moves came on the 'Curlew drag' that guards the finish at Sligo. When they reached the foot of the Curlews, the five main contenders were in front, in scattered groups – Connaughton, Kennedy and Nulty from Meath, and Flynn and John Mangan from Kerry. As is common in bike racing, the memory and interpretation of what happened over those final few miles differs for each of the contestants, but one thing is agreed – there was a 'battle royal' and, at the end, Flynn had won the stage but his team-mate, John Mangan, had lost the race lead to Nulty. Colm Nulty was the foremost of six brothers who all cycled. Another of the hugely promising Meath cyclists to emerge in the 1960s, he rode his first Rás in 1967 and finished an impressive sixth in two stages. Now in yellow, the Meath team had sorted itself out with Nulty as the apparent team leader. He was desperately determined to win and was seen to have the capacity to do so.

In the Kerry team, however, tensions had been building following events in the Curlews – John Mangan's interpretation was that Flynn, in his attempt to win the stage or gain time, had aided Nulty in taking the race lead from him. While this was not Flynn's view, it led to some resentment on Mangan's part and some tension between Flynn and himself.

Meath's team dominance and unity were to the fore over the next few stages, as the race moved south, and they defended Nulty's lead successfully – nineteen-year-old Noel Clarke won at Uachtar Árd and the unrelated Larry Clarke won the following stage into Milltown Malbay in County Clare.

The next day, the stage was split, with a 17-mile (28km) time trial from Milltown Malbay to Kilrush in the morning. It was a crucial day, on which tensions in the Kerry team were further exacerbated. Gene Mangan, who had abandoned the race because of tonsillitis, was now travelling with the team and it was agreed that Paddy O'Callaghan would follow John Mangan in the time trial and provide spare wheels if necessary, and Gene Mangan would service Batty Flynn. However, during the course of the time trial, O'Callaghan left Mangan and went to check on Flynn, during which time Mangan punctured and was left without a spare wheel. It was to be a disastrous ride for John Mangan, as he got a second puncture and finished over 6 minutes off the leader on GC. Meanwhile, Flynn won the time trial, cutting Nulty's lead to just 65 seconds. Flynn, it now seemed, had established himself as leader in the Kerry team, but in acrimonious circumstances.

After finishing the time trial, the race had the novelty of a crossing of the River Shannon on a newly established car-ferry to Tarbert, on the southern bank. There, they began the afternoon stage to Dún Chaoin (Dunquin) in west Kerry. The Dún Chaoin finish was uncharacteristically rural – 'The stage stopped suddenly, in the middle of nowhere.' However, it typified the wider objective of the Rás in promoting the non-sporting NCA objectives. Dún Chaoin is the most westerly parish in Europe, at the heart of the Kerry Gaeltacht. As part of a government move to rationalise the National-school system at that time, the impending closure of Dún Chaoin's small school was announced. This became hugely controversial as, for supporters of the Irish language, the school represented the soul of the language and a bastion of Irish heritage. It became a *cnámh práine*, or *cause célèbre*, for supporters of the language and the parishioners undertook a high-profile march from Dún Chaoin to Dublin during the Easter prior to the Rás. As an expression of solidarity, Joe Christle decided to hold a stage end in Dún Chaoin and Séamas Ó Tuathaile, also a language enthusiast, liaised with a local, inexperienced stage-end committee.

When the race resumed at Tarbert, a break containing one of the Meath strongmen – Séamus Kennedy – went away soon after the start. The break had good riders, including Jim McConville from Armagh and Gabriel Howard. The time gap crept up steadily and Kennedy appeared to be threatening Nulty's lead. This led to some consternation in the main bunch as Nulty was apparently being attacked by his own team-mate. A messenger was sent up by car to tell Kennedy to stop working in the break, but he was forcefully rebuffed. Kennedy claimed that he went to mark the break and only started riding when he became race leader 'on the road'. It is generally believed, however, that Kennedy, who was always considered to be an impulsive rider, saw his chance of the Yellow Jersey and could not restrain himself from seizing the moment. For the bulk of the Meath team in the bunch, it seemed that Kennedy had turned maverick and was going for broke. They had two options – they could 'sit' and let Kennedy take over the lead, or they could chase and restore Nulty as race leader. But chasing was problematic, as

Flynn and Mangan were bound to 'sit in' and would be fresh to attack towards the end.

The break was also a concern for Kerry because, if it stayed away with a big margin, Flynn would lose his second place and both he and Mangan would be out of contention. The Meath manager, Anthony O'Reilly, cleverly exploited this, going back to the Kerry car and saying to O'Callaghan: 'Are you going to let Flynn lose his second place?' The implication, of course, was that Kerry would join in the chase with Meath and O'Callaghan favoured the plan. Gene Mangan was also in the car and, as team captain, strongly opposed the strategy. The Meath team, he argued, had split and the opportunity should be exploited – their own man had broken ranks and was attacking Nulty who was bound to chase Kennedy down – 'Let them roast and tear each other asunder', Mangan argued, and then, when the time was right, John Mangan and Batty Flynn should pounce and leap-frog them.

The bunch was just rolling along, with everyone watching the Meath and Kerry riders for a reaction. It became a game of tactical brinkmanship – 'It was a war of nerves.' Kennedy was up the road, 'burying' himself to build up his lead; Nulty, always a strong character, desperately wanted to chase and was trying to force the matter; Connaughton was cautious, trying to balance the merits of leaving Kennedy off or chasing for Nulty, while at the same time not allowing Kerry any advantage; John Mangan and Flynn were 'sitting', awaiting instructions; O'Reilly, the Meath manager, was trying to coax O'Callaghan into a joint chase; and O'Callaghan and Gene Mangan were rowing bitterly in the Kerry car over Meath's suggested strategy. Meanwhile, the gap was still growing.

O'Callaghan broke the stalemate or, in the words of one of the Meath riders, 'O'Callaghan cracked first'. To Gene Mangan's fury, he told the Kerry riders to chase with Meath. Even with the best Meath and Kerry riders working together, the hunt of the Kennedy group was a tough chase. There was a gap of over 5 minutes to pull back over a relatively short distance. After hard riding through the Dingle peninsula, over its spine at Gleann na nGealt, through Dingle and around Slea Head, they caught Kennedy just 3 miles from the finish. Jim McConville, who had been in the original break, won the stage.

Kennedy was utterly drained, physically and emotionally. He felt he had held the winning of the Rás in the palm of his hand but was chased down by his friends and team-mates. He had nothing to show for his efforts. There were bitter rows in both camps that evening, leading to 'open warfare' within the Kerry group. Tensions had been building and Gene Mangan's fury with O'Callaghan over a decision he believed had cost the Rás led him to abandon the team, advising both

Colm Nulty was a great all-round rider, with an honest, straightforward approach to racing. He wore the Yellow Jersey again in 1979 and is seen here leading Oliver McQuaid over Ballaghisheen in Kerry during that Rás. The main race cavalcade has not yet begun the ascent.

Flynn and Mangan to ignore instructions and make their own decisions for the rest of the race. John Mangan was also irate. His annoyance with Flynn over events in the Curlews and in the time trial was compounded by the happenings of the day, and he concluded that Flynn was the favoured rider by the Kerry management. And Flynn was dispirited, believing his chance was lost.

Similarly, there was a 'massive row' in the Meath camp – Kennedy was castigated and recrimination flowed. While Meath got over this relatively quickly and closed ranks around Nulty, it helped sow the seed of doubt in Kennedy's mind about ever winning a Rás while constrained in a team with so many possible contenders.

Batty Flynn was still second, just 61 seconds behind Nulty, facing the longest and toughest stage, 116 miles (178km), through the Cork and Kerry mountains to Castletownbere. It included four tough climbs. Yet, Mangan, who was over 5 minutes in arrears, argued that it should be he who would attack Nulty the following day. He asserted that if he got in a head-to-head confrontation with Nulty in the mountains, he would ride him into the ground, drop him and take over the lead.

Flynn was despondent because of the previous day's events and the consequent departure of Gene Mangan, and Jacko's argument prevailed. Along with this, there was some consensus amongst a few of the leading riders that Mangan and Nulty 'should be left at it' – 'They were strutting around like two prize cocks, each one muttering about what he wouldn't do to the other if he got him alone in the mountains – we contrived to leave them off and slog it out.' That was, more or less, what happened, even though it was a risky strategy for both sides. They were gone from the bunch within 20 miles (32km), along with Derek Carroll of Dublin and Garbriel Howard, a Meathman, also riding with Dublin. Some did not realise what was happening and were waiting for Flynn to make what they thought should be the logical move, but this never came.

What followed was one of the great head-to-head clashes of the Rás between two of the top men of their day, both of the 'hard-man' category. They were 7 minutes up at Killarney and this began to stretch further on the climb to Moll's Gap where Howard did much of the work in front. The dicing began in earnest on the 'Tunnel Road', from Kenmare, where Mangan launched a series of furious and sustained attacks. Seven attempts were recorded by one reporter, with Nulty countering each time. He began to taunt Mangan as he grew in confidence, clapping him on the back when he came up to him and telling him that he must eat more bananas and try harder.

Mangan launched more withering attacks on the climb outside Glengarriff. On one occasion, when he regained contact with Mangan yet again, Nulty rode up beside him, caught the front of his Yellow Jersey, shook it at Mangan and roared: 'You're not getting it, Jacko – you're not f---ing getting it.' Nulty, in fact, was riding supremely and it was probably the best stage of his Rás career. A Kerry team follower said that 'Nulty was dancing on the pedals', and one newspaper report declared it to be 'one of the greatest races of his life'. To cap it all, he won the sprint from Mangan into Castletownbere and Howard was third.

In the 5 hours and 20 minutes of the stage, they distanced the bunch by almost 20 minutes. This gap was aided by Meath's dominant influence in the bunch and its ability to frustrate any chase while one of their men was in the break; Mike O'Donaghue, who won the bunch sprint, declared to a reporter that he almost had to ask permission from the Meath riders to leave the bunch at the end. O'Hanlon also felt persecuted – 'I don't know what they have against me.'

In contrast to Gene Mangan, who viewed the previous stage to Dún Chaoin as the day the Rás was lost for Kerry, Paddy O'Callaghan, the Kerry manager, saw the stage to Castletownbere as 'the day of disaster'.

Nulty's great form and positive frame of mind was in evidence for the rest of the race. A great all-round rider, with an honest, straightforward approach to racing, he continued to show immense strength, confidence and competitiveness. Though 6 minutes 31 seconds ahead of John Mangan, he did not withdraw into a defensive role and, with good help from his team, continued to be active at the front. He was second to Batty Flynn on the next stage to Killarney and at the head of affairs again to Roscrea.

The final stage ended in Eamon Ceannt Stadium – Dublin's cycle track – and a leading group of eight arrived to the finish. Gene Mangan had coached both Flynn and John Mangan in the detail of the vital and tricky entrance to the stadium, helping Flynn get his fourth stage win. Mangan was second, a Frenchman – Gauthier – third and Nulty was fourth. Overall, Nulty won comfortably, Mangan was second and Gabriel Howard's wonderful ride to Castletownbere secured him third place – the highest finish of his twenty-one consecutive Rásanna. As in 1969, Meath won the team as well as the individual prize.

While Meath recovered from their internal difficulties quickly, the race was a frustrating and embittering experience for John Mangan. He felt that the management of the team had not worked in his favour and that his efforts were exploited by Flynn. He found the entire experience hard to accept. While such feelings were commonplace between county-team riders, Mangan was headstrong, single-minded and determined. He resolved to replay the scene the following year, but not within the confines of the Kerry team. This, he did, in what was to be a tumultuous and watershed year in Irish cycling.

11
CHANGE

'We'll never see
the like of Joe
Christle in Irish
cycling again,
that's for sure.'

1972 was the beginning of a period of great change in Irish cycling and was the last year in which Joe Christle was involved in the Rás. He organised the 1972 event as usual, but got a severe ear infection and the running of the event was overseen by a triumvirate of Gerry Keogh, Ronnie Williams and Pádraig Murphy. It had ten stages, two of which were split, and it also had a rest day for the first and only time.

Meath again had two strong teams, with Nulty, Kennedy and Connaughton as firm favourites. Things were more uncertain in Kerry. The three Killorglin riders, John Mangan, Batty Flynn and Pat Healy, had gone racing in France earlier in the year and the Kerry manager, Paddy O'Callaghan, told a local newspaper that John Mangan would not be coming home for the Rás and that Flynn would lead the team – 'There is nobody in the country at present who can ever come near him.' Mangan's absence gave rise to another report in the same paper that an appeal had been made to the Bishop of Kerry for him to try and persuade Mangan to return and ride for the county. Neither was Gene Mangan to be on the team as he was not selected. As it transpired, Flynn did not come home for the Rás, citing contractual obligations to his French Gitane team, but John Mangan did return, not to ride for Kerry, but to the small Setanta club in Dublin run by Gene Mangan.

Gene Mangan was vexed, not only on account of the previous year's events in the Rás, but because it was the first time he had not been chosen for the Kerry team, while available, since 1954. John Mangan also harboured a degree of resentment from the previous year and had a point to prove to both Kerry and Meath. Séamus Egan, a workmate of Gene Mangan's, was added to the Setanta team as a third man, but it was his first Rás and he was to play no active role. Personally financed by Gene Mangan, the Setanta Rás team was clearly an alternative Kerry team, ready for a showdown with a rival faction. To add to the complexity and possible scheming, Gene Mangan recruited Louis White and Jim Gorman as managers for the Setanta team. They had had a long involvement with the management of the Meath team, up to 1970.

Winning the race appeared a daunting prospect for John Mangan. The combined Meath opposition was indeed powerful and he feared O'Donaghue and O'Hanlon even more. The French were also expected to be very strong, especially Bernard Dupin who had earlier finished ninth in the Grand Prix de l'Humanité. At the other end of the scale, John Mangan had the help of Gene Mangan, well past his best, but still with speed over short distances and, perhaps more importantly, what was considered one of the best tactical brains in the Rás. In addition, along with months of French experience, Jacko's innate ability and toughness was bolstered by a determination driven by injured pride.

Many of the favourites came to the fore on the first stage to Dundalk – Séamus Kennedy of Meath won, followed by Pat Healy of Kerry. John Mangan of Setanta was third, two Frenchmen were next, followed by Colm Nulty of Meath. The second stage was split, with 49 miles (78km) of racing in the morning, into Belturbet. Another Meath rider, Noel Clarke, was first across the line. These split stages created extra challenges for the riders and team organisers, such as the need for special attention to diet and changes of race clothing, especially if the weather was bad. It sometimes involved uncomfortable waits between stages in less than ideal conditions. While some were well prepared for these contingencies – a few brought sleeping-bags and managed to find a spot to sleep – many teams were poorly prepared and performances suffered accordingly.

The afternoon stage was 79 miles (126km) to Donegal, and with the effects of the morning's stage being felt in the riders' legs, John Mangan's strength and resolve came to the fore in very hard racing. He took over the race lead from Kennedy who was dropped by a leading group in the mountains. To add to Kennedy's misfortune, he fell on a slippery bridge near Ballintra, about 15 miles (24km) from the finish and came in over 10 minutes down. Noel McGuill, from County Louth, fell on the same spot and hit the bridge's parapet. It was prior to the compulsory wearing of hardshell helmets and he sustained serious head injuries. He later died in hospital.

McGuill's death stunned the Rás, and though there was a question as to whether the race should be cancelled, it left for Dungloe the following day, albeit in subdued mood. The racing quickly cranked up to its normally frenzied pace and Mangan had to withstand fierce attacks from a combination of Meath riders, especially Kennedy, Nulty, Larry Clarke and John McNally. The race continued in this vein for three days, with Dupin, O'Donaghue and O'Hanlon all joining the assault on Mangan.

Gene Mangan's speed could help in closing gaps over a few miles, but his main assistance to John lay in his 'wheeling and dealing' – brokering help and contriving to divide the opposition. He considered Colm Nulty, also back from France, as Jacko's main threat and, early in the race, deliberately set out to impair and provoke Nulty with the intention of diverting his attention away from Jacko and converting it into anger and retribution focused on himself. Though Kennedy was out of contention for the overall prize due to the time lost when he crashed, he was a powerful ally of Connaughton and Nulty. Mangan therefore tried to remove him from the equation as much as possible by intimating that Setanta would not chase him for stage victories, provided his moves did not assist John Mangan's main opponents.

With his lead wavering between 30–55 seconds, Jacko withstood all assaults for the first four days that he wore the Yellow Jersey. In the meantime, most of the leading men got stage wins – Kennedy and Noel Clarke got two each, and Dupin, Nulty and O'Donaghue also won.

It was anticipated that Mangan would get some respite from the 26-mile (42km) time trial from Ennistymon to Kilrush, as either himself or O'Hanlon were expected to win and make significant gains. However, Mike O'Donaghue was the surprise winner, even though he had started 20 seconds late due to a puncture during his warm up. An objection claiming irregularities was not upheld and O'Donaghue's performance, helped somewhat by the adrenalin and tension generated by his delayed start, put him in second place on GC.

The next stage finished in Killorglin where Mangan arrived in the Yellow Jersey and was, of course, fêted as a local hero. The situation was, nevertheless, awkward because the obvious question arose as to why neither of the Mangans were riding for Kerry. Furthermore, the following day was a rest day in the town, allowing the question to simmer. Continuing with his manoeuvring, Gene Mangan went directly to some of the Kerry riders, appealing for their assistance, not for Setanta, but for John Mangan. The result was that when the race left Killorglin for Kinsale, everything had become slightly blurred – John Mangan was officially embraced by the Kerry team which was now riding, it was announced, to get a Rás win for a Kerryman.

This rest day proved unpopular with the riders and was not repeated. Some went for a 50-mile spin, and those that did not found themselves with stiff legs facing the longest and hardest day of the event, the 111-mile (177km) stage to Kinsale during which Meath made the last major throw of the dice. Shortly after Killorglin, there was an attack in force, led by Kennedy, Noel Clarke and Tom O'Reilly from Meath. The group also had Dupin, Peter Sargeant from Cork and Gabriel Howard, who was riding with Dublin.

They were 3 minutes 45 seconds clear on the first major climb after Killarney, where O'Reilly, Sergeant and Carroll dropped away. John Mangan led the chase by the Kerry–Setanta group on the downhill run to Kenmare, and on the summit of the 'Tunnel Road', they had reduced the gap to 1 minute 30 seconds. Dupin punctured after Glengarriff and the break withered. When the main group made contact, Kerry was expecting a counter attack from Connaughton who had been sitting in, but this never came. Connaughton, having been attacking Mangan all week, now realised that he could not be broken.

O'Donaghue was still lying second and, on the very last day, going through his home territory of Carlow, he launched a blistering attack and sustained a

John 'Jacko' Mangan (right) with Gene Mangan and supporters following the 1972 Rás. Both Mangans had been on the Kerry team the previous year but, due to tensions on that occasion, were not in the 1972 Kerry team. They rode as Setanta – Gene Mangan's Dublin-based club – but were, in effect, an alternative Kerry team. John Mangan won.

tremendous pace for most of 15 miles (24km), burning off all but a few. It proved futile, however, and no strategy or alliance of riders was likely to overcome Mangan's strength, grit and determination. While the Kerry group continued to ride hard for him, and Pat Healy and Matt Lacey made some important interventions, Mangan was able to control much of the race himself and his superiority was evident to all. One of the great, strong riders of his era, he eventually finished over 2 minutes ahead of O'Donaghue.

On the second-last day of the 1972 Rás, when John Mangan was containing attacks on the road from Kinsale to Carrick-on-Suir, Noel Taggart, from Banbridge in Northern Ireland, was in the process of winning the ICF Irish Road race Championship, on his own, by over 3 minutes. He was a great rider in tremendous form. Though a member of the NICF, he was expected to represent Ireland in the Munich Olympics the following September. This was possible because of an arrangement whereby riders from both the ICF and NICF could represent Ireland in international competition, while both federations would otherwise confine their activities to their respective jurisdictions. From the NCA perspective, this was a partitionist settlement – a conveniently hypocritical arrangement that excluded NCA riders who stood for a genuine 32-county entity. Thus, while Taggart, from a Protestant background in Northern Ireland, could represent Ireland in the Olympic Games, John Mangan, a nationalist from Kerry who had just won the Rás, could not.

Joe Christle had decided to again highlight the partition of Ireland – and Irish cycling – by organising a protest at the Munich Olympics of 1972 similar to those at the World Cycling Championships in Rome in 1955 and the Melbourne

Olympics in 1956. He had initiated plans to send at least one NCA rider to the Rome Olympics in 1960, and had asked Shay O'Hanlon to get a passport and prepare to travel. O'Hanlon, who was just eighteen at the time, had some difficulty with this as his parents were abroad on holiday, but he forged a letter of consent and obtained a temporary passport. However, this plan never materialised. It is not clear why Christle resurrected this form of protest after a lapse of sixteen years, but there were at least three coinciding factors that may have contributed.

Firstly, much tension and rancour had developed in Irish athletics in the late 1960s when the NACA, the 'unofficial' 32-county athletics equivalent of the NCA, merged with the AAU (Amateur Athletics Union), the 'official' 26-county body, to form the BLE (Bórd Lúthchleas na hÉireann). BLE was then the official 26-county organisation. This was a major setback for republicans in general, and especially for the NCA because of its close historical and ideological connections with the NACA. The structure of these ties meant that the NCA was, in theory, part of the NACA, and it was therefore very much involved in the merger process. At a special NACA congress held in Jury's Hotel in Dublin in April 1967 to ratify the merger, opposition was led by the NCA element, with Joe Christle as the main spokesman. As well as opposing it on grounds of principle – for example, that it would cast the dissenting northern element of the NACA into the 'wilderness' – he also fought it on technicalities, claiming that the special congress was illegal and had no standing in law. Nevertheless, the merger was approved.

With a resonance of wider splits in Irish politics, Christle was one of those who led a number of dissenting delegates in re-establishing the NACA. The re-formed NACA was very weak and the NCA played a central role in supporting it initially. NCA cyclists were encouraged to compete in NACA cross-country competitions during the winter, and the first revived NACA athletics track championships were organised in conjunction with the NCA cycling track championships.

As an illustration of the complexities of the time, and Christle's extensive web of contacts and supporters, the considerable bill for the prizes for these championships, for which the NCA had no funds, was covered by a cheque from Charles J. Haughey, organised by Christle. Haughey was then a minister in Jack Lynch's government, and Lynch himself was considered a supporter of the BLE initiative.

These emotive developments in athletics were especially tumultuous in some parts of rural Ireland, to the point of divided parishes, and further cast the NCA in the role of defender of the 32-county principle.

A second factor that may have raised the protest issue in Christle's mind was that four of the 'new wave' of NCA cyclists had gone to France in 1972 – the three Killorglin riders, Mangan, Flynn and Healy, and Colm Nulty from Meath. The question of licences, which had not been a significant issue since Shay O'Hanlon's return in 1963, arose again. John Mangan was especially viewed as having a realistic chance of surviving on the continent, but he was a strong supporter of the 32-county stance in cycling. Along with this, strenuous attempts were being made, at the most senior levels, to prevent the Killorglin riders from racing in France. Lord Killanin, who became president of the International Olympic Committee later that year, was one of those involved in blocking the Killorglin riders.

A third possible factor was the tense political situation throughout the island, arising from the Northern Ireland situation which had escalated from a civil-rights campaign in 1968 into a violent, bloody and sectarian conflict by the early 1970s. The Rás programme in 1971 was dedicated to 'political prisoners', demanding their immediate release, and again reasserted the principles of the race:

> Primarily, it [Rás] is a celebration of Irish nationality, and identification by the National Cycling Association with the highest ideals of Irish life consonant with its main aim as an organisation – the promotion of Irish nationality.

In January 1972, this situation reached a new intensity when thirteen civil-rights protestors were shot dead by British troops on Bloody Sunday. There was enormous outrage in the Republic, exemplified by the burning of the British embassy in Dublin and the recall of the Irish ambassador from London.

Whether or not the atmosphere created by these various developments contributed to Christle's decision to send a protest team to Munich, they do clarify the context in which the protest, and the subsequent fall-out, occurred.

It was an elaborate plan. Christle had discussed some of the arrangements with John Mangan during the Rás, and Séamas Ó Tuathaile and Benny Donnelly were also involved in the planning. Healy, Flynn and Mangan were already based in France, and drove from Rennes to Ostend, where they met up with the group that had travelled in two cars from Ireland – Gabriel Howard, T. P. O'Reilly, and two from Belfast whose names were kept from the press 'on the grounds that it might endanger them at home'. Benny Donnelly acted as the manager and chief spokesman.

From Ostend, the group drove in a three-car convoy to their base – a house on the outskirts of Munich. As in Rome and Melbourne, a group was to infiltrate the start and try to race. If they were caught, they would distribute leaflets and generally make known the point of their protest. However, a second group was to lie concealed in a wooded area, out on the course, and were to try and join the race as it passed. All had clear instructions not to engage in any violent activity.

They went to their positions, unaware that all Olympic events for that day had been postponed due to the massacre of eight Israeli athletes by Palestinian gunmen. Having learned that the race would be held the following day, they returned to the house. Isolated at their base, and not understanding the language, they were unaware of the full scale and impact of the events, and the resultant atmosphere of revulsion to violence and reaction against political interference in sport that the massacre had created. Therefore, they were blindly stumbling into a situation where their protest could expect little understanding or tolerance.

Healy, O'Reilly, Howard and one of the Belfast riders went to the start. They had special tricolour jerseys but, lacking numbers, only Healy managed to start by wearing a track-suit top and warming up on the course until the last minute. He was to crash out on the second lap. When the others were stopped, they distributed leaflets in English, French and German detailing British involvement in Ireland and its effect on sport.

Mangan, Flynn and the second Belfast rider were concealed along the course and succeeded in leaving their hiding place and joining the race as it passed. One of them caused some consternation when he went to the front and opened a lead. He was recognised as an intruder because of his lack of a number and police on motorbikes soon brought him to heel. Then, in the bunch, Kieron McQuaid was the first member of the official Irish team to see John Mangan. He rode beside him and words were exchanged. McQuaid warned his team-mates to watch out for trouble. A short time later, he saw Mangan and another of the official team, Noel Taggart, side by side ahead of him. Then, to his astonishment, 'Mangan literally caught Taggart, pushed him off the road and then held onto him'.

Mangan subsequently explained the incident as an unplanned, isolated row, unconnected with the main protest, and claimed that Taggart being from the North of Ireland was incidental. The quarrel simply arose in the heat of the moment when, according to Mangan, they exchanged words and Taggart made offensive remarks to him. If he did, it was very untypical of a naturally modest and retiring man who, contrary to later suggestions from NCA individuals, had no connection whatsoever with the Northern Ireland security forces. Indeed, he was generally considered to have had little or no interest in politics – 'He hadn't a political bone in his body.'

Whatever the immediate background, it was a defining moment in Irish cycling – one Irishman pulling a member of the Irish team from his bike while competing

Above: Brian Holmes, one of the NCA protesters at the Munich Olympics, struggles to free himself from an official holding him from behind while other officials move in on him. Holmes was a republican activist and one of two protesters from Belfast whose names were kept from the press 'on the grounds that it might endanger them at home'.

Left: John Mangan being detained by police at the Munich Olympics after he pulled a member of the Irish team from his bike during the Olympic road race. It is considered a pivotal event in the modern history of Irish cycling that helped provoke a process which eventually led to the re-unification of the sport. Batty Flynn was also removed from the race and detained – he was handcuffed to a van at the side of the road, sporting bruises from his encounters.

for Ireland at the Olympic Games – and all because of an ideological issue, unconnected with sport. The NCA could not have hoped for the level of publicity achieved, but it backfired as a PR stunt since Mangan's action was interpreted as a deliberate part of the protest. Benny Donnelly's attempts to play down the incident, claiming that the protest was intended 'to be passive and without violence', was swamped by outraged reaction. Given the international atmosphere created by the massacre of the Israelis, it was an unfortunate incident that happened in the wrong place at the wrong time and the NCA message was largely lost in the furore. It made world headlines, helped by a widely syndicated photograph showing Mangan being detained by police. 'Despicable' was used in screaming newspaper headlines on both sides of the border, and the Taoiseach, Jack Lynch, who was at the Games, made a statement that the Irish team 'were cycling for Ireland and this interference was a travesty of sportsmanship and reflected no credit on the country'.

Outrage amongst ICF riders and the resultant increased bitterness and entrenchment of opinion was compounded by Taggart's nature – although a tough man on a bike, he was normally of a mild-mannered disposition. At that time, the Olympic road race was an amateur event and there was a consensus that Taggart had a realistic chance of a medal. Much fund-raising had taken place locally to help him in his Olympic bid and, at thirty-one years of age, it was to be his last race. 'Utterly distraught', he subsequently avoided discussing the detail of the incident, even with his family or closest friends, and made every effort to avoid conveying any sense of bitterness or acrimony.

Viewed in context, and in the light of subsequent events, 'Munich' is considered by many as a pivotal event in the modern history of Irish cycling. Paradoxically, it prompted a process which would eventually lead to the reunification of the sport and bring major changes to the Rás. The clash between Mangan and Taggart, it is argued, highlighted the depths to which the division of cycling had reached and shocked moderates on both sides into an appreciation that 'something had to be done'. Even one of the Northern papers, carrying the headline 'Black Day for Banbridge Rider', thoughtfully commented in the midst of the outrage that it was 'sadder still in that it reflects the waste and strain of the rift in Irish cycling'. Reflecting on Munich in later years, Batty Flynn made a simple but telling observation: 'There was a craziness in Irish cycling then.' Munich, it is contended, helped create a mood in which subsequent moves to defuse that 'craziness' would find broad support on both sides.

Prior to Munich, however, elements within the NCA were becoming increasingly dissatisfied on a number of fronts. Joe Christle had a policy of encouraging younger men into administration so as to have better representation for the cyclists. However, this younger blood became a force for change and individuals such as Billy Kennedy, Dermot Dignam and Mike O'Donaghue came to question Christle's habit of doing things without reference to normal executive procedures.

The Munich protest was an example of this – the NCA team had left for Germany before some of those in senior positions were even aware of the plan, despite Christle having organised and fund-raised in the name of the NCA. The unquestioning loyalty that his personality had until then commanded was coming under some strain, leading to tensions within the organisation. Billy Kennedy, who had become General Secretary of the NCA at the age of seventeen, sought more transparency both in the Rás and the NCA. A member of one of the two Carrick-on-Suir clubs with 'Carrick Wheelers' a component of their names – one NCA, the other ICF – he felt an acute need to move the situation forward constructively so that his friends and club-mates in the NCA Carrick Wheelers could compete on a 32-county basis and internationally, as did their fellow cyclists in the ICF Carrick Wheelers.

Shay O'Hanlon and Dermot Dignam had also begun to question the NCA – its methods and its values. Their own attitude to the national question and the role of cycling in politics was also examined. Doubts about the NCA had arisen for O'Hanlon some years earlier, in 1962, when talks between the NCA, CRE and NICF broke down far too easily. Conscious of the sacrifice he was making by remaining in the NCA, he had been hopeful of the sides resolving their differences. But O'Hanlon formed the impression that there was little determination within the NCA leadership to pursue such discussions tenaciously, and that their resolve was not proportionate with the sacrifice that riders like him were making.[43] Why, he asked, should he be making such a sacrifice for the sake of a principle if the officials were not prepared to make their best effort to find a negotiated solution to vindicate the same principle? In his typically meticulous fashion, O'Hanlon took a sheet of paper and wrote down two sets of arguments, examining his options from the two different perspectives. Having sought an opinion on his document from his mentor, Shay Murphy, O'Hanlon concluded that he should remain in the NCA. Though he settled into the routine of the organisation, he no longer believed blindly in the leadership and would become disgruntled from time to time. Around this time, his good friend and training companion, Seán Dillon, 'went over' to the CRE and some in the NCA developed a sense that O'Hanlon had wavered and, perhaps, was not entirely trustworthy in the cause.

Dermot Dignam, on the other hand, had entered the Gate Cycling Club in the 1950s as a young man attracted by its republican ethos. His thinking evolved during the 1960s and he had come to question whether the NCA's methods were really the best way of promoting the republican cause of Irish reunification, or whether they were, in fact, creating more barriers and causing further divisions. Two events, in particular, set him thinking. Firstly, he witnessed Tom Hughes, a significant rider from the National club, being told that he was being dropped from the Dublin Rás team because he had trained with CRE riders. Dignam thought this extreme and unfair. Secondly, there was the 'Rutland dinner' affair.

The Rutland, a popular bike shop in Dublin, catered for racing cyclists. Though its two owners were associated with the CRE, the shop was frequented by some of the top NCA cyclists, including Mangan and O'Hanlon, both of whom were friendly with the proprietors. In 1968, the Rutland hosted a dinner to celebrate the business' twenty-first anniversary. Three NCA champions – all Rás winners – Gene Mangan, Ben McKenna and Shay O'Hanlon – were invited and attended. The dinner was interrupted by two NCA men who publicly castigated the riders and demanded they leave what they considered to be a CRE event. Mangan, McKenna and O'Hanlon refused to leave, prompting a move within the NCA to have them expelled. Dignam's support for the expulsions was sought, but he instead fought the move, believing the individuals concerned had sacrificed greatly for the NCA and that to expel them would be completely inappropriate. The matter was eventually dropped, but Dignam was further convinced that the direction of the NCA needed to be altered.

Though O'Hanlon and Dignam had been in rival clubs, their work in the NCA administration brought them together. They became friendly, discussed their respective concerns, became bent on changing the thrust of the organisation and developed a strategy to do so. Jim Killean had been the long-time unopposed president of the NCA. An old republican, he was a respected figurehead, and provided stability and continuity within the organisation. He and Christle effectively directed the NCA even though Christle never sought, or held, any of the very senior positions. Killean had suffered from ill health for a number of years and had been threatening not to allow his name go forward for president, but each time would be persuaded to stay on. In autumn 1972, Dignam approached Killean, discussed his concerns and outlined how he thought the organisation should develop. He put it to Killean that the NCA was perpetuating Partition by allowing divisions persist between cyclists and that, as republicans, they had an obligation to try and bring the others in rather than maintaining the divide they believed was imposed and sustained by Britain. Somewhat to his surprise, Dignam found that Killean agreed with the thrust of his argument.

Dignam suggested that, at the next AGM, O'Hanlon should take over as president and promote a new agenda within the NCA. Killean again agreed in principle but requested a meeting with O'Hanlon. Killean brought Kerry Sloane to this meeting – O'Hanlon described it as an 'interview' – even though Sloane then had no involvement in cycling administration. Apparently satisfied with O'Hanlon's views and assured that the core 32-county principle would not be compromised, Killean agreed to Dignam's proposal.

The established procedure was that nominations for elections at the AGM had to be submitted in time for the final Executive meeting prior to the AGM. Dignam had the arrangements carefully orchestrated. The meeting was under way, with the final preparations being made for the AGM, when there was a knock on the door and O'Hanlon's nomination produced. It was initially treated with some ridicule, but then Killean announced that he would not be going forward. Christle was stunned and tried to dissuade Killean, his former comrade-in-arms. Killean, however, would not be moved, even when it was suggested that assistants might be appointed to help him. He insisted that it was time to bring in new blood. Too late for any further nominations or counter measures by Christle, it was a *fait accompli*. Dignam and O'Hanlon had taken the first major step in re-focusing the organisation.

Reaction was mixed, with suspicion of the motivation and some distrust of the possible direction of the new administration. The response of Gene Mangan, who was to follow as president after O'Hanlon, was fairly typical:

I sat down with O'Hanlon when he became president. I told him I wasn't particularly happy but I'd go along with them as long as they stuck to the 32-county principle. We remained friendly.

Dignam and O'Hanlon, now secretary and president of the NCA respectively, intended to initiate discussions with the ICF but, needing to avoid alienating sections of the NCA, they developed their strategy cautiously and no formal proposals on the matter were put forward at this time.

One Sunday morning in January 1973, when the training season began, they rode to Crossgun's Bridge in the Dublin suburb of Phibsborough, one of the traditional gathering places for training runs on winter Sunday mornings. Barry Lacey, the secretary of the NCA, was also with them. It had long been common for NCA and CRE/ICF riders to train together, but the Crossgun's Bridge group mainly consisted of ICF riders, and attitudes had hardened considerably since

Munich. Kieron McQuaid was there, and saw them arriving. Part of the great McQuaid cycling dynasty from the 'other side', he had witnessed the Munich incident and was very bitter. He became irate at the sight of the three leading NCA men. 'I'm not cycling on the same road as those fellows,' he said to his companions, and moved away. Others managed to placate him and the group moved off. Dignam, O'Hanlon and Lacey went with them.

These winter training spins are normally carefree and pleasant affairs, with good banter. Riding in two lines, they move as a chain doing 'bit 'n' bit', with different riders taking turns at the front and all the riders cycling beside each other at varying stages. The talk is relaxed and companionable, about events of the year past, plans for the coming season and riders trying to mislead each other about their respective levels of training and fitness. Not surprisingly, there was tension in this group, but McQuaid eventually had to ride beside O'Hanlon and Dignam. This is his memory of what happened next:

> At one stage I ended up beside O'Hanlon – I had a problem riding with them because I knew they were senior figures in the NCA and Noel Taggart was a rider that I had great, great respect for. So I decided that I'm saying nothing to this man and looked straight ahead. Then he said to me, in his distinctive Dublin drawl:
>
> 'Isn't it a bit ridiculous that we can go out training together but we can't race together.'
>
> I thought, 'What's happening here?' Then I said: 'Are you telling me that you're trying to do something about changing that?'
>
> 'Yeah.'
>
> 'You mean sit down around a table and talk about it?'
>
> 'Yeah.'
>
> We then talked a little bit and I said: 'Okay, leave that with me.'

A threshold was crossed – the initial connection made, on bikes, during a winter's morning training spin. It was a landmark step in the eventual reunification of Irish cycling. They rode, perhaps, a hundred miles that day, with Dignam raising the issue with other riders and general conversation taking place on the matter. Kieron McQuaid then brought the details of the discussion to his uncle, Paddy McQuaid, vice-president of the ICF.

The process initiated in the first month of 1973 would take seven years to reach completion. A symbolic milestone was reached in 1974 when reciprocal teams from both federations were welcomed in the Rás and Tour of Ireland.

The Tripartite Committee at a dinner to mark the finalisation of the unification of Irish cycling during the winter of 1978–79. 1. Karl McCarthy (ICF), 2. Gerry Keogh (NCA), 3. Shay O'Hanlon (NCA), 4. Dermot Dignam (NCA), 5. Jim Traynor (NCA), 6. Jack Watson (NICF), 7. Paddy O'Callaghan (NCA), 8. Des Mooney (NICF), 9. Kieron McQuaid (ICF), 10. Gene Mangan, (NCA), 11. Morris Foster (NICF), 12. Bert Slader, (SCNI: Sports Council of Northern Ireland), 13. Tommy Campbell (ICF), 14. Steve Lawless (ICF), 15. Joe McCormack (ICF), 16. Frank Kelly (SCNI), 17. Donald Lavery (NICF), 18. Michel Jekiel (FIAC – now UCI), 19. Liam King (NICF), 20. Ivan Towell (NICF).

This resolution of the conflict in Irish cycling, initiated behind the scenes and later formalised by a 'power-sharing' tripartite committee of representatives from the three cycling bodies on the island, bore striking similarities to the later attempt at resolution of the wider conflict – the conflict which had spawned the problem in cycling. It was characterised by an evolution of thought regarding traditional principles; the coming to the fore of courageous individuals who were prepared to take risks; suspicion and some hostility from elements on all sides; tenacious leadership determined to overcome setbacks and committed in the long term to the process; a willingness to accommodate other interests through compromise while maintaining certain principles; and the careful coaxing along of the general membership of the organisations. Outside influence was important, too. The Sports Council of Northern Ireland played a crucial role and, through contacts made when the Russian team competed in the Rás, Paddy O'Callaghan later travelled to Moscow in order to try and bring UCI influence to bear on the situation.

The process was copper-fastened by the formation of the Irish Cycling Tripartite Committee (ICTC)[44] in 1978. Stephen Roche won the first Rás run under the umbrella of the new body. In common with the 'Peace Process' of later years, bitterness was slow to dissipate and 'dissidents' continued to resist developments. The Rás was to become an important means for cementing the unification as it brought all concerned together to work closely in the congenial atmosphere of the Rás. In 1995, for example, at a stage end in Dingle, Kieron McQuaid observed Noel Taggart and John Mangan at opposite ends of a hotel function room. Recognising an opportunity, he brought both men together for the first time since the fateful day in Munich twenty-three years earlier, and they shook hands.

The change of president of the NCA in 1972 coincided with Joe Christle becoming increasingly occupied with another sporting activity. While his three sons had cycled with success at junior level, their main sporting interest lay in boxing and the Christle family approached this as thoroughly and effectively as it had addressed the Rás. On one memorable night, for example, in the National Stadium in 1980, Christle's three sons – Terry, Joe, and Mel – each won an Irish national senior boxing championship. Christle had been running the Rás for nineteen years and a certain level of fatigue was inevitable, especially given his other interests and commitments. He withdrew from cycling affairs and, having satisfied himself that the 32-county principle was not going to be compromised, left the new administration carry on its work without interference.

It was the end of the Christle era in the Rás – a vibrant and sometimes turbulent chapter in Irish sport. Gratitude is the sentiment that comes across strongly from those who experienced the Christle era: 'We have a lot to thank Joe Christle for.' Equally, while a few ponder the wisdom of their allegiance to the cause he championed, the passage of time has generally not diminished the stature of the character in the eyes of those who knew him. Colm Nulty, a Rás winner in 1971 who later moved to the ICF, summed up a common sentiment: 'We'll never see the like of Joe Christle in Irish cycling again, that's for sure.' For those who promoted cycling, his inspiration, organisational ability and especially his gift for promotion, were missed most – 'What would Joe have done in this situation?'

One of the first challenges facing the new leadership of the NCA was the organisation of the 1973 Rás, now rudderless without Joe Christle.

12

BEGINNING OF THE MODERN ERA

Mike O'Donaghue, winner of the Rás in 1973, represented a new wave of riders who emerged in the 1970s.

Joe Christle's departure created an immediate vacuum in the running of the Rás – nobody else had detailed knowledge or experience of the organisational logistics. In spite of this, and of the lack of resources and experience, it did not seem to occur to anyone that there might not be a Rás in 1973. An NCA organising committee was formed – its leading figures were Barry Lacey, Dermot Dignam, Gabriel Howard and Shay O'Hanlon. Having appointed Jim Kelly as Race Director and Dermot Dignam as Route Organiser, the committee set to work, making the usual contacts with key individuals throughout the country. A smaller number of advertisers than normal was approached, but with a request for a substantial £250 each. The organisation of the event gradually made progress and it ran under much the same template as Christle had developed.

One significant difference, with the unity talks in progress, was that the Rás and its programme lacked the normally strong nationalist tone. There was a consciousness of the delicacy of the unity talks at this early stage and giving offence was carefully avoided. Also, in deference to the sponsor, the traditional nationalist and republican messages were to give way, over the next few years, to cheerful descriptions and flattering pictures of the regions that the Rás was visiting. In fact, the era of the Rás being used as an overt medium for highlighting the division of Ireland was at an end.

Mike O'Donaghue, from Carlow, finally won the Rás in 1973 when he least expected it – he had come to accept that his day in the Rás might never arrive. Since first riding the event in 1964, he had consistently finished in high positions – eighth, sixth, fourth on two occasions and second in 1972. Notwithstanding this impressive record and his status as one of the country's leading riders, his lack of team support and style of riding militated against stage-race success. He got married in 1972, was busy building his house during 1972–73 and did not consider himself well prepared – he did not even buy his customary new set of wheels for the Rás or get his regular haircut for the event. The new wheels and haircut were part of O'Donaghue's fastidious approach to racing and he was noted for his attention to appearance. His bike was always sparkling, he was one of the first to get sponsorship and ride in his own trade shirt, and he sported a tan and sunglasses before either was common.

Although born in Kildare, close to the Carlow border, Mike O'Donaghue was always associated with Carlow, a county with little cycling tradition. He got into cycling by accident – his youthful interest in motorcycle racing led him to cycle to see the Leinster 200 event in County Meath in 1959. The fourteen-year-old found that he enjoyed the 100-mile round trip and he later did some touring.

Left: Garret O'Donaghue, Mike's father, performing a final check before the Rás in 1964. Mike's father's home-grown vegetables were part of O'Donaghue's diet – an important aspect of his fastidious approach to preparation.

Below: Mike O'Donaghue, aged nineteen, on the Ring of Kerry on his first Rás, with Ned Flanagan. He finished sixth overall in spite of having broken a chain.

Mike O'Donaghue was a great all-round rider. He could ride alone, climb well, had great speed over the final miles and an exceptional sprint. Always lacking in team support, he was regarded as shrewd, learning to measure his effort and exploit the energies of stronger teams. Considered to be a 'flashy character' of the Rás in his time, he regularly sported sunglasses and a tan before either was common or fashionable. He is seen here getting one of his nine stage wins, into his home town of Carlow in 1969.

A local newspaper attracted him to a race for beginners in Monasterevin, 23 miles (37km) away, and he cycled to it. Con Carr, one of the great Kildare riders from the 1950s, spotted him arriving and took him to his house for a meal. Without a proper racing bike and, in spite of his long ride, he won the event and continued competing in the grass-track scene in the Carlow/Wicklow/Wexford area.

The Rás became a huge ambition and he followed it as a spectator in 1962 and again in 1963. In 1964, as an accomplished rider at the age of nineteen, he was initially selected for the Kildare team as there had never been a Carlow team in the event. Joe Christle, however, recognised O'Donaghue's potential for promoting cycling in Carlow and persuaded him to ride in a County Carlow team. To coincide with this, he organised the first stage end of the Rás in Carlow town. Gene Mangan, who was then making a comeback following a break from cycling, joined O'Donaghue's team and duly won the stage into Carlow by making his notorious move on the footpath. O'Donaghue was sixth, an impressive finish into his home town for a nineteen-year-old in his first Rás. Full of youthful aggression and energy, he finished sixth overall that year, in spite of losing time after his chain broke near Kenmare.

The race came into Carlow again the following year and he was determined to do better. On 'draggy' roads from Clonmel to Carlow, he broke away early with a bunch of about twenty, which had been whittled down considerably by Carlow. He won the sprint in front of the home crowd, enhancing his already growing local profile. He sustained his progress, finishing fourth overall in 1966 and 1967.

Like many of the top Rás riders of the period, O'Donaghue was largely without guidance as regards training, and Fausto Coppi's mantra of 'miles, miles and more miles' was his main influence. Supported strongly by his mother, he did enormous training, regularly covering distances of up to 120 miles, and his life followed the élite amateurs' simple cycle of working, eating, training and sleeping. He developed into a great all-round rider – he could ride alone, climbed well and had an exceptional sprint. Always lacking in team support, he was regarded as shrewd, learning to measure his effort and exploit the energies of stronger teams. Unlike many of the great, strong riders of the time, he would not try to jump away from competitors or burn them off. Instead, he would combine with them and benefit from their efforts for as long as possible before unleashing his great speed. This style amassed seven stage wins by the start of the 1973 Rás and two more that year before the decisive sixth stage into Belmullet.

Denis Mangan from Kerry, the younger brother of John 'Jacko' Mangan, won the first stage, into Carlow. O'Donaghue won the second, into Waterford, and Mick Nulty, the younger brother of Colm Nulty, won the third, into Macroom. During this early part of the race, the Yellow Jersey was for the most part contested by the two kings of the Rás, O'Hanlon and Flanagan – O'Hanlon took the Yellow Jersey on the second day; Flanagan took it from him on the third and was defending it well, with the usual able support of his brother, Ned. Paddy and Ned Flanagan had returned to the NCA just a short while earlier having originally defected to the ICF in 1967 at the time of its high-profile name change from CRE. While the Flanagans were well liked and greatly respected, riders who had 'gone over' to the CRE were sometimes initially received on their return with some coolness by elements within the NCA. Often, there was an unspoken consensus that there would be a period of penance – the 'loyal' riders would be favoured for a time or, at least, a certain statement of rebuke would be made to those who had been 'disloyal'.

The sixth stage in 1973, into Belmullet, was the furthest west the Rás had ever ventured into Connacht. It was very long – 120 miles (192km) – and much of it over narrow, poorly surfaced roads through bleak and exposed bogland. The stage left from Gort in County Galway and, as was natural in the Rás, the riders from

Mayo and Galway were determined to make a good showing. A break of about twenty soon developed. It contained some of these riders from the western counties and also included a core of strong men, including O'Donaghue, Jack Murphy from Dundalk, the Frenchman Bernard Dupin, Mick Cahill from Cork, and Larry Clarke and Christy Reynolds from Meath.

O'Donaghue saw an opportunity with this break, though a break of such size is normally unwieldy – there are too many individuals and interests to become forceful. O'Donaghue rode very hard and drove the group, urging the Galway and Mayomen to lead the Rás through their homelands. Back in the bunch, Ned and Paddy Flanagan moved to protect the Yellow Jersey, but it soon became clear that they were not going to get any assistance from most of the top men. A decisive moment came – Ned Flanagan made a long and hard turn at the front, bringing the break within reach. Then he pulled over to let somebody else in the line take up the work. Nobody went through. Everyone just sat up and the chase faltered.

Circumstances began to work in O'Donaghue's favour, and the strong riders in the lead group, realising that the gap was opening, redoubled their efforts. Back in the main bunch, the argy-bargy grew and it became obvious that there was no general willingness to work with the Flanagans. The leading group drove on, with the Galwaymen dropping away as they rode through Ballina and into unknown Rás territory beyond Castlebar. The gap grew steadily, reaching 11 minutes at one point. To cap Flanagan's misfortune, he punctured with 15 miles to go and there was an immediate charge from the front of his bunch, capitalising on his ill luck. The break eventually came in 7 minutes 27 seconds ahead of the main bunch – Larry Clarke won the stage – and Flanagan was another 2 minutes 45 seconds behind. O'Donaghue, by a quirk of tactical chance typical of the Rás, went into yellow for the first time in his Rás career, Dupin was in second position overall and Mick Cahill was third.

O'Donaghue now had a team of sorts, by default – the top six riders in GC had been in the break into Belmullet and, while not concerned with defending O'Donaghue's Yellow Jersey, it was in their interests to uphold the status quo by containing riders who might challenge their positions and push them down on the GC – a top-ten position in the Rás was worth much suffering and sacrifice. It was developing into a typically complex Rás chess game, requiring an intimate knowledge of the roles, strengths and abilities of the various players.

O'Donaghue was now going to be under severe pressure, especially from O'Hanlon, Flanagan and John Mangan. Mangan had come back from France for the Rás but had pulled a muscle in his chest while helping with farm work at home just before the race. While in poor form early on – he had to have hospital

John Mangan (right) just pips Noel Clarke at the end of the ninth stage in Navan, 1973. Mangan also won the next stage. His brother, Denis, won the first stage. Noel Clarke won a total of eight Rás stages.

treatment after the second stage – he was recovering form and began attacking O'Donaghue on the following stage, into Donegal town – the longest of that Rás at 123 miles (196km).

On a bad, rainy day, O'Donaghue was countering attacks from many quarters and quickly closed down any move that he saw as a danger. Then, while already under severe pressure, he got a puncture and John Mangan attacked again. O'Donaghue regained contact quickly and got some respite by happily sitting in the back of the bunch. Not getting news through the bunch that O'Donaghue was 'back on', Mangan kept driving in front and prevented further attacks. That 'free ride' for O'Donaghue lasted almost 20 miles (32km) before further attacks went away and he had to counter again. Nonetheless, he benefited significantly from the efforts of those who had been in the leading break the day before and wanted to retain their positions.

The racing continued at a hectic pace, without respite, and John Mangan made another determined effort between Sligo and Bundoran. He powered away, dropping O'Donaghue and gaining over a minute. Without team support, it was a critical moment for O'Donaghue, and the race hung in the balance. Then Flanagan, who previously had been attacking him, came up beside him and simply said: 'Come on, we'll get him back.' They regained contact with Mangan in a furious chase that Flanagan later described as one of the hardest rides he ever did. Flanagan was in great form and later left the leading group with apparent ease to win the stage on his own.

Why Paddy Flanagan helped O'Donaghue to such an extent is not clear, but it is known that Flanagan was vexed at the treatment he had received the previous day when he lost the Jersey and he had identified John Mangan as one of those riders who had hindered him. Even though there was no obvious friendship between O'Donaghue and Flanagan, there was a certain empathy as O'Donaghue was born in Kildare and had sometimes trained with Flanagan. Consequently, it has been speculated that Flanagan, peeved at the previous day's events and now out of the reckoning in the overall classification, had thrown in his lot with the underdog, O'Donaghue, because of this empathy but also to deprive any of the contenders who had thwarted him on the stage to Belmullet. The casual alliance that formed between Flanagan and O'Donaghue, arising from the kind of unplanned and confused scenario that often develops in the 'fog' of stage racing, was typical of the Rás. It was to be even more crucial the following day.

The stage from Donegal to Clones was neutralised for the first 7 miles (11km), as far as Ballintra, where a minute's silence was observed at the site of the accident that had caused the death of Noel McGuill the previous year. It was a day of brilliant sunshine, with a following wind, and the bunch was rolling along steadily when O'Donaghue punctured again. A group of riders then launched an all-out attack at the front, while O'Donaghue got a disastrous wheel change – as well as being slow, the wheel was badly fitted, forcing him to stop again and get a second wheel. When he eventually got going, the bunch was almost 2 minutes ahead.

Without a team, it should have been the end of O'Donaghue, but Paddy Flanagan again came to his assistance. Along with Ned, he waited for him and they again began chasing furiously. A Meath trio also waited, but this act of apparent generosity was reportedly inspired by one of them having drawn O'Donaghue's name to win the Rás in a local cycling-club sweepstake and he had recruited two other Meath helpers in order to protect his possible winnings! Their benevolence was unwise as O'Donaghue and the Flanagans rode away from them, leaving them with their own battle to conserve time. In an epic Rás chase, O'Donaghue and the Flanagans eventually made contact with the bunch and Paddy told O'Donaghue to get to the front and exert his authority. Although drained, O'Donaghue did so and there was no further attack by any of the main challengers.

This stage also saw one of the countless acts of extraordinary fortitude that the Rás inspired. Joe McAloon, from Antrim, who had been in the decisive break into Belmullet two days earlier, was descending a steep hill when his chain came off the front chain ring. He put his hand down to re-fit it and remembered nothing else until he regained consciousness in an ambulance on his way to Manorhamilton hospital. He had crashed badly, but insisted on leaving the hospital and returning to the spot where he crashed. He remounted another bike and rode the final

80 miles (128km) on his own, in bad condition, just to try and complete the Rás. He finished away outside the time limit but a discretionary blind eye was always turned to such exceptional cases in the Rás. He managed to complete the next stage, into Navan, where he was seen by a doctor. Again, in spite of advice, he finished the final stage and was taken to the Royal Hospital in Belfast on his way home.

Flanagans' and O'Donaghue's chase on the road to Clones was the last decisive act of the 1973 Rás – Mick Nulty later escaped to win his second stage and John Mangan's recovery was demonstrated by his victory in the final two stages.

There is no doubt that O'Donaghue was a beneficiary of what one competitor described as Flanagan being 'marked to extinction'. However, this was common in the Rás and, in O'Donaghue's case, 'fortune favoured the brave'. He was a worthy winner in his own right. As in all sport, the Rás has its list of 'should-haves' – great riders seemingly destined to win the Rás but never doing so – Ronnie Williams in the 1950s, Dan Ahern in the 1960s, Alan McCormack in the 1980s. Given O'Donaghue's undisputed stature, he would definitely have joined the list of 'should-haves' had he not won the Rás in 1973.

With moves on unity in progress, the ICF had invited a team from the NCA to compete in the Tour of Ireland in 1973. The invitation was issued at short notice, there was much suspicion on all sides, and the proposal was declined, citing lack of notice as an excuse. During this period, advocates of unity held some 'unofficial' races that included riders from different sides, and there was a growing current of agreement for joint racing amongst the general body of riders.

At the same time, the Rás was taking its first major step into the commercial world. In 1974, the Rás name was associated with a corporate sponsor – Bórd Fáilte. Brian Connaughton had received sponsorship from Bórd Fáilte for a county team in 1973 and had developed a good working relationship with a Bórd Fáilte

Mike O'Donaghue, winner of the 1973 Rás, with his arm around Paddy Flanagan. They are flanked on the right by Ned Flanagan and on the left by Liam Cannon. Flanagan threw in his lot with O'Donaghue in the 1973 Rás.

Mike O'Donaghue never had a strong team in the Rás and his style of riding militated against stage-race success. Though he had consistently finished in high positions in the Rás – eight, sixth, fourth on two occasions and second in 1972 – he thought that he might never win it. Then, in 1973 – when he least expected it – Mike won the Rás. Second was the Frenchman, Bernard Dupin (right), a member of the French FSGT team. Also alienated from the UCI, the FSGT teams provided important international competition for the NCA during this period of the Rás. Mick Cahill (left), who was in the break with O'Donaghue into Belmullet, was third.

executive, Paul Glynn. It was proposed to Glynn that Bórd Fáilte might become involved in the Rás the following year. With falling tourist numbers from abroad because of the violence in Northern Ireland, Bord Fáilte had launched its 'Discover Ireland' promotion to encourage Irish people to holiday at home, and the Rás fitted this particular strategy. It became the 'Discover Ireland Rás Tailteann' for 1974, the first of a series of name changes necessitated by the growing commercial involvement.

Glynn was knowledgeable about sport and quite aware of the split in cycling and athletics, and of the NCA's historical republican association. This he had chosen to ignore as there was no overt republican connotations by that time and the race director, Jim Kelly, had no apparent political agenda for the event. Furthermore, Glynn made the suggestion that a team from the ICF might participate in the Rás and, while this was initially unimaginable to some within the NCA, an invitation was issued just two weeks before the race began.

An ICF team was at that moment competing in the two-week Tour of Britain and, with further major events looming ahead for the ICF – the Tour of Scotland, Isle of Man event, Tour of Ireland and World Championships – the timing was described as 'inconvenient'. Nevertheless, the invitation was accepted, though on condition that approval be granted by the world governing body. John Lackey, the chief figure in the ICF side, revealed in later years that he had received a telegram from the UCI on the eve of the Rás refusing permission, but had torn it up and later said that it had arrived too late. It was also agreed that a reciprocal team from the NCA would ride in the ICF's Tour of Ireland. The NCA also issued an invitation to the NICF, but it was declined.

This first ICF Rás team included some of the most distinguished and experienced racers in modern Irish cycling – men from a cycling tradition with a somewhat different outlook and experience to that of the NCA. Peter Doyle, who was to eventually win the event, was an international amateur racer of high international calibre, having ridden in seven Tours of Britain, six Tours of Scotland, nine Tours of Ireland and two Olympic Games. He had won the Tour of Ireland and both the points and KOH competition in the Tour of Britain in 1968. The team also included Pat and Kieron McQuaid from the great McQuaid cycling dynasty begun by their father, Jim, an international cyclist. Cycle racing, at the highest possible international level, was the main focus of the McQuaid household and the younger generation absorbed cycling – and an expectation of success and international representation – from the earliest age. By 1974, Kieron McQuaid had competed in the Olympics, whilst Pat had represented Ireland numerous times and was about to turn professional. The two McQuaids, as members of a family that had been central to the development of the CRE, represented the heart of the 'old enemy'. Mick Toolan, Brendan Madden and Seán Lally, also very experienced, made up the rest of the very strong ICF squad. Having so recently competed in the Tour of Britain, the experienced and well-organised ICF team was in top form.

Some NCA figures realised that so strong an ICF team might dominate the racing and cast the NCA riders in a poor light. In these circumstances, they argued, there should be a corresponding NCA team. This did not materialise and a previous pattern was repeated – an 'outside', top-class, disciplined and focused team, with an enormous wealth of international experience, was matched against a plethora of county teams which, despite having brilliant individuals, lacked strategic cohesion or strength in depth and were constrained by structural and organisational limitations. They also suffered from the lack of regular, high-level competition.

The Rás became a nine-day event in 1974, shortened by a day so as to make it easier for riders to get time off work. The decisive move came on the very first stage. A group of eight arrived at the first stage end, at Carrick-on-Shannon, 4 minutes 20 seconds ahead of the bunch. Peter Doyle won and was followed by Colm Nulty, Seán Lally, Brian Connaughton, Paddy Flanagan, John McNally, Martin McKenna and Mick Nulty.

Peter Doyle receiving the winner's prize from P. V. Doyle in 1974. Doyle was a member of the first ICF team to ride in the Rás, and was the first man to win both the Rás and the Tour of Ireland. 1974 was the first year in which the Rás had a major commercial sponsor and it became the 'Discover Ireland Rás Tailteann', sponsored by Bord Fáilte. P. V. Doyle, founder of the Doyle Hotel Group, was then associated with Bord Fáilte.

Séamus Kennedy grabbed the second stage into Westport, but the top six remained at the same time on GC and the ICF team decided to put more distance between Doyle, Lally and the rest of the field. At the very start of the next stage – 90 miles (144km) to Galway – they planned to take advantage of a steep hill outside Westport and send four men away from the start. Doyle waited at the line, hand on Kieron McQuaid's shoulder and both feet strapped in tightly. The four sprinted flat out the moment the race began and 'pandemonium' broke out in the bunch when they saw the move. The break got away and opened a gap, but Brian Connaughton and Séamus Kennedy led a chase that brought the race together. Their ability to bring back four of the best ICF riders came as somewhat of a surprise to the ICF team and the race held together until a bunch sprint in Galway, won by Pat McQuaid. With no bonuses for stage placings, Doyle remained in yellow for the first three days even though he was on equal time with six others who finished together on the first stage. Because of this, the organisers decided to award the Yellow Jersey on points and his team-mate, Seán Lally, took it over on the fourth stage, to Kilkee in west Clare.

The pattern of the race was now well established. The ICF team would only let breaks go that contained riders who were down on time. Even then, or when dangerous men got away, they had the strength to send riders to mark them and chase them down later in the stage. The ICF's Peter Doyle, though past his best and near retirement, was a brilliant rider. His team was disciplined and ably managed by the experienced John Lackey. Two of them – Mick Toolan and Kieron McQuaid – won the next two stages and Doyle reclaimed the Yellow Jersey when he got away on a circuit race in Killarney town, gaining vital seconds. Their instructions from then on were relatively simple – to look out for Doyle to within 30 miles of the finish when he could then look after himself.

In spite of the ICF's apparent dominance, the race was regarded as a huge success by the majority of the riders – a most significant development in terms of the sport's history. Doyle was especially respected and the top NCA riders were glad of the opportunity to race against him. Equally, while the ICF team had approached the event with some caution and remained somewhat aloof, they found no general animosity directed towards them. The beautiful weather during the early part of the race also helped the atmosphere.

There were incidents – Pat McQuaid and Colm Nulty got entangled in a fight – but these arose more from the normal heat of competition than from hostility. With excellent cycling competition predominating and with some weariness after years of turmoil, the event helped create a general groundswell of support for unification, vindicating the unity moves which were then generating a very lively debate amongst the riders. It was an important moment in the mellowing process and aided the progress towards the Rás' apolitical outlook.

On the seventh stage, to Cobh, a determined NCA move saw eight riders open a gap of 90 seconds. Doyle closed it, largely by himself. Nonetheless, Martin McKenna of Meath broke the cycle of ICF stage victories when he won a sprint finish. The following day, to Tramore, the NCA again made what *The Irish Times* reporter, Jim McArdle, called 'a desperate bid to recoup some prestige'. Noel Clarke and Shay O'Hanlon led the effort, helped by Gabriel Howard and Jim Keogh from Cork. The ICF tactic followed the normal pattern – an ICF rider, in this case Pat McQuaid – got up and 'sat on them' in an attempt to haul them back, while Doyle led the remainder of the ICF team in keeping the main bunch within safe reach.

For the second time in the race, Pat McQuaid popped out at the line, to pip O'Hanlon who had been doing most of the work on the road. His brother, Kieron, also got a second stage win the next day, raising speculation as to which one of the McQuaids would win the final stage and get a third stage win in the Phoenix Park. O'Hanlon, however, president of the NCA, was the first man over the line.

Comparisons were inevitably drawn between the ICF and NCA riders at this time and also between the Rás and the Tour of Ireland. Some of this analysis helps to illustrate the nature of the Rás. Both camps found the riders from the other side to be somewhat better than expected, obviously due to propaganda whereby each side depicted the other as inferior. There was general agreement that there was no major difference in the standard of the top ten riders in the Rás and the Tour of Ireland. However, with a much higher proportion of foreign riders in the Tour of Ireland, the standard of the remaining bunch was generally higher. This gave rise to more orthodox, high-speed racing and a greater number of potential winners. The Rás, on the other hand, had much more 'jumping' and its own peculiar tactical pattern that was often more physically and psychologically demanding.

Given the very experienced and organised nature of the ICF team in the 1974 Rás, the results suggested a greater difference in standard than actually existed. Doyle's main advantage was gained on the Killarney circuit. Flanagan and Connaughton were third and fourth overall, behind Lally, but the three of them were on the same time – 20 seconds behind Doyle – and the difference in placings was based on points.

Commenting on the relative merits of both sides, the journalist Jim McArdle concluded: 'The question has not been properly answered … they [NCA] had in the field, county and club teams in competition with the Irish International selection which was led by Peter Doyle and included vastly experienced continental and Olympic riders.' While many NCA riders agreed with the statement of one of its riders that 'it was pointless trying to take on Peter Doyle with the form he was in', an ICF rider also acknowledged the reason for the apparent gap: 'It was not the riders, it was their lack of experience and poor organisaton.' This lack of organisaton, or management, is a thread running through the early part of the Rás' history. It had many facets, some of which are touched on by Gene Mangan's observation:

> It was hard to manage any fellow in this country. We had no management structure. You would have managers for a day or a week but they weren't readily available or very experienced. Meath was better than most. Good management was decisive in most of the Ráses. Often it is difficult to manage a good team – not so difficult to manage a team with a single outstanding rider. Management was poor in the first half of the Rás' history, but was better in the second – we progressed. You must take into account that, for thirty years, the two associations were at variance. Half of the NCA's energies were spent in dealing with the 'war'. The 'war' overshadowed cycling a bit.

Despite their Rás success of 1974, and the ongoing, if faltering, unification process, ICF cyclists did not ride in the Rás again until unification officially began under the Irish Cycling Tripartite Committee in 1979. Examined together, 1973–74 was a milestone period in the history of the Rás – the end of the Christle era, the embryonic commercial involvement, and the participation of the 'old enemy'. It marked the beginning of the modern era of the Rás.

13
FLANAGAN

'Paddy Flanagan
was one of cycling's
true gentlemen …
one of the greatest
racers the country has
ever known … a gritty
road man.'

An NCA team was formed for the 1975 Rás, possibly as a result of the lesson learned the previous year at the hands of the ICF team. It consisted of Shay O'Hanlon, Séamus Kennedy, Noel Clarke, Bobby Power and Mick (Michael) Nulty. With the unity talks at an early stage, there was no ICF team to challenge, but there were teams from Algeria, France and West Germany, as well as the usual county teams. Seventeen years after his first Rás, Paddy Flanagan – still fiercely competitive and powerful at the age of thirty-six – was to beat them all. His third Rás win was achieved with little support.

Flanagan was a legend, even before his third win. Cycling lore tells us that it all began one evening in 1955 when the sixteen-year-old Paddy was cycling, on a common bike, from his home in Kildangan, County Kildare, to the nearby town of Monasterevin. He was passed by six riders from the local Midland Cycling Club who were on a training spin and the young Flanagan tucked in behind them. They rode on and, as the spin quickened towards its conclusion, Flanagan was still on their wheel. They sought to dispatch the young upstart but, as the speed increased even further, it was other riders who began dropping away. The remnants of the group were led into Monasterevin by two of Leinster's leading riders at the time – Paddy Doyle and Jack Crowe – and, when they finally reached the town, only the sixteen-year-old Flanagan was left with them.

Doyle and Crowe 'recruited' Flanagan and introduced him to the local cycling scene. As was usual for boys from regular modest backgrounds at that time, he was already out at work – labouring on the bogs for Bord na Móna – and he saved £21 for a second-hand bike. He entered the world of competitive cycling, absorbing its skills and strategies, and learned the craft well. Paddy Flanagan won the second road race he entered and quickly established a formidable presence on the then thriving grass-track scene.

Only seventeen, he rode his first Rás in 1958 and made an immediate impression, coming second to Gene Mangan in the fifth stage and holding second place on GC until the 139-mile (222km) sixth stage to Castlebar, where he dropped to twelfth place. He finished eleventh overall. He had improved considerably by the 1959 Rás and, with a ride of great determination, came second to Mick Murphy on the second stage, and finished fourth overall.

Always a wonderful time trialist, Flanagan liked to do much of his riding in small groups, away from the bunch. The first of his eight Rás stage wins came on the second stage, into Castlebar, in 1960. With 25 miles (40km) remaining, he broke away with two others, finished 14 seconds in front, went into the race lead and donned the first of his seventeen Yellow Jerseys. With the help of other great Kildare riders, such as Con Carr and Eamon Ryan, and in the first of many epic battles with Shay O'Hanlon, he successfully defended his lead for the remainder of the race.

Flanagan's win in the Rás Tailteann made him an instant hero in the cycling stronghold of Kildare. A bonfire was lit for his homecoming to Brownstown, his club base, but to the disappointment of the crowd, there was no sign of Paddy at the festivities. Off the bike he was reserved and somewhat shy in those days and, when eventually found at home, he could not be persuaded to attend the celebrations.

In 1961, Flanagan emigrated to England for work. He missed home, returned in 1962 and resumed racing. The 1964 season was one of his best ever. Following the birth of his twins a few days before the Rás, he won the Yellow Jersey on the second stage. On the following day, the riders were confronted by vile weather conditions as they traversed the mountainous roads between Cork and Kenmare. Strong wind and driving, bitingly cold rain caused many abandonments. This was the kind of environment in which Flanagan thrived – he welcomed hardship, not for what it did to him, but for what it was doing to everybody else. He was sustained by his belief that he could endure more suffering and affliction than his rivals. While Mike O'Donaghue initially tore the field asunder, Flanagan capitalised on the appalling conditions and went on to win on his own by a minute.

Paddy Flanagan, with his wife Alice, after his 1964 win. They had twins earlier that week.

Above and right: Paddy Flanagan receiving the Corn Cathal Brugha from Jim Killean, 1964. Murt Logan is on the right. The trophy was presented by the GAA and modelled on the McCarthy Cup presented to the winners of the All-Ireland hurling final. It was named after Cathal Brugha, an IRA leader in the War of Independence and member of the first Dáil. Later, an East European winner failed to return the trophy.

Below: A section of the massive crowd that saw Paddy Flanagan get his second Rás win – the *Cork Examiner* estimated it at 40,000 people.

He lost the Jersey to Ben McKenna on the fifth day, but recovered it on the 25-mile (40km) time trial on the second-last day. In the Phoenix Park, in front of a crowd estimated by the *Cork Examiner* at 40,000, Flanagan made Rás history by becoming the first man to win the event twice. Having won numerous other events in the various cycling disciplines that year, he was given the prestigious Caltex Award.

Flanagan remained one of the leading riders in the Rás up to 1969, getting two stage wins and three top-five finishes. That same year, he 'went over' to the ICF with his brother, Ned, and some other Kildare riders. When the CRE changed its name to ICF in 1967 as part of its high-profile and well-organised campaign to increase its membership, there had been an expectation in Kildare that many riders, even entire clubs, would join the ICF, but this did not happen. The failure to induce this significant groundswell of support made the Flanagans' defection a more pronounced and prestigious coup for the ICF. Naturally, there was some resentment at his departure and one particularly unpleasant episode occurred when three NCA officials went to his home to repossess NCA trophies.

Flanagan rode well in the ICF – he competed in one Tour of Ireland and finished fourth despite being directed down a wrong road while leading a stage. Some of his NCA supporters claimed this was done deliberately to prevent him from winning, but the suggestion was never given much credence. Pat McQuaid of the ICF provided an insight into Flanagan's motivation and *modus operandi*: 'He was very aggressive – he would look at everyone in the field and have this huge aggression to beat them all. Then he would attack and attack and keep driving until he wore out the opposition.'

While most of the other Kildare riders drifted back to the NCA fairly quickly, the Flanagans did not return until 1973. In fact, Paddy stopped racing in 1972 and 'retired' for a year while discussion took place within the NCA about his wish to return. He continued training during this period. The suggested reasons for his return to the NCA vary – it was said that he disliked the long journeys involved in competing in the ICF's more limited and dispersed calendar. Notwithstanding this, it is clear that he greatly missed the camaraderie and spontaneous sense of fun in the NCA, and the bigger involvement of the public at its races – 'He found the NCA more homely'; 'There was more *craic* and fun at the NCA races'; 'The NCA was a kind of a family'. These observations throw an interesting light on the NCA ambiance and, by association, on the qualities of the Rás. Jim McQuaid's understanding of the reasons for Flanagan's departure further illuminate this difference as seen from an ICF perspective:

The main thrust of the ICF through the 1960s, 1970s and 1980s was international bike riding. The NCA were more parochial in the same way that the GAA is – the club promoted at the ground level – it didn't matter how good or bad you were, you could still ride in the Rás. That was different to the way we thought – when the Tour of Ireland came around there would have been only twenty Irish riders riding in it and the rest were internationals. There was no hardcore local country-type support at ICF bike races. Paddy would have found that hard and I could understand how he would have found it difficult. The way that the NCA operated would have been more to his liking. It wouldn't have been a fact that he wasn't doing well in the ICF or that the races were any harder for him.

The elementary nature of Flanagan's love for cycling meant satisfaction was derived from the quality of his own performance and the thrill of battle rather than from the prestige of events. Unlike most young and successful racers, he harboured no ambitions of continental success and never considered moving to Europe. Flanagan was therefore more content within his own geographical and social roots, and in the competitive, yet social atmosphere of the NCA. These intimate satisfactions held sway over the attractions of the ICF – even over international competition.

He suffered a rebuff from some of the leading riders on his return to the Rás in 1973, much to Mike O'Donaghue's advantage, but was quickly absorbed back into the NCA fold and remained totally dedicated to bike racing. He developed a structured, exacting and intense training regime – his friend and racing companion, Emanuel Thackaberry, commented that 'Paddy trained so hard that he found racing easy', and Gene Mangan, a keen observer of bike racers, summed up his preparation thus – 'He did long, hard miles and had great knowledge of his body.' An interesting feature of his routine was high mileage when the season was over so as 'not to let the legs go stiff'.

Many qualities are generously attributed to Flanagan by those who knew him as a racer – 'dedication', 'strength', 'competitiveness' and 'love of the bike'. Lightly built but with disproportionately muscular legs, he had an average sprinting ability, was an exceptional time trialist and could climb well. He was an 'open-road' man, less comfortable in a *criterium* or bunch sprint, and his forte was driving small groups in tough, difficult conditions. In the break, he would sometimes maintain a constant chatter of encouragement as he rode up and down the line.

This combination of strength and determination lasted right through his career. In 1977, for example, almost twenty years after his first Rás and beyond the peak of his ability, he took the fight to a Russian team that contained riders of international calibre, such as Lavrushkin, winner of the Tour of Yugoslavia, and Chelpakov, who was to win a gold medal at the Moscow Olympics. He attacked the Russians' lead on the sixth stage into Clonmel, and was in a break with Lavrushkin and Frans Croon from Belgium. Beyond his prime, Flanagan drove the break and then held out as the foreigners 'worked him over' during the final 25 miles (40km). There were other Irish riders in the break, including Martin McKenna, Larry Clarke, Tommy Mannion and Gearóid Costello. Costello, the only Irish rider to survive to the finish with Flanagan, remembered the stage end:

> They attacked him repeatedly and couldn't shake him. The Irish guys were doing their best for Flanagan. We were sacrificing our chances because this guy would have been our hero of sorts. Just having the privilege of being in the break with him and being able to help him was almost better than having a chance of winning a stage, such was the regard he was held in and the reputation he had built up. Lavrushkin eventually got away with about 2 miles to go and Paddy just drove on after him, keeping the gap down, with Frans Croon and myself sitting on.

Perhaps the most-often-stressed characteristic of Flanagan is 'intelligence'. His contemporaries describe him variously as 'wily', 'cute', 'crafty'. He was renowned for his astute assessment of riders, not only of their racing ability, but of the inter-personal currents that perpetually flowed within the bunch and how they could be turned to his advantage – 'He had a great head on him'; 'The Dublin fellows used to call him a "bogman" in the early days but he could buy and sell them'; 'He was able to psyche people out and get the best out of them'; 'He could get people to work for him and they didn't even know they were doing it'; 'Paddy was a master of psychological warfare'.

Anecdotal stories of Paddy Flanagan's 'cuteness' come to the fore whenever his Rás career is discussed by those who rode with him. Bobby Power, who rode in his first Rás in 1975 as a young member of the Irish team, gave a typical example of how, in the latter part of his career, Flanagan manipulated two younger and supposedly better opponents. Though his story refers to a Rás Connachta, it exemplified Flanagan's ways in the Rás very well:

> Paddy Flanagan was the cutest rider … he'd play everyone off against each other … Denis Devin and myself were two young fellows on the Irish team. The two of us were clear in a Rás Connachta stage with Paddy and, of course, each of us was trying to figure out how the stage would end. Paddy turns to

me and says: 'You'd want to watch Denis, he'll jump with a mile to go, watch out for him there.' We came towards the finish and, sure enough, with a mile to go, Denis takes off like a rocket. I'm onto him straightaway. I come around him and try to beat him in the sprint. Then, who comes sailing past me in the last 100 yards but Paddy, and he wins the stage. Denis and myself were after going much too soon. I said to Denis afterwards: 'You went fairly early,' and he replied: 'Paddy told me that if I attacked with a mile to go he wouldn't chase me.' Paddy had set up both of us – either of us should have beaten him hands down in a head-to-head sprint. But that was typical of Paddy.

A young Philip Cassidy saw it as a privilege to be on the same team as Paddy Flanagan in 1981 when, at the age of forty-three and riding with a Meath team, Paddy again took the Yellow Jersey, becoming the oldest man ever in the Rás to wear it.

Paddy was the nicest man, he was so relaxed and easy going and unassuming, you wouldn't think you were with a champion. He was as cute as a fox – he'd cycle around town in a low gear in the evening, after his massage and dinner, and he'd be chatting to everyone – he'd be telling Costello to watch Kennedy – 'He's going to go for it tomorrow' – and then he'd go and tell Kennedy to watch Costello. He'd have everybody watching each other and then he would go for it himself. He was a marvellous man.

Nevertheless, there was much more to Flanagan's ability to exploit the abilities of others than mere roguery. Séamus Kennedy said of him: 'Paddy Flanagan was a fellow who made loads of friends. He rode hard against you but he would ride fairly – most of the great riders were honest.' This sense of Flanagan's fairness comes across strongly – Gearóid Costello, who rode with him towards the end of his career, noted that 'he was a very fair guy – he didn't like anybody sitting on him and coming around him at the finish and you certainly wouldn't do that to him – you'd ride with him for as long as you could … he'd never want to win or be placed where he hadn't worked his share.'

This very fundamental sense of fairness resulted in one notable outburst in Clonakilty in 1981. Flanagan had just ridden into the Yellow Jersey in a long break during which Seán Lally had 'sat in'. Lally's lack of contribution could be explained by tactical prudence as his team-mate was in yellow further back. However, when he came around Flanagan in the final sprint and won the stage, Flanagan's sense of justice was severely offended and he lunged at Lally, pushing rider and bike up against a shop window. It took three bystanders to restrain Flanagan and prevent the incident from escalating.

Apart from his 'cuteness', he was remarkably intuitive – 'He had a sixth sense about riders – out of a bunch of twenty, he could look at them and know which was the most dangerous.' This sense of judgement also applied to his analysis of the road and his knowledge of race routes – 'Flanagan was a master at reading the road.' While many riders depended on raw speed or strength to break away, and Flanagan could do it when needed, he had a skill of sliding away from the front of bunches. Choosing his place, often on 'draggy', 'dead' roads, he would apply pressure gradually, suffering in the knowledge that everyone else was feeling at least as bad. Then, while heads were down and minds dulled by fatigue and pain, Flanagan would gradually slip away from the front.

Flanagan's racing intelligence also had great breadth, producing a strategist able to analyse a complex race like the Rás. A close observer and admirer, Mike O'Donaghue, noted:

> Like the snooker player who sees the next four or five shots, Flanagan would see the next four or five stages of the race … although cycling is as individualistic a sport as you can get, Flanagan realised the importance of teamwork – people working together, though not necessarily from the same team. In stage racing you can win the battle, or stage, and lose the war, or race. Paddy knew which was the more important.

Flanagan's third Rás win, in 1975, exemplified this. O'Hanlon was the hotly-tipped favourite. He was in great form, having won the 100-mile Championship, and was racing in a strong Irish team – the other members, Séamus Kennedy, Noel Clarke, Bobby Power and Colm Nulty, had just returned from the Grand Prix de l'Humanité. Kennedy got into the decisive break on the first stage and won the sprint from a group that also contained Marzek Zekei of Algeria, Josef Zebisch of Germany, Paddy Flanagan and Mick Cahill of Cork. While Kennedy was now the race leader, he had no time advantage over the other four.

Another German, Thomann, won the second stage, into Letterkenny, but Kennedy, Flanagan and Zebisch still remained locked on top of GC on the same time. There was much speculation and apprehension about the following stage in the Donegal mountains and, especially, the potential effect of the notorious Glengesh Pass. Rumours of its exceptional steepness lead to much discussion about the need to reduce gear ratios on the machines. The Kildare team did not have the luxury of a selection of gear sprockets and, when they were discussing what to

Two of the great Rás riders at the start of a time trial – Ben McKenna (standing) and Paddy Flanagan in the Kildare lily-white jersey (date and location unknown).

do, Flanagan suggested they would walk up it. This is exactly what they did – they walked or ran three different sections for want of equipment. The lost time had to be clawed back later on the stage, which was described as a great one for the Irish team – Noel Clarke and Shay O'Hanlon come first and second, and Kennedy retained the Jersey. But still Kennedy, Flanagan and Zebisch were not separated on time difference.

The deadlock was broken briefly on the following stage, to Castlebar, when Flanagan – having punctured – was penalised by a minute for taking a wheel from a car other than his team car. Though only an enforcement of the rules, it led to much controversy and, on appeal, Flanagan's time was reinstated for the following stage to Galway, and the three leading riders were back on level terms.

The Irish team were apparently riding well – Kennedy, Clarke, Nulty and O'Hanlon had won five of the six stages, and successfully defended the Jersey from Flanagan and Zebisch. Nevertheless, the wisdom of defending the Jersey, with no time advantage, was not considered by the Irish team. This was pertinent because there was a time trial on the morning of the last day and, going by form, Flanagan should comfortably beat Kennedy. Did Flanagan, therefore – who had been harrying Kennedy all week – simply need to stay with him and then overtake him in the Wicklow Mountains or in the time trial on the final day, just as he had done to Ben McKenna in 1964? Or should other Irish-team riders have been taking the fight to Flanagan and Zebisch, rather than just defending?

Some saw the writing on the wall and Flanagan was described as 'a coiled spring, waiting for his time to strike'. As always in the Rás, individual riders attempted to exploit the openings generated by the bigger battle and go for glory – Billy Kennedy of Tipperary broke away on his own after Oranmore, on the next stage, to Limerick, but railway gates at a level-crossing closed, splitting the race, and it had to be stopped. Joe Cashin of Tipperary succeeded. He went clear near Scariff, with 30 miles (48km) to go. In spite of a determined chase by eight riders, he finished on his own. The seventeen-year-old Eamon Connolly, from Meath, made a similar bid on the next stage to Kilkenny but was caught by an Algerian, Malek Hamza, inside the last mile. Meanwhile, there was still no change on top of the GC classification.

On the following stage, to Naas – with the Wicklow Mountains looming – everyone was anticipating a decisive showdown between Flanagan and Kennedy. Flanagan, however, did not read it quite so simply. He knew Kennedy and his form, and was aware that he had expended much energy in his defence of the Jersey. Flanagan was confident, therefore, that he could at least stay with Kennedy in the mountains and take him in the time trial. It was the German he was most concerned with – he calculated that Zebisch had not shown his full hand during the week. Zebisch certainly had exasperated Kennedy who claimed 'Zebisch never did a stroke … he bled me to death'. With Zebisch an unknown quantity at time trialling and probably with something in reserve, Flanagan decided he would have to be challenged and tested in the mountains.

The stage to Naas was 85 miles long (136km) and included the climbs of Aughavanagh, Drumgoff and the Wicklow Gap. Before the start, Flanagan slipped onto his bike a pair of light time trial wheels, borrowed from Mike O'Donaghue – an indication, perhaps, that he expected to be alone, presumably at the front. Early skirmishing by opportunists came to nothing and the leading bunch became considerably thinned out by Aughavanagh. The front group included Kennedy and his team-mates, Mick Nulty and O'Hanlon, as well as Flanagan and Zebisch. Then, after eight days of stalemate, Flanagan threw down the gauntlet on the dramatic ascent of the Wicklow Gap. He attacked Kennedy and began to distance him. Zebisch also escaped. Nulty and O'Hanlon initially stayed with Kennedy, supporting him in the chase, but Kennedy was struggling to keep up with them. With Flanagan gaining, O'Hanlon abandoned Kennedy and went after Flanagan.

O'Hanlon, in fact, had been very frustrated during the week with a tactic he described as 'the defence of a non-existent lead'. Given the apparent inevitability of Flanagan's superiority over Kennedy in the impending time trial, and with Kennedy having no time advantage on Flanagan, he felt that opportunities which arose for other Irish-team members to take the Jersey from Flanagan had been squandered. Now, with Kennedy losing ground to Flanagan, he 'decided to disengage from defensive responsibilities and ride for the stage win'. O'Hanlon caught Flanagan near the summit and joined up with Mick Cahill from Cork for the final, critical section of the race. With O'Hanlon 'sitting in', Flanagan and Cahill began working together and Zebisch failed to make it across to them. When O'Hanlon received word that Kennedy was losing more time, he also began to work.

With about a mile to go to the stage end, O'Hanlon noticed, to his relief, that Cahill's rear wheel was going soft. This helped him to win the sprint which Flanagan, true to form now that he was race leader, did not seriously contest. Further disaster struck Kennedy when he punctured on the run in and lost 2 minutes 13 seconds on Flanagan. Relegated to third place, behind Flanagan and Zebisch, and with yet another Rás having slipped through his fingers, Kennedy was bitterly disappointed. He turned his ire on his team-mate, O'Hanlon, over his tactics on the Wicklow Gap, and they fell out for a number of years as a result – yet another episode of the Rás that remains controversial.

Flanagan won the time trial. Over 7 miles, he took 7 seconds off Zebisch and seconds from Kennedy, proving that he had had the winning of the Rás in the time trial all along. Noel Clarke won his third stage in the final circuit race in the Phoenix Park and Paddy Flanagan came in safely in the bunch, hands raised, for his third Rás Tailteann win. Given his age and the circumstances in which he overcame powerful teams, it was considered Flanagan's sweetest Rás win – his wife, Alice, noted that 'Paddy smiled a lot after 1975'. It was an exhibition of all Flanagan's strengths and a demonstration of that combination of characteristics which produces a classic stage racer – he was strong, fast, shrewd, determined and combative, all day, every day.

No discussion on Paddy Flanagan can take place without consideration of the role of his younger brother, Ned, also called Eamon or the 'Butt'. Most of their contemporaries agree that Ned was significant in Paddy's career – 'You were always racing against two Flanagans'; 'Ned did a lot of his donkey-work'; 'Ned would know when to let the elastic snap and let the break go with Paddy.' Ned Flanagan was a great Rás rider in his own right – he won stages in 1966 and 1967 – and some would claim that although he had the same athletic potential as Paddy, he lacked his ambition, organisation and single-mindedness.

Ned needed something … you saw Ned at his best when someone, probably from Dublin, was after saying 'Ah, the men from the bog' or 'Ye culchies', or something like that, and then Ned would get mad and there would be no stopping him. He won a stage into Ballyjamesduff – the roads were up and

Paddy Flanagan with his mangled bike following a crash in 1976 while he was wearing the Yellow Jersey. He was favourite for that Rás and finished the stage, but had to have an operation for a broken bone in his arm that evening.

down, very hard to get going on – and Ned got away with a break of about ten people and there was nobody left at the end – they were all scattered all over the place because he was so powerful when he got going. But he needed something to switch him on. Ned was a very honest racer.

Ned was uncomfortable in bunches and descents, and it is thought that he never fully recovered his confidence following a bad crash on the descent from Moll's Gap in 1960 when he went over the edge at the notorious 'Round-of-Beef' bend and fell a considerable distance. While Paddy did benefit greatly from Ned's efforts, it would be inaccurate to describe Ned as his *domestique*, in a servile sense. Rather, Paddy gave purpose and direction to Ned's great ability and Ned, in turn, found satisfaction and expression for his talent through devotion to Paddy.

Longevity in the Rás was a quality common to several Rás legends and Paddy Flanagan was an example – 'Flanagan seemed to go on forever.' While other greats – Mangan, O'Hanlon and McKenna, for example – continued to ride in the Rás for many years while past their best, Flanagan competed at a consistently higher level for longer than anyone else. From the retiring individual of his youth, he grew in personal confidence and carried his fame with modest ease.

Nevertheless, Flanagan developed a sense of his own stature and would not have been satisfied to ride just for the sake of participation. He retained a huge competitive urge. While managing the demands of work and a large family of seven children, he succeeded in remaining totally committed to the schedule of an élite athlete and his regime was as exacting in his forties as it was in his twenties.

He held the race lead again in 1981, at the age of forty-three, and finished fourth. Some who rode in that Rás think he might have won it if he had had more confidence in his own ability then. He finished tenth the following year, at the age of forty-four. He won eleven stages in all during his career, and wore seventeen Yellow Jerseys, with an interval of twenty-one years between the first and last.

There is no doubt that, for a very long period, O'Hanlon and Paddy Flanagan were kings of the Rás and had enormous public stature. Their careers were closely intertwined – for Flanagan and O'Hanlon, defeat was often at the hands of the other and victory at his expense. Yet, their rivalry never seems to have gone beyond the pure sporting challenge and they held each other in deep respect. This great Rás rivalry continues in another form – the inevitable debate amongst Rás followers as to who was the better, O'Hanlon or Flanagan? While O'Hanlon's Rás record is objectively superior, despite having never benefited from the same degree of assistance as had Flanagan, the question is essentially futile. Though there are similarities – Rás longevity, ability, competitiveness and love of the Rás – the differences in style, outlook, support, opposition and the personal circumstances of their amateur lives make any real objective comparison impossible. Each rode at his peak at different periods, but given their exceptional longevity as racers, there are very few who observed at first hand both men through the duration of their careers. It might be easiest to say that each possessed a unique and inimitable greatness.

Paddy Flanagan's death in 2000 prompted many accolades. The journalist, Paul Kimmage, writing in the *Sunday Independent*, summarised some of his characteristics:

> Paddy Flanagan was one of cycling's true gentlemen … one of the greatest racers the country has ever known … a gritty road man.

A tribute written by one of his great rivals from neighbouring Meath, Brian Connaughton, perhaps best captures the essence of Flanagan, and vividly conveys the affection and emotional appeal he generated. It also provides an insightful glimpse into the meaning of the Rás, and the centrality of its role in the fellowship of Irish racing cyclists:

> The sudden death of Kildare cycling legend Paddy Flanagan has cast a huge shadow on the sport throughout the country.
> Three times winner of the Rás Tailteann and a Caltex Award winner in 1964 surely prove the calibre and ability of the man for those who hold a passing

A typical strategy of Paddy Flanagan – generating the break on a selected stretch of road and then driving ceaselessly from the front. This scene is the second-last stage, near Gorey, in the 1977 Rás. Flanagan, at the age of thirty-eight, was the main Irishman to take the fight to the dominant Russian team. He had attacked them the previous day and got into second place, 1 minute 35 seconds behind Lavrushkin. Here, he challenges for the lead before the Wicklow Mountains. Three of the Russian team are directly on his wheel, including Lavrushkin (third man, partly hidden). The rider on the back, at the outside, is Jack Murphy, a member of the only veteran team to ride in the Rás. Flanagan eventually slipped to third place.

interest in the sport. For those of us who raced with him or against him, we know that awards and victories were only peripheral niceties in his approach to his beloved bike racing. It was so obvious to us that the hum of the tires, the smell of the wintergreen, the banter in the dressing room or on the roadside, the training sessions where competitors could be tested and psyched were the genuine ingredients of what he really was.

He was no different from any of us in that he liked to win, but it was the manner of the winning that was all-important for him. We knew too well that his motto was 'attack when you are feeling the pinch because the others could be feeling a bit worse', and invariably we were. For Paddy, bike racing was a craft to be practiced to the absolute fulfilment of enjoyment and satisfaction. To achieve this, his bike and body were tuned and honed to the zenith of perfection. These assets, combined with a fantastic racing intelligence, delivered to us a master craftsman.

He rode countless races all over Ireland, Europe and beyond, sometimes winning but always giving the last ounce of his vast reservoir of strength, stamina and courage. However, it was riding the Rás that put that extra elixir in his veins. For Paddy, the Rás was a sacred place, a sacred thing. He held it in awe, he gave it total respect, he spoke of it lovingly. The weakest competitor, the most irritating official, were all to be respected and obeyed.

He rode it many, many times with sponsored, county and national teams. I will remember him most of all in the white of County Kildare, a concentrated look of determination in his eye and his brother Ned by his side. After his first Rás victory in 1960 he asked Ned to close the dressing room door as it was a little draughty. 'Close the flippin' thing yourself,' said Ned, 'haven't I closed enough gaps for you all week.'

Riding and winning the Rás in that Lily-white jersey, accepting the applause and sharing the joy with his team, was heaven for Paddy. He loved to revisit that heaven with family, friends and team-mates, on long winter nights and on long winter training sessions when the moves that won and lost the Rás were analysed, bisected and dissected.

He was such a rare individual. He treated his 'danger-men', on and off the bike, with total regard and in return was, one could really say, revered by them. He loved competing with them. His accounts of battles with Shay O'Hanlon and Peter Doyle would make a winter night seem not so long. Racing and training was the life he loved and it gave him the people he loved. With his bike, his health, his loving wife and family, his life was complete. Sadly that is all finished now.

He has attacked again, slowly disappearing into the distance on a hilly, windswept road in that white Kildare jersey. I know he wants us to let him go this time, but some other day we will reel him in.

14

Séamus Kennedy who won the Rás in 1978 after a 'long wait'.

The 1976 Rás started outside of Dublin with a 2-mile (3.2km) time trial in Sligo. This was only its second time starting outside the capital, the first being in Navan in 1967. Paddy O'Callaghan was now Race Director. A member of Kerry Rás teams in the 1950s, O'Callaghan was a stalwart of cycling in Kerry, a staunch NCA man who was involved in the unity process and a socialist republican of a similar persuasion to Joe Christle.

With the unity talks in progress, there was speculation about the possibility of an ICF team attending the Rás, but this failed to materialise. A newly-formed Irish developmental 'Youth Squad' took part – Bobby Power, Denis Devin, John McNally and Mick Breen. For the first time, 'hot-spot sprints' were contested, at surprise locations, with the riders getting notification by flag 200 yards beforehand. The race had ninety-two starters, considerably larger than the fields of around seventy that had been the norm over the previous decade. There were five separate teams from Meath, along with the usual foreign contingents which included the fancied Josef Zebisch of Germany, runner up to Flanagan the previous year.

Flanagan was riding as well as ever and was a favourite. Devin won the opening time trial and Kennedy won the second stage, with Fons Steuten of Holland, a world veteran[45] champion, going into the race lead. Paddy Flanagan cut loose on the third stage – between Clifden and Lisdoonvarna – attacking in the first few miles, and there followed a classic Rás day of hectic jumping, chasing, counter attacking, and more jumping and chasing. Flanagan was the chief powerhouse behind it all, winning the prime at Maam Cross, chasing down a leading group on Corkscrew Hill, and eventually winning on his own by 1 minute 26 seconds The performance gained him the Jersey, at the expense of the Dutchman, and the consensus was that he was going to be very difficult to dislodge.

A major crash the following day, after only 20 miles of the stage, to Listowel, ended his hopes. Involving about twenty riders, it split the race badly. When Flanagan got going again, he was in obvious distress, with his left arm 'hanging'. He drifted back to the team cars and asked Pat Healy in the Kerry car to tug at it, probably in the hope that a dislocation might be repaired. He managed to finish the stage and lost only 7 minutes, but was taken to hospital in Tralee that evening and operated on for a broken bone in his elbow. He was out of the race.[46]

At the finish that day in Listowel, the young Bobby Power from Carrick-on-Suir won the sprint and Séamus Kennedy went into yellow, yet again. The next day, the race travelled onto Valentia Island via the new bridge that had opened in 1970. In another day of frantic racing, the Frenchman, Jean Claude Breure, won the stage and went into yellow.

The fifth stage, through the mountains of Kerry from Valentia to Kenmare, was controversial even before it began, with riders and managers declaring it too dangerous. Nevertheless, the stage went ahead as planned, though race instructions included a warning about 'extremely dangerous bends and very narrow twisting roads'. Six riders were taken to hospital during the stage and two were detained. There were many more 'walking wounded', among them the race leader, Breure, who limped into Kenmare 24 minutes behind the stage winner, a sorry sight with bandaged head. Its many perils aside, there had also been concern about the severity of the stage, which proved equally well-founded. Six major climbs were crammed into a relatively short 66 miles (106km), beginning very near the start, and the field was eventually scattered to bits with the sixty finishers strewn out over 20 miles (32km) of road.

While the stage might have overwhelmed the unfortunate, the less cautious and less strong, it proved a magnificent setting for the top contenders and was the scene for a virtuoso performance by Mick Nulty and Bobby Power. Nulty broke away on the very first climb, Coomaneaspaig, within 2 miles of the start, and Power followed immediately. With crashes splitting the main group on the descent, they gained a 3-minute lead at one stage. But a determined chase was launched on Moll's Gap and the lead began to close. Nevertheless, they stayed away for the entire stage, with Nulty, the better climber, leading the ascents. They went over six major climbs together before finishing 1 minute 12 seconds in front of the next group of riders. Power won the sprint and went into the race lead.

Power was in only his second Rás and not with a good team, but he was riding strongly and defended well the next day into Mitchelstown. A dangerous three-man group had gone clear before Macroom – John McNally from Antrim, Larry Clarke and Mick Cahill – but it fell apart after Coachford when they began to row over the sharing of the work and a bicycle pump was swung in anger.

Power again defended into Carlow and was confident facing the Wicklow Mountains on the second-last stage to Bray. Chance deprived him, however – he punctured on one of the descents, but support cars had been held back because of the risk of riders and cars becoming dangerously entangled on the descent. Fons Steuten attacked him during the wait, became race leader in Bray, and defended it well, especially against the Nultys on the final stage, back over the Sally Gap and into the Phoenix Park.

Fons Steuten had been one of Holland's leading amateurs before he turned professional and rode in the Tour de France and Tour of Spain. Power was a relative novice, in his second Rás. Though obviously disappointed at the manner in which he lost,[47] he was young and confident, facing a bright racing future. As with many such young and promising riders in the Rás, disappointment was tempered by optimism and an expectation that his day would yet come. But like so many others, he was to discover that winning opportunities are rare in the Rás. He remained one of its leading riders into the 1990s, winning a total of six stages and six Yellow Jerseys, but 1976 was to be the nearest he ever came to an outright win.

The 1977 event was the twenty-fifth Rás, again under the direction of Paddy O'Callaghan. The sponsorship arrangements had been strengthened, with the involvement of the Department of Health under its 'Be Active Be Alive' health-promotion campaign. It also had a new trophy – the George Plant Perpetual Memorial. The original Rás trophy – Corn Cathal Brugha – was never returned by one of the teams from behind the Iron Curtain, and the George Plant Trophy, originally dating from 1958, was re-engraved and remains the winner's trophy to this day.[48] The tone of the Rás programme was conciliatory. An article about the NCA referred to the 'unfortunate split' in Irish cycling and added: 'There is good hope if the Irish Cycling Bodies are left to work out their own destiny …'

Fons Steuten, the winner from the previous year, was back, leading a Dutch team, but the Russians were expected to dominate. Given their colossal status in international sport, their arrival again brought great prestige to the event, and their reputation, along with the memory of their total dominance in 1970, gave little hope to an Irish team that would normally have been considered quite strong – Flanagan, Power, Kennedy and Devin. The absence of the once-mighty Dublin team indicated the continual shift in the balance of county-team power in the Rás. The Nulty brothers were also conspicuously absent, having changed over to the ICF – they were riding with an Irish team in the Tour of Britain as the Rás was beginning.

In one sense, nothing seemed to have changed in the approach of Irish riders to world-class rivals and Bobby Power's memories reveal remarkable parallels with the naïvety shown by previous leading Irish riders when they first encountered a top foreign team in the Rás, as far back as 1963:

The tactics of those guys [Russians] put us to shame … They were so disciplined – their tactic was to get the Jersey early on and then sit on everything. Then their lowest man on GC would go up the road and he would keep jumping people. When they would get up the road they would drive it. They didn't mind losing the Jersey because there would be another fellow up the road. They had the strength and depth to be able to do it. I was with two of them going into Macroom – they showed me some tactics. They kept attacking and attacking until one of them would get away and then the other

Fons Steuten from Holland, winner of the 1976 Rás, flanked on the left by Colm Nulty (second) and Colm's brother, Mick (third on the right). The Nulty brothers were the main challenge to the Dutch team. Sally Ryan, a marketing executive, is on the left – she has played an important role in the Rás since 1975. On the right is Tommy Sheehan, a Rás announcer and a significant figure in Tipperary cycling.

fellow would sit on you and wait until another one came up. Then they'd start attacking you again. I was with two of them about 3 miles before the finish and they started to talk to each other in Russian. Then, the fellow on the outside just lay in on top of me and tried to pin me into the ditch. All of a sudden I was fighting to control the bike and the other fellow just took off. They were ruthless.

Yet, in another sense, much had clearly changed. While the Russians were obviously extremely strong – effectively 'professional' riders competing full-time around the world (Chelpakov, for example, won a gold medal in the 1980 Olympics) – the Irish had advanced from the negative 'sitting' response of previous encounters with such teams and were not afraid to take the fight to the Russians. Brian Connaughton took the Yellow Jersey by over 4 minutes in a remarkable break on the third, 102-mile (163km) stage from Nenagh to Boyle. Kennedy won the next stage, into Castleisland, refusing to yield to unrelenting pressure from the Russians on the Barnagh Gap, and Connaughton retained the Jersey with a reduced margin of 1 minute 44 seconds His defence collapsed on the next tough stage, to Macroom, when the Russians' power and strength in depth became overwhelming. Yuri Lavrushkin, who had won a stage in 1970, went into the lead.

Paddy Flanagan then took up the challenge. Aged thirty-eight, he was most exceptional in that Rás, taking the fight to the Russians and moving into third place on the sixth stage to Clonmel. In another day of fierce racing to Courtown, he moved up into second. Now just 1 minute 35 seconds behind the leader, there was much hope that he could snatch the lead on the penultimate stage in the mountains to Newbridge but, after two hard days and facing the combined power of the Russians, he eventually slipped back into third, 1 minute 45 seconds behind the winner. The next best-placed Irishman was Eamon Connolly of Meath, in fifth place. The winner, Lavrushkin, who had won the Tour of Yugoslavia since first competing in the Rás in 1970, noted the difference from the previous visit, and a newspaper report quoted him as saying that the Irish riders had 'improved greatly'.

In this respect, the 1977 Rás was a noticeable benchmark in the evolution of the Irish team as a force in the event.

By 1978, Séamus Kennedy had set a Rás record of sorts – since his first Rás in 1965, at the age of seventeen, he had lost the Yellow Jersey more times than anyone else, before or since. He had worn it for a total of thirteen days and won eight stages, but had lost it four times without winning. Undoubtedly one of the best Irish riders of the previous decade, and an ever-conspicuous and influential force in the Rás, it remained the only major title to elude him.

Kennedy was a wonderful rider, with a very professional attitude and a meticulous approach to his preparation, diet and any aspect of his life that impinged on cycling. While not an exceptional climber, he was fast, focused, aggressive and ruthless in the sprints. He was a classic single-day racer – a feared rider who never gave an inch, always generating breaks, staying away and winning the sprint. For a number of years in the 1970s, he was arguably the most outstanding one-day rider in the NCA. Yet he simply was not a natural stage racer. The type of strength needed to win a stage race did not come to him until later in his career, and some of those qualities that made him an exceptional one-day rider thwarted him in the Rás: 'Kennedy rode on impulse'; 'If a hundred attacks went up the road, he'd try to be in every one of them'; 'Kennedy had a tendency to put his head down and ride too early, and not leave enough for the closing days.'

My problem was that I couldn't hold back and I'd go in the break the first day and ride everybody off the road. Then I would go through one bad day and lose 5 minutes.

The general consensus was that Kennedy could not stick with a multi-day strategy as he was unable to restrain himself during the early stages of the Rás – he usually had little in reserve for the final few days. Nor did he have that forceful character that can sometimes dominate and intimidate the bunch, and his uncompromising style of racing, more suited to single-day events, sometimes conflicted with the interests of team-mates and was not conducive to developing the kinds of alliances that are necessary in the Rás.

Being a member of the powerful Meath team was a double-edged sword. A powerhouse of Irish cycling during the 1970s, Meath teams always had a number of possible contenders and this led to a lack of clear goals and clashes of interests. Tensions and divided loyalties inevitably developed, and became most manifest in 1971 when Kennedy and Colm Nulty battled with each other for the Yellow Jersey on a stage to Dún Chaoin. According to Kennedy:

> From 1968 on in Meath, we were head and shoulders above any other county. Meath should have won more Ráses, but because we got so strong we were riding against one another half the time.

While Meath had an abundance of good riders, Kerry cycling had been in the doldrums since John Mangan's win in 1972. Kennedy was a frequent visitor to Kerry as his father was from that county, and Kerry began to court Kennedy. Paddy O'Callaghan persuaded him to ride for the county in 1977, but Kennedy changed his mind. For a number of years, Gene Mangan had also been attempting to entice him. He worked with Kennedy in Dublin and they regularly had coffee with Colm Christle, winner of the first Rás in 1953. Much of the talk inevitably turned to cycling and Kennedy found some consolation in Christle's philosophy that the deserving rider will eventually win provided he is ready to take his chance when it presents itself. Mangan would try to persuade and coax him – teasing and half-jokingly, and sometimes seriously, suggesting that he would never win the Rás until he rode with Kerry as a clear team leader, with no obligations to anyone else. And he would be restrained in the race until the time was right.

Kennedy had a warm memory of Mangan from the shattering day in 1975 when Paddy Flanagan snatched the Rás from him on the stage to Naas:

> I learned a bitter lesson that day – journalists and TV cameras were chasing me all week but I was on my own after that stage into Naas – they didn't even report that I had punctured. I learned one thing – when you are down, nobody gives a damn about you. I was sitting on the footpath on my own and then

Gene Mangan came up to me and said, 'Don't worry Séamus, we'll go back to the drawing board.' I never forgot that.

Paddy O'Callaghan approached him again for the 1978 Rás, pointing out that Kerry would provide strong riders to work solely for him:

I had looked at the Meath team and I knew there were too many men capable of winning in Meath … but for me, time was running out. Paddy O'Callaghan asked me again would I ride on the Kerry team and I said yes … I remember thinking that I must start using the head.

The involvement of Bord Fáilte signalled the first significant commercial sponsorship of the Rás. This was bolstered by the involvement of the Department of Health.

Now named the 'Discover Ireland – Be Active Be Alive Rás Tailteann' due to its strengthened relationship with the Department of Health, the race began in Shannon, County Clare. For the first time, it had an entry of over a hundred. Dermot Dignam was Race Organiser.

It was Kennedy's thirteenth consecutive Rás start and he was feeling strong and relaxed, having just returned from the Tour of Tunisia – nine days of good racing in pleasant weather. Gerry Keogh came with Kennedy to the Kerry camp, and joined Paddy O'Callaghan in back up. The other three Kerry riders – Anthony O'Halloran, Mick Breen and Donal Clifford – were facing their clearly prescribed role with enthusiasm.

It seemed an ideal team arrangement. Yet, as in so many Rásanna, a reasonable county team, with an exceptional leader, was not, in itself, an adequate platform from which to win the event. Good fortune also had a part to play, and Kennedy's luck first emerged on the second stage, in Galway, a circuit-race on the second part of a split stage. He fell on a corner – there was no optional 'lap-out' then – but was uninjured. Standing at that very spot was his manager who straightened the handlebars between his knees and got him going quickly. Kennedy's ability to regain contact gave him further confidence.

Foreign riders were strong. Fons Steuten, the 1976 winner, was back again, but foremost among the Continental contingent were Helmut Willer of Germany and Albert Kesters, a Belgian – they both won stages and shared the Yellow Jersey for seven days. However, it remained close on top of GC for the first five days of very hard racing, and only 46 seconds separated a group that also included Bobby Power, Denis Devin, Flanagan, O'Hanlon, Clarke and Kennedy.

With Gerry Keogh playing a strong restraining role, Kennedy was, as planned, 'keeping his powder dry' and staying in contention. His plans nearly unravelled over what should normally have been a minor detail of planning. It was a 98-mile (157km) stage, from Bundoran to Letterkenny over the Glengesh Pass. He knew the route thoroughly, was thinking about a possible attack on the Jersey and gave explicit instructions on where he was to get food. Just before the appointed feeding place, however, Fons Steuten – in a bid for victory – launched a withering attack. Kennedy and Kesters were in an all-out chase, both trying to contain Steuten, when they passed the feeding spot – Kennedy grabbed the food bag in full flight. It was a plastic bag, securely knotted. The scene that ensued might appear comical in retrospect but was very serious for Kennedy at the time. He was riding furiously with the bag in one hand, trying to hold Kesters and chasing Fons Steuten, whilst simultaneously making desperate attempts to undo the knots. Then he realised that the bottle had spilt and his drink was sloshing around the bottom of the bag, mixing with the food. In disgust, he threw it into the ditch and continued the pursuit without food or drink. He suffered badly as a result – on the climb at Meenabolt, a combination of over-high gearing and lack of food resulted in Kesters' escape and stage victory. Kennedy was swallowed up by a following group, lost the advantage of the chase and dropped 20 vital seconds from Kesters.

The broad Kerry team plan was that, if reasonably fresh and in contention, Kennedy's restraint could be discarded on the next stage, from Letterkenny to Warrenpoint. With just two days to follow, and the longest stage of 101 miles (162km) through the smooth roads of Northern Ireland, it would be the ideal time and place for Kennedy to be unleashed on the race. Now in eighth place and 2 minutes 10 seconds seconds down on the leader, Kennedy got on his bike in Letterkenny feeling in good form and remembering the words of Colm Christle: 'Your day of reckoning will eventually come.'

Early attacks, led mainly by O'Hanlon, were nullified after about 40 miles (64km) of racing beyond Omagh where the race stewards had to manage traffic control without any RUC assistance or co-operation. Then commenced the coincidence of factors that swung the direction of the race in Kennedy's favour. The leader, Willer, punctured just as a strong break launched from the front and

Miserable weather does not dampen spirits as Race Director, Paddy O'Callaghan (on the left in black), prepares to start a stage. The first- and second-placed riders in 1978 are in front of the group – Séamus Kennedy (right front) and Bobby Power (left front). The tall rider in the centre (white cap) is Mick Nulty. The rider on the far right is the Dutchman Henk de Hey who won a stage of the Grand Prix de l'Humanité shortly before the Rás.

By 1978 Kennedy had worn the Yellow Jersey for a total of thirteen days and won eight stages, but had lost the Jersey four times and it appeared that he might never win the Rás. His eventual victory in 1978 – on his thirteenth attempt – was one of the most popular in the history of the event. In a way, Kennedy's victory drew down the curtain on part of the NCA's history.

Kennedy was the first recipient of the George Plant Perpetual Memorial, the current Rás trophy. Dating from 1958, it was dedicated to the memory of George Plant, a highly regarded official of the Gate Cycling Club (not to be confused with another George Plant – an IRA-man who was executed by the Dublin government during the Second World War). It was originally awarded for the 'Annual Guinness 100 kilometres Massed Start Cycle Race', but was re-engraved for the Rás Tailteann in 1978.

the speed increased. He was having a torrid time trying to regain contact on his own and, to add to his woe, the *commissaire*, in an unusual move, held back the cavalcade of cars from the rear of the bunch. This deprived him of the advantage and shelter of being able to 'ride the cavalcade' back up to the bunch.

Regardless of this, the break was gone, with Kennedy in it and without any of the leading seven riders on GC. It contained thirteen altogether, including the inevitable 'passengers', but had that vital combination of interests that were collectively driven by the gain it promised for each. A strong Tipperary group was at the heart of the break, trying to put Bobby Power into contention and take the lead in the team classification. Along with Bobby Power, there were three of his club-mates in their first Rás – Larry and Paddy Power and Bobby Sheehan – and they were riding their hearts out for their club and for Bobby. John O'Sullivan from Cork was also riding hard to keep his NCA Irish team ahead in the team competition. Kennedy, the highest man on GC in the group, was riding all out to take over the race lead. The German in yellow behind provided further strong motivation – Kennedy rode up and down the bunch exhorting them to 'ride for Ireland lads, ride for Ireland'.

They did ride exceptionally hard and it was to be an extraordinarily fast stage, averaging 28 mph (44 km/h) for over 100 miles (160km). Equally significant were the dynamics in the main bunch which inhibited any cohesive chase. The seven top men did not organise a pursuit, each for his own reason – Willer was probably too tired and his strongest team-mate had crashed out earlier; O'Hanlon could find no allies to take up the chase; Devin was happy to see an all-Irish bunch get away with the prospect of an Irish win. All in all, it was one of those days where a certain weariness and resultant apathy descends on the bunch – there had been five days of very hard racing up the west, it was the longest stage of the race at 101 miles (163km), and the weather was warm.

The break came into Warrenpoint 7 minutes 54 seconds ahead of the main bunch. In one decisive move, Kennedy went into yellow and still could not resist winning the stage. He was now 62 seconds ahead of second-placed Bobby Power. Willer, who was stranded in the main bunch, was now third, well back at 5 minutes 44 seconds.

The second-last day was Kennedy's thirty-second birthday, and he was inevitably feeling under some pressure with Rás victory, yet again, within his grasp. But there was to be no real threat over the final two days. His Kerry team-mates had risen to their task – the occasion of the Rás could always inspire exceptional performances. Kennedy's praise of them was as enthusiastic as his style of riding: 'They rode their hearts out for me … they would have left their bodies on the road for me.' He also acknowledged the role of the Tipperary team on the crucial day: 'Fair play to the Tipperary boys …' The unusual route also helped. Coming into Dublin from the north, there was no major mountain stage during which he could be threatened.

Even if there had been a serious attack on him, Kennedy would probably have held out anyway. Apart from his own strength and the support of his team, his prospective victory was one of the more popular in the Rás. With his contribution over thirteen years, it had been a long wait and richly deserved and he would have received plenty of assistance on the final days if needed. He was therefore able to enjoy something of a 'cruise' into Dublin, and could even restrain himself from contesting the perilous bunch sprint. While, naturally, there was regret amongst Meath cyclists that Kennedy had not won the Rás while in his native county team, there is no evidence of any resentment – an indicator of the looseness of the county-team ethos at this time. Kennedy's eventual win was widely welcomed.

Looked at retrospectively, that victory drew down the curtain on part of the NCA's history. Following the formation of the Irish Cycling Tripartite Committee, 'Unity' was to formally commence the following year – Kennedy was therefore the last NCA man to win the Rás under the old regime.

15

UNITED AND FORWARD

Stephen Roche, (left) wearing the race-leader's jersey, and Colm Nulty, wearing the points-leader's jersey, 1979.

1979 was a watershed year in Irish cycling with riders from the three cycling bodies able to compete together. This followed the setting up of the Irish Cycling Tripartite Committee in 1978 – the first formal structure to facilitate the unification process that had been in train since 1972. Under this arrangement, the three cycling organisations still existed as independent bodies and ran their own events, but all members could compete in races organised by the others. It was a huge breakthrough, an emotional time for some, and the 1979 Rás was a landmark event as it brought together many of the top riders and senior officials in Irish cycling for the first time in decades. While open to all, the Rás was run by the NCA under the new arrangement and this was to continue until the unification process was progressed further in 1987 when the three bodies amalgamated to become the Federation of Irish Cyclists (FIC).

Each of the three organisations had its own team in the 1979 event. The NCA team – under the name 'Ireland' – was comprised of Séamus Kennedy, Paddy Flanagan, Denis Devin and Pat McHugh. The ICF team included Tony Lally, John Shortt, Oliver McQuaid, Alan McCormack and Stephen Roche. The Northern Ireland Cycling Federation sent two teams – its A-team consisted of Billy Kerr, Brian Stevenson, Pat McGarrigle, Aidan McKeown and Pat Shearer.

The unification process also helped to boost funding from the Department of Health and it had been marketed as the 'Health Race' from the previous year. While still depending on its volunteer base, this brought a very professional marketing element to the race and its organisation benefited accordingly. For the first time, there was over 100 riders in the event.

In spite of the new and exciting developments, the event got off to a rather ignominious start. The first stage from Dublin to Longford was 40 minutes late in setting off and there was confusion about results at the finish. Worse was to follow at the evening time trial when the results were found to be unreliable. After much confusion, it was announced that the results were scrapped and the stage did not count. Officials explained that gaps in the starting order caused by riders who had entered but not started had not been allowed for. The débâcle understandably caused much annoyance to riders.

Aside from this difficulty, and it being the first 'unity' Rás, the 1979 event is best remembered for the performance of the nineteen-year-old Stephen Roche. He was not hotly tipped prior to the event – all the ICF riders were considered potential winners, while Billy Kerr from the NICF team was probably favourite – but Roche's performance, in terms of both physical and mental strength for one so young, left a lasting impression on those who witnessed the front of the race for its duration.

Stephen Roche winning a stage, aged nineteen, 1979.

His main opposition eventually came from within his own team – something the manager had obvious difficulty in controlling. Alan McCormack considered himself to be the established leader and felt that Roche was challenging him. Roche went into yellow on the fourth stage, to Caherciveen, but two days later, on the road to Carrick-on-Suir, he had to do hard riding at the front of the bunch to stay in touch with team-mates, Oliver McQuaid and Alan McCormack, who had gone away with a French rider. McCormack had another go on the second-last day, to Navan, but Roche dismissively nullified the threat with a devastating surge out of the bunch, across to McCormack.

One of the biggest sensations of the Rás was Roche's defeat of Billy Kerr in the 16-mile (26km) time trial on the morning of the final day. Such was Kerr's time trialling reputation, pre-Rás predictions had anticipated he might win the race on this stage. Roche, however, beat him by 11 seconds and did so with apparent ease, cheerfully waving to the crowd on the run-in and even finding time for a few words for the veteran reporter, Jim McArdle, as he passed by car. Indeed, McArdle's

1979: Nineteen-year-old Stephen Roche leading from Michael Nulty and Aidan McKeown. 'Roche made it all look so incredibly easy,' declared one newspaper report, but Roche's main opposition came from Alan McCormack. Roche's Rás win was an important stepping stone on his route to the continent.

final headline of the event summed it up: 'Roche made it all look so incredibly easy', and he went on to state that Roche 'was the most impressive winner of any of the big stage races I have seen'.

There was a great wave of enthusiasm amongst the riders for the joint participation in the 1979 Rás – 'It was a breath of fresh air' – and there is little doubt that this enthusiasm was important in sustaining what was still a fragile unification process. To the younger riders especially, less aware as they were of ideological differences, it seemed to make utter sense that all should be competing together. Roche reflected this when he said that 'the main question was why this hadn't happened before – it was a magnificent event'.

Roche, of course, was heading for greater things. But his Rás victory was an important stepping stone on that journey. His winning of the event, at a critical time in his development as a person and as a rider, was an important element in raising his expectations and setting his sights on the continental cycling scene. Eight year later, in the glorious year of 1987, he became assured of cycling immortality by becoming the only rider to emulate Eddie Merckx's feat of victory in the Tour de France, Giro d'Italia and World Championship in one year. Given such eminent world stature, it would be understandable if the memory and significance of the teenage win of a remote, amateur bike race in Ireland had slipped into the deeper recesses of his memory. This was not the case. When Merckx first met Roche after his triple win in 1987, Merckx congratulated him, saying: 'Congratulations Stephen, we are equal now.' Roche, in his typically mischievous way quipped: 'No, we're not Eddie – you've never won the Rás.'

The progress of the unification process was further in evidence in 1980 when a joint Ireland team was entered by the Tripartite Committee, consisting of Paddy Flanagan, Billy Kerr, Pat Healy and John Walsh. This was the first all-Ireland road race team in over thirty years, in the sense that it was chosen from all the riders on the island. Roche was not back to defend his title as his Paris-based team would not release him, but much interest lay in John Mangan.

After winning the Rás in 1972 and the subsequent events at the Munich Olympics, Mangan appeared to have a possible career in France. But the hitch of his being in the NCA and therefore ineligible for a licence created the usual problem. Furthermore, he was close to Joe Christle and a committed NCA man. However, with the approval of Christle and with the assistance of John Lackey in the ICF who smoothed the process, Mangan took out an ICF licence and thereby, in theory, defected from the NCA to the ICF. Unusually, this created little stir. Christle's acquiescence goes some way to explaining this – itself an interesting indication of his thinking then – but Mangan also managed to turn his membership of the ICF into a quiet form of passive opposition: he remained aloof from the organisation in Ireland, never attended any of its functions or meetings and never raced in any of its events.

Mangan's toughness quickly became evident in France. Not only did he defy the established cycling 'mafia' through sheer strength and doggedness, he quickly established a controlling interest and came to dominate racing in Brittany – an accomplishment in itself, and lucrative, too. He had not returned for the Rás in the interim, and his prospects now prompted much speculation.

Alan McCormack took the Yellow Jersey in the first stage and held it until the fourth day when there was a sensational development in Donegal. He won the sprint but was disqualified for taking both hands off the bars as he crossed the line and his name did not appear on the GC sheet that evening. The infringed rule was an NCA one and not one applied in ICF events, but, as the Rás was being run under NCA jurisdiction, the rule was applied. The disqualification led to huge controversy, further heightened by the fact that McCormack's father and manager, Joe (J. J.), was a leading ICF figure. Perhaps it was a case of NCA *commissaires* and officials making a stand as a newspaper report from the previous Rás noted that Peter Morton had raised both hands crossing the line in Mallow and Dermot Dignam had announced it would be the last time this infringement would go unpunished.

On appeal, McCormack was reinstated, as was probably originally intended once the point was made, but the problem again arose two days later when John McQuaid raised his hands as he beat John Mangan in the sprint into Thurles. After further controversy, McQuaid was penalised by a minute, depriving him of the stage win which was credited to Mangan. Mangan himself was penalised a minute for continually taking drinks from a motorbike but this was re-instated on appeal.

While these difficulties were evidence of the many teething problems encountered during the unification process, the main story of the 1980 Rás was Billy Kerr. An exceptionally good rider of international class, then coming towards the end of his career at the age of thirty-five, he was powerful and forceful and took the race lead on the fifth stage, from Donegal to Roscommon, after McCormack apparently became ill during the night.

Kerr had to defend against very strong riders, but the anticipated battle with John Mangan never really materialised. Mangan, undoubtedly a better rider than in the year he won it, did have bad luck – he had a number of punctures, his back wheel collapsed at one point and he crashed on the second-last day – but he also rode a tactically poor race, doing enormous amounts of work at the front of the bunch for very little reward. What's more, he complained much about the bad weather. While he won the points competition and finished fifth, it was regarded as a disappointing result. Many felt that he treated the race somewhat lightly and that, perhaps, his sojourn in France had dimmed his comprehension of the real challenge of the Rás.

It was considered fitting that a rider of Kerr's stature should become a Rás winner, and he became the first Ulster rider, and the first rider from the NICF, to win the event. He also joined Peter Doyle as one of only two Irish riders to have won both the Rás and the Tour of Ireland.[49]

The Rás faced a financial crisis after the 1980 event as the Department of Health discontinued its funding. This was a major blow as it was understood that the Health Education Bureau was committed to significant and long-term funding of the Health Race as part of its health promotion strategy. Officials from the Scottish health promotion organisation had even come to Ireland to observe the strategy at work and the role of the Rás. However, an economic decline during this time brought cuts in health spending and it is understood that, whatever about the merits of health promotion, a political decision was made that it would be politically unwise for the Department of Health to be seen to support a bike race, in a high-profile way, at a time when hospital wards were closing. Tirolia – a firm that traded in domestic heaters – stepped in and the event became the 'Tirolia Rás Tailteann' for 1981.

Norman Lindsay, a 21-year-old Scot, and Paddy Flanagan, the 43-year-old Kildare man riding with a Meath team, dominated the first two stages and shared the same time on top of GC, with the Scot wearing the Yellow Jersey on points. The Jersey reverted to Gearóid Costello and Aidan McKeown for the third and fourth stages, and John McQuaid won the fourth stage, making up for the penalty that cost him the stage win the previous year. The fifth stage, from Bantry to Clonakilty, was a unique day, with veterans taking both the stage and the race lead. Forty-year-old Seán Lally won the stage, while Paddy Flanagan went into the race lead.

Flanagan's taking of the Jersey at his age was remarkable, especially as it had not come from an opportunistic or lucky move. In typically aggressive fashion, he jumped from the bunch and, with the help of John O'Sullivan, bridged a minute gap to a leading group against a stiff headwind. He then drove the break, repeatedly attacked and dropped riders of the calibre of Mick Nulty and Paul Mahon. There was a row between the two veterans at the finish – Flanagan felt that Lally had contributed little to the break before jumping ahead for the stage win. Lally, however, was a team-mate of Costello – then in contention – and it would not have been in his interest to ride with Flanagan.

A *criterium* in Clonakilty that evening provided further controversy. Gearóid Costello described the racing as 'savage', John Mangan and Oliver McQuaid had a row in the middle of it and a big crash split the field. A number of the riders who fell took a lap out but rejoined a break which had developed in the meantime, rather than the main bunch. Their placings were questioned and it was late in the night before it was sorted out – they were relegated to the bunch time. Costello regained the Jersey from Flanagan and Tony Lally won the stage, making it two Rás stage wins in the same day for the Lally brothers.[50]

A number of observers of that Rás contend that Flanagan was lacking confidence in his ability to defend the Jersey in the mountains towards the end of the race and that he was happier to lose it at that stage. He was sharing a room with the young Philip Cassidy, who was on his team, and Flanagan did indicate to Cassidy that he – Cassidy – should concentrate on his own race because Flanagan felt it unlikely that he could hold the overall lead. As it transpired, Flanagan rode well in the mountains and it is speculated that he might have won his fourth Rás, in his mid-forties, had he possessed more belief in himself and fought to defend the Jersey. Others who knew Flanagan as a cyclist hotly dispute this suggestion or any theory that Flanagan would not have given his utmost to preserve his Rás lead: 'That just wasn't Flanagan'; 'Paddy would have fought to the bitter end for tenth place, let alone first'; 'It wasn't in the man to compromise like that.' Also, it was a Rás racked with divisions – within the Irish team, and between John Mangan and the McQuaids for example – and Flanagan would have recognised the opportunities that might have arisen in these circumstances.

Aidan McKeown and Archie Cunningham were challenging Costello. McKeown took the lead and held the Jersey for two days until the second-last stage, from Courtown to Trim, where Jamie McGahan, a former Scottish champion, took the race lead. Cunningham's crank snapped on the Sally Gap, resulting in a dislocated kneecap and an end to his race. McKeown made a desperate attempt to regain the Jersey during the time trial on the second-last day, and came to within 12 seconds. It was not enough and the Scot was victorious.

There was much recrimination in the Irish camp which was said to be in disarray, and poor teamwork by an Irish team was blamed. However, there were many 'wheels within wheels', as can be gleaned from the following comments of the reporter, David Walsh, written after the final stage:

John Mangan was linked to the controversy. His relationship with the other Irish riders has been strained all week. Yesterday there was no reconciliation as Mangan was bitterly accused of deliberately helping McGahan to retain the Yellow Jersey. Mangan would argue, that, after eight days of 'war' with those same Irish riders, that he owed them absolutely nothing. In all the arguments, there was a great number of losers and only one winner, Jamie McGahan.

Also, McGahan was the first man from Great Britain to win the Rás, but he was from Scotland and that was not considered too bad!

Dermot Dignam bowed out of the organising group of the 1982 race and Billy Archibald became Race Director. The Irish team dominated from early on. Managed by Pat McQuaid, it included Billy Kerr, Martin Earley, Dermot Gilleran and Paul Tansey. Gilleran and Kerr shared the Jersey for the first four days, but Philip Cassidy took it on the fifth stage, from Tralee to Ballybunion, and defended it in an evening stage to Kilkee. The Irish manager then cracked the whip and placed Earley, Gilleran, Kerr and Tansey in a pecking order for the following day. Kerr and Tansey were to mark Cassidy, while Earley and Gilleran were to attack and get away.

The plan worked. Cassidy had a weak team and he stayed with Kerr, presuming Kerr wanted to win his second Rás and would therefore make a move. When the break was well gone, Cassidy put it to Kerr that he should start riding if he wanted to stay in contention. Kerr, uncomfortable with the task assigned to him, revealed that he had been instructed by McQuaid to say put. Later, they combined to break out of the bunch, repeatedly taking every second turn to attack, and eventually escaped. But it was too late for Cassidy – in spite of the fact that both Gilleran and Madden collided and crashed with 12 miles (19km) to go, Gilleran took the Jersey.

The next stage finished in Drogheda and there was a circuit race at nearby Tullyesker that evening. It was preceded by a parade, led by a band, but the riders refused to join because of a downpour. For this display of insubordination, the *commissaire*, Ben McKenna, announced he was halving the prize money for the final stage to Dublin. The riders decided on a go-slow and rolled out of Drogheda at their ease. They sent Gabriel Howard up the road to collect the prime going through his home town of Stamullen. Next, the two riders at the bottom of GC were sent to collect the next three primes. They finally started racing for the prime at Navan.

Gilleran had sealed his Rás win in a wonderful ride on the second-last day when a fierce attack by McGahan brought him to within 27 seconds. There was no major change on the final day and Gilleran retained that advantage. Some disciplined team riding, under the direction of Pat McQuaid, had been crucial in Gilleran attaining and saving the race lead – an early example in the Rás of a top-class Irish rider being expected to sacrifice himself for the sake of a team win. Not everybody approved. Kerr, a rider of immense stature at the end of his career, and the type of 'up-front' rider so admired in stage racing, was not happy with the role he had been assigned in taking the Jersey from Cassidy – 'It wasn't my style of riding … if I was to be beaten, I wanted to be beaten on the road, fair and square, by a better man.' Comments of Jim McArdle in *The Irish Times* also had an air of disapproval:

> Although the ruthless 'execution' of Cassidy when he was leading, with Kerr having to sacrifice his chance, is new to Irish cycling, it was apparently a case of the Irish team having to win regardless of who won out.

McQuaid's strategy, perhaps seen as exemplary twenty years later, did not comfortably fit within the prevailing ethos then – a further interesting landmark in the tactical evolution of the Rás.

Another associated and equally subtle evolution took place in the early 1980s. With the best riders of three organisations distilled into one, a new cohort of 'young guns' was emerging, with little respect for the reputations of earlier Rás greats or the established conventions of the bunch. The Rás bunch, during the 1970s, came to be dominated by a powerful group of élite riders. They were hard, rugged men – highly individualistic and singular in character. They were viewed with a certain awe by many and some had iconic status amongst the ordinary county riders and followers of the sport. A certain pecking order developed, a form of respect where those of higher rank were deferred to. Perhaps Séamus Kennedy's win in 1978 marked the end of their era but, certainly by the early 1980s, an entirely new cohort of riders, with a fresh attitude, had arrived on the scene – Roche, of course, was an exceptional example, but there were many others, among them Philip Cassidy, the McQuaids, the McCormacks, the Kimmages, the McCanns, Martin Earley, Gary Thomson and Dermot Gilleran. Part of the Kelly–Roche era, this cohort of young riders swept across the Rás during the 1980s. With the best young riders of three federations coming together, there was, according to John McCormack, 'a hidden tension', but the end result was that 'it galvanised the game of cycling'.

A computer was used to help compile results for the first time in the 1982 Rás. Record cards were used prior to that, with each day's time added on. Above is Mike O'Donaghue's card from 1972. Note that the card uses the more common 'O'Donoghue', as opposed to the correct 'O'Donaghue'.

The background of some of those who came from the ICF was a definite influence. While many of the great cyclists stumbled into the sport and learned their craft through hard experience or through a form of apprenticeship served under the wings of established masters, a core of ICF riders at this time had been reared in cycling dynasties – their cycling knowledge and ambition was absorbed by being immersed in families whose lives revolved around the sport. They arrived into the senior ranks with insight, skill, ambition, confidence and high expectations.

The McQuaids were prominent in this regard and were a hugely significant family in Irish cycling. They also achieved much international representation, probably more than any other family in Irish sport. Jim McQuaid, originally from Dungannon in County Tyrone, was a successful track and road cyclist in the 1940s, and rode as an international. For himself and his brother, Paddy, top-level international competition was the primary focus; Paddy had been instrumental in the founding of the CRE in 1949 so as to have an international outlet.

The family moved to Dublin in the 1940s and Jim McQuaid imbued all his sons with a great sense of ambition. A large family, with seven boys, they absorbed the ambition and assimilated the wherewithal to realise it. Their main aspiration, which clouded everything else, was to ride at international level:

> As far as he was concerned, if you were at this game, it was a bloody hard game and you'd have to put a lot into it. If you weren't getting anything back from it, there was no point – do something else.
>
> It's a very complex game and to acquire knowledge of it takes years of suffering on wet, dirty, hard roads. Also, we always heard elders who knew what they were talking about. We soaked up knowledge both ways.

Six of them eventually became international riders. Pat was the oldest and most successful. He won the Tour of Ireland twice, gained much international experience[51] and turned professional with the Viking team in England. The others followed – Kieron, Oliver, Jim, Paul and Daragh.

> It wasn't pumped into you – you just followed suit. I was going to bike races from the time I was a baby. I watched my older brothers racing. When it came to my turn, I didn't ask if I would race and nobody asked me. I had a bike and that was it – it was the natural thing to do – it was my turn to start racing.

The McQuaids first competed in the Rás in 1974, as members of the first ICF team in the event, and Pat and Kieron won two stages each. They had no further involvement until the ICF competed again in 1979 and, from then on, the McQuaids were to be very influential, both as riders and managers. Pat won three stages in all, Kieron won two and Oliver one. Their first cousin, John, had six stage wins, won seven Yellow Jerseys and came third to Paul McCormack in 1988. In all, the extended McQuaid family won a total of thirteen Rás stages in spite of a gap, between 1974 and 1979, during which they could not compete in the Rás. Paul McQuaid won the Rás in 1995.

The McCormack brothers – Alan, John and Paul – came from a similar stable. Their father, Joe (J. J.) McCormack, was from County Offaly but his background was somewhat obscure. Orphaned at an early age, he was reared by a neighbouring family who purchased a bike for him to go to school. That was the beginning of his cycling career. He went to Dublin in the early 1950s, doing various labouring work initially and became a great racer. Originally in the NCA – he was its national grass-track champion – he joined the CRE and represented Ireland many times. He became a central figure in the CRE, and founded the Junior Tour of Ireland. Alan and Paul McCormack were to win a total of ten Rás stages and Paul won two successive Rásanna in 1987 and 1988.

The Kimmages – Paul, Raphael, Kevin and Christopher – had a similar cycling background. Their father, Christy, was an international cyclist who switched allegiance to the NCA in order to ride the Rás in 1963. He won two stages against the dominant Poles, but went back to the CRE the following year, citing discomfort with the political dimension to the NCA. The four Kimmage sons were reared on tales of cycling – 'We were bred into it' – and, even though there was no parental pressure, they 'took to it like ducks to water – it was cycling at breakfast, dinner and tea – nothing else mattered'. Between them – the father, Christy, and sons Kevin and Raphael – they won six Rás stages, with Kevin winning the Rás outright in 1991.[52]

These cycling families contributed greatly to a vibrant cycling fraternity in the 1980s and 1990s, when Irish cycling thrived in the glow of the Kelly–Roche successes. The top riders had a more professional approach than ever, moved with ease in the international scene and a number were to advance to professional careers. They played a major role in the development of the Rás and 1983 may be seen as a milestone in the event's development. That year, Philip Cassidy was the first of this new generation to win it, Dermot Dignam was offered full control of the Rás and a sponsorship deal was agreed – an arrangement that was still providing financial stability and continuity twenty years later.

DIGNAM TAKES OVER

The winning move, 1993: Philip Cassidy on the solo, 20-mile (32km) break into Tuam. Such was his apparent ease at riding away from the race that he called the lead car back and asked them to put some music on its loudspeakers to entertain him.

The Rás was in need of greater funding than that provided by Tirolia in 1981 and 1982 and discussions took place with a marketing executive, Sally Ryan, with a view to possible sponsorship for the event from the National Dairy Council (NDC). Ryan, then working for the advertising company that handled the NDC's account, had worked on the Rás during Bord Fáilte's sponsorship in the mid-1970s. As well as promotion, her functions included the arranging of accommodation on the route and providing race clothing for all the teams. She therefore had a detailed knowledge of the logistical workings of the event.

Ryan developed a proposal for the NDC to sponsor the Rás, beginning in 1983, but made it conditional on Dermot Dignam's return as Race Organiser. She felt the event required his management if it was to achieve the organisational level necessary to justify her client's support. Dignam agreed and the 1983 event was called the 'Dairy Rás Tailteann'. The following year, Ryan brought the FBD insurance company into the race as a co-sponsor with the NDC and it thus became the 'FBD Milk Rás', the title it still had on the event's fiftieth anniversary two decades later. This partnership – resting on the four cornerstones of NDC, FBD, Sally Ryan and Dermot Dignam – was to prove remarkably stable and resulted in one of the longest, continuous sponsorship arrangements in Irish sport.

Dignam made no dramatic changes but gradually and astutely developed the event. In contrast to Joe Christle's style, Dignam kept out of the limelight and was appeasing, conciliatory and cajoling in his approach. He nevertheless followed Christle's example of keeping close control of decision making and strategy, and avoided the complications of trying to run it by committee and consultation. This was possible because, as with all races, the event was run by a club – effectively Dignam's club – now called Cumann Rás Tailteann. Created by an amalgamation of the Gate and Clann Brugha clubs, which had gone into decline and become inactive, Cumann Rás Tailteann concentrated on the organisation and running of the Rás. In the words of one observer, 'Dignam and Christle were complete opposites, but with the same end result'.

In assuming responsibility for the Rás, Dignam envisaged the event becoming a vehicle for reconciliation and unification within Irish cycling. Rather than allowing it to remain as an ex-NCA enclave within the relatively new FIC, Dignam purposely invited helpers and officials from the other two former organisations to become involved in running the event. That inclusive mix, and the resultant close association of individuals for over a week in an amiable atmosphere and with a common purpose, did succeed in helping to break down old stereotypical assumptions. Within a few years, individuals who were once entrenched in diametric camps were working together on the Rás with a sense of friendship, fellowship and camaraderie.

In a rather ironic way, though the Rás developed during this period, its public profile was somewhat diminished by the huge popularity and success of Irish cycling at that time – success brought about by other high-profile events, such as the Nissan Classic and the Kellogg's Series, which tended to overshadow the Rás. They had large budgets and the participation of top Irish and continental professionals including Stephen Roche and Seán Kelly. Although these events were fleeting by comparison with the decades-old Rás, they caught the imagination of the public and the media, and the amateur Rás was somewhat eclipsed by comparison.

There was much interest in the prospects of Paul Kimmage prior to the 1983 Rás. He had created a sensation beforehand in the Tour of Britain when he was leader on the second-last day before a puncture and a fall probably cost him the race. His Irish team-mate, Philip Cassidy, also created a great stir on the final day when he led for much of the stage with a magnificent solo break. They were spoken of as potential successors to Stephen Roche and rode on the Irish team for the Rás, along with Gary Thomson and Davie Gardiner.

Both Kimmage and Cassidy had ridden in the Manx International two days before the Rás and were feeling the effects on the first stage. Kimmage missed the critical move and lost 2 minutes, but Cassidy was luckier, being the last man to join the decisive break. He stormed into the Yellow Jersey on the next day with a fantastic performance on a stage between Killeshandra and Tuam. With an aggressive, forceful style that was to be the hallmark of his career, he broke away from the start with the 1981 winner, Jamie McGahan, who was riding very well and had the support of a strong Scottish team. They were joined by about twenty others after 16 miles (25km), but Cassidy, with his unrelenting pressure, launched yet another attack and went away with Pat McHugh and Martin Drain.

With 20 miles (32km) remaining, the break received word that Paul Kimmage was coming up. Cassidy welcomed this because Paul was 2 minutes down and would be expected to help Cassidy in extending the break and thereby put him into the race lead. However, when Cassidy glanced back, he saw that Kimmage was indeed making his way up, but his younger brother, Raphael, was coming up with him. Raphael was not on the Irish team and was therefore a threat to Cassidy. The Kimmages considered Raphael to be the best rider in the family and, for Paul, loyalty to his brother apparently took precedence over loyalty to his team on this occasion. This was part of the 'behind the scenes friction' in the Irish team that year, but Cassidy's simple response was to take off and his solo ride into Tuam is one of the legendary solo breaks of the Rás. He drove on relentlessly for most of 20 miles (32km), steadily increasing his lead, and was not seen to change down from the massive 53 /12 gear that he was pushing. He appeared at ease, knowing he was riding into the race lead, and was in triumphant mood – at one stage, he sent word up to the lead car to play music on its loudspeakers. He came in 2 minutes 40 seconds ahead of McGahan, with the main chasing group at over 3 minutes behind.

With the burden of the Yellow Jersey after just the second stage, Cassidy was advised to conserve his energies and defend his lead judiciously. Such a strategy ran counter to his naturally combative nature, but the reliability of his team support was also suspect and a conventional defence might not have been prudent. He remained in attacking mode for much of the middle section of the race and had to keep a constant eye on his own team-mates. On the fifth stage, to Blarney, while under threat from McGahan and his Scottish team, Thomson attacked him with 40 miles (64km) to go and gained almost 2 minutes. With little assistance from Kimmage or Gilleran, Cassidy had to recruit help from outside of his team to bring Thomson back.

Cassidy faced further difficulty on the stage to Carrick-on-Suir, when he failed to contain an attack by the Scottish pack. His lead was diminished and left McGahan poised at 1 minute 45 seconds. Cassidy did get help from his team on the next stage, to Wexford, and there was much anticipation of McGahan's challenge in the Wicklow Mountains on the penultimate day. However, it was to be his Irish team-mate, Thomson, who pressed him, with McGahan dropping out of contention in the battle between the two Ireland riders. The stage went over Aughavanagh and Glenmalure, and finished on top of the Wicklow Gap, but Cassidy retained his lead and won his first Rás.

Like most Rás winners, Cassidy showed outstanding ability. There was, however, an extra, somewhat indefinable dimension to his performance. He had exceptional stature, an authoritative presence, best articulated by Bobby Power when he commented on the 1983 Rás: 'Cassidy became the Godfather of the Rás then.'

1984 was an Olympic year and the inevitable speculation about selection for the Olympic team added further interest to the Rás. In spite of the eagerness of the top riders to impress, it was an unfancied rider, Stephen Delaney, who came to the fore. It began with a prologue time trial in the Eamon Ceannt Stadium, where Seán Kelly gave a guest performance. The first four stages were dominated by a variety of riders, including Dermot Gilleran, Paul Tansey, Séamus Downey, Bobby Power, John Shortt and Stephen Delaney. Davie Gardiner, a favourite, had

Philip Cassidy (right) stormed into the Yellow Jersey on the second day of the 1981 Rás. He broke away after the start at Killeshandra with the 1981 winner, Jamie McGahan (left), and Cassidy rode the last 20 miles into Tuam on his own. There was much tension in the Irish team and his team-mate, Gary Thomson (behind), attacked him later in the race.

a bad crash on the second stage and suffered a fractured skull that ended his cycling career. Séamus Downey held the Jersey for four days but lost it to Bobby Power. The decisive break for Delaney occurred on the sixth stage, from Castletownbere to Mallow, when a group of fourteen broke away soon after the start. With Delaney and Shortt doing the lion's share of the work, the break came in almost 9 minutes ahead of the bunch and Delaney – as best-placed rider of the group – went into yellow.

The eighth stage, from Enniscorthy to Gorey, was an unusual 18-mile (29km) team time trial with bonuses of 15, 10 and 5 seconds for each individual member of the fastest three teams. Only the second team time trial in the history of the Rás, it had little relevance to teams with no hope of being in the top three, and riders who did not have full teams remaining just fell in at the back of some other team. Raphael Kimmage, for example, the only survivor in the Irish team, rode with the Nottingham team.[53] It was won by the Dublin team and the result put Paul Tansey into second place, a position he would lose again to John Shortt in the mountains near Carlow. Kimmage dropped to third.

Delaney held his lead until the end, with Shortt coming second and Kimmage third. Though Delaney lacked a strong team, his aggressive approach to the defence of his lead, and the strength and confidence of his riding, left a great impression and an unfulfilled expectation that he would become a formidable force in Irish cycling.

The Soviet team was expected to dominate the 1985 Rás, which began with a prologue time trial on the Hill of Howth, won by Michael Walsh. Seán Kelly and Stephen Roche made guest appearances. The English rider, Chris Lillywhite, won the first stage to Navan, and the Russian, Nikolai Kosiakov, took the race lead.

This was the beginning of the anticipated Russian dominance and it was sealed in the fifth stage, from Athlone to Kilkee, when they took to the front in force from the start and put three men into the first three places on GC.

Stephen Spratt provided the main Irish challenge from then on. On the seventh stage – the same day that three Irishmen were starting the Tour de France – he challenged for third place in the mountains between Caherciveen and Bantry. The Russians had to tactically outmanoeuvre and outnumber him, but he was still only pipped at the line. Spratt gave another remarkable, indeed extraordinary, performance for a first-year senior when he lapped the entire field in the final stage around Parnell Square in Dublin.

The Soviets took all the top awards and the comment of David Peelo – a strong county rider who spent years on the Rás – had a resonance of similar reactions from Rás men of earlier eras – 'You couldn't handle the Russians – it was a matter of trying to hang on to them.' The winner, Nikolai Kosiakov, who had won the Tour of Yugoslavia and ridden the Tour of Spain, was a physical-education teacher, a presumed euphemism for 'professional' when talking about Soviet riders at that time.

Stephen Spratt's display against the Russians was but a foretaste of the type of rider he would become and he achieved the first of his two Rás victories the following year while riding with the Tipperary team.

Cycling in Tipperary was centred on Carrick-on-Suir, one of the great nurseries of Irish cycling. The Carrick Wheelers Cycling Club, commonly referred to as Carrick Wheelers, was founded in 1954 and was affiliated to the NCA. Led by Tommy Sheehan, it developed into a proud club and contributed to a strong Tipperary influence in the Rás. Tom Kiely, Mick Woods and Seán Welsh exemplified riders who contributed to a proud county tradition in the event and who lived up to the expectation that Tipperary riders would be competitive.

In 1968, a prominent member of Carrick Wheelers, Tony Ryan, left the club, formed the Carrick Wheelers Road Club and affiliated to the ICF. There were now two Carrick Wheelers clubs in the town, and it was the ICF club that the young Seán Kelly chanced to join in 1972. He therefore never rode the Rás as he had become a professional rider in France by the time the ICF began participating in the race in 1979. Unlike the situation in Dublin, the divisions in cycling did not affect Tipperary riders during the winter training months and Kelly was one of a group of Carrick riders from both federations that began a tradition of heavy winter training in the south east. A group of riders, including Kelly, Bobby Power, Tony Ryan and Martin Wall, did a regular Saturday 95-mile (152km) route from Carrick, through Clonmel, Dungarvan, Waterford and back to Carrick.

Seán Kelly and Stephen Roche making guest appearances in 1985. Seán Kelly never rode in the Rás because he was a member of the ICF and had gone abroad before the unification of the three cycling bodies in Ireland.

Others joined along the route and this tradition of good winter preparation was an important factor in the development of many formidable Rás riders from that part of the country.

By the mid-1980s, the Tipperary Rás team, based around the Carrick Wheelers, had evolved into one of the best-managed county teams ever in the Rás. Led by Billy Kennedy, a former Rás rider and a discerning manager, organiser and financier,[54] the team operation had become highly developed, with meticulous logistical preparation beginning months in advance of the Rás. There was strong resolve that a Tipperary team, with Carrick at its core, would win the county team prize in the Rás. The club had spent years in fostering and developing riders, and its regime of training and racing was primarily dedicated to this end. This dream was to be eventually fulfilled, surpassed even, in 1986.

While the 1986 team rode under the Tipperary county banner, it was, in essence, a club team, and a strong sense of loyalty to Carrick Wheelers was an important element in its success. The two unrelated Powers, Bobby and Larry, were Carrick men. Bobby, the senior rider in the team, might have won the Rás in 1976 but for a puncture and came second in 1978. He had amassed six stage wins in all by then. Larry Power was a powerful rider and dedicated club man, prepared to sacrifice for the club when the need arose.[55] Vincent Kelly, a brother of Seán, also came from Carrick and was a very strong rider. Stephen Spratt was the undisputed team leader and a rider of immense potential – Seán Kelly is reputed to have commented: 'If only I'd had Spratt's class …' Though a native of

The Rás bunch negotiates a stream on the stage to Dingle, 1986.

Dungarvan in County Waterford, Spratt was very much part of Carrick Wheelers, having ridden with the club since he was an under-age rider. A fifth rider, Andrew Hitchens, was recruited from England to strengthen the team.

The race was somewhat confused and controversial. The Yellow Jersey changed hands five times in the first five stages. Hitchens complained about negative tactics amongst the Irish during the second stage and Gary Thomson, one of the Irish favourites, publicly promised Hitchens that he would have to 'eat those words before the end of the week'. Spratt took the Yellow Jersey on the fourth stage, from Kanturk to Dingle, but lost it to his team-mate, Hitchens. He, in turn, lost it to the eighteen-year-old Laurence Roche, younger brother of Stephen.

Roche, riding with the Young Ireland team, went into the sixth stage with a slim, 2-second lead and an apparent understanding that he would not be attacked by the main Irish team. However, he was left very much on his own and such was the desperation and determination of his defence that it was some time before he regained the use of his speech after his arrival at the stage end in Kilkenny. In spite of his efforts, Spratt regained the Jersey from him.

Mick Kinsella, a twenty-year-old on the Irish team, launched a ferocious attack on Spratt in the mountains the following day. He started 2 minutes 32 seconds down, in tenth place, but scattered the field in Wicklow and came to within 18 seconds of Spratt. He tried once more on the morning of the final day, again in the Wicklow Mountains. Conditions were terrible, with heavy rain and poor visibility on the Wicklow Gap and sixteen riders were involved in a crash on the descent. Kinsella's efforts moved him into second place, but Spratt retained his lead and won the race.

The outcome was a wonderful triumph for the Tipperary team. In addition to Spratt's outright win, they won not only the county team prize, but beat all the national teams to win the overall team prize. They also got three stage wins. The performance was a vindication of years of careful preparation and management, and an illustration of what a county team could achieve with the right combination and in the right circumstances.

17
TWO RACES, TWO WINS

John McQuaid, before he lost the race-leader's jersey in 1988. He was part of the great McQuaid cycling dynasty that won thirteen Rás stages and one overall victory.

Paul McCormack has a unique Rás record. He competed in only two Rásanna and won both, back to back. The first time was 1987 in a Rás that was to be controversial, with the press declaring the Irish team performance to have been 'pathetic' and a 'fiasco'.

McCormack had been racing on the US circuit and had never ridden in the Rás. His reputation suffered in Ireland somewhat when he pulled out of the World Championship race in Colorado the previous year and this contributed to his motivation to return:

> I wanted to see my family, ride in this great race and try and re-establish my name after pulling out of the Worlds [Championships] – people were saying I was just a *crit* [*criterium*] rider – a sunny-day racer.

He would have preferred to have been on the McQuaids' team but it was full and, in the normal manner of late arrivals to the Rás, he was given a choice of county teams with spare places. He chose Longford on a whim – it was near to where his parents had come from – but he soon found the team to be rudimentary. They had no team kit so he rode in a plain cycling jersey. They had no car so he stowed his gear in the truck that transported the marshals' baggage. He was essentially on his own – when he arrived at the end of a wet second stage in Derry, there was no accommodation arranged and a policeman pointed out the direction to the tourist office. Cold and wet, with his bags draped across his bike, he rode to the office, booked accommodation and rode to a bed and breakfast for the night. Nevertheless, what he lacked in support he made up for in temperament and class – Gearóid Costello, a contemporary of his, described him as 'a typical McCormack

Paul McCormack (right) and John McQuaid were good friends and represented two great Irish cycling families. However, the 1988 Rás was to severely test that friendship.

– tough as nails, very dogged and with plenty of talent'. Along with Gerard Irvine from the Irish team, he was snapping at the heels of the Yellow Jersey holder, Philip Cassidy, over the first few stages.

Much of the controversy in that Rás arose from tensions between Cassidy and the Irish team, of which he was not a member. Cassidy had won the second stage into Derry, went into the race lead and held this for four days. McCormack made a strong move on the fifth stage, from Roscommon to Tipperary, and got away in a good break that was over 5 minutes ahead at one stage, making McCormack the clear leader on the road. The break expected him to do the bulk of the riding, but he reserved his effort somewhat, not wanting to show his hand so early. Cassidy and Irvine joined forces and recruited help to bring the break back. However, friction developed between Cassidy and some of the Irish team over comments that Cassidy made about them after the stage. Some of the Irish team were resentful of such public criticism, though Cassidy said he was misunderstood.

On the following stage, to Mallow, McCormack again slipped away with a group of more than twenty riders that contained neither Cassidy nor the leading Irish-team riders. Now in fourth place and 1.5 minutes down, McCormack felt this was the time to strike and drive the break. Meanwhile, behind, the Irish team and Cassidy 'started looking at each other'. There were tensions from the previous day and some of the Irish team felt that Cassidy's strategy was dependent on staying close to Irvine as the Irish team would chase for him. Both sides lost focus and personal animosities took precedence over strategic aims. According to *The Irish Times*, 'tempers flared, there were even occasions when they were going so slowly that some riders had to put a foot to the ground to avoid toppling over'.

McCormack rode into yellow, with the bunch coming in almost 20 minutes behind – a size of gap that had not been seen for many years in the Rás. It was a humiliation for the Irish team and the row continued after the stage with Cassidy being told in anger that his international prospects were over and he would not be on the Irish Olympic team. Cassidy retorted that he would, because he would be the national champion, and he was to be right on both counts.

McCormack was now race leader and eventually had a support car, driven by his father who had come to support him. To some muttering around the Rás, J. J. McCormack, a former CRE/FIC stalwart, was now driving the leading car in the cavalcade, having apparently parachuted into the middle of the first Rás he had made an appearance at. In spite of the lack of an effective team, McCormack defended well to Tramore and, at the end of the stage, his father quizzed him about the degree of help he had had from various individuals during the stage. Paul asked why he was so interested in the performance of these riders and his father then revealed that Karl McCarthy had given him £500 in Mallow to help obtain support for Paul to defend the Jersey.

Karl McCarthy, from Cork, was one of the original high-profile NCA riders to defect to the CRE in the early 1950s. He had become a very successful businessman and was very friendly with J. J. McCormack, often staying in his house in Dublin while on business in the city. He had come from Cork to meet him at the stage end in Mallow. Paul learnt that his father had already parted with £150 before the stage to Tramore. In Paul's view, the recipients had been of no help to him and he asked his father for the use of £200 himself for the vital next stage, in the Wicklow Mountains. McCormack later claimed that he had used none of it and that he did not benefit in any way from McCarthy's money. He did display exceptional class in the mountains and increased his lead further in the following day's time trial up the Devil's Glen.

He got a bad scare in the final *criterium* when, in a lead group with 40 seconds advantage, he fell with just three laps remaining. His father happened to be at the corner where it occurred and he helped him back on his bike in time to join the main bunch. He retained the Jersey, achieving a notable win for the McCormack clan, especially welcome as his brother, Alan, had made such efforts previously, without success, to win both the Rás and the Tour of Ireland.

In spite of his win, McCormack was informed by the National Team Director that he was unlikely to be riding in the World Championships. But there was to be fall-out from the poor performance of the Irish team in the Rás and this changed matters. Cycling standards and expectations were very high in Ireland at the time, with up to eight professional licences being issued by the FIC annually and almost 200 juniors entering the Junior Tour of Ireland. Attempts to change the management of the Irish team were the focus of continued reporting and speculation in the sporting press for weeks after the Rás, and this did eventually come about, with the result that McCormack rode in both the World Championships and the Nissan Classic later in the year.

Following the Nissan Classic, McCormack returned to the US and resumed his life there. The following year, 1988, having received word that there was to be a training camp in Ireland in February in preparation for the Seoul Olympics, he returned home in order to get on the Olympic squad. At the camp, the team manager listed the races on which the selection of the Irish Olympic team would be based. They were all in Europe, giving McCormack no option but to stay at home if he was to have a chance of Olympic selection. He pleaded his case but got no concession. It was a turning point in his life – a decision between the life he had been building in the US – where he had an American fiancée and a cycling

John McQuaid won the third stage, into Clifden, and took the Yellow Jersey. Paul McCormack won the next stage, to Ennis. Here, McCormack, in the stage winner's jersey on stage 5 to Killarney, is trying to get clear of McQuaid (left) who has a 16-second advantage on GC.

contract – or a chance at representing Ireland in the Olympics. He was distraught at the dilemma and resentful of being put in such a position – his brother, John, said that it was the only time he ever saw Paul in tears. He made the decision with the help of his fiancée – she insisted, by phone, that they could get married at any time but he had only one chance to ride in the Olympics. He therefore elected to remain at home – 'We both took an unknown road.'

McCormack was picked for the Irish team for the 1988 Rás, a particularly important edition with Olympic selection still at stake for him and his three team-mates – Cormac McCann, Philip Cassidy and Stephen Spratt. While McCormack had a point to prove the previous year, it was his friend, John McQuaid, who had a bone to pick in 1988, having been omitted from the Olympic panel and the Irish Rás team. From two great cycling families, McCormack and McQuaid were friends, but the pivotal incident of the 1988 race was to test that relationship severely.

McQuaid won the third stage and went into a slender, 16-second lead from McCormack. Ian Chivers and Paul Madden, riding with the Young Ireland team, closed the gap to just 9 seconds by the sixth stage, to Clonakilty. A 12-mile (20km) time trial loomed in Dungarvan two days later and was considered ominous for McQuaid as McCormack was expected to overtake him. However, McQuaid

The decisive move, after the Devil's Glen incident, stage 9, 1988: tremendous pressure as Stephen Spratt, with Paul McCormack behind, drives the break to try and increase the lead on John McQuaid. The third rider is Vladimir Berka from Czechoslovakia.

Below: David Peelo getting attention from Dr Philip Brady after a crash on stage 5, 1988.

Above: John McQuaid (left) has just lost the race lead to his friend, Paul McCormack (right) on the second-last stage into Wicklow. From McQuaid's perspective, McCormack breached an understanding they had. McCormack disagreed.

produced an epic ride to Dungarvan to extend his cushion on what was a long stage of 108 miles (173km). Held in atrocious weather, there were many crashes and eighteen riders abandoned. McQuaid fell twice himself but, at the end of a splendid ride, was 67 seconds ahead of McCormack on GC, facing the crucial time trial the following morning.

McCormack did cut back the margin to just 29 seconds, but the gap was expected to be adequate for McQuaid and he faced the mountains with confidence – he had held the Jersey for seven days, valiantly warding off all attacks, and had the protection of a strong team. 'If I lose now it will really crack me,' he told a reporter. By this point, McCormack and McQuaid had agreed that neither would attack the other in the event of a mishap – McCormack had punctured going into Killarney on the fifth stage and McQuaid had not taken advantage of it.

Following the time trial, there was a respite over the earlier miles of the afternoon stage to Wexford – the last man on GC was allowed up the road to claim the first two primes – and there were no major changes on GC. All changed dramatically, however, in the Wicklow Mountains on the ninth and second-last stage, from Wexford to Wicklow. McCormack claimed that he said to McQuaid on the starting line that he had to 'go for it' that day, thus indicating his intent. These intentions were based on an elaborate plan by the Irish team to take the lead from McQuaid on the Devil's Glen, a short but very steep climb in Wicklow. McCormack's fellow Irish-team member, Philip Cassidy, was to go in an early break. Cassidy was not a noted climber and the intention was that he would get up the Devil's Glen early and then wait for McCormack. Meanwhile, another team-mate, Cormac McCann, was to soften up McQuaid by driving hard to the foot of the climb. A third team-mate, Stephen Spratt, who was a good climber, would go on the climb with McCormack. Then, at the top, they would hopefully have gained a vital gap on McQuaid and would join up with Cassidy for the decisive run in to Wicklow, where they had to make up at least the 29-second deficit to McQuaid.

Cassidy got away in an early break, according to plan. Equally, McCann drove the contenders and their entourages to the foot of the climb, where he pulled over to let McCormack make the critical challenge. Then, as they were beginning the climb, John McQuaid called out that his bike was giving difficulty. He believed that McCormack would not attack, in accordance with what he thought was their agreement. McCormack, however, never looked back and went as hard as he could. McQuaid's bottom bracket was apparently giving trouble and he got off and exchanged bikes with another rider. The vital gap was now opened even before the climb began.

McCormack claimed that he was justified in continuing the attack on a number of accounts. He had an obligation to the Irish team and the move was planned; he had warned McQuaid of his intentions on the starting line; had he not cycled as he did, Andy Hurford, an Englishman riding in the Limerick team – just 49 seconds behind McQuaid – would have gone into the lead. Finally, he contended, McQuaid had overreacted, a point borne out by the fact that his bike was ridden to the finish by another rider without apparent difficulty. Whatever the merits of the various arguments, it was a costly episode for John McQuaid. Noted for being meticulous in all aspects of his bike racing, with the exception of bike-maintenance, he lost 63 seconds on his friend from there to the finish and slipped into third place.

McCormack had won a second, consecutive Rás, the only person apart from Shay O'Hanlon to do so. It had been a particularly tough Rás – only 77 of the 149 starters finished and just one member of a fancied Czech team completed the race. The friendship of McQuaid and McCormack came under considerable strain and they did not speak to each other for some time after the race. However, McQuaid's efforts had not been totally in vain as, along with the four members of the Irish team in the Rás, he represented Ireland in the Seoul Olympics. By that time, he and McCormack were somewhat reconciled. Following the Olympics, Paul McCormack married his fiancée in Dublin and they returned to the US where he resumed his professional career.

Rumours about exchanges of money – McCormack's experience in 1987, for instance – had crept into the Rás during the 1980s. It's thought that the origin of this practice lay in the habits acquired by some of those riders who were spending periods racing abroad around this time. At home, this Continental practice had a touch of sophistication and was seen as modern, clever and a form of semi-professionalism adapted to the Irish circumstances. As well as this, there was a lot of money coming into the sport, with some riders even getting cash to appear in races in Munster. It was probably also related to the fact that certain county teams were being controlled by individual sponsors and, in reality, were the preserve of those sponsors rather than the counties they were meant to represent. This conflict was never fully resolved in the Rás. Some of these sponsors had prestigious teams and were prepared to go beyond normally acceptable practices in the sport. Prize money had also become a factor in cycling – a winner, for example, was expected to share his prize with team-mates who had worked hard for him. This culture of exchanging money was confined, but a minority of riders favoured normal limits being pushed out. Some rule changes helped stamp out the problem – for example, the practice of bringing foreign riders to supplement county teams was banned.

By the late 1980s, the practice of paying riders to work for an individual or team was largely a thing of the past.

The Soviets returned for the 1989 Rás and the most immediate impression was made by the condition of their bikes. Described as 'rust-buckets' and 'gates', their machines were old, with rust on the frames and components that were considered obsolete by the Irish. They were a source of derision for some of the younger riders who assumed that the quality of the Soviets' riding would mirror that of their machines. Older and more knowledgeable riders, who knew about 1970, 1977 and 1985, warily suspended their judgement until racing began.

True to previous form, the Soviets took the race lead on the second stage when Robert Vinovsky went into the Yellow Jersey, but only on points difference from John Tanner of the Great Britain team and Ger Madden of Cork. Tanner took over the Jersey on the third stage, into Tuam, the highlight of which was a solo break by Declan Lonergan that won him the stage in impressive style.

Vinovsky regained the Jersey in the fifth stage and the Soviets were heading all the classifications and occupying the four top places on GC at the end of the next stage, through the Cork and Kerry mountains. They continued to dominate in spite of their clear lack of resources, though they did seem to have an abundance of tubular tyres which they used as barter for goods of all sorts, especially electrical items such as Walkmans.

Vinovsky, the only one of their team to have a decent bike, lost his lead in misfortunate circumstances on the second-last day, when he collided with a police motorbike near Waterford. Although injured and delayed, he regained contact with the front group, got over Mount Leinster and retained his lead. However, an X-ray that evening revealed two broken bones in his foot and he had to withdraw, becoming the only rider to abandon while in yellow since Gene Mangan withdrew on the second stage in 1964.

Dainis Ozolse, a Russian in second place, became race leader for the following morning's time trial on the second-last day, in Carlow. While many riders were now

Dainis Ozolse, the 1989 Rás winner and only member of the Russian team to have a decent bike. He was a former stage winner in the Peace Race and in the amateur Giro d'Italia, and went on to win an Olympic bronze medal.

using low-profile frames, disc wheels and streamlined helmets, the Soviets started the time trial on their old bikes yet still took the first two places – Declan Lonergan deprived them of third. Ozolse, a former stage winner in the Peace Race and in the amateur Giro d'Italia, retained the lead to the end. He went on to win an Olympic bronze medal in 1992.

By 1990, the Rás had grown considerably, both in scale and complexity, under Dermot Dignam's direction. Fields had swelled to around 140 – double the entries of the previous decade – and, with equally increasing numbers of support personnel and race officials, the logistics were causing problems. Chief among these was the cost of accommodation and the difficulty of finding sufficient beds in stage-end towns at the height of the tourist season. Tourist traffic on some of the stages was also a difficulty. Because of a clash with the soccer World Cup, the race was moved to mid-May – the 'official' reason provided was that now it was an event in the UCI international calendar, it had to be moved so as to fit in with the UCI schedule.

The early part of the race was dominated by a French team – CMA Paris. They won the first two stages and held all the jerseys. Declan Lonergan was the best Irishman, in fourth place. Despite their early dominance, the French were not tactically prepared for the Rás and tried to control it in continental fashion, chasing breaks, keeping the bunch together and letting the sprinter pop out at the finish to win the stage. They kept it up for two days before they began to wither under the repeated and sustained assaults of the Irish riders. All the French finished over 12 minutes down on the third stage, into Ennis, won by Kevin Kimmage, while a Belgian, Klaus de Muynck, took over the lead. From then on, the French began losing men from the drain of their misplaced efforts and only one was to finish.

The fourth stage went to Killorglin from Listowel, via the Conor Pass and Ian Chivers of the Irish team was in an early break that tried to gain an advantage before the climb. Declan Lonergan bridged a gap of almost a minute to get across to the leaders and they got over the Conor Pass ahead of the Belgian. After hectic racing from Dingle, Lonergan won into Killorglin and Chivers took over the race lead.

With internationally qualified *commissaires* now presiding over the event, a rigid interpretation and application of the rules was evident. This led to a protest by riders after an incident in Clonmel on the sixth stage. Barry Sutton was first over the line but was later penalised 20 seconds for 'brief pacing' while getting back onto the race after a puncture. The same day, seven others were penalised and one disqualified. The following morning at the starting line, word was put

Anthony Dineen attacking the bunch on stage 5 between Killorglin and Macroom, 1990. Dineen was one of the great riders to emerge from Blarney in the 1980s – he won a stage into Clonakilty in 1988 and his club-mate, Richard O'Gormon, won a stage into Killarney the previous day. These back-to-back wins were the highlight of a thriving cycling scene in Blarney in the 1980s. Inspired by Patsy and Donal Crowley who were legendary in Cork cycling (Donal won two stages in 1982), a thriving under-age structure was developed and bore fruit in the senior ranks from the mid-1980s. Besides O'Gormon and Dineen, other Blarney-based Rás riders from that era included Ger Madden, Brian Osborne, Noel Holmes, Tommy Madden and Brian Lenihan. The drawing of their best riders for Cork county Rás teams, and for Irish teams, was a considerable annoyance to the club at that time.

Above left: Ian Chivers finished fourth behind three Russian riders in 1985, just a year after he won the Junior Tour of Ireland, and was fourth again in 1988. Here, he defends his Yellow Jersey in a time trial in Clonmel in 1990, the year he won.

Above right: Ian Chivers in the decisive break before the Conor Pass, 1990.

around through the bunch to stay put when the lead car moved off, in protest over Sutton's demotion. The protest quickly fizzled out and the race got under way.

Chivers remained in control to the end, despite hints of disharmony in the Irish team. Described in a later Rás programme as 'a chirpy little Belfastman', he had only gained a place on the Irish Rás team when the national champion, Paul Slane, had to drop out. In 1985, a year after his victory in the Junior Tour of Ireland, he had finished fourth behind three Russian riders and was fourth again in 1988. He never won a stage in the Rás but his strength lay in his consistency, suited to stage races.

The 1991 Rás took a southerly route from Dublin with an ascent of the Wicklow Gap on the first day, en route to Enniscorthy. The first prime was near Tallaght, at the edge of Dublin city, and many expected the field to fragment on the very first day. This did not happen and Gethin Butler of the Great Britain team won the stage and went into yellow. Having declared that he had no intention of defending, he sat in the bunch on the second day, to Midleton. A minor incident occurred on the approach to the finish, without anyone realising its significance at the time, when Declan Lonergan had an altercation with another rider at a roundabout. He was seen by a *commissaire* and penalised 30 seconds. Robert Power won the stage and Donal O'Halloran from Waterford, riding with the Tyrone team, took over the Yellow Jersey.

O'Halloran, who had spent three years in France, won the time trial in Midleton the following morning. The afternoon stage, to Limerick, was to be one of those renowned Rás stages: the three leading men on GC – O'Halloran, Stephen Spratt and Robert Power – were left stranded in the bunch as a group of more than thirty riders came in to the finish in Limerick over 5 minutes clear. Declan Lonergan also lost out, while a Dutchman, Jos Wolfkamp, went into yellow.

Gethin Butler reclaimed the race lead on the next stage, to Clifden, and retained the Jersey for four days despite a very determined effort by Kevin Kimmage on the sixth stage, from Clifden to Ballina, when he broke away with a small group early in the day, did most of the work and won the stage.

The following stage, to Letterkenny, was variously described as 'farcical' and 'ridiculous' in the press. Farcical it might have been in a normal stage race, but eccentric stages were thought inevitable in the Rás from time to time and, as long as they did not cause major upsets in GC, were an accepted element of the event. Consequently, the 1991 stage to Letterkenny is fondly recalled more with humour than with the kind of annoyance that was conveyed in the press. Some of the more dominant riders apparently came to a consensus that there had been very hard riding during the previous days and that the stage to Letterkenny would be a

After days of hard racing, Stephen Spratt called a 'piano' on the sixth stage, to Letterkenny, and 50-year-old Seán Lally (right) was sent up the road. Another lowly placed rider, the 36-year-old 'Tosh' (Thomas) Lavery (left) who had taken up riding just the year before and was in his first Rás, was sent with Lally 'to keep him company'. However, the bunch had underestimated the pair and Lally almost sneaked a stage win. Seán Lally rode four consecutive Rásanna in his fifties and is thought to be the oldest Irishman to complete the event.

'handy day'. Stephen Spratt, one of the few riders who could command the necessary authority in the bunch, called a 'piano' and serious racing never really got under way. Benevolence was bestowed on Seán Lally, previously one of Ireland's leading riders but then fifty years of age. He was 'given the nod' and jumped out of the bunch. Another lowly placed rider, 'Tosh' (Thomas) Lavery – a 36-year-old who had taken up riding just the year before and was in his first Rás – was sent with Lally 'to keep him company'.

The bunch were in festive mood – even singing a few songs. Lavery and Lally were riding hard to build up their lead. Some Donegal riders, who were having a hard time to stay in the race and were now in their home county, were then sent away to have their day of glory. But they failed to make progress to the leaders and fell back into the bunch. The lead went to 2 minutes before an English rider, Tim Schools, broke the piano, went after the leaders and soon made contact. Lally, realising that Schools would not be allowed to gain time on the bunch and that his presence would inevitably invite further chasers, made his opinions clear to Schools. Obviously impressed by the persuasiveness of Lally's case and not unmoved by the forceful manner in which it was expressed, Schools turned around on the road and rode back the way he had come and into the shelter of the bunch.

Lavery's and Lally's lead eventually grew to 13 minutes and their ride, though described as 'ridiculous' by the press at the time, quickly grew in Rás lore to become an even greater epic than it actually was. Within a few short years, Rás legend had it that the leading riders, realising the humiliation they would suffer if beaten by a fifty-year-old, organised a furious chase that cruelly pursued Lally and, with

This picture, showing Lally (left) arriving into Letterkenny in the chasing bunch, was published with some newspaper reports, giving the impression that the fifty-year-old almost won the stage.

increasing panic, caught sight of him inside the last kilometre. Even then, Lally was deprived of a glorious stage win only by the uphill incline of the finishing straight in Letterkenny. It's unfortunate that history should spoil such a dramatic Rás story, but the fact is that Schools recruited reinforcements in the bunch and four riders set out on the chase after Sligo. Given the changed circumstance, it was inevitable that the piano would collapse. The two breakaways were eventually caught by a chasing group after surviving on their own for most of 70 miles (112km); 'It was a case of a hill too far,' declared Lally. Lavery fell away on the Barnesmore Gap and the stage might not have achieved such notoriety had Lally not amazingly managed to remain with the leading group for the remaining 30 miles (48km) to finish in thirteenth place, despite having been passed by a number of riders in the final uphill stretch.[56]

Schools came second for his efforts, but the stage caused no major changes. There was further controversy the following day when a leading group of five suddenly came up, from behind, on another group that had been chasing them! The leaders had been led on a wrong route and were brought back into the race behind the chasing group. The race had to be stopped while officials sorted out the confusion.

During the course of the 1991 Rás, it appeared that Kevin Kimmage was well out of contention on a number of occasions. His eventual victory was one of those wins that arose from exceptional grit and determination, and a refusal to accept the apparent inevitability of a situation where all seemed lost.

The next day, Enniskillen to Navan, was decisive and produced outstanding rides from Declan Lonergan and Kevin Kimmage. Lonergan, who showed massive power throughout the event, dropped Butler and Kimmage, the two leading riders, and became leader on the road. Kimmage, who 'didn't believe in defending second place', forced Butler into chasing and then jumped away from him. Clear of Butler, he chased down Lonergan and went into yellow in Navan. After something of a chequered Rás career, one of the Kimmage clan was now in yellow in the Rás.

In 1987, Kevin Kimmage had gone straight into the Irish team for the Rás in his first year as a senior rider. That Irish-team performance was considered a débâcle and Kevin found it a difficult experience in other respects: 'It defied all, it was crazy, like no other race – there was no pattern to it.' Following years of intensive competition, he took a break from cycling over the winter and early spring prior to the 1988 Rás, and entered the race with limited preparation. In his own words, he was 'legless' after two days and rode a time trial wearing a woolly hat and a Walkman. He was eliminated after the stage, supposedly for being outside the time limit, but he suspected it was because of his apparent display of indifference. Humiliated and peeved at being eliminated in the Rás, he 'boycotted' the 1989 event, but came back in 1990 and won a stage into Ennis, an event he regarded as enormously significant for himself and his family.

Now in yellow, he appeared to be within grasp of the biggest prize in the sport in Ireland. But Declan Lonergan, who had won the fourth stage, to Clifden, was in second place and 'desperate' to win the Rás. His efforts brought him three consecutive stage wins in the final days, but he could not bridge the gap to Kimmage. Given Kimmage's final margin of 28 seconds, the 30-second penalty Lonergan received a week earlier in Midleton had possibly cost him the race. On the other hand, while Kimmage's victory can be clearly traced to the eighth stage, to Navan, he saved that Rás with some outstanding displays, away from the front of the race, when it appeared that all was lost. The fourth stage, into Clifden, was one such day, when he found himself not alone missing the break, but also at the back end of a split bunch. Where many riders would have accepted the apparent inevitability of the situation, he rode with exceptional grit and determination, and limited his losses to near 5 minutes. As with so many Rás winners, the race was saved before it was won, out of the limelight and with a strength of character that can make the decisive difference.

Some of that strength could, no doubt, be attributed to his family background, as implied in Kevin's interpretation of the significance of his win: 'It didn't matter that I won – it was the fact that a Kimmage won. It was a massive thing for the family – it made a point.'

18

A COUNTY TEAM

Mark McKay (right) and Bill Moore en route to Carlow, stage 8. McKay is now over 4 minutes up and leader on the road, while Kerry are desperately organising the chase behind.

The central role played by the county teams in the early Rásanna had become less relevant by the 1990s. By then, some of the weaker county teams were having places filled by disparate categories of cyclists – riders who could not get on their own county teams, riders from a county not fielding a team, or foreign-club riders who were seeking a berth on the great Rás. The County Board structure had collapsed throughout much of the country, leaving no administrative framework to select teams in many counties. Some county teams were essentially club teams, flying under a flag of convenience. Others were run by sponsors who could offer superior conditions and better organisation, and could therefore attract better riders from other counties. In short, pride in representing one's county and the prestige derived from wearing the county jersey were no longer the significant factors they had been in the 1950s and 1960s.

Part of the problem lay in the nature of the Rás itself – riders from different clubs who competed against each other regularly were thrown together in teams where there were no pre-defined roles or expectations and where sporting rivalries and jealousies often came to the surface. Each rider wanted to achieve his own best possible result in the Rás and might be reluctant to sacrifice this for the sake of allegiance to the team or to a particular individual within it. A large section of the Rás was, in reality, a mass of individual riders, each with his own goals and aspirations for the event. While this went some way to accounting for the unique nature of the racing, it militated against effective team racing. The professional system, where the team is paid to work for a team leader, is much less complicated.

John Mangan began sponsoring the Kerry Rás team in 1997. He had won the Rás in 1972 and spent a decade racing very successfully in France before returning to his home town, where he established a successful business. The team rode as Kerry Irish Baltic Trading, from Mangan's company name, and he provided significant funds for the team, ensuring good support and conditions. As in many such cases, when the request for sponsorship came in, his goodwill towards the Rás and the county team prevailed over sound commercial judgement.

Following the 1996 Rás, some of those involved with the Kerry team were uneasy about the lack of any significant results and the idea was floated that Andrew Roche might ride with Kerry following his win in the Kingdom Series – a very successful series of races in Kerry every August. Roche had completed a number of Rásanna and had won a stage into Dungarvan in 1992, and it was felt he had the potential to become a Rás leader. Although Roche was from the Isle of Man, his grandparents were from Kerry and he had taken Irish citizenship. He stayed regularly in Kerry and competed in the Kingdom Series. With the now acceptable ambiguity about such matters, the Kerry cycling fraternity would be happy to adopt him as a Kerryman. The approach was made through another Kerry rider, Fionán (Finn) O'Sullivan, as he and Roche had raced for the same professional club in Belgium. On the basis of O'Sullivan's assurances that Roche would be joining a well-managed team, Andrew Roche accepted the offer.

Even with Roche, Kerry Irish Baltic Trading was just an average Rás team. John Blackwell was the team veteran, competing in his eighth Rás. At the age of nineteen, he was one of those promising young riders who left for France and competed well in many amateur continental stage races. When he had returned for the 1989 Rás, he was in super form, having just won a stage race in France. He harboured secret ambitions of winning and expected at least a stage win, but the realities of the Rás came as a shock and he completed only three stages. The Rás, however, had cast its spell on him – he suffered a year-long sense of inadequacy at not having completed the event, but kept coming back.

Though still one of the country's top riders in 1996 and riding at his best at twenty-six years of age, Blackwell had become reconciled to not having that combination of strength, speed and power necessary to win the Rás. However, he had always been a significant player in the event – he had a number of top-ten stage finishes – and still dreamt of that elusive stage win, an event that would be the pinnacle of his career and set him apart in Irish cycling. Every success of a distinguished cycling career would willingly have been swapped for just one Rás stage win. It was also significant that his cycling career had developed in the influential shadows of some of the legendary Kerry riders of the 1950s and 1960s – such as Paddy O'Callaghan and Gene Mangan – men for whom loyalty to the team and county was paramount.

Fionán O'Sullivan also came with considerable pedigree. He wore the Yellow Jersey in the Rás in 1995 and he had raced professionally in Belgium. Feeling that his form was not at its best that year and that a win was highly unlikely, he was satisfied to ride as a *domestique* for Roche. However, he was to be lost to the team in the Kerry mountains when he was eliminated, following a series of mechanical problems.

The two other Kerry riders were Denis O'Shea and John McCarthy. Denis O'Shea had ridden very well the previous year – he was leader on the road at one point and finished tenth overall. He was typical of the county riders in the Rás – unpredictable and courageous, always 'having a go' and capable of a day's performance that might have a significant influence on a stage outcome, or even the final race result. John McCarthy was young and in his first Rás. His mission was just to finish the event and he was not expected to contribute significantly.

Going for the home win. The Dutch rider, Slagter (left), and John Blackwell, in the break heading for Moll's Gap.

All in all, they were a reasonably good group of riders, but the team left for the Rás with no high expectations.

For the Kerry team, it was one of those Rásanna where everything went right from the beginning. One or other of its riders was getting into breaks and Kerry was soon leading the county-team category. After three days, Roche was in the top six, Blackwell in the top ten and O'Shea in the top fifteen. The Kerry car had moved up to a prestigious number six position in the cavalcade and the support team was in the rare position of being able to see some of the race. Things were looking up.

The new team manager, Brian Connaughton, had brought a professional dimension to the squad, a feature that was often absent from county teams. Having won the 1969 Rás, he was now an experienced manager. When Paul McCormack won in 1988, it was as a member of the Irish team managed by Connaughton. McCormack described him as one of the best managers he had ever had: 'He was very level-headed, understood the sport and had a human touch.' Connaughton first met the team in O'Connell Street, at the start of the first stage. The riders realised things were going to be different when he went through their food bags and dumped anything he considered to be junk – most of the contents. He imposed a strict diet and regime, and watched over the riders at dinner, where they were confined to one dessert. The usual Mars Bar and Coca-Cola at stage ends were considered sacrilege. Instead, drinking two litres of water became a ritual. They began to lose weight and John Blackwell woke one night with a hunger pain in his stomach – he bitterly complained that it was bad enough to be getting the knock on the bike but that it was a bit much to be getting it in bed! However, the approach paid off, both physically and psychologically. A positive and professional ambience developed around the team and the riders noticed they were retaining both their physical and mental strengths as the days wore on.

When the race hit home territory in Tralee, following a 106-mile (170km) run from Lisdoonvarna, the team had retained its overall position but was disappointed at having failed to put on the all-important good show for the home crowd. Kerry local radio was interviewing Kerry riders and one, in bravado, remarked that the team was going to attack the race the following day, take the Yellow Jersey and win the stage into Killorglin. The comment, taken as team intention, was broadcast. Close observers of the race also began to see Andrew Roche as a potential winner. Fionán O'Sullivan was rooming with him and was building Roche's confidence. The team manager observed Roche's recuperative powers and recognised him as a likely winner. Pressure mounted.

While driving to the stage start in Killarney next morning, Connaughton threw the team out of the car at Farranfore and made them ride the 10 miles to the start. Having raced 106 miles (170km) the day before and facing the Kerry mountains en route to Killorglin, they were a bit aggrieved, but when Blackwell rode away from the little group on one of the drags, Roche suggested he had the legs to do something on the stage that day.

The race left Killarney for Moll's Gap and Blackwell was gone on his own at 2 miles. A Dutch rider came up to him and they had a 2-minute lead at the first KOH at Ladies' View. They were still clear at Moll's Gap and again at the Gortadown KOH. They were joined by other riders, including Ray Clarke and Micheál Fitzgerald from the Irish team, along with Tommy Evans and the English rider, Mark McKay. When the group was still away at the final KOH, at Coomakista, Blackwell began thinking that this might be his final chance for that elusive stage win.

A home-town stage win is a dream of all competitive cyclists and for Blackwell – as for many Kerry riders – a win in Killorglin was the Holy Grail. Killorglin is the gateway to the Kerry mountains and the key to many Rásanna. The finishing stretch of road, beyond the Laune bridge and up the hill to the finish in the town square, is one of the great theatres of Irish cycling. Blackwell knew every inch of it after fifteen years of racing there, from under-16 through to senior. He had won six races into Killorglin in previous years and had never been beaten. He knew what lines to take in the bends, what position in the road would put him out of sight of pursuers, he knew what gears to use, where to kick, and he knew the exact number of pedal strokes from the bridge to the finishing line. However, he had been driving the lead bunch in the mountains for the entire day and did not have the confidence to beat Fitzgerald in a close sprint. So he planned to take a flyer.

The final act of the stage began with 2 miles to go. Tommy Evans and the Dutchman made early attacks but were chased down. At the 1km sign, Blackwell risked all and took off. He chanced one glance back and saw a significant 10-second gap, but he did not know that Clarke was sacrificing himself behind, burying himself to get Fitzgerald up in his slipstream. Blackwell swung around the final corner, onto the foot of the finishing hill. The crowd saw the green-and-gold Kerry jersey and went wild. Blackwell was convinced that the stage was his and that a lifetime's ambition was about to be fulfilled. But he knew that he did not have the normal strength in his legs that usually swept him up the hill on a 52/15 gearing – he changed down into a 17 sprocket and hit the final 50-metre rise. The loudspeakers were blaring, the spectators were hanging over the barriers and screaming, the chequered flag was waving just in front of him. Then, with 30 metres to go, Fitzgerald swept by to win, followed by McKay to take second place and the Yellow Jersey. Blackwell just saved third position. It was, at once, both the best and worst moment of his cycling career. What he had lost would always haunt him, but he had got his best-ever Rás result – a place on the podium on home territory. And he had increased the team lead.

There was an extra buzz around Killorglin that evening, a feeling that Kerry might really do something. Kerry radio was there again and wise old champions were sought out to give expert opinion. John Mangan, who that week was celebrating the twenty-fifth anniversary of his Rás win, abandoned his business and joined the support team.

The pattern for the team continued on the following stage, to Bandon, when Denis O'Shea got into a break and again consolidated the team's lead. Ciarán Power went into yellow and tried to hold his lead the following day on the road to Tramore. He tore the race apart in a vicious cross-wind, but made a fundamental Rás mistake of letting a group go. It included McKay, along with the Frenchman, Stephane Calvez. Andrew Roche rode aggressively to bridge a minute gap to get to this lead bunch before the finish, when a seemingly small event proved to be a decisive turning point in the race.

The chasing bunch en route to Moll's Gap. Anthony Doyle (left), Gary Adamson (centre), Kieran McMahon (right).

John Blackwell, just metres from a home win, swings around the final bend in Killorglin and hits the bottom of the finishing hill. Though riding with Kerry, he is wearing the shorts of his Kanturk club.

At once, both the best and worst moment of a county rider's Rás career. Micheál Fitzgerald and Mark McKay swept past Blackwell before the line, denying him the coveted Rás stage win. He just saved third place, the best stage result of his career and his only time on the Rás podium.

The run in to the finish had a ferocious descent, followed by a sharp bend and an uphill finish. With his usual managerial thoroughness, Connaughton had warned Roche about the danger of the bend, but McKay came into it too quickly and had to come to a complete stop and take his foot out of the pedal to avoid a crash. The Frenchman won the sprint, but McKay's lost rhythm and momentum cost him about 7 seconds, the Yellow Jersey and probably the Rás. Andrew Roche came seventh and Kerry gained the Yellow Jersey for the first time since Séamus Kennedy had won the Rás in 1978. And they were still leading the county category.

The joy in the Kerry camp was tempered by the knowledge that the Yellow Jersey would be very vulnerable in the next stage – 94-miles (151km) to Carlow – and that various plans and scenarios were being conceived by opposing teams that evening. It was, indeed, to be an epic stage for Kerry. The team went to the front in the morning in order to keep the speed up and prevent attacks, but a strong group got away and McKay slipped into it. John McCarthy, making his

John Mangan, winner of the 1972 Rás and sponsor of the Kerry county team, starts stage 6 in Killorglin, 1997. Mangan was celebrating the twenty-fifth anniversary of his own win, but the county team had been in the doldrums since then. Now, there was a keen sense of anticipation that they could do something in the Rás. John Blackwell, the Kerry rider who came third the previous day, is behind.

first move in the race, went with it. The gap increased to 4 minutes and McKay became the leader on the road. Kerry tried to counter the attack to save the Jersey but could make little impression on its own. Appeals to other teams to help with the chase fell on deaf ears – it was Kerry's dilemma and they would have to do the suffering.

With the Yellow Jersey seemingly lost, Blackwell took the initiative and went back to the team car to get approval for a course of action. He then went up and down the bunch, picking out strong men who were low on GC and who had no stake in the final outcome. He pleaded his case in the ways of amateur bike racing. He knew who to remind of past favours and whom to promise future favours to. He knew which riders would be susceptible to the patriotic appeal to join in a do-or-die effort to deprive the Englishman, McKay. He knew how sheer sporting instinct would react to an opportunity to be a significant actor in the Rás at a

Andy Roche defending his Yellow Jersey on the 'Butts' during the morning time trial of the final day. He held off Mark McKay by 9 seconds, a fragile lead before the final *criterium*.

critical juncture. And whatever other inducements were necessary, he promised them. Eventually, himself and O'Shea got a few others around them at the front and cranked up the chase.

The finish at Carlow was guarded by the Corrabut Gap and Mount Leinster, and the group had to bring Roche to the foot of it with fresh legs and as small a gap as possible to have any hope of catching McKay. They drove on, with Roche sheltering. O'Shea and Blackwell rode superbly, fully realising that their efforts would inevitably lead to them dying on the climb and sacrificing their team and GC positions along with the county team prize.

Roche hit the climbs with reserves in his legs and rode away from the group, along with Gethin Butler and Peter Daly. They, in turn, dropped him on Mount Leinster, leaving him chasing on his own in 'no-man's-land'. The race reached the relatively flat 30-mile (48km) run in to Carlow and a group of random riders came up to Roche. None had an interest in the final destination of the Yellow Jersey but, in typical Rás fashion, each had his own agenda and motivation – the points jersey, team placings, a place in the top ten on GC – all had an interest in driving on. It developed into a cohesive group riding flat out and eventually closed on McKay with just 3 miles to go. Roche was completely drained with the effort and knew he would be dropped again if McKay counter attacked. Deciding on a bluff, he rode up beside McKay and looked at him as nonchalantly as possible. McKay did not attack and a dramatic day's racing had saved the Jersey with a 38-second cushion.

McKay won the mountain time trial on the 'Butts', near Carlow, on the second-last day and reduced Roche's lead to 9 seconds. McKay was an English professional with a good *criterium* pedigree and top experience in the Kellogg's Series. He also had the help of a strong team and could be expected to claw back the 9 seconds in the hot-spot bonus sprints. The outcome would again depend on third parties and Micheál Fitzgerald – one of the riders to have deprived Blackwell of his win in Killorglin – was approached for help.

There was ferocious racing on the *criterium*, and the field was split into pieces. Fitzgerald dominated the hot spots and denied McKay. Clarke, Blackwell and others tried to take the minor placings. McKay got one placing and clawed back 2 seconds. The time gaps swung with the fortunes of the sprints, but when Roche came third in a sprint, he knew he had won the Rás.

Andrew Roche had won a clever Rás. He rode a low-key race, was consistent, conserved his energy in the early stages and did not show his form. He probably benefited from the low profile that being in a lowly county team can sometimes provide. The Kerry team could not have dominated the race, but they allowed the race to come to them and then flogged themselves to the limits of their abilities. It contained all the elements of a classic stage-race win – a good rider, good management and organisation, intelligence, courage, suffering, sacrifice and luck. With the help of resourcefulness, guile and 'friends', a mediocre team had produced a winner.

The celebrations, centred in Killorglin, were reminiscent of the scenes following the famous Kerry victories of the 1950s. While acclaiming and honouring the victor of the Rás, the festivities were primarily fuelled by the accomplishment of the county team. The sporting public perceived the team as *its* team, representing the pride, traditions and sporting aspirations of the county on the roads of Ireland. For the native Kerry riders especially, it was a triumph. They were local boys who had won nothing, but were champions in their own community because they were seen to have performed and sacrificed for the county cause. The Rás had briefly returned to its roots and re-connected with the public in the way intended by its founders. It had created new heroes from county pride and added a new episode to a proud county tradition.

Nevertheless, the manner in which the win was achieved highlighted the weakening of the county team as a force in the Rás. The era in which a county team could control a Rás was now over. The cyclist who might be capable of winning the Rás was restricted by the limited support a county team could provide and, while a good county team might be able to defend a race leader for a day or two, it could never be strong enough to withstand an all-out assault from the national teams. Andrew Roche's 1997 win was a wonderful success for the Kerry team, but it also begged the question as to whether the county-team model was any longer the best structure to serve the Irish rider, or the Rás.

19

THE ITALIAN AFFAIR

Cresting Musheramore, 1993.

The Rás of 1992 was probably the most publicly controversial of the event's history. A blatant violation of the basic principles of sportsmanship left a bitter taste in many mouths and an opinion that the Rás' reputation was tarnished. Others took an opposite view, claiming that, in the harsh world of bike racing, the outcome was a triumph for tough and pragmatic team management.

Three parties were principally involved. Stephen Spratt, winner of the 1986 Rás, was hugely talented but considered temperamental and lacking in the necessary ambition and focus to fully realise his potential. He had been in the Irish team for the 1986 World Championships in Colorado, but his former mentor in Carrick-on-Suir, Billy Kennedy, was involved in pulling him out of the team twenty-four hours before the event, on account of his behaviour. Spratt subsequently moved from Carrick Wheelers. Next was Jim McQuaid, an experienced and successful team manager in the Rás, then in charge of the Dublin Emmelle team for which Spratt now rode. The team was sponsored by Kieron McQuaid who was involved in distributing Emmelle bicycles in Ireland. In short, it was a McQuaid team and generally known as the 'McQuaid outfit'. Thirdly, there was a very strong Italian national team with riders of the calibre of Giuseppe Guerini, Wladimir Belli and Gian-Matteo Fagnini – riders who later progressed to highly successful professional careers.[57]

Bobby Power won the first stage, with Spratt coming second and Guerini fourth. The Italians demonstrated their form on the second stage when three of them made it into the first four places and Guerini went into yellow. However, the Rás factor struck on the third, relatively short 82-mile (132km) stage, from Oughterard to Ennistymon, when the Italians, in wind and rain, were left behind as Philip Cassidy and David Hourigan initiated a decisive move within the first mile. Spratt eventually won the stage, with Colm Bracken taking the Yellow Jersey from Guerini, who slipped into third place, almost a minute down. As with many foreign teams, the Italian manager was irritated by the nature of the racing and complained about what he called the negative tactics of the Irish. He was especially critical of the Irish team's lack of effort in the chase. One newspaper commented on his outburst: 'Welcome to the Rás.'

Yet the Italians adjusted well and, unlike the unsuccessful French in 1990, did not attempt to tactically control the race. They rode somewhat like the Irish, putting riders into breaks and letting the race unfold rather than having the team chase every break. Guerini, in particular, was displaying his power, jumping between bunches and exploiting any chances that arose. Possessed of great bike skills, the Italians were all very strong, both on the flat and in the hills, and were ruthless in jockeying for good positions.

Spratt's form was as good as expected and he decisively took the Yellow Jersey on the fourth stage, into Killorglin, taking a lead of 2 minutes 38 seconds. He defended it well but lost time to Guerini when he punctured on the seventh stage, to Gorey. The next stage, to Naas – the second-last day of the Rás – produced an epic struggle in the Wicklow Mountains. Spratt began with an advantage of 1 minute 39 seconds over Guerini and contained the initial attacks to the foot of Aughavanagh. At that point, Guerini and his team-mate, Belli, began piling on the pressure. Spratt contained them initially but soon yielded to the onslaught and was distanced by 1 minute 18 seconds on Drumgoff. The Italians increased this margin to 2 minutes on the Wicklow Gap and added another 10 seconds at Slieve Corragh, 9 miles (14km) later. Their advantage now gave Guerini a 32-second overall lead on the road.

A furious chase developed, driven by Spratt and other riders – among them Robert Power and Steven Maher from Tipperary – and they reduced the Italians' lead to 1 minute 47 seconds by the finish at Naas. This put Guerini back into the Yellow Jersey by just 8 seconds and, ahead of the final *criterium* in Dún Laoghaire,

Peter Daly (left) and Gian-Matteo Fagnini (right) lead a bunch in 1992. Craig Sweetman (left) and Paul McKenna are in the second row.

1992 was one of the wet Rásanna – Paul Kiernan (right) and David Peelo (left) at the head of the chase. No. 64 (with glasses) is Paul McKenna; to his right are Declan Lonergan and Martin Maguire.

Philip Cassidy (left) and Giuseppe Guerini of Italy getting to know each other on the first stage, 1992.

Spratt conceded defeat, believing the 8-second gap to be insurmountable. Although there were 15 seconds available in bonus sprints, he admitted to the sports journalist, Jim McArdle: 'It's over now. I've not got the speed for the sprinting required in the final stage.'

Another journalist – and former rider – Paul Kimmage, did not even wait for the last stage before announcing the final result in the *Sunday Tribune* the following day. Reporting from Naas at the end of Saturday's penultimate stage, he said: 'The Italians produced an exemplary team display to take stage and overall honours.'

In spite of everyone's assumptions, Spratt's manager, Jim McQuaid, saw things differently and assured Spratt that 'it isn't over yet'. Like most, Kimmage's judgement had been premature as McQuaid planned to play one last card. Kimmage's follow-up article on the Sunday after the Rás gave an overview and judgemental analysis of the final dramatic events at the *criterium* in Dún Laoghaire.

Recruitment started the night before. Most of the riders enjoyed a drink before bed and as they sipped, a member of Spratt's entourage moved amongst them to canvas support. Steven Spratt himself was not involved.

'It was orchestrated,' one told the *Sunday Tribune* this week, several Irish riders were approached before the stage and asked, 'to do whatever it takes'. 'These Italians are all going to turn pro soon, they won't want to go home in bandages' was the line being used.

Some pledged support out of a fondness for Spratt, a popular figure in the *peloton*.

Above left: 'Welcome to the Rás'. The Italian team initially found the tactics disconcerting, with the manager complaining to the press. The Irish riders thrived during the middle part of the race – here, Declan Lonergan wins the fourth stage, into Killorglin, where Stephen Spratt went into yellow.

Above right: Declan Lonergan (left) and Robert Power (in yellow) trying to save the Yellow Jersey on stage 2, 1992. Bobby Power won the first stage but Robert Power got the Yellow Jersey on time bonuses. The Italians attacked in strength on this stage and three of them escaped, along with a Belgian. Lonergan is riding an Allsop bike.

Next day, the intimidation started from the drop of the flag – niggly, petty stuff that soon degenerated to the nasty and dangerous. Guerini's big mistake was letting the Irishman out of his sight. Once Spratt had gone clear his fate was sealed.

Jumping at the opportunity for 'Ireland', they obstructed the Italian at every opportunity, forcing him onto the footpath and swung out of his jersey – as near as they will ever come to holding it.

Where were the 'macho' men the day before in Wicklow when real courage was needed? Unfortunately it is easier to throw your weight around than carry it across a mountain, easier to pull the brakes than pedal.

As the intimidation increased, the most frightening was witnessed by National Team Director, Alasdair MacLennan. He saw the race leader being forced into the gutter, then punched as he tried to prevent himself from falling by leaning on his aggressor.

In a week of inquisition, allegation and denial, those dishing out the penalties must look most closely at themselves. Given that nearly every spectator on the circuit had an idea what was going on, why did it take them so long to react? And why, given the level of abuse that the leader had been subjected to, was that reaction so weak?

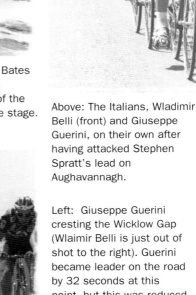

Gian-Matteo Fagnini (right) and a Belgian, Philip de Bates escaped on the second, wet stage from Carrick-on-Shannon to Oughterard and were 'away' for much of the day. They came first and second respectively on the stage.

Above: The Italians, Wladimir Belli (front) and Giuseppe Guerini, on their own after having attacked Stephen Spratt's lead on Aughavannagh.

Left: Giuseppe Guerini cresting the Wicklow Gap (Wlaimir Belli is just out of shot to the right). Guerini became leader on the road by 32 seconds at this point, but this was reduced to 8 by the stage end. The *commissaire* in the car is Jack Watson.

Applying menial penalties on riders who were hours behind was a joke. At the end of the day who was penalised most, the guilty or Guerini?

A thorough investigation is clearly required.

Spratt's manager, Jim McQuaid, was the 'member of Spratt's entourage' referred to by Kimmage. McQuaid, however, disagreed strongly with Kimmage's interpretation. From his perspective as a manager, Guerini's 8-second advantage should not, as was generally assumed, assure him of victory. Spratt was an undoubtedly brilliant and proven *criterium* rider. Guerini was a climber, small and light, and unsuited for the high speed and aggressively close racing that would be involved in the twenty-eight laps of the tight, 1-mile circuit.

In his recruitment of good sprinters and *criterium* riders, McQuaid did say the Italians 'won't want to go home in bandages'. This unfortunate comment, he argued, was taken in isolation and not seen in the context of his strategy which was based on the notion that if the racing became confused and dangerous at the front, the Italians – heading for professional contracts – would not risk career-threatening injury for victory in the lowly Rás. If the right conditions could be legitimately created, the Italians would back off:

> I picked men who could make it tough and dangerous around corners. One of them was … a good galloper but pure awkward – I knew he'd frighten the daylights out of a world-class Italian.

This, in McQuaid's view, was the reality of top-class bike racing and, if the roles had been reversed and Spratt had been leading a race on the continent under similar circumstances, he would receive similar treatment. He agreed, nevertheless, that 'it got a bit over the top', but argued this was outside his influence and attributed it to the pent-up animosity towards the Italians that had been festering all week. While the Irish riders had respected the Italians as supreme bike riders on their way to professional contracts, they also sensed an arrogance on their part and, more importantly, a lack of respect for the Rás and for the Irish as bike riders in their own right. This, according to McQuaid, had also motivated his intervention:

> The Italians were very stand-offish and arrogant. They thought they were at a bog-race. I saw them laughing at the condition of some of the Irish county fellows at the start of the race.

Other riders agreed that the Italians had been aloof and strutted their talents, that they'd helped nobody and hindered many. There had been a number of incidents that led to muttering and a strong build up of resentment and anger. 'They showed disrespect' is a typical comment of Irish riders in that Rás. Paul Kimmage, in his article from the stage end in Naas, had hinted at something unusual, reporting that the Italians' method of taking the lead 'was somewhat questionable', but he did not elaborate. To some extent, this background must explain the degree of venom unleashed upon the Italians in Dún Laoghaire. Such antagonism had never been a feature of any prior Rás, even against far more dominant foreign teams.

Guerini's major tactical mistake was, of course, to have left Spratt out of his sights. Spratt, in fact, had escaped from the main bunch on his own, going across to a small leading group and, as described by Kimmage, the 'intimidation' started immediately. Riders who had not been approached by McQuaid became involved. Some of these say that their contribution was legitimate or, at least, borderline and that the Italians gave as good as they got. Many witnesses disagree, and the worst of the 'action' took place on the back of the course, out of sight of the main body of spectators or *commissaires*. One of those involved gave a vivid description of what happened as McQuaid's plan got out of hand:

> The entire thing degenerated into a rolling brawl – a belting match that continued around the circuit at high speed. It stretched across the road, holding up the race behind. The only pause was for the corners, where hands had to go back on the handlebars to negotiate the bends. It was entirely out of control and driven by temper and passion rather than reason.

Officials could do little to stop the high-speed mêlée as it careered around the course at up to 30 mph. A motorbike *commissaire* was sent back from the leading group to the main bunch but, on such a tight circuit, he could get to the front of the bunch for only very brief periods before having to back off for the safety of the riders.

With Guerini being impeded in the affray, the gap to Spratt's leading group grew to 40 seconds, with Spratt also taking some of the bonus sprints. Some riders tried to restore order in the bunch – Bobby Power, then thirty-seven and somewhat of a father figure, was especially vocal in pleading for fair play for Guerini. But the Yellow Jersey holder never had a chance and eventually became too frustrated to chase.

Bobby Power, considered an 'elder statesman' of the Rás at the age of thirty-seven, was one of the riders who tried to restore order in the bunch. Subsequently, he was very vocal in his criticism of the tactics used against the Italians. It was one of Power's best Rásanna – he won the first stage and held the points jersey for a number of stages.

The leading group approached the finishing line with Spratt unaware of what had happened in the rear. In a typical display of showmanship, he dropped back from the group and rode alone across the line with both hands raised in celebration of his second Rás victory. Guerini arrived 24 seconds behind. When the bonus sprints were calculated, Spratt had won by 22 seconds.

The fall-out was far reaching. The Italian ambassador, who was on the podium, took the microphone in an attempt to protest but was hurriedly ushered away. As tempers cooled and heart rates slowed, the implications of their actions dawned on some of the riders involved. There was no jubilation and little celebration of Spratt's win. The furious Italian manager lodged an objection, calling for the stage result to be nullified. When his appeal was rejected, Guerini declined to take his place on the podium as second-placed rider.

Top: In a typical display of showmanship, Stephen Spratt dropped back from the group and rode alone across the line with both hands raised in celebration for his second Rás victory. It was unfortunate that his win was tainted by the unsavoury deeds of others, a victory that he might have achieved anyway against a world-class Italian team.

Bottom: John Blackwell (left), one of the Irish riders penalised for their role in the 'Italian Affair', remained tight-lipped after the *criterium* in Dún Laoghaire. He later agreed that a legitimate strategy had got out of hand but claimed that he 'got the first belt' following his role in one of the bonus sprints. The ultimate cause of the strong reaction against the Italians, he said, was the apparent 'contempt' they had shown to Irish riders during the week – 'we weren't proud of it, but it had to be done'. Jason Meredith is the rider on the right.

Dignam announced that he would be inviting the Italians back, but no Italian ever again rode in the Rás. Though action was taken against six riders, some considered the penalties to be derisory and meaningless.[58] However, while most agreed that the Italians were impeded by a confused mass of dangerous riding, there was difficulty in identifying specific rule infringements by individual riders as they passed *commissaires* at high speed. Guerini was critical of the *commissaires'* lack of strong action – 'I asked a *commissaire* [afterwards] what he was going to do but he said he saw nothing – that was impossible.'

Press reaction was strong. An *Irish Times* headline, for example, cried 'Rás discredited'. For many with a close affinity with the event, this disgracing of the Rás caused much offence and sadness. Over a decade later, the 'Italian affair' still invokes a strong sense of shame and outrage amongst many. Along with what most considered to be basic bad sportsmanship and a breach of fundamental principles of fair play, a threshold had been crossed in the pursuit of sporting victory that brought the Rás into a sporting realm they did not want it to be a part of. This reflects a wider difference of opinion regarding sport – the balance, on one hand, between the value of victory, no matter what the pragmatic means of its attainment or, on the other hand, the nature of the individual's sporting endeavour in pursuit of success. The latter consideration had traditionally been held in high esteem in the Rás, but the 'Italian affair' possibly reflected the far reaches on the spectrum of sporting value. Yet, for some, Jim McQuaid's status as manager was greatly enhanced by the way in which victory was snatched from almost certain defeat.

To some extent, Stephen Spratt also suffered, despite having won the Rás. One of the leading riders of his generation, he had performed brilliantly with only the support of a small team and was lying just 8 seconds adrift of a rider who was about to become a world-class professional and had the support of a team of élite, world-class riders. Spratt was not implicated in the unsavoury events of the final day and his reputation was intact. He had maintained his focus and taken his chance. The irony is that his victory, which might have been achieved anyway, was tainted by the deeds of others.

With the passing of the years and the advancement of his career, curiosity is the only residual sentiment in Giuseppe Guerini's mind: 'Nothing like that ever happened to me again – I don't know why they did it – I would just like to meet those men and ask, "Why?"'

The escalating costs of drug tests under the UCI's protocol led to the withdrawal of the Rás from the UCI calendar in 1993. It would have cost approximately £15,000, a sum not available.

David Hourigan and Robert Power were dominating domestic racing, and were seen as strong contenders for that year's event. The English professional and twice world pursuit champion, Tony Doyle, was also a favourite. Yet, all the pretenders were to be sensationally upstaged by a nineteen-year-old in his first year as a senior rider.

Mark McKay, riding with a Liverpool team, led for the first two stages but, on the third day, from Dungloe in Donegal, a strong wind split the field early and, after just 16 miles (25km), the race was split into six separate groups spread over 4 minutes. Three members of the Irish team were in the front group – David Hourigan, Paddy Callaly and Eamon Byrne. McKay finished 6 minutes down and Hourigan went into yellow. The roads had been taking their toll on the Irish team's bikes – Robert Power's forks broke on this stage, while Eamon Byrne had broken a pair the previous day – and the team had to send to Dublin for spare forks.

On the fourth day, from Sligo to Nenagh, Byrne moved into second place at just 12 seconds. On the next stage, from Nenagh to Listowel, a break of eleven riders, including Byrne, got away in the ring road around Limerick. Byrne rode into yellow while Hourigan was left in the bunch. Hourigan expressed relief at being rid of the burdensome Yellow Jersey, saying he would bide his time before recovering it, but he never did, and Byrne defended it to the end.

David Hayes trying to ride to the stage end at Boyle without a saddle, 1994.

Nineteen-year-old Eamon Byrne (front) had all the appearances of being a phenomenal rider following his Rás performance, but he suffered health problems the following year and never again reached the heights of 1993. He is followed by Paddy Callaly (right) and John Tanner (left). Tanner was a prolific British performer in the Rás, winning three stages and two Yellow Jerseys.

Eamon Byrne, only drafted into the Irish team when another rider pulled out, had all the appearances of a phenomenal rider in the making but suffered health problems the following year, and never again reached the heights of 1993.

'You will be the greatest Irish rider never to win the Rás', the Irish Team Director, Alasdair MacLennan, was saying to Declan Lonergan prior to the 1994 Rás. Lonergan, a top-class rider, had won a stage in his debut Rás in 1988 when he was just nineteen. He came third overall in 1990 and second in 1991, a race that he might have won had he not been penalised 30 seconds following a tiff with another rider. He had amassed nine stage wins altogether by 1994, including four in 1991, three of which were consecutive.

Lonergan, however, carried a bitter memory of the 1992 Rás when MacLennan had informed him, in a car at the side of a street, that he was not selected for the Irish Olympic team. Lonergan was 'devastated', both by the message and by its timing and mode of delivery. He had been declared the 'Champion of Champions' by the cycling federation the previous year, but conceded that, in Olympic year, 'There was so much politics, pressure and strain', and he had not been riding as well. Undoubtedly one of the country's leading riders over the previous years, he was now denied Olympic participation. Wholly disillusioned with the Irish scene, he 'fled the country' for the US and it was thought that he would never race in Ireland again.

During the following year – 1993 – Lonergan's and MacLennan's paths were to cross again at the prestigious Commonwealth Bank Classic in Australia. Lonergan was on a composite international team, managed by MacLennan, and he won three stages, two of which were in sprints against the newly-crowned world amateur champion, Jan Ullrich. He also won the points jersey. It was a fantastic performance and had the dual effect of giving Lonergan the confidence that he could win the Rás while leaving MacLennan in no doubt of his true potential. Though relations with MacLennan remained strained, Lonergan agreed to return for the 1994 Rás.

In spite of his undoubted talent, MacLennan feared that Lonergan might be another of what he referred to as 'Munster-heads'. Cycling was thriving in Munster then, but MacLennan had seen a succession of great Munster cyclists fail to win the Rás because it meant so much to them – generating pressures that distorted their normal good judgement when it came to the Rás. Lonergan's reflective comments seem to support this: 'For the Irish riders, the Rás is just the biggest race there is – they are in a completely different mind set in it.' Also, Lonergan was a big rider, the type susceptible to one 'bad day' in a stage race, perhaps by losing a minute or two in a mountain stage.

David Hourigan won the first stage of the event, from Dublin to Drogheda, but a subsequent drug test proved positive and the stage was awarded to Paul Slane. While a Belgian rider tested positive in a later Rás, these were the only positive drug tests in the history of the event and there is no evidence of a drug culture ever having existed in the Rás.

Although Tommy Evans held the Jersey for two stages, a Dutch team was dominant in the early stages and came to the fore in a hectic third stage, from Boyle to Westport, with Danny Stam taking yellow. Racing remained very tight and, by the time they got as far as Kerry in the fifth stage, the top thirteen riders were within 1 minute of each other, with England, Holland and America filling the top five places. Declan Lonergan was best of the Irish in sixth place, at 28 seconds.

The climbs of Ballaghisheen and Coomaneaspaigh on the sixth stage failed to produce the expected gaps on the road to Caherciveen, where Englishmen moved into the top two places, Lee Davis wearing yellow. For the third time in the race, Lonergan was beaten into second at stage ends. Davis' team-mate, Steve Farrell, took over the lead on the seventh stage, to Macroom, but only a few seconds separated the top riders, making for a dramatic and tension-filled final two days.

The eighth stage, to Carrick-on-Suir, was the longest of the race at 114 miles (182km), and Lonergan began just 3 seconds behind Farrell. A break containing the earlier Dutch leader, Stam, went over 2 minutes clear and he seemed to have the race in the bag. However, the break was chased down and the stage concluded with a sprint amongst the top men. After viewing film of the finish, the judges concluded that Lonergan had gained the 3-second deficit on Farrell. The English

Steve Farrell of Great Britain in yellow (left) with a 3-second advantage over Declan Lonergan (right) on a circuit of Macroom on stage 7. Lonergan had come second on three earlier stages and was to gain the 3 seconds next day. He took the Jersey on points and went into the final stages on equal time with Farrell. The outcome was to be decided on the final circuit in Swords. Lonergan punctured before entering Swords but Farrell chose not to attack him. Lonergan gained 3 seconds on the final circuit and took the narrowest Rás victory ever. Lonergan and Ben McKenna were the only riders to get first, second and third places in the Rás.

Philip Cassidy (right) in a typical attacking move out of Dingle on stage 4, 1995. Cassidy is urging Paddy Callaly on. Cassidy was in the Yellow Jersey and defying conventional wisdom with such aggressive tactics. He was to lose the lead to his team-mate, Paul McQuaid, two days later.

team objected, claiming that a loose dog had caused a dangerous obstruction, but the result stood, with Lonergan and Farrell going into the final stage on equal time – Lonergan wore the Yellow Jersey on points difference.

The final, 68-mile (109km) stage went from Naas to Swords, with laps of a finishing circuit that included now-vital bonus sprints. There was further drama when Lonergan punctured just before the final circuit. Farrell chose not to attack the Yellow Jersey while in difficulty and Lonergan was quickly back on with the help of his team. On the final laps, he won second and third placings in the bonus sprints and thereby won the Rás by just 3 seconds, the smallest-ever winning margin.

It was the only Rás in which he rode that Lonergan did not win a stage, but this probably reflected his maturity as a rider, with his eye on the bigger prize. After two previous near misses at Rás victory, Lonergan was 'ecstatic' and declared himself to be 'numb with happiness and relief'. He left Ireland three days later to pursue a professional opportunity in America.

1995 is remembered by riders as 'a real bad, wet Rás' – one of those events where continuous days of rain, wind and mud-soaked spray can bring untold misery to riders. For the second year in a row, a strong challenge was expected from a British pro-am team, with Chris Lillywhite, one of Britain's top professionals, expected to make an impact.

After two days, however, the Irish team occupied four of the top five places with Micheál Fitzgerald in the Yellow Jersey. This passed to Finn O'Sullivan on the third day and, following two wheel changes on the Conor Pass while en route to Dingle on the fourth day, he lost it to Irish-team member, Philip Cassidy. Cassidy, in great form, continued his policy of attacking the race while in yellow and, on a miserably cold and wet fifth stage, with strong cross winds, he retained the lead into Clonakilty. In spite of his apparent dominance, many felt that Cassidy's normal attacking tactic was not prudent while in the lead and with the support of the Irish team.

The sixth stage, to Clonmel, was decisive. Cassidy was heavily marked and a promising break escaped. Cassidy's Irish team-mate, Paul McQuaid, was sent to mark it. The gap grew – some thought that Cassidy had gambled on the foreign riders chasing McQuaid because he may have over extended himself during the previous days. This did not happen and, in the meantime, McQuaid was gaining time at the back of the break.

With his team-mate up the road with the break and gaining time, Cassidy was now in a classic dilemma – he had the Yellow Jersey on his back but his team-mate was becoming race leader on the road. Should Cassidy chase to protect his lead,

should he try to slow the bunch to protect his team-mate's lead, or should he send instructions for his team-mate to come back and help in the chase?

McQuaid received instructions to ride for himself and went into the Yellow Jersey at the stage end in Clonakilty. He was a strong rider, a good climber and defended well. On the second-last day, he survived a strong attack from Wexford through the mountains to Newbridge.

Paul McQuaid, from Ireland's greatest cycling dynasty, won the Rás in 1995, twenty years after his brother, Pat, won the Tour of Ireland. In all, the extended McQuaid family won a total of thirteen Rás stages in spite of a gap, from 1974–79, during which they could not compete because of the divisions in Irish cycling.

Tommy Evans (right) leading his Derry team-mate, David McCann (left) over the line on stage 4 into Castlebar, 1996. The nature of the finish gave rise to speculation that there was an agreement between both riders. Evans, however, also went on to win the race, in which the Derry team excelled.

With the assistance of team-mate, Mark Kane, he minimised his loss well on the Wicklow Gap and descended brilliantly. At the end of the final stage in Swords, he was exactly 1 minute ahead of Dave Williams from Liverpool. Twenty years after the eldest of the McQuaid brothers, Pat, first won the Tour of Ireland, it was significant that another member of the McQuaid clan had now won the Rás.

Another notable outcome of the 1995 Rás was that it was the third consecutive year that an Irish-team member had won under the direction of Alasdair MacLennan, with none of the winners taking a single stage.

MacLennan chose four French-based riders for the 1996 team – Micheál Fitzgerald, Peter Daly, Mark Hutton and Leslie McKay – but it was the Derry team-mates, Tommy Evans and David McCann, who produced the main story of that year's Rás.

The first big shake up occurred on the fourth stage, from Nenagh to Castlebar, and the decisive move occurred within a few miles of the start, involving David McCann, Denis O'Shea, Finn O'Sullivan and some foreign riders. A few miles later, they were joined by four others, including Tommy Evans and an eighteen-year-old German, Marcus Lemm. The gap exceeded 4 minutes at Loughrea and there was a reluctance on the part of the Irish team to commit itself to chasing alone.

With about 30 miles (48km) remaining, a chasing group finally broke away, first with over twenty riders, then reduced by half. Three of the Irish team were in it, but these again got little help in chasing and the leading group stayed clear. Over the final miles, the Derry team-mates, Evans and McCann, jumped clear and came to the line on their own. McCann did not seriously contest the sprint, enabling Evans to realise his first Rás stage win which he declared was the fulfilment and culmination of six years of training. The German, Lemm, went into yellow, but the real talking point amongst the riders was whether there was an understanding between Evans and McCann as regards the final spoils of the race.

The young Lemm retained the Jersey for three days but, in the mountains between Buncrana and Donegal on the seventh day, he succumbed to the pressure and finished over 15 minutes down. Evans made his move and went into the race lead, while McCann finished second on GC, 1 minute 48 seconds behind his Derry team-mate.

The final two days became a battle between these two for the final honour, leading to further speculation, this time suggesting that if there had been a deal between the two, there now appeared to be no compromise. On the second-last day, from Donegal to Newry, McCann became leader on the road and there was a frantic chase by Evans into Newry to try and retain his lead. He arrived 1 minute 23 seconds behind McCann, enough to retain the Jersey by 25 seconds.

McCann attacked him again in the final circuit in Swords, gaining 10 seconds at one stage, and Evans had to go to the front to reel him in so as to ensure victory.

It was a marvellous performance by a Derry team that, along with first and second overall individual prizes, also won the team prize and three stages. Along with Evans and McCann, the other members were Paul Giles, Barry Monaghan and Denis Easton. One of the main talking points about that Rás remains the Evans-versus-McCann showdown – 'David could definitely have won the race that year – he had the legs – but Tommy went away on one of those savage breaks.'

Another of the main talking points was the somewhat questionable arrangement between the Derry team and a number of other riders, including the third-placed rider, Ben Luckwell from England. He had entered as an individual and won the third stage, to Nenagh, but the following day, he was fined the equivalent of his winnings – £100 – for collusion with the Derry team. The next morning, he was interviewed by *commissaires* and officials, fined a further £200, penalised 20 seconds and given a final warning. The offence of collusion is so difficult to prove, yet the *commissaires'* penalties were emphatic, suggesting that there was more to the victorious Derry 'team' than that which appeared in the programme.

20
BLASTING AWAY

Philip Cassidy 'blasting away'. Cassidy was one of the riders who continued the traditional Rás style of racing into the modern era.

avid O'Loughlin was one of the most aggressive riders in the early stages of the 1998 Rás but got scant reward for his efforts, as the early spoils were divided among foreign riders. The Irish team was having little success and much criticism. Temperatures soared to the high twenties and the third stage included three climbs in a spectacular circuit of Achill Island.

Tommy Evans, also riding with the Irish team, answered the critics with victory in the mountainous fifth stage, from Listowel to Castletownbere. He was now menacingly poised, just 12 seconds behind Sigvard Kukk, the Estonian race leader, while Ciarán Power was third at 57 seconds. Paul Griffin took the sixth stage, to Mallow, without any overall change.

Power had endured many difficulties up to that point – his front forks broke and he suffered one crash – yet he nevertheless made a move on the seventh stage, from Mallow to New Ross. David Hourigan instigated an early break and was joined by Power, along with Stephane Rifflet, a Frenchman, and Richard Hobby of England. Hobby could not maintain the pace as the gap to the main field grew to over 4 minutes, making Power the leader on the road.

The three-man break drove on, but a strong wind worked against them and their lead was gradually whittled down. By Waterford, they were a mere 30 seconds ahead but continued to battle on. Approaching the stage end in New Ross, Micheál Fitzgerald jumped across to take the stage, but Power's group held their slim advantage. For almost 80 miles (128km) of effort, Power had gained just 40 seconds, bringing him to within 17 seconds of Kukk. Evans was still second at 12 seconds.

Given the immense effort involved in that ride, there were doubts about Power's ability to recover and mount a challenge in the penultimate stage, in the mountains to Ballymore Eustace. Paul Griffin escaped in an early break, posed a threat, but was pinned back. After 65 miles (104km) – beyond Rathdrum – a group of twenty-seven formed at the front. Along with Evans, Kukk was stranded in a trailing group, with a deficit of 3 minutes at one point, again making Power the clear leader on the road. On the Drumgoff climb, three Irish-team riders went to the front – Brian Kenneally, Karl Donnelly and Power. Jeff Wright, from England, then challenged and the power of his effort reduced the bunch to six. Paul Griffin suffered two punctures and lost contact, but the Irish-team riders stayed in charge over the Wicklow Gap and maintained Power's advantage.

In the meantime, Evans managed to evade Kukk, organised a chase and set off in pursuit of Power's group. At Slieve Corragh, with 5 miles (8km) remaining, Wright launched a stage winning attack and finished with a 6-second lead over the remainder of the leading group, which included Power, who now went into

Micheál Fitzgerald's fifth Rás stage win, in O'Connell Street in 1998. Riding with the Usher-sponsored Dublin team, Fitzgerald 'blew up' on the fifth stage and decided to abandon. However, his manager refused to take him into the car, threw him a jacket and said he'd see him at the finish. He also instructed other team cars not to pick him up. Fitzgerald survived and went on to win the next day into New Ross, as well as this final stage in Dublin.

Ciarán Power (right) and his Irish team-mate, Tommy Evans, crossing the line in Dublin together to come first and second respectively in the 1998 Rás. Starting the second-last stage the previous day, Evans was second on GC, ahead of Power, but Power got into the decisive break and became 'leader on the road'. Evans chased, but Power retained the lead. Power praised Evans's effort in the final *criterium*.

A high-speed pile-up during the bunch sprint for second place at Sligo, 1999.
All continued the next day.

the lead. Evans' chase brought him to within 56 seconds of Power, putting him into second place overall.

The final circuit was held around O'Connell Street, where Tommy Evans was particularly vigilant in keeping the pace high for Power and thwarting any threatening escape attempts from the bunch. Micheál Fitzgerald won the sprint, getting his second stage win of that Rás, the sixth of his career. The Irish team had secured the first two places, with 22-year-old Ciarán Power winning his first Rás, the threshold of a blossoming career.

The new, British-based, Linda McCartney professional trade team injected some extra interest and glamour into the 1999 event and were expected to make a big impact. True to expectations, Ben Brooks – one of their number – won the Yellow Jersey on the first day. Although only eighth over the finishing line, Brooks took the Jersey through 10 seconds of bonus sprints achieved during the stage. This placed him 5 seconds ahead of Eugene Moriarty of the Irish team, with Stephen O'Sullivan another second behind.

Brooks' team-mate, Jon Clay, took over the Jersey on the second stage, with Brian Kenneally 2 seconds behind on GC. This led to speculation that Kenneally's day may eventually have come in the Rás. A great Carrick rider, Kenneally was one of those much-fancied Rás contenders for whom nothing seemed to go right, with their Rás careers turning out to be a sequence of frustrated potential.

The Dutch team took the first three places on the following stage, to Killaloe, without any overall changes at the top, and the fourth stage – 88 relatively flat miles (141km) to Ballinrobe – was expected to produce little change.

The ever-enthusiastic Philip Cassidy, along with Paul Helion, broke from the very start, and they were joined by two others initially and then by six more at 10 miles (16km). Clay was left in the main bunch, probably marking Kenneally, who was probably happy there in the expectation that the McCartney team would lead

the chase. While those behind eventually did organise a pursuit, a leading group stayed away and David McCann took what was to be the only Irish stage win of that Rás. Erki Putsep from Estonia went into the race lead, while Philip Cassidy, riding with the Irish team, moved into second place at 68 seconds.

The race was now developing a pattern of some familiarity: a powerful foreign team – Linda McCartney in this case – was dominating early but soon began to wilt under the collective pressures that the Rás can bring to bear. The McCartneys lost their grip on the race and gradually began to lose men.

Putsep had a difficult time defending his Jersey on the fifth stage, to Sligo, with a variety of riders, including Kenneally and Mark Lovatt, leading threatening breaks. The bunch did stay together as expected, but this resulted in a spectacular mass crash just short of the finishing line. Colm Bracken touched a barrier while trying to break through, and both he and his bike rebounded into the path of the bunch and brought down five other riders. The photo-finish camera recorded Bracken's bike crossing the line, but without its rider, while some of the riders who were placed actually slid over the line. Pádraig Marrey and Denis Easton finished up under the judges' platform.

The Irish team attacked from the start of the mountainous, 89-mile (142km) stage to Killybegs, attempting to propel Philip Cassidy into yellow, still in second place at 68 seconds. Eugene and Patrick Moriarty, Ray Clarke and Cassidy drove the race and, when a bunch of over twenty regrouped after the Glengesh Pass,

The crash in Sligo, as photographed by the finish camera.

20 miles (32km) from the finish, the Yellow Jersey was a minute behind, leaving Cassidy just 8 seconds adrift of the lead. They drove towards the finish but, with 10 miles (16km) remaining , Eugene Moriarty punctured, the break lost vital power and Cassidy failed to take the Jersey, given a deficit of 18 seconds. Irrepressible as ever, Cassidy threatened 'I'll be blasting away again tomorrow and making it difficult for everyone'.

In his inimitable style, blast away he did, from the very start of the seventh stage to Cootehill. He broke clear with Mark Lovatt and an Estonian rider, Raido Kodanipork. Three others joined them, including Kenneally, and they were over two minutes up when they crossed the border at Pettigo. Another group of six joined later, while others dropped away. Approaching the finish, a group of four broke clear – Cassidy, Alges Massikmets from Estonia, along with Richard Hobby and Jeff Wright from England. The Estonian, who had been 'sitting in', won the first of two consecutive stages. Cassidy, who had been driving the break all day, went into yellow with a lead of 2 minutes and 11 seconds. He declared it to have been 'just like a training spin'.

Cassidy became quite ill overnight with gastrointestinal trouble, but his team did not allow this news to leak out. Having slept little and probably dehydrated, he set out for Drogheda with his main competitors having no inkling of his vulnerability. He was never lacking in help, retained his lead and took his second Rás win the following day in the Dublin *criterium*, with over 2 minutes to spare on Dermot Finnegan.

Then aged thirty-seven, Cassidy had amassed two Rás wins and two stage wins over a nineteen-year period. Notwithstanding his other distinguished achievements over a long career, this result, taken in isolation, could hardly have elevated him to the illustrious ranks of all-time Rás 'greats'. Yet, when fellow riders – normally unsentimental people – refer to this still-competing contemporary as a 'legend', it is clear one is dealing with a phenomenon who has made a very deep impact and whose status in the Rás cannot be gauged by a result-count alone.

Ultimately, the stature of any rider can only be fully determined by the opinion of his peers – those whose impressions were formed while embroiled in the heat of the front-line action. Paul McCormack, who triumphed successively in his only two Rásanna, said that the real source of his satisfaction was 'to leave the race knowing that everybody else realised that you were a factor in it'. Cassidy was always a factor in the Rás because, again quoting Paul McCormack, 'he races the races'. In other words, he always produced honest, competitive effort, with every day likely to be a battling day. This, along with his ability to push the threshold of suffering beyond that which most of those around him could endure, and to have the steely will to do so consistently, left a lasting impression on everybody, whether those efforts were successful or not.

By 1999, Cassidy had changed much from the happy-go-lucky cyclist who began his winning ways twenty years before. As a youth, he was a competitive swimmer but was convinced to try cycling by his friends and, motivated by their many trophies, lined up at the start of an under-age race in Dunboyne in 1976. An official, whom he later learned to be Brian Connaughton, saw that he was a beginner and decided to give him and another boy a handicap. Cassidy won and the attractive trophy he received convinced him to change his allegiance from swimming to cycling. At this time, Cassidy had a casual approach to the sport and that first victory was to be his only one for three years. Even when the Rás passed his house the following year, he did not bother to go to the side of the road and watched it instead through his living-room window. Neither was he an outstanding junior: 'During the summer I had to work with my father during the week, and I didn't have time to train. I used to turn up on Sunday for the races and just go for it.' He nevertheless won the NCA National Junior Championship.

He rode his first Rás in 1980, his first year as a senior and, in his own words, was 'all over the place'. He attacked from the line on the second stage, to Strabane, stayed away in a break for over an hour, was caught and got spat out the back. He finished so late that even the judges' platform was gone. Unperturbed, he finished fifth into Gorey five days later. 'I was a bit brainless at the time – it came from an impatience and wanting to have a rattle. I had no patience to sit around and wait, or no real understanding of tactics – I'd be gone from the drop of the flag.'

Cassidy had obvious raw, robust strength at this early stage – illustrated in 1981 when he became seriously ill with glandular fever during the Easter period. He spent three weeks in hospital and had to receive intravenous cortisone while in intensive care. Yet, defying advice, he lined out for the Rás a few weeks later and finished second behind Brendan Madden on the fifth stage to Dungarvan.

His career began to flourish and he produced some outstanding international performances. But, in the view of some observers, his potential was not realised in these early years. He had a rather haphazard approach to training, with form coming mainly from racing, and he remained tactically immature for some time:

> I had little savvy in the early years ... some would say that I was pretty thick really as a kid in the '80s. There wasn't strong team management at that time ... Brian Connaughton was a big help – he would try to talk some sense into me but more often than not I'd forget his advice once the action started.

Part of the group that eventually gathered around Philip Cassidy on the stage to Cootehill. It was the decisive break of the Rás. (left–right) Jeff Wright, Amr El Nady, Mark Lovatt, Philip Cassidy, Alges Maasikmets, Raido Kodanipork.

Numerous great cyclists of his era came from cycling 'stables' – the McQuaids, the McCormacks and Kimmages, for example – whereas Cassidy lacked that background immersion in cycling which induces both the knowledge and attitude to facilitate maximum performance. While he spent time in France, the full-time cyclist's 'treadmill' did not appeal to him and he found it difficult to discipline himself adequately. He had no sense of himself as a cyclist in essence – rather, he was Philip Cassidy who did some cycling.

His attitude changed gradually. There was always, of course, the 'Meath factor' and, while he was not born into the tradition of Meath cycling, his pride in being a Meathman influenced his riding: 'I was always proud of my heritage and to be a Meath person – representing Meath that time was as important as representing my country.' He gradually began to develop what he called 'tunnel vision', and Brian Connaughton became a significant influence, ensuring structure and balance in his preparation. As with Connaughton's own career, this wasn't so much a high-tech, formulaic approach, but based on that element of common sense which seeks to achieve an optimum training input while allowing for an equilibrium between cycling and the other aspects of one's life. This might involve a reduction in training time, but with a more focused, targeted purpose. This became one of the hallmarks of Cassidy's later career – his dedication and success in racing, and ability to make an impact, whilst maintaining work and family commitments. Cassidy's 'new' training formula led to much speculation, especially as he was apparently not a slave to the accepted canons of training. For example, he seemed happy to enjoy a few drinks at night-time during stage races, without any apparent adverse effects on his performance.

Cassidy came to be a figure of stature and authority in the Rás bunch. Bobby Power, commenting on Cassidy's 1983 Rás win, said 'Cassidy became the Godfather of the Rás then' – a reference to that rare and potent combination of presence, stature, authority and respect that can make an individual a leader in the *peloton*. Though an elusive and non-quantifiable quality, some elements can be clearly identified to account for Cassidy becoming a true *patron* of the race. As Cassidy evolved as a rider, his style changed little. Some regard his style of endlessly 'blasting away' as somewhat primitive and misguided – some even claimed it cost him the 1995 Rás. Yet more was achieved than lost through this style and there is little doubt that he left his mark as one of the most influential riders in the Rás over the two decades prior to his second win in 1999.

This is one of the features of the 'greats' – to be a creator, to 'make' the race and not merely to be opportunistic or reactive to the creative efforts of others – 'Cassidy is a man who can make things happen.' While his unrestrained, all-or-nothing style appears straightforward, it was not deployed mindlessly and Cassidy's racing intelligence is frequently commented on – 'His knowledge of the race is one of the best assets he has going for him … tactically he is very good.' Equally, the comments of riders project Cassidy's great stature and authority in the bunch, with telling references to his 'presence': 'He has a great presence – he puts a fear into riders – he fears them to work.'

Respect for Cassidy also arises from his loyalty to team-mates and his willingness to sacrifice for others. Very few possess both that will and ability to ride oneself, for others, literally to a standstill, but this is what he did while trying to get Eugene Moriarty into yellow in the Kerry and Cork mountains in 2001 –

'He was in bits when we caught up to him,' recalled one of the main bunch which swept past him when his effort finally collapsed. He always had that ability to drive himself to extraordinary limits – so extreme were his efforts in winning a stage into Derry in 1987 that he remembered little of the final uphill section into the Diamond.

Like many of the great Rás riders, Cassidy's ability seemed to endure and his influence to persist. The combination of these qualities – style, intelligence, sacrifice, longevity and authority – made him a natural leader, the animator of many decisive moves. One of the enduring images of Cassidy is as the leader in the break, erect, chest out, looking around with one hand off the bars, thinking and calculating – the dominant wolf surveying the territory and heading the pack.

These traits, of course, worked in Cassidy's favour in terms of the inter-personal dynamics of the Rás, especially in later years. He often found willing helpers. His climbing, for example, though good, was not outstanding. One of the leading riders, commenting on Cassidy's 1999 Rás win, said of him: 'He was suffering on the climbs but he always had the numbers around him – he always had people to ride with him to help him get back up.'

Cassidy could hardly have survived such a long period at the forefront of the Rás without provoking some degree of controversy. In the 1992 Rás, he was one of those penalised for being implicated in the unsavoury treatment of the Italian rider, Giuseppe Guerini, and this, in the view of some, was an unfortunate blot on an otherwise distinguished career. Cassidy, however, disputed the interpretation of his involvement and claimed that he was, in fact, attempting to get more order in the bunch so that the support for Spratt would be more organised.

Probably the most telling statement about Cassidy, from one of his peers, was that 'Cassidy is a Rás rider'. Perhaps this means that Cassidy shares some of those essential qualities of the Rás – a unique style with a certain abandon and passion for racing – but it would be more accurate to say that Cassidy and the Rás complemented each other: the Rás was the great stage for Cassidy's abiding performances and he, in turn, was the leading modern representative of a style of riding that gave the Rás some of its colour and uniqueness.

In spite of his age, Cassidy's second win in 1999 was not to be the last of his memorable contributions to the Rás.

Philip Cassidy was a strong favourite for a third Rás win in 2000, but lost much time on the first day after a group of seventeen riders gained over 4 minutes on the first stage, to Longford. Another large breakaway was allowed to escape on the second stage – to Newport – leaving many of the pre-race favourites over 7 minutes down. The stage belonged to Brian Kenneally who, after five previous frustrating

Rásanna, had nothing to show for his considerable talent. But when his day did eventually come in the Rás, it was a courageous and memorable one – he broke clear on the first-category Windy Gap and did a 25-mile (40km) solo ride to the finish. Three riders were now on the same time on top of GC – Mark Lovatt from England, who won the Jersey on points, Stephen O'Sullivan and Kristoffer Ingeby from Sweden.

Even more damage was inflicted on the contenders on the third stage, to Oughterard. A relatively short and flat 75-mile (120km) stage, there was expected to be little decisive racing, given the 120-mile (192km) marathon to Listowel the following day. Contrary to expectations, there was ferocious racing over the length of the stage, leading, in the words of the sports writer, Shane Stokes, to the sight 'of a long, straining main bunch in single file, desperately struggling to remain in touch'. Lovatt retained his lead but more damage was inflicted on the top of the GC.

Nobody had any doubt that an attempt was going to be launched to get a stage win for Eugene Moriarty into his native Listowel, but the 120-mile (192km) length of the stage caused some trepidation. A group of thirty riders went clear early, but many of the leading riders adopted a cautious approach, remaining in the bunch in the hope that the length of the stage would wear down the break. It was a costly decision for many, including the leading three riders – Lovatt, Patrick Moriarty and Stephen O'Sullivan. In front, Tommy Evans, Eugene Moriarty and Philip Cassidy rode ferociously hard, first to drive the break and then to contain riders who were lunging from its front as they approached Listowel. Moriarty failed to land the dream home win, finishing fifth, but moved into third position on GC behind the Italian-based David O'Loughlin, who took over the Yellow Jersey.

The 106 miles (170km) and five climbs on the road to Kenmare the following day did not produce the expected shake up, but the sixth stage – to Mitchelstown – saw an upheaval, with the four top riders losing out on the steep Musheramore climb. Here, the strong UK riders came to the fore and, from there to Mitchelstown, four of them effectively did a team time trial to the finish – Mark Lovatt, Wayne Randle, John Tanner and Julian Winn. This effort put Winn, who was with a Welsh team, back into yellow.

The young and gutsy O'Loughlin launched a determined attack to retake the Jersey at the beginning of the next stage, to Enniscorthy, driving a group of eleven clear and becoming leader on the road at Carrick-on-Suir. Two English teams, Surrey and Pro-Vision, combined in the chase and preserved the lead for Winn. The Irish had received a dose of their own tribal medicine amidst mutterings of deals being done between the three UK teams.

O'Loughlin again mounted a number of assaults in the Wicklow Mountains the next day, and received tremendous help from David McCann. The effort was in vain, with the British riders keeping tight control. Tommy Evans and Eugene Moriarty salvaged something when they were placed first and second in a bunch finish on the final *criterium* stage, but Julian Winn from Wales won the millennium Rás.

Dick Barry at the start of the 1958 Rás. His bike and equipment were typical of those in the early Rásanna.

There is, of course, no such thing as an average Rás man – one who might personify the typical rider in the event over a fifty-year period. Yet some comparisons and contrasts can be drawn to illustrate both similarities and changes during that time. Dick Barry was a Cork rider who rode in four Rásanna, from 1957–60. He could be classified as an average Rás rider of his day and, as a subject, can help to make comparisons with modern Rás riders.

Equipment is one sphere that illustrates a distinct difference between a modern rider and his counterpart in the mid-1950s. While the bicycle has changed little in its essential layout, and though riders in the 1950s and 1960s, by and large, used the best equipment available then, a modern racing cyclist would consider the gear used in the early Rásanna to be primitive in the extreme.

Long before hardshell helmets were compulsory, Barry wore the soft peaked cap that was still common amongst professional riders. A net-type helmet, made of leather, was sometimes worn on the track and a few riders wore these in road races. They called them track helmets and, while they might protect the scalp from abrasions in a crash, they offered no resistance to impact.

His jersey was woollen, knitted locally in one of the many small hosiery industries of the day. Hot and irritating to the skin in fine weather, the wool became sodden, heavy and cold in the wet. Its open weave trapped the wind – when leading racers began to use silk in the 1970s, gains of up to two minutes in a 25-mile time trial were claimed due to the reduction in wind resistance. With the pockets at the back, Barry's jersey had a modern appearance in the mid-1950s – many still had pockets in the front as well, a residue of the continental style where huge quantities of food had to be carried on very long stages. Riders still carried large amounts of food on longer stages of the early Rásanna and it was not uncommon to see their jerseys almost rub the back tyre when dragged down by the load of food, especially when a wet jersey stretched.

The shorts were also woollen. They lost their shape after a few washes and flapped in the wind. They had a soft insert, or 'shammy' – a 'chamois'– originally a piece of pliable, soft leather made from the skin of the chamois, a goat-like European antelope. The shammy lost its natural oils in the wash, making it brittle and hard if not treated carefully. It soaked water and became soggy in wet conditions.

With poor shorts, indifferent hygiene and leather saddles, 'saddle-corns' were a constant problem and there were many home remedies. Friar's balsam, mixed with methylated spirits, was a popular concoction and would be applied before and after a ride. Most riders would suffer from some degree of saddle soreness after a stage race.

Riders had to be self-sufficient as regards food, drink and puncture repair in the early Rásanna. At a time of long stages, it is now thought that they ate too much inappropriate food and drank too little too late – Dennis O'Connor of Dublin is well loaded with food as he sets out to defend his Yellow Jersey over 125 miles (200km) in the Cork and Kerry mountains, 1955. Note the bell on his bike.

The majority of riders would have just one pair of shorts and one jersey and, in the houses of the 1950s – lacking washing machines or dryers – washing gear between stages was not always possible.

The shoes, made of leather, were heavy, with flexible soles. They were ridden with bare soles when new, until the pedal left its imprint, and this provided the mark for an attachment that would grip the pedal. Dick Barry considered himself lucky to have a pair of proprietary aluminium shoe plates that his local cobbler tacked to the sole. Most of his friends just got the cobbler to tack two strips of hard leather in line with the marks. The shoe was attached to the pedal by a toe clip and leather strap. The strap would be tightened in the lead up to a sprint and had to be opened by hand before a rider could release his foot from the pedal.

Dick Barry (in white cap) with the Cork team at the start of his first Rás in 1957; (left–right) Gerry Rea, Willie O'Brien (manager), Pat Hickey (no. 30), Tom Scanlon, Dick Barry and Don Noonan. Note the spare tubular across Noonan's shoulders, as well as the drinking straws and pump. Tom Scanlon is wearing the type of cravat worn by some riders in the early Rásanna. The manager, 'Big' Willie O'Brien, won two consecutive stages in the first eight-day Rás in 1954.

Barry's machine was purchased second-hand from Harding's bike shop in Cork, one of only a handful in the country to cater for the racing cyclist. A new machine of its type would then have cost between £15 and £20. His was a Rutland bike, made by the Hercules Bicycle Company in Dublin and marketed by the Rutland bike shop in Dublin. The frame was made from steel tubing, lugged and brazed. By modern standards, it had a long wheel base of around 42 inches (107cm) and gentle angles of 72°, producing a comfortable ride and predictable handling, but not very stiff for forceful riding or climbing.

Steel wheel rims were still common, but aluminium was becoming popular. Though lacking a quick-release mechanism, the large wing nuts could be opened with a kick or a blow of a stone. Tyres and tubes were most commonly used, even though 'tubulars' were known to be faster and could take higher pressure than the 60 pounds a tube could then sustain. Tubulars, however, were expensive – in the early 1950s, the cost of a leading tubular, the Dunlop road racing no. 2 tubular for example, was £5. 2s. 6d., more than an average week's wage. Most riders opted for the slower tyres and tubes, some of them quite wide and heavy.

With race fields often widely scattered and riders left unsupported, competitors had to be self-sufficient. A few still carried a spare tubular or tube wrapped across their shoulders in the early Rásanna, but most had them strapped to the rear of the saddle with a spare toe-strap. Everybody carried a pump – Barry, in accordance with the fashion of the time, carried his on the front of the down tube. A quick tube change could be completed in around 2 minutes. Barry's bike had Weinmann side-pull brakes, very ineffective in the wet, at least until friction dried both rim and brake-block to some degree.

Some of Barry's friends still rode fixed-wheel bikes, but all Rás riders had gears. Shortly before winning the first Rás, Colm Christle had ridden the 100-mile Tour Revenge on a fixed-wheel bike with 83.9-inch gear (50 x 16 sprockets approx.), but rode a bike with gears in the first Rás. He described gears then as an 'unreliable novelty'. Two gear systems were commonly available by the mid-1950s, Simplex and Benelux. Dick Barry's bike carried the Benelux type – the Simplex was not available in Cork, so Barry rode to Dublin with a friend, Tommy Scannell, in order to buy a Simplex in the Rutland bike shop. The front changer was operated by a lever above the crank and the rider had to lean down to switch the chain between the 46- and 48-tooth front rings that were then commonly used. The five rear sprockets – 14, 16, 18, 20 and 23, were operated by a lever on the down tube. Neither was indexed and the chain had to be centred on the sprocket by feel and instinct. The ten speeds gave a much narrower range than the twenty available today, and the closely spaced front rings were commonly used for getting intermediate gears. The 27-inch (690mm) wheels, used with tyres and tubes, were slightly smaller than the modern 700mm wheels and produced marginally lower gearing.

Barry's bike had an aluminum and plastic bottle, one on the handlebar and the other on the seat tube. This set up reflected a change in fashion that saw bottles moving from the handlebars to the seat tube. Some bottles had long straws extending from the lids and riders could lean forward and drink from the bottle still in place on the handlebars. Barry's bottles had provision for this but did not carry the straws.

The Brooks' leather saddle was most popular, and Barry's was a Brooks' Shallow Sprinters' Saddle, normally used for track racing. Leather saddles had to be broken-in.

Initially very uncomfortable, they gradually adopted the profile of the rider's anatomy but became distorted when wet. Some riders would then wrap them in newspaper and tie them with a toe-strap in a bid to recover the shape. The more diligent regularly treated them with Neatsfoot leather-oil, which was available for horse harnesses.

The saddle was normally positioned at the same height as the handlebars, or slightly higher. Along with the extended wheel base and shallow frame geometry, this produced quite a different riding position to the one in use fifty years later and was similar to a modern, soft touring set up.

Barry's Rutland weighed about 25 pounds (11.3kg), almost twice as heavy as the 13.4 pounds (6.8kg) minimum weight set by the UCI in 2000. When he bought it, he would have expected it to last perhaps ten years. Riders like Barry usually had nothing extra – no extra bike, wheels, shorts or jerseys; just one of everything, apart from a tube or tyre.

The bikes and clothing used in the fiftieth Rás of 2002 represented the dramatic technological evolution of fifty years. Hardshell helmets are compulsory and most riders will change them every year or two, mainly to keep abreast of changing fashion and developments in ventilation. Sunglasses change from year to year, again largely depending on style. Clothing, manufactured from a variety of synthetic fabrics, is light, hugging the rider's profile and providing minimal wind resistance. It does not absorb moisture and quickly whisks away sweat and rain.

Frames, in most cases changed every year or two, are made of lightweight materials, such as aluminium, carbon fibre or titanium. Frame angles have steepened, normally to 73°. With this frame geometry, shorter wheel base and stiffer materials, the modern bike is much more responsive – producing giddier handling – and is better suited to climbing and sprinting. It also produces a harsher ride, with more of the shocks and bumps of the road being transmitted to the rider than was the case with the bikes of Dick Barry's era. Riders are much more conscious of aerodynamics and set the saddle as high as possible. The overall effect is for the rider to sit much higher than the handlebars, in a shortened position.

With steeper and shorter frame geometry, more gears and a higher saddle position, riding styles have changed somewhat. In the early Rásanna, riders spent much more time on the 'drops' – the bottom part of the handlebars, while the modern rider will spend more time on the 'hoods' – the tops of the brakes. By and large, the modern rider will use higher gears, with less of a 'pedalling' and more of a 'pushing' style.

Gear levers are integrated with the brakes, giving fingertip access to twenty gears. Wheels are stronger, lighter and the fewer spokes offer less wind resistance. They are fitted with narrower tyres, holding more than twice the pressure of Barry's time and offering much more resistance to puncture. Shoes are firmly attached to pedals with clip-on attachments. Most riders will have some form of tachometer that gives various digital read outs, such as speed, average speed and highest speed. Some riders will have a heart-rate monitor, providing a read out of their current heart rates. A few will have yet a further read out of their power output, in watts, measured from a device in the crank. In the more sophisticated teams, this data is stored during the stage, downloaded to a computer and then analysed. In the case of some of the larger foreign teams of recent years, this information is e-mailed to a coach at the team's headquarters overnight, where the results are analysed before being sent back to the team prior to the following stage. This provides the team manager with a clearer idea of the physiological state of each of his riders – something to be considered when making decisions during the stage or before instructing his riders on strategy by radio.

This ever-developing, high-tech scenario is far removed from the conditions of the 1950s and threatens to take away much of that element of the race that depends on riders' good judgement and intuition – their ability to 'read' the race.

For the average rider in the fiftieth Rás, the bike was purely a racing machine, upgraded regularly, tended with great care and becoming obsolete within a few years. Most likely, a second bike will be used for training on wet, dirty winter roads. In Barry's time, the same bike was often relied upon for daily commuting, and riding long distances was commonplace. Barry and his friends often stayed in youth hostels and a typical weekend might include a journey to Killarney or Thurles to see a football or hurling match. They would ride to most of the races around Cork and Kerry, and even further afield. In 1961, for example, four of them rode to the Tour of Ulster. They left Cork on a Wednesday, overnighted in Portlaoise and Dundalk, and arrived in Belfast on the Friday. Over the next three days, they raced to Derry, Monaghan and back to Belfast on the Monday. They then left, retracing their route, to return to work in Cork the following Thursday.

Significant changes have also come about in food – riders in Barry's time had no scientific knowledge of the dietary demands of long stages. By modern standards, their diet was woefully inadequate. In the various houses they stayed in, they would eat 'whatever we could get'. They had never heard of pasta. Breakfast might be a fry or simple bread and butter with, perhaps, a boiled egg. Food during stages was equally inadequate. Fruit, for example, was popular.

Riders had their own preferences for drinks – glucose and tea were common, and Barry mixed honey with his drink. By modern standards, they ate too much food of little suitability and drank too little. Money was always scarce in the 1950s and 1960s, and some riders have vivid memories of being hungry during the Rás – in 1963, for example, in Ballyjamesduff, Gabriel Howard recalls getting a 'pass-out' for the Rás dance and selling it in order to buy a sandwich. By contrast, every rider in the modern Rás will have a keen awareness of dietary requirements. Food and drink, especially during stages, is appropriate and concentrated, much of it specially manufactured for cyclists' purposes.

Many modern riders will also be much better prepared than their earlier counterparts. Dick Barry gave a summary of his training in the 1950s:

> Starting in the spring, we used to train two nights a week – Tuesday and Thursday nights. We would meet at the monument in the Grand Parade. There was about ten or twenty of us together, and we would go down to Castlemartyr and back. That would have been about 40 miles. Saturday we would go to Mallow and back – about 40 miles. We could do up to 80 or 100 miles on a Sunday. That would be early season. Then the County Board would have races on Wednesday nights. They would also have time trials – 10s, 15s, 25s. There were festival races as well. The road racing calendar was small down in Cork and I would go hostelling at the weekend instead of going to sports [grass-track racing]. I would often go away on the Saturday and come back on the Sunday …

By contrast, Brendan Doherty from Belfast outlined the training that one of the better-prepared riders would have undertaken for a Rás in modern times:

> I would ride from October to Christmas, hard, on the mountain bike. Starting on Boxing Day, I would get ten days in a row on the road, 3 hours a day. Starting on 1 January, a group of riders would meet every Saturday and Sunday – it's dead easy to train with them – 4 or 5-hour runs by the time you get into February. Two nights a week in the gym from mid-January and two nights a week on the road from mid-February. In the latter years, I would spend two weeks in Majorca in March and then I started riding the Tour of Majorca in April – that sets you up for it …

The sophistication of Doherty's team's organisation also contrasts with what was often a haphazard set up in the 1950s, with little money, little experience and little knowledge. Getting a vehicle or a few spare wheels was a difficulty for many county teams of those early years. Most, for example, would not have had a spare bike.

Entering the twenty-first century, many of the teams had become highly refined. The Ulster team, for example – run by Frank Campbell – had reached a high degree of sophistication for a non-national team. When the riders finish the stage, they are met by the equivalent of the professional *soigneur* who provides a towel to clean their faces, a warm top and directs them to their accommodation. There is no confusion when they arrive – their names are on the doors of their rooms and their bags in place. After a shower, tea and sandwiches are ready. Then it's back to bed for a rest and the round of massages begins. Meanwhile, bikes are serviced, bottles sterilised and refilled. The riders have nothing to do but race, eat and rest. This is one of the great attractions of the Rás for many Irish riders – the opportunity to devote themselves exclusively and professionally to bike racing for just one week of the year.

Despite its apparent backwardness when compared to the modern setting, the Rás scene in the 1950s – when Barry's team knelt down together to say the Rosary each night – should not be viewed as a dull and colourless picture. On the contrary, the Rás men of the 1950s were exceptional in their day and might be regarded as a lot more adventurous, often venturing into the unknown – there was always a great sense of fun and camaraderie. And like many Rás riders up to more recent times, Barry enjoyed at least one good night out during the Rás.

Dick Barry had experiences similar to a succession of riders down through the years. Like many, he found the event to be a learning process – 'It takes a couple of years to get it right.' During this process, he identified his own strengths and limitations, and adapted his riding accordingly. Most crucially, he learned that while he could be competitive for three days, it was a matter of survival thereafter. As with many of the rank-and-file riders down through the years, Barry found it to be not so much a race against the opposition as his own, private quest – 'It was a personal challenge to me.'

Barry was fourth on the second stage of the 1957 Rás, but had to withdraw following a crash on the sprint into Clonakilty. With no Cork team entering in 1958, he rode as an individual. This time, he was determined to finish and rode cautiously – he was even able to stop going through Cork to say hello to his parents at the roadside. His arrangements were uncomplicated:

I got the train to Dublin the morning of the race. I rode the race and as soon as the final stage ended in the Phoenix Park, I got my bag, rode down to the station and changed my clothes in the toilet – I had to be back for work in the morning. That was it.

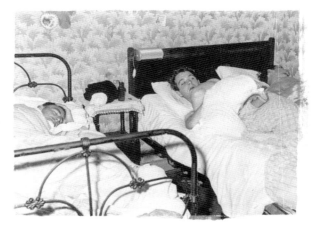

Conditions were often rough and ready for riders in the early decades of the Rás, even for visiting foreign teams, as illustrated by members of the Exiles team sharing beds (1962) and members of the Polish team (Janzy and Linde) sharing muddy bath water (1963).

He returned with a Cork team in 1959. As happened often in the Rás, though an ordinary rider without any hope of featuring high in the final results, he played his role in influencing Rás history. Ben McKenna was leading on the sixth stage that year, with Ronnie Williams hot on his heels. McKenna fell near Fermoy and Williams attacked him. When McKenna remounted, quite gashed, Barry went to his assistance, along with Gerry Keogh. There was no single reason for this – he was feeling good, the Yellow Jersey holder was hurt, he knew Gerry Keogh well – but he rode hard with McKenna and Keogh in pursuit of Williams. When the GC results were calculated, McKenna had retained his lead by just 1 second. With a minute bonus for the race leader at each stage, Barry's work helped gain the equivalent of 61 seconds and secured McKenna's eventual victory.

The modern rider has clear advantages in terms of equipment, food, conditions and support, and most will also be better prepared. The fact that the modern Rás is almost 25 per cent shorter than its 1950s equivalent makes these contrasts even more pronounced. Many of the earlier riders also comment on how 'clued-in' modern Rás riders are by comparison, apparently possessing a much keener tactical awareness.

In spite of the obvious differences, the one unalterable truth running through the history of the Rás is that the bike has to be pedalled and the race has to be raced. The motivation to finish has remained just as strong and this contributes much to the hardship experienced by the average rider. The degree of that difficulty, the personal, hidden journey that each individual has to undergo, is difficult to comprehend for the non competitor. The sheer hardship is compounded by that dread of not finishing. Eugene Murtagh, following the 2002 Rás, articulated it as follows:

> In a normal race, you might pull out if you get dropped or if you're having a bad day. You can't do that in the Rás, even though every stage will be harder than the hardest race you will normally ride during the year – but you have to ride eight of them in a row.

Another rider, commenting on the 2001 Rás, said: 'It's a frightening thing to see a hundred riders in a line.' Only a rider could appreciate the full meaning of this observation or comprehend the cumulative desperation, suffering and fright that exists in such a 'line' in the Rás. The following extract, from the work of the sports writer, Shane Stokes, provides an insightful glimpse of a moment in the race. When it is considered that such a moment is replicated many times over eight days, it may provide some insight into this hidden Rás experience for the average rider:

> Imagine it. You are two-thirds of the way down a snaking line, a wriggling arrow of riders which hugs the sheltered side of the road. Eyes fixed on the spinning wheel in front, a spray of filthy water channelling up onto your face, into your eyes, into your gaping, oxygen-hungry mouth. The water obscures your vision but still you persist, remaining desperately in the sanctuary of the slip-stream. Just an inch or two from being exposed to the cruel wind which would rip your screaming legs apart. Just an inch or two from tipping that shimmering rubber strip in front of you and plunging out of control to the ground.

Concentrate. Concentrate on holding your place. Concentrate on avoiding the lethal hazards on the road surface which suddenly appear in front of you. A distant, disembodied voice up ahead roars 'Hole – left', and you swing outwards, narrowly missing the crater which would send you smashing into the ditch. Behind you, you hear a thud, a curse and the hiss of air which jets from a tubular, ripped asunder by the same hole. Poor bastard. Forget him. Concentrate.

You grip the bars, hunched low over the bike. A sore back, aching shoulders and burning chest eat into your resolve, dwarfed only by the torture taking place in your lower limbs. Ease back, they plead. Sit up. You ignore the protestations. Concentrate. Seeking to distract the mind, you focus on the digital displays before you. One tracks the exertion of your heart, the transmitter strapped to your chest relaying the signal to the monitor and telling you that the straining pump is working overtime at 180 beats per minute. Beside it, a record of that other crucial parameter, which confirms what your legs are going through. Thirty-two miles an hour. Thirty-two point five. Thirty-three. The speed climbs as some insatiable sadist forges off the front. You curse. You spit. You hang on for grim death.

Then the gaps appear. Not directly in front of you, for you are locked tight to that spinning strip of rubber ahead. But two or three riders up the line, daylight is poking its way through the links in the chain as one struggles. You hear his breathing, hear the futile crunch of his gears as he searches desperately for more pace, see the rock of his shoulders and the useless, ominous swing of his head. 'Not now,' you think, 'God not now.'

He swings to one side, spent, useless. The next in line dips his head, grits his teeth and the ten feet become eight. The eight become six, then four. The gap closes. Legs on fire, lungs tearing themselves apart, you bury yourself as the line becomes one again. Then, in a moment of sudden lucidity through the ravages of lactic acid, that old phrase comes back to you. 'Spent the day chewing the handlebars.' It suddenly makes perfect sense. You'd laugh if you didn't have another 80 miles to endure in this purgatory. You'd laugh if you weren't so set on becoming one of the 'Men of the Rás …'[59]

22

THE BRITISH PERSPECTIVE

Paul Manning became the first Englishman, and the first member of a Great Britain team, to win the Rás. He is seen here in 2001 on the Corribut Gap where a wonderful ride put him back into the Yellow Jersey after he lost it the previous day in controversial circumstances. He also won a stage in 2002.

The British presence in the Rás has become increasingly significant in recent years. In the golden-jubilee event of 2002, sixty riders from mainland British teams competed. In all, four British-based riders have won the Rás.

Riders from England first appeared in the Rás in the 1950s but these were made up of Irish emigrants organised in Exiles' teams. The first Englishman to ride is thought to have been John 'Geno' Goddard from the Kenton Road Club in London – he was co-opted onto an Exiles' team in 1963. Against very strong opposition from a Polish team, Goddard wore the Yellow Jersey for one day. He suffered heavily for his participation as he was suspended for six months for competing in what was then an illegal race according to UCI regulations. His ban began in January 1964, effectively taking a year out of Goddard's career.

Geno (John) Goddard is thought to be the first English rider to compete in the Rás. He wore the Yellow Jersey for one day but was later suspended for six months for riding in the event. He is seen here with a local admirer at the end of the stage into Castleisland, where he took the Yellow Jersey from the Poles in 1963.

With British road racing coming under the umbrella of the UCI during the 1960s, there was no further significant participation from across the Irish Sea until after the unification of Irish cycling in 1979. Jamie McGahan, a tough, wiry Scot who now resides in Ireland was the first rider from mainland Britain to win the event, in 1981, when he competed with a Scottish team.

Further involvement was slow – the Rás was not an attraction for national Great Britain teams because it was not in the UCI calendar. Many British riders came to the event with high expectations but found their ambitions frustrated by a combination of hostile factors – the character of the racing, the unforgiving roads and terrain, and alliances of Irish riders that sometimes worked against potential foreign winners.

It was 1997 before there was another victory for a rider from Great Britain. Andrew Roche, from the Isle of Man but with Irish roots, won while riding with a Kerry team. Three years later, Julian Winn, riding with a Welsh team, won the millennium Rás. The following year, with the event in the UCI calendar, Paul Manning became the first Englishman and the first rider from a Great Britain national team to win the event. Other British riders, such as Mark McKay and

Steve Farrell, can consider themselves unlucky not to have won – Farrell, for example, in 1994 suffered the narrowest losing margin ever in the Rás at just 3 seconds.

Apart from the four outright winners, individual British riders have made a very strong contribution over the past two decades. Jeff Wright was a prolific stage winner, taking six stages over a ten-year period, and four others have won three stages – Jamie McGahan, Mark McKay, Chris Newton and John Tanner.

Phil Leigh was another distinguished British rider and he accelerated the influx of British talent. He rode nine Rásanna, mostly under the umbrella of CC Bowland. The squad first rode the Rás in 1986 and made an impression by that 'go-for-it' attitude so respected in the Rás. Not many breaks were without a CC Bowland rider that year and Dave Ferguson took the Yellow Jersey after two days before pulling out with tendinitis. Tim Schools and Andy Crawshaw were also never far away from the action, and both continued to make their presence felt in later editions.

During his début Rás in 1986, Phil Leigh moved steadily up the GC to second overall, 2 seconds off the Jersey held by Stephen Spratt, the eventual winner. However, a bout of sickness the night before one of the hardest stages, through the Wicklow Mountains, destroyed his form and he eventually dropped to twelfth overall. He improved on that by claiming seventh overall the following year, along with fifth in 1990. However, he always felt that he came closest to claiming the 'prize' in his first Rás.

As well as his contribution as a rider, Leigh was also responsible for introducing other British talent to the event, including Jeff Wright. Once Gethin Butler had made his England début in the Rás, it was Leigh who ensured his continued involvement by bringing him over in his 'teams' during the following years. After riding his last Rás in 1995, Leigh returned for his tenth Rás in 2002 as manager of the Compensation Group Road Team, with Jeff Wright along as mechanic. His former team-mate, Tim Schools, was the man behind this team and it's interesting to note that these men, who have earned the distinction of becoming 'Men of the Rás', were now plotting to win that one race which is most dear to their hearts.

Returning to the Rás in 2002 as a team manager, Phil Leigh said that it was 'like coming home', such was the welcome he received. With such a long involvement at different levels, Leigh's British perspective on the Rás provides a useful insight into the more subtle characteristics of the event:

It is hard for an Englishman to make a 'real' impression on the Rás, especially if he only rides the race once or twice. Obviously, all the British riders who

Julian Winn (right) in the points jersey, surrounded by some of the British riders that helped him win the 2000 Rás. Left–right: Wayne Randle, Mark Lovatt, David McCann (drinking), Julian Winn, John Tanner (partly hidden).

have won the race demand the utmost respect, but to be really respected in the Rás, in an Irish sense, you somehow have to do something a bit more than 'simply' turn up with a strong team and win! Certainly, Jamie McGahan and Andy Roche, with their Irish connections, had this 'Irish' advantage.

However, while Paul Manning and Julian Winn are held in awe as winners, they will have to have a few more Rásanna under their belts before they will be classed as true 'Men of the Rás'. It is with this in mind that I mention two riders who didn't even win a stage but who have completed twenty-four Rásanna between them – Steve Howells (fourteen) and John Cosgrove (ten). These two riders were omnipresent during the 1990s, with Steve creating a record for a UK rider by competing in his fourteenth event during the golden-jubilee Rás of 2002. He views the Rás as 'a unique mix of old-fashioned amateur racing and the modern … in a form which makes it one of the most sought-after races in the world despite the modest prize fund.'

Phil Leigh (second from left) was a British rider who was strongly influential in increasing British involvement in the Rás. Beginning in 1986, he rode nine Rásanna with a best overall place of fifth. He continued his involvement as a manager. Both as a rider and manager, he adopted a style of racing that was both respected and effective in the Rás. He is seen here with his Compensation Group Team before the final stage of the 2002 Rás: (left to right) Mark Lovatt, Phil Leigh, John Tanner and Kevin Dawson. Lovatt held the Yellow Jersey for two days in 2000 and finished second. Tanner held it for two days in 1989 and won stages in 1993, 2000 and 2002. Dawson finished third in 1997.

Steve is a rider who closely resembles the average Irish county rider – not frightened to have a go but aware of his limitations and, while he may never have climbed the steps of the podium, has a very wise Rás head on his shoulders. Steve 'knows' how to optimise his talents so as to complete the event year-on-year, no matter which superstars are making the race harder than he would prefer.

Another gutsy rider from the UK to have made a big impression on the Rás is Gethin Butler, son of the former British professional champion from the 1960s, Keith Butler. Gethin has a decade of Rás finishes to his name, along with two stage wins, and has finished in the top ten on six occasions without ever quite reaching the top spot on the podium. He rued his bad luck during the final time trial in 1997 when a puncture put paid to his best chance of overall victory. Of all the riders ever to come from the British mainland to contest the Rás, Butler has to be counted as probably the British rider whom the Irish have most taken to their hearts. For sheer guts and entertainment value, he has proved himself to be a genuine 'Man of the Rás'.

Before coming to the Rás, I was totally unaware of the impact it would have on my life and cycling career. The Rás became the focus of my seasons for the next few years and, racing apart, the thing that impressed me most was the camaraderie among the whole 'caravan' involved with the Rás. The Rás is simply one big 'family' and I was taken into its heart like the prodigal son. I suppose, really, I could not get over how much I was appreciated as a rider because of my efforts 'up the road' – after 25-plus years of racing in the UK, I am still waiting in vain for a similar emotion.

I remember one event, from the early 1990s, that might illustrate one aspect of this Rás 'ethos' which values the participation of all the riders: Steve Howells and his team were stranded 15 or 20 miles out of a stage start with a vehicle breakdown. Their absence was noted and the race was delayed for as long as possible, but it eventually had to get under way without them. However, when they finally got to the start, 20 minutes late, they discovered they had not been forgotten and 'arrangements' had been made. They were eventually able to get onto the back of the bunch in a fashion that would not have happened in any other stage race! It is this kind of act that epitomises just one of the unique characteristics of the Rás – the shepherding instincts of not unnecessarily losing any of the flock. If such an occurrence had happened in the UK there would have been an outcry for the riders concerned to be thrown out of the race, but I do not recall a single voice of objection from the Rás convoy!

The double winner, Phil Cassidy, must get more than a passing mention in the modern history of the Rás. I rode my nine Rásanna between Phil's two victories and, while I always prided myself on my ability of reading a race, it was that man, 'Cass', who invariably would be alongside me in some 100-mile breakaway from the gun. I learnt a lot about how to ride the Rás by observing and competing with the man, and many British riders who came to the Rás with ideas of winning had their plans undone by his tactical approach and local knowledge.

I have talked to many British riders who have become 'Men of the Rás', from successful riders such as Wayne Randle and Roddy Riddle, to the many UK riders who, despite never featuring high on GC, had the racing experience of their lives. In every case, the Rás is the race that holds some of their fondest memories of our sport.

23
A NEW RÁS?

Denis Lynch, David O'Loughlin and Ciarán Power (left–right) ride steadily as Philip Cassidy (out of shot) contests a KOH. These four were the remains of the initial break and then almost seven minutes ahead of the Yellow-Jersey group.

Having withdrawn from the UCI international calendar in 1992 because of the increasing costs involved, the Race Organiser, Dermot Dignam, resolved in 2001 to have the Rás re-established in the UCI calendar. As well as a source of UCI points for Irish riders – the accumulation of which determines participation in international events such as the World Championships – Dignam saw it as a further step in the necessary process of renewal and progress that he had fostered for almost twenty years.

Since his initial involvement in the Rás as a rider in 1959,[60] Dignam had worked as an official in various capacities and first became Race Organiser in 1975 at a time when various committees and individuals were taking charge of the event following the departure of Joe Christle. He again became Race Organiser in 1983 and has held that position since then. The 'quiet man' of Irish cycling, Dignam earned great respect from those in the Irish cycling community who understand his role in keeping the Rás alive, and the fact of its very existence is generally attributed to the adeptness of his stewardship. Irish cyclists never have to ask 'Will there be a Rás next year?' – like the coming of the swallows, the Rás is anticipated as an inevitable part of the year's cycle.

Beyond preserving the event, Dignam has gradually developed and adapted it to a modern context, whilst astutely respecting and preserving the traditions of the Rás. In spite of its prominence in Irish cycling, he did not allow the Rás to become a sacred cow and never lost sight of the fact that it exists to serve cyclists and cycling, rather than the reverse.

The sophistication and scale of the event presided over by Dignam in 2001 – as the Rás entered its sixth decade – was in marked contrast to earlier eras. A year-long liaison with domestic and foreign teams brought a field of 189 riders, along with an even greater number of team-support personnel and officials. The requirement of almost 500 beds at each stage end created a monumental organisational task.

As always, the selection of the route and the organisation of stage ends was the main task. Much the same considerations applied as before – to bring the Rás to a new location, perhaps, and to produce an interesting route: mountain and flat, fine road and more typical country road – that delicate balance on which the uniqueness of the race depends, and which may influence the final outcome. Even when the route is decided, it has to be travelled several times in order to prepare the Race Manual which documents every significant junction, the expected time of arrival of the Rás in every town – allowing for varying weather conditions – and other such technical considerations. Local authorities have to be consulted to ensure roads will not be dug up when the race is due to pass, and stage-end

Left: Dermot Dignam (left) and Myles Cullen at a stage end in Longford, 1959. Dignam had an accomplished Rás career as a rider. His competitive career spanned thirteen years; he came second on a stage behind Paddy Flanagan and came fourth on six different stages.

Right: The 'quiet man' of Irish cycling, Dermot Dignam has earned great respect from those in the cycling community who understand his role in keeping the Rás alive. Beyond preserving the event, Dignam has been astute in the way he has respected and preserved the traditions of the Rás while, at the same time, gradually developing and adapting it to a modern context, and on a scale that can be sustained on modest commercial support.

committees have to be visited, up to five times for the less experienced ones. These are provided with clear guidelines regarding stewarding, parking and so forth.

The procedure of preparing the race is, therefore, much the same as before, if more elaborate. However, bringing the race, uninterrupted and safe, from start to finish each day is an entirely different operation. When Joe Christle declared in a press release in 1966, on the occasion of motorcycle Gardaí joining the race for the first time, that 'traffic control is one of the major problems of such a race', he could scarcely have envisaged the complexity of the task facing his successor in this regard. Not alone facing increased traffic, road works and traffic-calming measures, but also having to consider increased health-and-safety requirements, along with greater organisational expectations from all concerned, the Rás machine has to be complex and efficient to meet its modern challenge.

This machine is made up of a number of diverse units, each put in place and orchestrated by the Race Organiser. At the beginning of each day, long before the race begins, various crews leave the race headquarters. One will set up the barriers and podium at the stage ends. Another will erect and staff the photo-finish camera, and yet another will mark every junction along the route. A myriad of other elements fall into place; four lead cars and three equipped neutral-service cars provide support for the various bunches that may develop on the road; two cars with doctors, and two ambulances and their crews, take care of medical emergencies; motorbike judges must be in place for the primes and hot-spot sprints; a blackboard official must provide the vital time gaps for the riders; press, radio and TV crews, as well as sponsors, have to be accommodated, and the crucial judges and timekeepers take their respective positions. The 'broom-wagon' will be the last vehicle in the cavalcade, sweeping up abandoned riders.

The stage begins with the ceremonial donning of the Yellow Jersey. When the Race Organiser drops the flag to formally start the stage, control passes over to the *Commissaire* President, an international *commissaire* appointed by the UCI. He has the assistance of two other *commissaires* in cars and a further two on motorbikes. These are linked by radio.

The *commissaires* also command the team cars in the cavalcade. The drivers, in the same way as the riders, 'sign-on' and thereby commit themselves to the race rules and the control of the *commissaires*. Long gone are the *laissez-faire* days described by Joe Christle when he wrote of the 1965 Rás: 'It has been commented that the cycle race itself is tame compared to the driving and manoeuvring of the team cars behind. "The cavalcade is getting like Le Mans," remarked one of the team managers last year.' The neutral observer will marvel at the understanding between experienced drivers and riders, especially when the race becomes confused and constricted on the more remote country roads.

The task of getting the entire rolling ensemble through towns and villages, over mountains and across bog roads, is daunting. It might be a mile long and travelling at 45km/h, or it could be spread out over 30 kilometres of road with an hour separating the front from the rear. Responsibility for controlling the passage of this throng, uninterrupted, through the country lies with the Chief Marshal. He travels ahead of the race, and communicates with the *commissaires*, the motorbike police accompanying the race, the different police divisions that the race passes through and with the Chief Motorbike Marshal. His squad of around fifteen motorbike marshals forms the backbone of the marshalling effort. Working from the Race Manual, they steward every significant junction and back up the Gardaí in performing a 'rolling road closure' – a procedure to minimise disruption to other road users by closing down the road just ahead of the race and reopening when the race has passed. The co-operation of the Gardaí is probably the single most crucial element in the running of the event.

No matter how meticulous the planning, the unexpected inevitably arises and the history of the Rás is littered with hard-luck stories arising out of freak

No matter how meticulous the planning, the unexpected inevitably intervenes and the history of the Rás is littered with hard-luck stories caused by freak encounters between riders and all variety of obstruction. Here, in 2002, the entire race is blocked by unexpected roadworks.

Garda Colm Cullen poses for a Rás photographer, 1992. The co-operation of An Garda Síochána is one of the most important elements in the successful running of the Rás.

encounters between riders and all variety of obstruction – sheep, horses, cows, dogs and cats, and vehicles of all kinds have ended the hopes of many riders. The entire race has even gone astray on a number of occasions. Ultimately, it is the responsibility of each individual rider to find his way, along the designated route, from start to finish.

By international standards, the Rás is run on a shoestring, without many of the superfluous trimmings in evidence at other stage races. The British magazine, *Cycling Weekly*, in wonder at the Rás' longevity, has noted the economy of the event:

> There are no blazers or uniforms to be seen – although officials do get a T-shirt and a cap. The race doesn't rely on a major vehicle sponsor, with many helpers using their own cars. Finish-line arrangements are basic – no grandstand and the podium is the back of a lorry. The media provide their own cars and there are no press rooms or phones provided. There are no publicity vehicles or advertising giveaways, and the Rás uses just one PR person and one public address announcer.

An RUC motorcycle escort lines up at the border as the race leaves Northern Ireland for the Republic, 1999. The relationship between the Rás and the RUC in Northern Ireland fluctuated with the swings in Anglo-Irish relations caused by the stresses and strains of the 'Troubles' during the 1970s and 1980s. Co-operation has been excellent in more recent times, and the RUC effort has been admired and appreciated by the riders.

Yet, while the trimmings might be lacking, the core elements are not compromised and the race is run efficiently with the budget provided by the sponsors and the Sports Council of Ireland. Dignam undertakes the main administrative work on a voluntary basis – with the assistance of his family – and the event itself is run by a tight-knit group of experienced and committed volunteers. Most view it as a privilege to be working on the Rás.

This is the Rás that entered the élite UCI calendar in 2001, a year before its golden jubilee. It could be described as a snug event – intimate and friendly, comfortable and confident, with the essence of its long tradition still intact. Its growing complexity and international involvement had evolved in tandem with the country's economic and social development, and the increased participation of Ireland in international affairs. The event remained nicely proportioned in relation to the size of the country, the scale of cycling in Ireland and the capacity of a voluntary team to organise and run it. While its public profile had diminished due to the ever-increasing media coverage of wildly diverse sporting events, it had changed little in essential qualities. The event still enjoyed its status and reputation, and retained its magnetic attraction for Irish riders.

With the race awarded a status of 2.5 on the UCI calendar, stronger teams than usual arrived to the 2001 Rás, including professional outfits from Switzerland, Poland, South Africa, Canada and Germany. The Swiss GS Fisconseil team, for example, included David McKenzie, a stage winner in the Giro d'Italia the previous year, and the USA team included Joe Miller, who won three US national championships. The Deutsche Telekom team from Germany was also expected to be very strong and Julian Winn was back to defend his title at the head of a Welsh team. The Irish team was also strong, including Mark Scanlon, former World Junior Champion, the CCC-Mat professional, David McCann, the ex-professional Morgan Fox, the former Rás winner, Tommy Evans, and Aiden Duff.

In spite of its elevated status, Dignam promised no major changes, though the race had to be reduced to eight days to slot into the UCI calendar. A foot-and-mouth outbreak in Britain, potentially ruinous for Ireland's economy if spread, threatened the participation of riders from Great Britain, but this was averted by the agreement of a strict disinfectant protocol.

David McCann won the first stage, from Navan to Ballaghadereen. His comments afterwards, to journalist Gerard Cromwell, provide an insight into the changed nature of the 2001 Rás:

> There was a break of eleven guys, so it meant that a lot of teams missed it … we got almost 3 minutes and I knew there had to be some reaction. When it did come it was astounding, because we had 3 minutes and it just came down on us like a ton of bricks. I had only 3 seconds at the end.

The trend continued on the second stage, to Portumna, with breaks being closely marshalled. Deutsche Telekom took the stage with its nineteen-year-old rider, Dirk Reichl, going into yellow and Morgan Fox just 4 seconds behind. In one of Europe's leading squads and hoping to become a member of its top professional team, Reichl declared after just two days: 'This race is very fast, very hard.' The third stage, to Castleisland, was the longest at 115 miles (184km) and, again, a promising break had an advantage of almost 4 minutes at 75 miles (120km) but was chased down by a combination of teams. A brave solo effort by Ray Clarke ended just 6 miles (10km) from the finish.

The fourth stage went to Killorglin, via the Conor Pass and Dingle. In another day of beautiful weather – which lasted for most of the event – there was more difficult racing. The stage was won by Mark Scanlon and Fisconseil's David Chassot took over the Yellow Jersey, apparently with some trepidation: 'The race leader is very vulnerable in this race, no matter who it is – it's such an attacking style of racing.'

While the aggressive racing persisted, the event, in fact, was adopting a pattern alien to the Rás; the change was something of a shell-shock to many of the Irish riders. The breaks just were not able to stay away and the speed was very high. At a certain point in the stages, the combined foreign teams would go to the front of the bunch, crank up the pace and chase them down with massive power that left many in the bunch at the outer limits of their endurance to cling on. It was transforming into classical, continental-style stage racing dominated by strong teams, with the bulk of the home riders playing a secondary role. In spite of McCann's and Scanlon's stage wins, the Irish were making little impression. While six riders had the same time on top of the GC sheet, none were Irish, and the best placed until then, Morgan Fox, had an injury that forced him to retire later. Although the top Irish riders were not far off the pace, it seemed as though the race was out of their control and being dictated by the foreign teams.

Killorglin is the threshold to the crucial Cork and Kerry mountains. During the Rás' first forty-nine years, numerous plots were contrived there, both in hope and desperation, and many Rásanna had been won and lost on the roads that radiate from it into the various mountain routes. Philip Cassidy, aged thirty-nine but described as 'incredibly bullish throughout' by one participant, decided that 'something had to be done', and sat down with his team, ostensibly a Meath outfit but in reality a trade-team sponsored by a business he part owned, Cycleways.

Cassidy's style of racing was highly admired in the Rás – relentless, attacking, unpredictable, uncompromising – in stark contrast to the formulaic continental style now coming to the fore in the Rás. Cassidy was critical of Irish riders for being cowed and lying under the whip. He felt there had to be a gamble; there were a number of Irishmen just 30 seconds off the Jersey but they had no hope of jumping away from the foreign team to make up the time at a stage finish – 'Teams of Olympic and world-class athletes just won't let that happen.' The pattern had been for the foreign teams to set a strong pace early on and eliminate the weaker riders. A counter strategy had to be deployed 'to soften them up early'.

The Meath Cycleways team rose to the challenge on the 94-mile (150km) stage to Skibbereen, which included three category-one KOHs and numerous lesser climbs. Eugene Moriarty was the best-placed rider on the team, lying twenty-ninth at 1 minute 20 seconds. Though riding with Meath, he was a Kerryman, now in his home county and this was still a significant factor in the Rás.

Riders were crowded around Dermot Dignam's car as the race left Killorglin – as soon as he took the flag in the window, the volley of attacks began from the front. A formation emerged within 3 miles. Cassidy and Moriarty had escaped, along with Denis O'Shea who, in his native county, had similar ideas. A typically strong county rider who had some tremendous Rás stages without ever figuring on the podium, O'Shea was tired of playing a secondary role and was gone from the beginning in an all-or-nothing effort. Ray Clarke, typically adventurous, and Nicholas White from South Africa were also in the group.

In blistering heat, the five riders powered down the road to Killarney. In typical Rás style, Denis O'Shea was very influential in home territory. They had 1 minute on the bunch at the first KOH at Ladies View after 24 miles (38km). A strong, six-man chasing bunch developed, followed by the main bunch. At Moll's Gap, they were still over a minute ahead of the chasing group with the main field over 3 minutes in arrears. Moriarty and Clarke, on the same time on GC, were now joint leaders on the road.

They charged down the mountain, into Kenmare, and began the climb of the Tunnel Road for Turner's Rock. The main bunch began to disintegrate on the climb and the chase was cranked up on the rolling, hilly roads before Schull. The strong foreign teams again combined and turned on the power at the head of the chasing bunch while the four Irish and one South African drove on in front.

It was, perhaps, a pivotal moment in the history of the Rás – a clash of two racing cultures on the road to Skibbereen. The Cassidy group represented the best of Rás tradition – a disparate band, in a conspiratorial, opportunistic and audacious move that defied conventional tactical logic by attacking the Yellow Jersey from the beginning of the most difficult mountain stage. In contrast, they were being chased largely by paid professionals riding to the well-managed, calculated formula of continental racing and receiving their instruction via radio from their managers behind. This, perhaps, represented the future face of the new, international Rás. Or could the traditional Rás prevail and would an Irishman be launched into the Yellow Jersey by dint of an heroic and epic break in the best tradition of the event?

The break began to falter. First, O'Shea dropped away and then, dramatically, Cassidy's effort collapsed. He almost stopped on the road and the main bunch swept past him. Clarke, Moriarty and White kept going and held a slim 40-second advantage at 10km. In Skibbereen, the front of the *peloton* just caught them and Christian Knees from the Deutsche Telekom team won the sprint. Paul Manning of the Great Britain team took the Yellow Jersey.

Over 18 minutes later, Cassidy staggered in and collapsed in a heap after crossing the line. In many eyes, he had made the last great mistake of his career in attempting a Rás too far, and the sight of the proud hero being attended to on the street in Skibbereen was probably the ignominious and unfortunate end of one of the most distinguished of Rás careers.

The race continued in the same vein. Manning lost the Jersey the following day after being penalised for taking a hand sling – a TV crew recorded the indiscretion – but he regained it brilliantly on the penultimate day when he and Nicholas White finished over a minute ahead of the main group. It was the only significant break in the Rás – the next biggest margin was gained by a group of four on the fifth stage when they finished just 4 seconds ahead of the bunch. The Rás breaks, always a feature of the event and measured in minutes, were now down to seconds.

Manning, an Olympic bronze medallist and World Track Championship silver medallist, was the first ever Englishman to win the Rás.

With its completely altered character, the 2001 Rás sparked off a debate about the changed nature of the event, the direction it should take and its role in Irish cycling. Almost with nostalgia, the expression, the 'old Rás', came into parlance and there seemed to be general consensus that the Rás was fundamentally changed. Had the 'old Rás' died on the road to Skibbereen in 2001?

Writing from the finish of that stage in Skibbereen, where he ended almost an hour behind the stage winner, Cian Lynch said:

> It's not the Rás we once loved – now it's suffering full-time – only the cream of Irish cyclists are able to mix it with the foreigners.

This was central to the debate – the role of the county rider in the Rás. The county rider, riding with his own or some other county team, had always been fundamental to the character of the Rás and it was that possibility, however remote, of having a role in the Rás that created such a magnetic attraction for the bulk of the Irish riders. For the good Irish rider, to get into the top ten in the Rás, just once, might be a goal, and the snatching of that stage win always featured at the outer reaches of his dreams. He might ride five to ten Rásanna in pursuit of these ambitions, using those tactics that gave the Rás its unique qualities. And if he did not succeed, the trials and tribulations of his efforts, and the memories they induced, would sustain his sporting needs. He always knew that it was possible, but not anymore – his role in 2001 was reduced to continual punishment in a basic struggle for survival. Myles McCorry, another rider writing for a website, gave his observations on 2001:

> The pros are stylish, smooth and stupid, the county-team men are sweating and rocking. You can see who has talent and gets paid, who is suffering and following a dream.

Was the dream over and the Rás, which had basked in a tradition conceived by the creative pursuit of such dreams, now irrevocably changed by the event having taking its place in the international affairs of cycling? This was progress, argued some. Nothing can stand still and the Rás, now Ireland's national stage race, must raise its standard to challenge the best Irish riders even further, thereby helping to elevate the national standard and provide the best of international competition for élite Irish riders on Irish roads. To coincide with this, the orientation of the Irish riders must change to strong team efforts, and if the county or club riders want to compete, they will have to prepare accordingly. A commonly used expression was that 'The man who has to go back to work on the Monday morning after the Rás will have no business in it'.

The change was welcomed by many. The good and ambitious Belfast rider, Brendan Doherty, expressed this view:

> People had different goals in the old Rás. The new Ras has nothing to do with the old Rás. It's become more professional and that suits me. It has to advance because the country needs it. You compete in the Rás now because it is an international race and you want to get points.

For some, this did not even go far enough. With its stature, the Rás, as a platform for commercial exposure, was undersold. It needed to draw in more money, increase its media profile, be developed in all aspects and become a more commercially supported showcase. This scenario, if realised, represents an unfortunate change of direction for the Rás, argued the traditionalists. The Rás should serve the rider who has to work until 6 pm every day, who can manage to get 2–3,000 miles into his legs early in the season, do his additional interval training and pacing, and ride the early races in the calendar to try and find form. The cycling calendar traditionally revolved around the Rás and might this collapse if the Rás was not an option for the county riders? Few of the public were going to show up at stage ends to see unknown foreign riders competing for stage wins and the atmosphere of the Rás would be forever changed. It would no longer be the Holy Grail of Irish cycling; rather, the Irish riders would be reduced to mere cannon fodder in a convenient source of UCI points for foreign teams.

Countering the argument that the Rás, as a brand, was commercially under exploited and in need of further development, those with longer memories pointed to other cycling events that had taken that direction. The Tour of Ireland, the Nissan Classic and the Kellogg's Series had all come and gone. The Junior Tour of Ireland was even threatened. Equally, in Britain, the Tour of Britain, the Tour of Scotland and the PruTour were no more. These events expired because they were developed to a scale and sophistication enormously dependent on substantial but fickle commercial support. There was little appreciation, it was argued, of the effort in keeping the Rás in existence even as it was – that delicate job of balancing its

Shay O'Hanlon, the most successful of all Rás riders, working as a volunteer on the fiftieth Rás, 2002. The annual running of the Rás succeeds due to the efforts of tightly-knit groups of experienced volunteers who are highly committed to the event.

size and sophistication on a scale commercially sustainable in the long term, while feasible to run on a voluntary basis. That wonderful voluntary and co-operative element, originating in the spirit that conceived the Rás fifty years previously and faithfully sustained to produce the Rás annually since then, would quickly dissipate if the nature of the Rás changed fundamentally and moved away from its original concept. Anyway, it was argued, when followed to its conclusion, the commercial scenario ultimately reduces sport to an industry, run by executives, where market considerations dictate sporting decisions and athletes become mere advertising banners. Was the Rás to reach the stage where attacks were motivated more by the need to get TV exposure for sponsors rather than the pursuit of authentic athletic endeavour?

Nobody envied Dermot Dignam in his effort to balance these conflicting demands and expectations. The thoughts of Gabriel Howard, a passionate Meath rider who epitomises the Rás spirit and tradition, reflected the questioning at this crossroads. Howard rode twenty-one consecutive Rásanna – beginning in 1963 – and won a stage in 1965. He broke a bone in his wrist in a fall in 1975 but rode with it in plaster for five days just to finish. He continued in the Rás in one capacity or another and, in all, spent forty consecutive years involved in the Rás: 'The Rás has lived with us, it is part of our lives,' he reminisced; but his comments went on to reflect the dilemma now faced: 'I feel sad about the change … I'd love to see it being given back to the Irish riders. But perhaps change is inevitable – part of progress. There may be no choice.'

'There will always be a place for the Irish county rider in the Rás.' These were the words of Dignam prior to the golden-jubilee Rás of 2002. But the extent of that role was not clear – whether it would be a central role, or as mere extras in the drama, filling out the set on which other stars would shine. There was much anticipation, and some trepidation, facing into 2002.

Gabriel Howard (centre), with fellow Meath riders and supporters, following his stage win in 1965 – the high point of 21 consecutive Rásanna, a total of 205 stages. Howard epitomised the county rider whose efforts gave the Rás its essence. Are such scenes a thing of the past given the changing nature of the event from the late 1990s? (left–right) 'Mixer' (Mick) Collins (eating), Tom Reilly (wearing cape), Leo Collins (with cap; a long-time Meath and NCA supporter), Gabriel Howard (stage winner), Séamus Kennedy (no. 37, Rás winner 1978), Ben McKenna (Rás winner 1959). The tall man between Tom Reilly and 'Mixer' Collins is Larry Dunne, a stage winner in 1960. The man in front with the white cap is another former Meath rider, Jimmy Gough.

A very large field of 195 riders was entered for the 2002 event, which was dedicated to the memory of Joe Christle. In another poignant move, the stages were dedicated to deceased figures from the Rás' past[61] and the final stage was set to return to the Phoenix Park, the scene of so many crowd-filled finales in the past.

The Irish team was announced, with the 1998 winner, Ciarán Power, as team leader. He would be supported by the former world junior champion, Mark Scanlon, by Tommy Evans – based in France – and by the home-based Timmy Barry and Paul Griffin. Scanlon later developed an injury and did not start. He was replaced by Dermot Nally who in turn had to drop out because of illness.

The declaration of Power as team leader, with the implication that the others were expected to work for him, was an arrangement that could not have worked in previous times and an indication that, by the fiftieth Rás, Irish-team management had matured to a level consistent with the international status of the event.

Power was well suited to the role, arriving to the event in great form, extremely focused and with a maturity forged in the vicissitudes of the years since his previous Rás victory in 1998. That win opened doors and promoted confidence and self-belief in the 22-year-old. It raised his sights and, supported by his father, he entered into an even more rigorous training regime. He received invitations to ride in the British PruTour and the Australian SunTour, and produced authoritative performances with top-ten placings in each. Before the end of the year of his Rás win, he was offered a place on the new Linda McCartney professional team.

His career progressed further in 2000. As the Rás got under way at home, Power was riding in the Giro d'Italia, the world's second most prestigious annual stage race, and he produced astonishing top-five finishes on two stages. His future seemed secure and bright. Then, his professional life began to crumble. First, the Linda McCartney outfit suddenly collapsed in confusion, leaving him without a team. Next, he fell and broke his collar bone while trying to re-establish himself early in 2001. His career prospects were bleak and he spent much of the year adrift, pondering his uncertain future and the feasibility of his remaining in international cycling. At the end of 2001, Power received an invitation to join a professional squad in the US. Though somewhat reluctant to depart the European scene, he thrived in America and returned to the 2002 Rás in wonderful condition and with great respect earned from the general body of Irish cyclists.

The weather for the first week of the event was entirely different to the sun-drenched race of the previous year and this was decisive from the beginning when, after 42 miles (67km), on the road to Ballinamore, a break of six went clear and driving wind and rain prevented a co-ordinated chase. The British-team riders were present in strength, enabling Chris Newton to get clear to win the stage. Ciarán Power, the sole member of the Irish team to make it into the break, was second, 27 seconds behind. The main field arrived 7 minutes behind, eliminating many of the contenders for the top honour and setting Newton and Power as clear leaders of their respective teams. Consequently, the race would hinge, to a certain extent, on their respective team performances.

The second stage, to Nenagh, was again reminiscent of traditional Rásanna. In a day of further heavy rain and wind, attacks began early and the action remained furious and fluid for the entire stage. There was much attacking, with Power trying to claw back the deficit. Philip Cassidy, now forty years old, had obviously put the previous year's race behind him and finished just a second behind the British champion, John Tanner. Cassidy declared on the podium that he was going to keep attacking.

The leading break coming through a tunnel on the road to Skibbereen, (left–right) Denis O'Shea, Ray Clarke, Eugene Moriarty, Phillip Cassidy and Nicholas White.

Philip Cassidy collapsed at the finish in Skibbereen, 2001, following an epic but failed attempt to break the stranglehold of the foreign teams. It led to comment that Cassidy had made the last great mistake of his career in attempting a Rás too far. The stage apparently marked a symbolic transition from the 'old Rás' to the 'new Rás'.

Cassidy, in fact, had not been as dispirited by the 2001 Rás as others. He recognised that the fine weather and a favourable wind were an important factor in the high speed. In his opinion, the gap in standard between the Irish and foreign teams was more psychological than real – there just were not enough Irish riders prepared to challenge and suffer positively in front, rather than being recipients of the punishment in the bunch. They were not prepared to have a go, in the traditional way, and make it tough for the visitors. Moreover, Cassidy saw his own collapse on the stage to Skibbereen as the result of choosing an unsuitable stage. Not a gifted climber, he was riding to his limit on the ascents and could not contribute. Consequently, he had to make an extra effort on the downhill and flat, and was therefore riding at his limit continually. Despite the tactical failure of that stage, it had proven to be a morale boost for him and his team – unlike much of the docile field, they were contributing to the race, dictating the play and not merely reacting to others' strategies.

In 'unbelievably hard racing', the leading break drives into wind and rain, trying to gain time on the Yellow Jersey holder, Ciarán Power, in front, followed by David O'Loughlin and Ray Clarke.

In improving weather, Ciarán Power (right) and Philip Cassidy, the previous two Irish winners of the Rás in 1998 and 1999, drive on to Killorglin.

As soon as the 2002 route was announced, Cassidy chose the third stage to Killorglin as 'his' stage in the Rás, adding that he had the additional incentive of a Kerry co-sponsor to satisfy. His year's preparation, he claimed – every mile that he rode – was focused on that stage and, before leaving his room that morning, he wrote on the inside of his shorts, 'P. Cass. – first, stage 3, 2002 Rás'.

Much to Cassidy's satisfaction, the stage again began in rain and a strong head wind. He attacked from the line and was joined by Timmy Barry of the Irish team and David O'Loughlin. Cassidy immediately made it clear to O'Loughlin, the best placed of them on GC, that this was no mere speculative break – they were riding all the way and O'Loughlin would go into yellow. By 5 miles (8km), they had a lead of 1 minute. A little while later they slowed slightly and waited for a group that was trying to bridge across. It included Ray Clarke of Cassidy's team, Denis Lynch, a young Corkman signed to a French club, and Anthony Malarczyk from Wales. Ciarán Power, seeing the potential, also bridged across and was the last man into the group. Cassidy again reiterated to Power, now the best-placed rider and in a position to take the race lead, that this was an all-out effort.

They beat ahead into the driving wind and rain, holding the gap at around 1 minute. Power felt that the British team was toying with them, letting them dangle out there alone in the hostile elements and would reel them in whenever it suited. The British, in fact, had their team in front of the main bunch, trying to preserve Newton's Yellow Jersey, but they were making no progress on the leaders. The British team coach later admitted surprise: 'It was quite unusual, in most international races we would have brought them back – I was a bit surprised.'

The leading group's advantage crept up to 1.5 minutes and they redoubled their efforts with the realisation that they were gaining. Barry later described it as 'unbelievably hard racing'. On the open ring roads around Limerick, the bunch disintegrated under the combined force of the British-led chase and the howling cross winds. Spectators in following cars saw riders leaning sideways into the wind to stay upright. Eugene Murtagh, one of the county men, described it as 'horrendous'. With near gale-force winds and driving rain from the left-hand side, the field was strung out along the right-hand gutter. Without shelter, some riders were blown into the gravel verge, gaps appeared and the main bunch began to disintegrate. Groups tried to organise *echelons* but the Irish riders, unused to riding on wide, clear roads, took some time to get formations in place.

The leading group continued to open the gap on the chase, but some could not maintain the pace in front and, on the long drag to the first KOH at the Barnagh Gap after 55 miles (88km), Clarke, Malarczyk and Barry dropped away. By then, the Yellow Jersey group was almost 6 minutes down. It had been turning into a classic, traditional Rás break, possibly decisive, and the leaders began thinking about the stage-end outcome in Killorglin, just over 40 miles (64km) away.

Four Irish riders remained in front – Power, O'Loughlin, Cassidy and Lynch. If they stayed away, Power would go into yellow, but the stage win and the KOH Jersey were up for grabs. Lynch was the fly in the ointment – a young rider based with a French club who was not well known by the more established riders, he posed an unknown threat for the stage outcome. He had failed to finish the Rás the year previously, before going to France, but had been active and aggressive over the previous two days.

They contested the Barnagh Gap KOH and Lynch won it ahead of Cassidy, much to Cassidy's annoyance as he was anxious to have some result for his sponsor at the finish. In a way, the scene made a statement about the Rás. Cassidy, who had been at the forefront of a large cohort of brilliant young riders that emerged to challenge established masters twenty years earlier, was now, himself, being challenged by this relatively unknown young rider. The significant difference was that now, two decades later, Lynch was the sole young Irish rider either able or willing to mount a similar threat to the status quo.

The four drove on and Cassidy contested the next KOH alone. With 23 miles (37km) remaining, they were almost 5 minutes ahead of a small chasing bunch and an incredible 7 minutes ahead of the Yellow Jersey group. Realising that they were not going to get assistance and that the break was not going to be caught, the British manager had decided 'not to ride my guys into the ground on the third day', and they eased back on the chase.

At Castleisland, in improving weather, Cassidy attacked and split the leading four. Power joined him, leaving Lynch and O'Loughlin trailing. Cassidy and Power, the two Irish winners of the Rás in 1998 and 1999, drove on to Killorglin together and, in bright sunshine, Cassidy was first over the line to get his third stage win – his previous stage win had been back in 1987. His ambition realised and his strategic approach vindicated in the most emphatic of fashions, Cassidy declared that it was his last Rás. With the formalities on the podium concluded, he adjourned to a bar at the side of the street to celebrate the day. Power, by dint of a remarkable performance over 97 gruelling miles (155km), had wrenched the Yellow Jersey from the British team and went into the race lead with a comfortable cushion of almost 4 minutes.

With a disciplined team and a masterful personal performance, Power retained the lead. Though left isolated at critical times, he displayed tactical maturity and resolve. On the road to Arklow, for example, through his native Waterford, where a strong following wind helped to produce the second-fastest Rás stage ever – averaging over 32 mph (50 km/h) – he was left isolated in a front group with four of the British team and other contenders. It was a golden opportunity to work him over and snatch his Jersey, but Power's defence was to attack and split the group. He repeated this in the Wicklow Mountains where a memorable break by Paul Manning, lasting most of the stage, faded just 10 miles (16km) from the finish. While the British team dominated all other categories and stage wins, Power won his second Rás by over 4 minutes.

The golden-jubilee Rás had been secured on that remarkable third stage, from Nenagh to Killorglin – a classic Rás stage in every respect – and, in its analysis, *Cycling Weekly* noted: 'This was a traditional-style Rás with unpredictable racing, heroic breakaways, rain, wind and a home winner.' Many agreed and, even before the end of the race, Philip Cassidy declared 'The Rás is back to normal'.

24

JUBILEE IMPRESSIONS

Ciarán Power, winner of the fiftieth Rás. While it had been a vintage event with a traditional flavour, perhaps Power is the model of the future Irish Rás winner – a full-time professional, foreign based, riding with the cohesive, textbook support of team-mates who may also be increasingly foreign based.

The golden-jubilee Rás of 2002 offered contrasting impressions. The social and political landscape that spawned the Rás Tailteann fifty years earlier had, of course, changed completely, and the years of turbulence were past – the event no longer carried ideological overtones. In a curious way, this was perhaps best illustrated by the absence of Brendan Doherty. From a staunch republican background in Belfast – though not from an NCA background – Doherty had no sense of the Rás being a nationalist race; he was proud to compete in it as his national tour. He opted to forgo the 2002 Rás as it did not suit his preparation for the Commonwealth Games, his only opportunity to compete in a championships of such a scale. His participation in that event – a hesitant acknowledgement of the Northern Ireland created by the new 'Peace Process' – would have been unthinkable even a few short years before.

The Rás did, however, remain somewhat unique and distinctly Irish, and the comments of the foreign visitors strongly echoed the impressions their predecessors had gained for decades – they talked about the difficult and aggressive nature of the race, its friendliness and warmth, and the passion of the Irish riders.

On the surface, at least, it had been a vintage Rás and the trends of the previous year had been reversed. But still, questions were left unanswered. An Irish winner, yes, but the next best-placed Irishman, Patrick Moriarty, was in thirteenth place. The fact that he was so much admired and respected for having been able to achieve this while working full time was a demonstration of the changing nature of the race. While the winning stage into Killorglin was classic Rás, it was created by Philip Cassidy; if, as he said, the 'Rás is back to normal', it was mainly due to his own influence and contribution. But is Cassidy the last of the great Rás riders, in the traditional sense, with that mixture of qualities – unorthodoxy, incorrigibility, passion, talent, stature, longevity and amateur – qualities which may, in time, see him elevated in the opinion of his peers to the 'Great' Philip Cassidy?

The continuing tradition of the Rás: Colm Christle (left), winner of the first Rás in 1953, receiving a Cúchulainn statuette from Dermot Dignam at the site where the first Rás began, fifty years previously.

Philip Cassidy, at the age of forty, winning into Killorglin in 2002 after leading an epic and classic Rás stage. Is Cassidy the last of the great Rás riders, in the traditional sense, with that mixture of qualities – unorthodoxy, incorrigibility, passion, talent, stature, longevity and amateur?

On the other hand, is Ciarán Power and his Irish team the model of the future: full-time, professional, foreign-based – riding, in contrast to so many Rásanna of the past, with the cohesive, textbook support of team-mates who may in the future also be foreign based and with broadened horizons that diminish the significance of the Rás?

And if on that stage to Killorglin, a number of teams had conspired to work against the break, as had happened the previous year to Skibbereen, would the fiftieth Rás have been reduced to a battle between dominant foreign teams – just another tour on their circuit – with little relevance to the bulk of Irish riders or Irish cycling supporters?

The final scenes in the Phoenix Park also offered some contrasting and challenging images. There were the victor's laurel wreath and the Cúchulainn statuette trophies – emblematic of fifty years of tradition. On the podium, possibly representing the new Rás, stood the winning county team, 'Meath Lee-Strand Cycleways', but with only one rider from Meath; the pendulum had firmly swung from county loyalty to commercial support, but with raised standards made possible by that association. And the various other prize winners, increasingly full-time bike riders – suave, preened-up for the photographers, ready to move on to the next job – were these images a taste of the future Rás, orientated towards the media, commercial support and international-level riders?

By contrast, on the road below could be found the old Rás, the survivors, the county men in their assortments of teams. Dublin Ravens, for example, collectively over 8 hours down with only half the men of their two teams surviving, shattered but emotional with relief and achievement, an odyssey endured, now 'Men of the

Rás', dishevelled, posing for snapshots taken by their families and friends. These county riders were always the essence of the Rás. While the élite Rás riders emerged from their ranks, the county man always had a stake in the Rás. It was essentially his Rás. In the fiftieth Rás, the good county rider could still ride and finish, but he had little or no hope of making an impact – the gap between the top men and the average rider had widened significantly. Can the aspirations of both be accommodated and reconciled in the developing Rás?

And what of the forty-eight who failed to finish – dreams shattered and scattered along 1,000 kilometres of road. Were they failures in the modern world of sport which measures success by results? Or, in the tradition of the old Rás, did their numbers also include heroes, with epic, Cúchulainn-like efforts that were masked by the cold figures on the GC sheets – John Peppard, for example, an experienced and productive Rás rider with nothing to prove, who crashed badly in the second stage but, driven by that Rás tradition, somehow, incredibly, managing to finish the stage with two broken wrists and a broken collar-bone? Why, some might ask – it's only a bike race?

But it was always more than just a bike race. It is the nature of the human condition to explore its outer limits and that quest, which lifts the human spirit, often finds expression through sport. It is a personal thing and comes across strongly through the history of the Rás – Gene Mangan, that great student of the Rás, commented: 'The Rás for the riders has always been a measure of themselves.' Ultimately, it was always about that quest. In its origin and early evolution – in a spirited but isolated European backwater – the collective Rás somehow exuded that spirit – a test, struggle and achievement of epic proportions for ordinary men, who became extraordinary in the process. The public, in turn, was touched by that spirit and responded accordingly.

While nostalgia and tradition are powerful forces that can stunt development, they never prevented the Rás from changing, adapting and evolving – it marched closely in step with the inexorable changes in Ireland over fifty years. It will, no doubt, continue to do so. That future progress, whatever direction it takes in a world of changing attitudes to sport and personal fulfilment, will be on the foundation of a proud and solid tradition that has given the Rás a certain living identity and strength.

That living tradition continues to generate immense goodwill and to inspire the human spirit to extend itself; this, one feels, will ensure the Rás endures as a unique event, especially for Irish cyclists. To win the Rás will be the ultimate laurel, but the race itself will always be the real prize.

NOTES AND REFERENCES

1   The top placings were as follows: (1) Colm Christle, 9 hours 20 minutes 2 seconds; (2) Pat Kenna, 9.21.9; 3) Kerry Sloane, 9.21.40; (4) Jimmy Moran, 9.22.2; (5) Paudi Fitzgerald, 9.28.19; (6) Leo Collins, 9.31.28; (7) Willie Scannell, 9.31.55; (8) Cecil O'Reilly, 9.32.10; (9) Christy Dunne, 9.35.24; (10) Harry O'Toole King, 9.35.25.

2   The quote originates from Lalor in the *Irish Felon*, 1848:
    Who strikes the first blow for Ireland?
    Who draws the first blood for Ireland?
    Who wins a wreath that will be green forever?

3   From a 1968 Rás Tailteann publication.

4   From a 1968 Rás Tailteann publication.

5   *The IRA*, Tim Pat Coogan (Fontana, 1987), pp. 371–2.

6   Named after Cathal Brugha, an IRA leader in the War of Independence and member of the first Dáil. He took the anti-Treaty side in the civil war and was killed during fighting in Dublin.

7   According to legend, Setanta was the boyhood name for Cúchulainn.

8   Rásanna: the plural of Rás which is the Irish word for a 'race'.

9   Translated from the Irish, Rás Tailteann programme, 1956.

10 Jim Killean, 1959 Rás Tailteann programme.

11 The first question of his law exam was: 'What are the safeguards in the Constitution against armed insurrection and rebellion?' (cited in *The Secret Army*, J. Bowyer Bell, Sphere Books, 1972.).

12 The Yellow Jersey was generally worn by the race leader in the Rás but, for a period during the 1960s, the NCA Irish-team jersey was worn by the race leader. This was a white jersey with a tricolour band. However, for the sake of continuity, the expression 'Yellow Jersey' is used throughout this book to signify race leader.

13 Andy Christle had been selected for the Irish road-cycling team for the 1948 Olympics in London. He joined the CRE when the split came, but this did not apparently cause any division with his brothers – a strong Christle family bond transcended ideological differences.

14 From an article by Frank Baird, Ireland's best-known track rider of the pre-Rás era, in *Bikes and Bikemen*, 1960.

15 This was only a 10-mile event, indicating the underdeveloped nature of road racing in provincial Ireland at the time.

16 Pat Murphy had been the rider most prominent in the ceremonies during the first Rás in 1953.

17 It included Shay Elliott, who finished fifth.

18 Philip Clarke was elected MP for Westminster and not TD for Dáil Éireann. This was probably a subtle 'error' on Christle's part, as Clarke had pledged, as a condition of his nomination, that he would only take a seat in an all-Ireland parliament.

19 The 'Men of the Rás' expression, as a catchphrase, is generally attributed to Ray Kennedy, a one-time Rás rider who later became an announcer at stage ends.

Kennedy recalls how, at a wet and miserable stage end in Kilkee in 1982, with a small crowd and groups of dispirited riders dribbling to the finish, he first urged the crowd to 'put your hands together ladies and gentlemen – let's have it for the men of the Rás'. It immediately became a popular catch phrase and a clarion call in the Rás.

20 Very late drinking sessions by officials and followers of the Rás.

21 From a diary supplied to the author.

22 The longest stage of the 1959 Rás, for example, was 134 miles (214km), from Westport to Ennis. The average distance was 117 miles (187km). It was also the second-longest Rás ever, at 929 miles (1,486km), even though it was an eight-day event and nine and ten-day events came later.

23 John Lackey, one of the NCA's best riders who defected to the CRE in 1954, taking the entire original Tailteann club with him. His defection was a major blow to the NCA. He became a significant figure in the CRE and was Race Director for the Tour of Ireland.

24 Percy Stallard founded the BLRC and is considered the father of road racing in England. He was brought by the National Club to the first eight-day Rás in 1954 to manage its team. Bob Thom was manager of the professional Viking team in England. Ian Steele was a former winner of the Tour of Britain and of the Peace Race (otherwise known as the Warsaw–Berlin–Prague race – a long and hard race run by the FSGT).

25 A professional category, between amateur and full professional.

26 The placings were: (1) Tom Finn (Dublin) 43.05.19; (2) Ben McKenna (Meath) 43.05.46; (3) Shay O'Hanlon (Dublin) 43.09.15; (4) Mick Christle (Dublin) 43.09.28; (5) Seán Dillon (Dublin) 43.11.14; (6) Paddy Flanagan (Kildare) 43.15.28; (7) Dermot Dignam (Dublin) 43.18.48; (8) Denis Magrath (Dublin) 43.20.54.

27 O'Hanlon's room-mate was Seán Dillon, whose brother, Allen, was then race leader, but on another team. Seán Dillon and O'Hanlon were very good friends until Dillon's death in a race in 1963.

28 A brother of Louison Bobet, a French rider who won the Tour de France on three consecutive occasions, beginning in 1953.

29 Shay O'Hanlon started in twenty-three Rásanna and finished twenty-one, one of which he did not intend to complete as he could not get time off work – he rode for just the first weekend. He abandoned another due to illness.

30 The FSGT (Féderation Sportive et Gymnique du Travail) was a French left-wing, workers' organisation closely associated with the trade-union and communist movement, that ran sporting events, including cycling. It was outside the UCI. See chapter 7.

31 See chapters 1 and 7.

32 The following extract from *The Irish Times* on the day before the event lists the most regarded NCA men of the period and indicates dominance of the Dublin team:

> On glancing down the list of entries a short list (of favourites) automatically draws itself up: Garda Ben McKenna (Meath), Gene Mangan (Kerry), and Tom Finn (Dublin), winners in 1959, '55 and '61, will be trying to set up a record as nobody has won the race twice. Liam Baxter and Murt Logan (Kildare), Patsy

Wall (Tipperary), Mick Twomey (Cork), Pat Neary (Louth), Dan Ahern (Kerry), Brendan Magennis (Antrim), and the rest of the Dublin team, Sonny Cullen, Christy Kimmage, Jimmy Kennedy, Archie Williams and the captain, Mick Christle.

33 Strictly speaking, Goddard was not an 'Exile'. He strengthened a good Exiles team from England that had been managed by John O'Reilly in the 1962 and 1963 Rásanna. O'Reilly had been one of Joe Christle's right-hand men in the early 1950s, but had emigrated to England in 1956. His last mission for Christle, on the day he left, was to deliver passports, on a motorbike, to the group that was to protest at the Melbourne Olympics.

34 Dan Ahern emigrated to the US in 1964 in search of work. He was persuaded to return to cycling to compete in the US trials for the Tokyo Olympics. He won three road-race trial races and was to be on the team. However, it was discovered that his emigration papers had not been finalised before the Olympics began and he was unable to compete. He was presented with a special medal in recompense but he never raced again. It is also interesting to note as an indication of the economic conditions in Ireland at the time that, along with Ahern, all three winners of the Rás from Kerry in the 1950s emigrated – Gene Mangan, Paudie Fitzgerald and Mick Murphy.

35 Called after the Fenian leader, James Stephens.

36 This reached its peak at the 1980 Olympics in Moscow and the 1984 Olympics in Los Angeles, where West and East, respectively, boycotted the Olympic Games.

37 Born near Dublin into an Anglo-Irish family, Roger Casement was knighted for work in the British colonial service. Later, he came to believe in Irish separatism, was involved in the revolutionary movement and attempted to smuggle arms into Ireland for the 1916 Rising. He was subsequently hanged for treason.

38 Two IRA men who were hanged in England in 1940 for involvement in a bomb explosion in which five people were killed. Their level of involvement was disputed.

39 The 1913 Lockout in Dublin was a major conflict between trade unions and employers and probably the single biggest socialist-verses-capitalist struggle in Ireland.

40 The 'Battle of the Bogside' began in 1969 when the Bogside – a nationalist area of Derry in Northern Ireland – was attacked by loyalist crowds. The local population barricaded the area in response and a 'no-go area' was maintained until 1972. It became a symbol of nationalist resistance.

41 At this time, the Peace Race (Prague–Berlin–Warsaw) was regarded as the world's greatest amateur road race, but many of the participants were effectively professional riders from behind the Iron Curtain. At the Grand Prix de l'Humanité, NCA riders used to meet teams that had come directly from the Peace Race and there was a great awareness of it amongst Irish riders. It was a very tough race, usually held in poor weather in May, and was normally about thirteen stages, covering approximately 2,500 km. In atmosphere, the event was similar to the Rás. Ian Steele, from Great Britain, won it in 1952 and Joe Christle subsequently brought him to the International Tour Revenge in Dublin, which he also won.

42 Séamus Kennedy had been knocked by a Russian in the sprint into Thurles on the fourth stage. Unlike today, he was not allowed the same time as the winning group for crashing in the last kilometre. He lost almost a minute as a result.

43 An article in *Bikes and Bikemen* (an NCA publication), Easter 1962, referred to these talks in a somewhat cautious tone – 'care must be taken that the tail does not wag the dog' (the NCA was the larger organisation) – and went on to outline how the NCA had thrived from the split.

44 This evolved to become the Federation of Irish Cyclists (FIC) in 1987. Under this arrangement, the NCA, the ICF and the NICF amalgamated, but some of the old NICF clubs remained outside of the new order and continued as the NICF with allegiance to the British Cycling Federation. The FIC was renamed the Irish Cycling Federation (ICF) in 1998 and this, in turn, was renamed Cycling Ireland in 2002. The division still continues in Northern Ireland and is in a state of flux.

45 An over-35 age category at international level.

46 Flanagan was back training within a week. He was nervous on his first outing and asked his friend, Emanuel Thackaberry, to accompany him. Satisfied that he could control the bike, he resumed his normal training routine and rode with a plastered hand for five weeks.

47 In modern events, Power would probably have received service, as a service car would be put ahead of the race so that it could drop back behind breaks that form in the mountains.

48 Not to be confused with the IRA man who was executed by the Dublin government during the Second World War, this George Plant was a highly regarded official of the Gate Cycling Club, based in Guinness Brewery in Dublin, and the trophy was originally commissioned to his memory in 1958. The original inscription reads: 'Presented to the NCAI (National Cycling Association of Ireland) by the workers of Guinness Brewery, Dublin, for Competition in the Annual Guinness 100 kilometres Massed Start Cycle Race.' The new inscription reads: 'Presented to the winner of Rás Tailteann from 1978.' Between the disappearance of Corn Cathal Brugha and the dedication of the George Plant Trophy, various other trophies were presented to the winners, including Waterford Glass and silver platters.

49 They also won a National Championship each – Doyle's win was an ICF National Championship and Kerr's was under the auspices of the Tripartite Committee.

50 Tony Lally won the Tour of Ireland in 1974 and his brother, Seán, was hoping to win the Rás and make it a double for the brothers. He came second, however, 20 seconds behind his team-mate, Peter Doyle.

51 Olympic participation is one indication of the McQuaid's contribution to Irish sport: Pat did not ride in the 1976 Olympics as expected because, along with his brother Kieron and Seán Kelly, he was caught racing in South Africa in 1975, thus breaking the international boycott imposed over Apartheid. Kieron represented Ireland in the Munich Olympics in 1972; Oliver in 1976 in Montreal; none rode in 1980 because of the boycott of the Moscow Olympics; Pat managed the Irish team in Los Angeles in 1984. Their first cousin, John (son of Paddy), rode in the Seoul Olympics in 1988. Pat's son, David, became the first of the third generation of McQuaids to represent Ireland when he rode in the Junior World Championships in 1997. Kieron's son, Gary, represented Ireland at a World Championships in 2001 and Pat's second son, Andrew, began his international career as a Junior in the 2002 World Championships.

52 The eldest son, Paul, rode one Rás in 1983 before moving to France where he became a professional, and rode the Tour de France. He was author of the ground-breaking book on professional cycling, *A Rough Ride*.

53   Davie Gardiner crashed out, Séamus Downey had to have an operation on a saddle boil in Mallow and Dermot Gilleran got gastroenteritis.

54   Carrick Wheelers had a long-term sponsorship association with Cidona, going back as far as 1978. However, they were to be precluded from entering teams in the Rás under this sponsorship as it was seen to be in conflict with the interests of one of the Rás' sponsors. This has been a long-term difficulty for the club as its sponsor is denied exposure in the country's premier event.

55   Other Powers who rode in the Rás: Paddy Power, an influential rider, was brother to Larry but was not on the 1986 team; Raymond Power, who came second in the Rás, was also from Carrick-on-Suir but not related; Robert Power, who wore the Yellow Jersey in 1992 and had stage wins in 1991 and 1994, came from Dungarvan in County Waterford and was not related to any of the others; Ciarán Power, who won the Rás in 1998 and 2002, came from Waterford city and was not related to any of the others. It is interesting to note that four Powers, though unrelated, took the four top positions in the Rás – Raymond, fourth; Robert, third; Bobby second; and Ciarán, first (twice).

56   Seán Lally successfully finished the Rás and also finished the following three. He therefore completed four consecutive Rásanna in his fifties. He is thought to be the oldest Irishman to complete a Rás; Tony Woodcock of England was the oldest competitor ever to finish the Rás.

57   Giuseppe Guerini was third in the Giro d'Italia in 1997 and 1998 and also won a stage in 1998. He won a famous stage to the Alpe d'Huez in the 1999 Tour de France where, in the final stages, he was knocked down by an over-enthusiastic fan who stood out in front of him with a camera. Wladimir Belli was third overall in the Tour of Switzerland in 1998 and 2000. He also won a stage in 2000. He was dismissed from the 2001 Giro d'Italia, while in contention for the race lead, when a helicopter TV camera recorded him punching a spectator that he was passing. Gian-Matteo Fagnini became the main lead-out man for Mario Cippollini in the Saeco team and later for Erik Zabel in the Deutsche Telekom team. He was thrown out of the 1997 Giro d'Italia for dangerous riding.

58   John Blackwell, Philip Cassidy, Declan Lonergan and Finn O'Sullivan were penalised 90 seconds, being cited for dangerous riding. Paul Kennedy and Daragh McQuaid were penalised 30 seconds. McQuaid was the only one of them to be in Spratt's team. Lonergan and Cassidy especially protested their innocence, and Cassidy threatened legal action over an *Irish Times* article on the event.

59   'The Wheel Deal', *Himself*, May 1999.

60   Dignam rode his first Rás in 1959 and his final Rás in 1972. His best result came in 1961 when he finished seventh overall and was second in a stage, behind Paddy Flanagan. He came fourth in stages on six different occasions during his career.

61   Stages were dedicated to Noel McGuill, a young rider fatally injured in the 1972 race; Donal Roche and Andy Christle, fatally injured in motorbike accidents in 1963 and 1954 respectively; Jim Killean; former great winners – Joe O'Brien, Ben McKenna and Paddy Flanagan.

RÁS HIGHLIGHTS

Most Rás wins: Shay O'Hanlon won the Rás four times.

Most stage wins: Shay O'Hanlon won twenty-four stages.

Most Yellow Jerseys: Shay O'Hanlon wore the Yellow Jersey for thirty-seven days.

Most stage wins in one Rás: Gene Mangan won four consecutive stages in 1958. Four stage wins in one Rás were achieved on seven other occasions, but not consecutively. These were: Shay O'Hanlon (Dublin) 1962 and 1965; J. Zelenka (Czechoslovakia) 1968; Alexander Gysiatnikov (USSR) 1970; Batty Flynn (Kerry) 1971; Yuri Lavrushkin, (USSR) 1977; Declan Lonergan (Ireland), 1991.

Successful defences: Shay O'Hanlon, 1966 and 1967, and Paul McCormack, 1988.

Oldest winner: As far as is known, Philip Cassidy was the oldest Rás winner in 1999, at the age of thirty-seven.

Biggest winning margin: Shay O'Hanlon's winning margin of 19 minutes 4 seconds in the 1962 Rás.

Smallest winning margin: Declan Lonergan won the 1994 Rás by just 3 seconds. He began the final *criterium* on equal time with English rider, Steve Farrell, and won the race on the bonus sprints.

Youngest finisher: Mel Christle, son of Joe Christle, finished the Rás at the age of fourteen in 1971. A time limit was not applied.

Oldest finisher: As far as is known, the English rider, Tony Woodcock, was the oldest rider to complete the Rás. In 1999, he finished the race when aged fifty-eight. Seán Lally is thought to be the oldest Irish finisher of the Rás – he was fifty-four when he completed the race in 1994. It was his fourth consecutive Rás finish in his fifties.

Youngest stage winner: Gene Mangan's win in the third stage in 1955, at the age of eighteen, is thought to have made him the youngest-ever stage winner.

Oldest stage winner: Mick Grimes at forty-one, as far as is known.

Most number of starts: Shay O'Hanlon started twenty-three Rásanna.

Most number of finishes: Ben McKenna, Shay O'Hanlon and Gabriel Howard each finished twenty-one Rásanna. Howard's were consecutive.

Riders who finished first, second and third: Ben McKenna and Declan Lonergan.

Race leader for entire race: Shay O'Hanlon, 1965, 1966 and 1967; Alexander Gysiatnikov (USSR), 1970.

Most county-team wins: The Meath team won either the overall team or the county-team prize eighteen times.

First foreigner to win: Zbigniew Glowaty from Poland in 1963.

Longest stage: 246km (154 miles) from Clonakilty to Wexford in 1961, won by Shay O'Hanlon.

Longest Rás: 1,497km (936 miles) in 1968, over ten days, won by Milan Hrazdira, a Czech. Eighty-two started and fifty-five finished, an attrition rate of 33 per cent.

Fastest Rás: The 2001 Rás, at 27 mph (43.1 km/h)

Slowest Rás: The 1959 Rás, at 21.5 mph (34.4 km/h).

Stages abandoned/discounted: The second stage was abandoned in 1956 because of the 'Cookstown incident' and the results of a time trial in Longford in 1979 were not counted because of confusion with the results.

Argy-bargy: A colloquial term used to describe disagreement or rough play, but not out right fighting. (See 'pulling and dragging' as it refers to cycling.)

Bit 'n' bit (bit and bit): The sharing of the workload when riders take regular turns in the front of a group, each doing his 'bit' to break the wind.

Break (or breakaway group): A small group of riders that gets ahead of the main group.

Broom-wagon (*sag-waggon*): The vehicle that travels behind the last rider and picks up (sweeps up) cyclists who abandon the race.

Bunch (or pack or *peloton*): The main group of riders.

Cavalcade: The line of vehicles following a race.

Commissaire: The official who enforces the competition rules.

Criterium: A race held in a closed, tight circuit, with many short, fast laps. Usually in a town, it is an exciting public spectacle and suits fast, skilled riders.

Domestique: French for 'servant' – a rider whose main function is to assist another rider, rather than compete for himself. It normally applies to professional racing.

Drafting (sitting-in): An energy-saving tactic of riding closely behind another rider and using him as a windbreak. It can also be done behind vehicles (taking pace), which is not allowed by the rules. 'Sitting-in' has slightly negative connotations, suggesting that the rider may not be doing his bit.

Drag: An incline in the road, not steep or long enough to be classified as a hill.

Echelon: A diagonal formation of riders that stretches across a road to get protection in cross winds. It requires good co-ordination between riders to work well. Each echelon can only be as wide as the road, so that cross winds tend to split up bunches.

Galloper: Sprinter.

General Classification (GC): Overall positions in the race decided by the total accumulation time on each stage.

GC: See 'General Classification'.

Green Jersey (points jersey): The Green Jersey is awarded to the rider who wins most points in sprints. As time is not a factor, the Green Jersey rewards consistency and sprinting prowess.

Hand-sling: A technique used in some forms of track racing whereby a rider catches the hand of a rider behind him and 'slings' him forward. It is not allowed in road racing.

Hot-spot (sprint): A sprint during the course of a race, at predetermined points, for which time bonuses and/or points are awarded.

Hunger Knock: See 'Knock'.

Jumping: Aggressive acceleration so as to get clear away from another rider, or a group of riders.

King of the Hills (KOH): A competition for climbers – designated climbs have points that are awarded to the first riders over the climb. The Polka-dot Jersey is normally worn by the KOH leader.

Knock (or bonk): A state of severe fatigue and exhaustion reached from not eating or absorbing enough food during a long race.

KOH: See 'King of the Hills'.

Lap-out: When a rider crashes or punctures in a *criterium*, he may take a lap out and rejoin the race on the next lap.

Laughing-group: The last group of riders on the road who are trying to stay inside the time limit for the stage. They may be struggling or just taking an easy day, hence the expression.

Lead-out: In a sprint, the 'lead-out' man will sprint ahead of another rider to give him an initial advantage by sheltering him from the wind.

Leader on the road: A rider who would be leader on GC if the race ended at that point, or will be leader if he can maintain his advantage. It has no relevance in final results.

Neutral service: Vehicles in the cavalcade that provide service, such as spare wheels, to any rider who is unsupported by his own team car. The neutral service is directed by the race *commissaire* rather than by teams.

Patron: An expression from the Tour de France, the *patron* is the boss of the *peloton* – a dominant personality who commands favours, respect – even fear – from the other riders.

Peloton: A French term for the main bunch of riders.

Piano (riding piano): Riding 'softly', or gently, or slowly.

Pulling and dragging: A term used in Irish sport to describe untidy and rough play. In cycling, it normally refers to negative tactics, lack of co-operation or cohesion in bunches. In cycling, it does not normally involve physical contact. See also, 'Argy-bargy'.

Prime: A cash prize awarded to the first rider in a sprint in a town that the race passes through, or at the top of a hill.

Scrubbing (scrubber): A disdainful term in Irish cycling for a rider who shelters excessively behind other riders and does not do his share of work at the front, if considered able to do so.

Sit in: 'Sit' at the back of a group and not share in the work at the front – considered acceptable in some tactical circumstances, otherwise considered as 'scrubbing'.

Sit up: To stop working in a group – the rider will usually adopt a more upright position when the effort ceases.

Switch: A dangerous manoeuvre of pulling across another rider during a sprint.

Taking pace: See 'Drafting'.

Tempo (riding tempo): A steady and comfortable riding speed.

Tubular (tyre): A tyre and inner tube attached together as one.

Veteran: A category for riders over thirty-nine years of age in Irish competition and over thirty-five in international competition.

Yellow Jersey: The jersey worn by the race leader. For a period during the 1960s, the NCA Irish-team jersey was worn by the race leader in the Rás. This was a white jersey with a tricolour band.

NON-CYCLING GLOSSARY

Bórd Fáilte: Irish Tourist Board.

Border Campaign: A campaign conducted by the IRA, mainly along the border, from 1956–62. Six members of the RUC and eleven IRA men were killed during it.

Cúchulainn: A mythical warrior hero and a central figure in the Táin, one of the main epics of Irish historical folklore. The statue of Cúchulainn in the GPO, by Oliver Sheppard, is an important national icon.

Culchie: A derogatory term for a country person as perceived by Dubliners.

FCA: Fórsa Cosainte Áitiuil – the Irish army reserve force.

Fianna: Mythical warriors from the ancient Irish sagas.

Gaeltacht: Irish-speaking region.

GAA: Gaelic Athletic Association. The GAA was founded in 1884 to organise athletics along nationalist lines and the revival of the Tailteann Games was an early ambition. The promotion of hurling and Gaelic football became its main pursuit. It became a very powerful organisation, with a strong nationalist ethos.

James Fintan Lalor: James Fintan Lalor was a radical member of the Young Ireland organisation of the 1840s. He was an early nationalist and advocated socialist-type land distribution.

Pearse: Pádraig Pearse was a teacher, writer and leader of the 1916 Rebellion, after which he was executed.

Shoneen: 'Seoinín: a shoneen, jackeen or johnnie, an aper [sic] of foreign ways, a flunkey, a settler, a small farmer, a poor Protestant' (from Dinneen's *Irish/English Dictionary*).

Taoiseach: Prime Minister of Ireland.

UCC: University College, Cork, now NUIC – National University of Ireland, Cork.

ABBREVIATIONS

AAU Amateur Athletics Union
BCF British Cycling Federation
BLE Bórd Lúthchleas na hÉireann
BLRC British League of Racing Cyclists
BNCU British National Cyclists' Union
CRE Cumann Rothaíochta na hÉireann
ESB Electricity Supply Board
FCA Fórsa Cosainte Áitiuil
FIC Federation of Irish Cyclists
FSGT Féderation Sportive et Gymnique du Travail
GAA Gaelic Athletic Association
GC General Classification
ICF Irish Cycling Federation

ICTC Irish Cycling Tripartite Committee
IRA Irish Republican Army
NACA National Athletics and Cycling Association
NCA National Cycling Association
NCAI National Cycling Association of Ireland
NCU National Cycling Union
NDC National Dairy Council
NICF Northern Ireland Cycling Federation
RUC Royal Ulster Constabulary
UCC University College Cork
UCD University College Dublin
UCI Union Cycliste Internationale

INDEX